Walk for Peace
Transcultural Experiences in China

为和平徒步 — 中国之旅的转文化体验

Transcultural experiences with 'three eyes' Series Vol.2
Series editors: Lixing Chen and Xiangqun Chang
Walk for Peace: Transcultural Experiences in China
By The Rt. Hon. Lord Michael Bates; Edited by Lady Xuelin Li Bates

The Chinese-English version published by New World Press 2016
24 Baiwanzhuang Street, Xicheng District, Beijing, China
The English, Chinese and English-Chinese editions published by
Global China Press 2016 and 2017
4th Floor, Cannongate House, 64 Cannon Street, London EC4N 6AE, UK

British Library Cataloguing in Publication Data
A catalogue record for this book is available from the British Library

English version: ISBN 978-1-910334-38-6 (paperback); ISBN 978-1-910334-40-9 (hardback)
DOI https://doi.org/10.24103/TETE.en.2016.1
Chinese version: ISBN 978-1-910334-39-3 (paperback); ISBN 978-1-910334-41-6 (hardback)
DOI https://doi.org/10.24103/TETE.cn.2017.1
Chinese-English version: ISBN 978-7-5104-6029-6 (paperback)
English-Chinese version: ISBN 978-1-910334-44-7 (paperback)
DOI https://doi.org/10.24103/TETE.en.cn.2017.1

"三只眼"转文化系列丛书 第2卷 陈立行 常向群主编
《为和平徒步——中国之旅的转文化体验》
〔英〕麦克·贝茨勋爵著 李雪琳·贝茨勋爵夫人等编译

汉英合订本由中国新世界出版社2016年出版
中国北京市西城区百万庄大街24号
英文版、中文版、英汉合订更新版由英国全球中国出版社2016年和2017年出版
4th Floor, Cannongate House, 64 Cannon Street, London EC4N 6AE, UK

此书编入大英图书馆的公开数据中的图书馆编目

ISBN 978-1-910334-38-6 平装；英文版书号：ISBN 978-1-910334-40-9 精装
DOI https://doi.org/10.24103/TETE.en.2016.1
ISBN 978-1-910334-39-3 平装；中文版书号：ISBN 978-1-910334-41-6 精装
DOI https://doi.org/10.24103/TETE.cn.2017.1
汉英合订本书号ISBN 978-7-5104-6029-6 平装
英汉合订本更新版书号ISBN 978-1-910334-44-7 平装
DOI https://doi.org/10.24103/TETE.en.cn.2017.1

Transcultural experiences with 'three eyes' ②
"三只眼"转文化系列丛书 ②

Walk for Peace
Transcultural Experiences in China

为和平徒步 — 中国之旅的转文化体验

The Rt. Hon. Lord Michael Bates

Edited by **Lady Xuelin Li Bates**

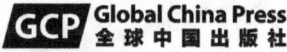
GCP **Global China Press**
全球中国出版社

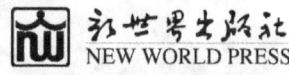
新世界出版社
NEW WORLD PRESS

Meet the couple – author and editor

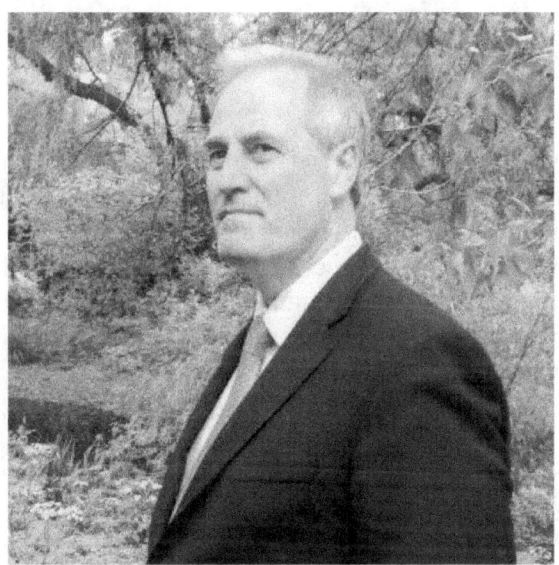

The Rt. Hon. Lord Michael Bates

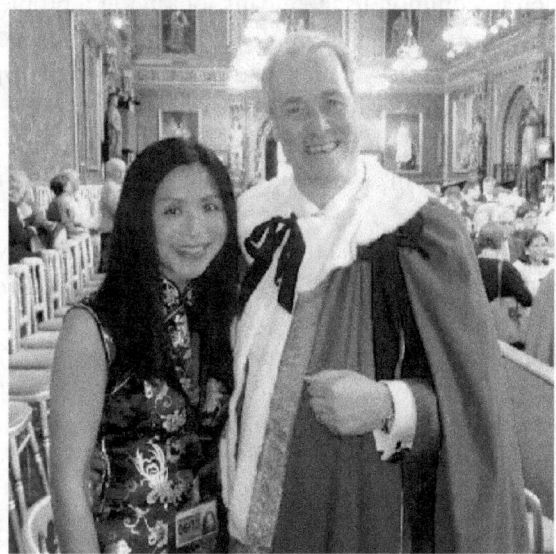

Lord Michael Bates and Lady Xuelin Li Bates
at the State Opening of Parliament in 2013

DOI https://doi.org/10.24103/TETE.en.cn.2017.1.1

General Preface

Transcultural Experiences with 'Three Eyes' Book Series

Over the past five centuries, encounters and exchanges between China and the West have grown ever more intensive. Owing to historical and cultural differences and the opposition between different ideologies, however, there are still misunderstandings and even prejudices on both sides. The rapid development of China in the nearly 40 years since the implementation of the reforms and opening up has attracted worldwide attention and raised high expectations of China to take its share of responsibilities and obligations in all areas of international affairs. In the last few decades, global society has undergone modernization, post-modernization, modernity, post-modernity, multi-modernity, globalization and post-globalization. We believe that the concept of transculturality, related to but distinct from cross-, inter-, intra-, and multiculturality, can become mainstream discourse in the near future. It could help us to abandon the prejudices of the past and re-examine each other objectively and rationally.

A person has two eyes, but both Western and Eastern mysticism talk about a 'third eye', which in common usage means looking at a problem from another point of view or perspective. For example, to political leaders from the United States, Europe, Asia and Latin America, the book *The Third Way and its Critics* (1998), by renowned social theorist Lord Anthony Giddens, which was translated into 25 languages, provides a new and unprecedented perspective on important international political debates. In essence, this is the work of Lord Giddens's 'third eye'.

However, from a methodological point of view, the 'third eye' is not simply a physical addition to a person's two eyes. The idea of the 'three eyes' that we propose is a popular metaphor describing a type of methodology. The expression originates from the 'three-eyed' deity Horse God (*Ma shen* 马神) in Chinese folk culture, commonly referred to as *Mawang ye* (马王爷), whose full name is Enlightened Ruler of the Grass Horses and full title is Clever Horse Marshal; he is also known as Three-eyed Brightness and Three-eyed Sunshine. He is a Taoist divinity, one of the immortal beings of Chinese folk religion. Thus, the 'three eyes' methodology entails looking at a problem using three main perspectives at the same time, which to a Chinese person means applying the perspective of the Chinese, of the non-Chinese and of professionals.

Within a single person, the three cultures can coexist, and can also be transformed into a different new type of culture, namely 'transcultural generativity'[1] or

---

[1] Shuo Yu. 2015. "'Universal dream, national dreams and symbiotic dream': reflections on

'transculturality'.[2] This kind of transcultural phenomenon can exist in an individual or in groups. The term 'transculturality' has been translated as *chaowenhua* 转文化 in Chinese, an unfamiliar word to most Chinese readers. Based on my understanding, the notions of 'cross-culturality', 'inter-culturality' and 'intra-culturality' should be translated as *kuawenhua* 跨文化, *jiwenhua* 际文化 and *neiwenhua* 内文化, respectively, which will be the subject of a forthcoming article. Culture does not know borders, and different cultures mutually influence one another. When a culture crosses into another culture, it sometimes coexists with it, giving shape to multi-cultural phenomena, such as the Chinese culinary culture that exists in the Chinatowns of many cities around the world: a so-called cross-cultural phenomenon. At other times, it overtakes the original local culture, developing a symbiotic relation with it, such that they merge to form a new culture, in which each culture contains elements of the other, thus originating transcultural phenomena such as combinations of Chinese and Western features: there are numerous transcultural products in the areas of clothing, food, architecture, transport, music and painting. As human society enters the age of the mobile Internet, the creation of transcultural products has a great impact on our ways of life and ideas. For example, the Chinese online payment platform Zhifubao, known by its English name Alipay, is widely used in many Asian countries, whereas English-speaking countries mainly use PayPal. The properties and functions of Alipay are basically the same as those of PayPal. Alipay was influenced by the technological culture of PayPal, and now an increasing number of countries are also using it, constituting a new payment system and a new consumer culture, in the same way as WeChat was influenced by WhatsApp. Some non-Chinese people have started using WeChat alongside WhatsApp, and this has become part of their lifestyle. It is clear that this type of 'transculturality', a new blend of cultures generated by elements from several cultures, is a notion that is similar to yet different from inter-culturality, intra-culturality or multi-culturality.

The reform and opening up that took place in China in the last 40 years coincided with the global ideological trends of modernization, post-modernization, modernity, post-modernity, multi-modernity, globalization, post-globalization and so on. In the early 1990s, some sociologists[3] initiated research projects on globalization. In 2016, the vote for the UK to leave the European Union and the election of Donald Trump as President of the United States marked humanity's

---

transcultural generativity in China–Europe encounters', *Journal of China in Comparative Perspective, 1(2)*.

[2] SHEN Qi. 2015. 'From cross culture, interculture to transculture: reading "universal dream, national dreams and symbiotic dream": reflections on transcultural generativity in China–Europe encounters', *Journal of China in Comparative Perspective*, 1(2); YU Shuo, 'Making space for "transculturality" – a response to SHEN Qi', ibid.

[3] Such as Martin Albrow, editor of the journal International Sociology at the time and author of *The Global Age* (1996).

entry into the post-global age[4], or the transcultural age.[5] In recent years, several scholars have looked into the limitations of the concept of globalization, hoping to find a conceptual tool that could interpret and analyse more effectively current and future global patterns, leading future trends of thought in philosophy, social sciences and humanities. These scholars have a very optimistic view of the notion of 'transculturality'. In the 1940s, Cuban anthropologist Fernando Ortiz[6] had already proposed the idea of transculturality, and a numbers of scholars started studying transcultural phenomena and concept of transculturality in the 1980s; but could the concept become an important theory and part of mainstream discourse in the near future? We need to conduct further research on this from a theoretical point of view.[7]

Transcultural Experiences with 'Three Eyes' is a series of popular and readable social scientific books, written either in Chinese or in English and launched in 2015 by the Global China Press (GCP). GCP is the world's first publisher focusing on bilingual publications about China in comparative perspective, Chinese perspectives of the world and human knowledge and non-Chinese perspectives of China in a global context. This series aims to act as a bridge in the areas of cross-border cultural communication and mutual understanding. The authors of this book series may be Chinese and non-Chinese living in China or abroad, Chinese and non-Chinese in a cross-cultural marriage, people of Chinese and non-Chinese mixed heritage and Chinese and non-Chinese with different backgrounds and in all kinds of professions. The triple perspective consists of their own understanding of Chinese culture, of non-Chinese cultures and of their specialties and sectors as professionals and practitioners. This understanding describes and explains the collision and confluence between different cultures and notions they experience in their everyday lives and work in China and abroad. The authors also use the 'three eyes' perspective to look at themselves, at China and at the world. The series adopts a comparative and narrative method to interpret prevalent misconceptions and prejudices from different dimensions, such as Eastern and Western ways of thinking, value systems and behavioural patterns, implicitly helping readers to achieve all sorts of realizations from within. The books are characterized by the

---

[4] GAO Bai. 2016. 'Is this the beginning of the post-global age?', *China Times* [GAO Bai. 2016: Houquanqiu shidai de kaishi? *Huaxia shibao*], 2016-1-11 http://www.chinatimes.cc/article/52971. html

[5] Karl Jirgens, 'Studying Canadian studies in a trans-cultural age', book review of Dirk Hoerder: *To Know Our Many Selves: From the Study of Canada to Canadian Studies* (Edmonton: Athabasca University Press. 2010), Spectres of Modernism, Special issue 209, *Canadian Literature* (Summer 2011): 162–163.

[6] Fernando Ortiz. 1940. *Contrapunteo cubano del tabaco y el azúcar*. Havana: Jesús Montero. English trans. by Harriet de Onis [1947] 1995 as *Cuban Counterpoint: Tobacco and Sugar*. Durham, NC: Duke University Press.

[7] Xiangqun Chang. 2015. 'Transculturality and the globalization of Chinese social sciences: vocabulary, invention and exploration', *Journal of China in Comparative Perspective*, 1(1).

'confessional' style typically used by Fei Xiaotong, a renowned Chinese sociologist and anthropologist, to rethink the problems of Chinese culture and their impact on globalization.

The Transcultural Experiences with 'Three Eyes' series is jointly edited by Lixing Chen and Xiangqun Chang. Lixing Chen is supervising all the operations related to the book series, while Xiangqun Chang is in charge of coordination between the publishing house and the authors, peer reviews and publishing arrangements. Each book runs to between 80,000 and 10,000 words, and each author may write one or more volumes. After passing through the hands of two co-editors, manuscripts are then passed on to the publishing house, where a meticulous checking and proofreading process begins. Before submitting their work for publication, authors are required to provide Global China Press with the title of their proposed book, a short biography (200 words), an abstract (1,000 words), a sample chapter and a complete table of contents.

The following titles in the series have been published or are in the process of publication:

- *What Has Been Lost in Contemporary China?*, by Lixing Chen
- *Walk for Peace: Transcultural Experiences in China*, by The Rt Hon. Lord Michael Bates, edited by Lady Xuelin Bates
- *Cultural Gene of the Institution: Experiencing American Campus Life and Thoughts*, by Sun Jiaming
- *Culture Gap: Social Life Experiences in China and the UK*, by Paul Crook
- *Conflicts and Communication in the Field of Transculturality*, by Yu Shuo

We hope that, by reading these books, Chinese people living both in China and overseas, as well as all readers interested in China and the Chinese and the children of overseas Chinese will deepen their understanding of the Chinese people and Chinese society, and of the social and cultural interpretation that others give to China, thus helping to build an international community based on complementarity, reciprocity and harmonious symbiosis.

Lixing Chen
Professor of Sociology, Kwansei Gakuin University
Former President of the Japan–China Sociological Society (JCSS), Japan

Xiangqun Chang
Director of Global China Institute and CCPN Global
Honorary Professor at University College London, UK

Revised June 2017

Contents

DOI https://doi.org/10.24103/TETE.en.cn.2017.1.2

Foreword

The English–Chinese dual-language edition of Lord Bates's *Walk for Peace: Transcultural Experiences in China* (original Chinese–English edition *Walk for Peace*, New World Press, 2016) was finally launched to readers all over the world at the 2017 London Book Fair. This is the result of the joint efforts of Lord and Lady Bates, respectively author and editor of the book, Ms Zhang Ming, in 2015 the head of the Public Relations Department of the Chinese Red Cross, who assisted Lord Bates during his walk across China, and colleagues at New World Press and Global China Press.

It has taken three years for this book to go from idea to realization. It was during a conversation with Lady Bates, Li Xuelin, wife of the author, the Rt Hon. Lord Michael Bates, back in 2014, that I learnt that they were in the process of planning Lord Bates's 2015 walk across China. I immediately expressed interest in publishing the journal of the 'Walk for Peace', and as the walk was underway I also forwarded the daily logs to our WeChat groups, China in Comparative Perspective Global and Global China Unit.

Global China Press was particularly keen to publish this *Walk for Peace* as part of our Transcultural Experiences with 'Three Eyes' book series. The general idea and message of this book series have already been set out in the General Preface at the beginning of this book. Here I provide a little further explanation on some related ideas, using the book as an example.

A British person, such as the author of this book, can also have three eyes. In 2015, Michel Bates undertook a walk across China on the occasion of the 70th anniversary of the Victory in the War of Resistance, walking from Beijing to Hangzhou, his wife's hometown. Lord Bates can be considered a son-in-law of China and, according to Tu Weiming's[1] classification, 'culturally Chinese'. Being a member of the British House of Lords and Minister of State at the Department for International Development, he is also a professional. In this triple role and using this triple perspective, he walked across China, recording in his blog everything he saw, heard and experienced on the way. The result is something very different from the traditional ethnographic fieldwork conducted in China by foreign anthropologists. But since it was able look at an issue from these three perspectives, could we not say that in a sense it opened the 'eye of wisdom' (慧眼)?

In publishing this book, we hope that a larger number of readers will gain new insights from it, helping them understand transcultural ideas. In his Introduction, the author writes: 'My wife is Chinese and we both respect and delight in

---

[1] Tu Weiming (杜维明) is an ethicist and a New Confucian. He is Chair and Professor of Humanities and Founding Director of the Institute for Advanced Humanistic Studies at Peking University, China. He is also Research Professor and Senior Fellow of the Asia Center at Harvard University, USA.

our respective adopted cultures. Culture connects us as human beings like nothing else: music, film, poetry, art, dance, literature, education, sport, cuisine, religion, language, social traditions, appreciation of the beauty and wonder of nature and sport. These are humanity's lowest common denominator and its highest value. The more we emphasize what we have in common, the more relations grow – in fact, the Latin and French roots of the word "culture" are all connected with nurturing growth.'

To date, Lord Bates has conducted walks across 23 countries, and what impressed him the most were not the cultural differences that have always been exaggerated but the great similarities that exist between different countries. Unquestionably, although similar practices and traits in different cultures may result from the autonomous development of similar items, from borrowing or diffusion, more and more transcultural phenomena contribute to 'the great similarities'.

One of our aims in publishing Michael Bates's book is to promote the reader's active participation in the social governance of global society. Nowadays, most Chinese leaders at every level and in all trades and professions have the aspiration of 'overtaking the UK and catching up with the United States', a popular slogan in the Great Leap Forward in the 1950s; during the Cultural Revolution, most of these individuals were sent to the countryside as 'educated youth'; back then, they wrily called everything they did 'embroidering the planet'. Now many things in China, such as the highways network, have already 'overtaken the UK and caught up with the United States'. In the transcultural age, what such people are doing can be considered to be building global society and taking part in global social governance. The participants in global governance range from individuals and groups and governmental and non-governmental organizations to multinational corporations and international organizations. Any person who, through his or her actions, mobilizes natural resources beyond a country, benefiting a group of people living in any area of national or global society, is participating in global governance.

Walk for Peace is a chronicle of multi-directional participation in global governance. Lord Bates's walk is an individual action, and his willpower to overcome its difficulties and hardships came from his firm belief in his inner force, as he himself points out in the Introduction: '[I] will do so in the hope that these steps may celebrate what connects the UK and China through culture and history. That they will raise funds to support the work of those who seek to bring peace and comfort in a world of conflict and pain. That we will demonstrate that we are not powerless in the face of suffering but powerful beyond measure. That idealism, passion and dreams are not the sole property of the young. That we do not need to live out our lives under the dark shadows, low expectations or cynicism of others.'

These hopes and goals are shared by many people from different cultural contexts. During the UK–China Year of Cultural Exchange, Lord Bates successfully completed a walk of 1,702.7 km across six Chinese provinces, raising £90,000 for charity projects recommended by the Chinese Red Cross. With this walk across

China, Lord Bates spread the notion of peace and set for all of us an example of 'transcultural cooperation for shared goals'.[2]

Last, I venture to add a personal comment. Fascinated by Lord Bates's story, I read the whole journal, log after log, and I was deeply moved and full of admiration for his perseverance and willpower in completing his walk, as well as of appreciation for his views on numerous topics. The most impressive entry, in my view, is that of 4 October, Day 70, 'Mother-in-law's question goes to the heart of the matter', which delves into the relationship between his walk, human nature and world peace.

'I believe we are on the verge of exposing the male lust for violence and the human glorification of war for what it is, "a primeval animal instinct". Its roots lie more in anthropology and tribal culture than in politics. Its antidotes are in the realms of competitive sport, education, cultural exchange and international systems of justice. My core theory is that "we are all the same", there is good and evil in the world, but it is not out there; it is in us. There are differences in culture, language and religion but these are explained not by some divine plan but by simple accident of birth and our tribal roots. The more we see each other as human first and our adopted culture second, the less we will distrust, the less we will feel threatened by difference, the less we will feel superior or inferior and the more we may seek to resolve disputes through agreed systems of justice based on the fundamental principle of the equal value, worth, rights and responsibilities of each and every human being. [...] I have yet to prove this theory or win an argument on its central premise [...]. I don't have the intellect or the words to even make the case, let alone win the argument, so I let my walk be my talk and hope.'

This passage calls to my mind the concept of 'cultural consciousness' developed by the renowned sociologist Fei Xiaotong. He interpreted the concept with 16 Chinese characters, which can be translated as 'cherishing one's own cultural beauty', 'openly appreciating others' beauties', 'letting different beauties coexist' and 'being blessed with *harmony but diversity* under the same heaven'. It means 'we are all the same' but 'we are all different'. True, we all have a tendency to love and hate; but we are all different in their proportions in us. We all experience fear, but some of us run away, some of us freeze and some of us fight. So, world order is not deducible from human nature, but from principles of organization that belong to the nature of existence for human society in its environment.

Xiangqun Chang
Director of the Global China Institute; Editor-in-chief of Global China Press
Honorary Professor of University College London
Revised in June 2017

---

[2] This is the theme of the Fourth Global China Dialogue, 1–2 December 2017 at the British Academy and UK Parliament.

DOI https://doi.org/10.24103/TETE.en.cn.2017.1.3

Preface

My heartfelt congratulations on the publication of *Walk for Peace*, Lord Michael Bates's journal of his walk through China.

This is no ordinary journal.

Lord Bates walked ten kilometres almost every day, for 71 days, and at the end of each tiring day he wrote an entry in his dairy. Each day's account is witty and humorous or contains deep reflections, and they represent the distillation of the author's tenacity, goodness of heart, enthusiasm and commitment to the value of his venture.

This was the first time since the foundation of New China that a British peer and Minister of State, equipped with a bamboo staff and a cloth bag, had travelled on foot for thousands of miles through China, exploring both urban and rural areas and writing stories of his first-hand experiences.

On July 10, 2015, to commemorate the 70th Anniversary of the Global War against Fascism and the first UK–China Year of Cultural Exchange, Lord Michael Bates, then Minister of State at the Home Office, embarked on his Walk for Peace, from Beijing to Nanjing and then to Hangzhou. The Chinese Red Cross acted as the backup team for the Chinese portion of the Walk for Peace, providing Lord Bates with technical assistance and logistics support to enable him to complete the itinerary to the best of his physical abilities, and, as the person in charge of this project, I was fortunate to accompany him throughout, becoming both a participant and a witness of this remarkable journey.

Lord Bates's Walk for Peace started right before the 2012 London Olympics, when he walked from the ancient city of Olympia, in Greece, to the then host city of the Olympic Games, London: he walked for 10 months, passing through 14 countries, covering a distance of 4,693 km (2,933 miles), and publicizing the Olympic Truce wherever he could. Michael Bates is not an athlete; you could not even say that he is a hiking enthusiast: up until that point, his walked distance in a day had never exceeded 16 km. With a demanding job in Parliament, in his fifties, he was already a grandfather and he was overweight. However, he pursued his ideals, which meant challenging his personal physical limits, and his impressive feat to appeal for world peace moved everyone. The United Nations Secretary-General, Ban Ki-moon, the then president of the International Olympic Committee, Jacques Rogge, and former Pope Benedict XVI expressed their sincere admiration upon meeting him. Afterwards, Lord Bates insisted on using the summer recess for Parliament for his Walk for Peace, also launching a charitable appeal for donations to help victims of conflicts, and walking more than 10,000 km (6,250 miles) in five years. He decided to come to China partly because of his wife, Xuelin, who is originally from Hangzhou, Zhejiang Province. She graduated from the Department of Architecture of Zhejiang University, and is a successful architect and entrepreneur. Although she has resided in the UK for the past 27 years, she has always been animated by patriotic feelings, and in 2015 she suggested that her husband continue his Walk for Peace in China.

The Walk began on July 27, 2015 in Beijing, passing through the provinces of Hebei, Shandong, Jiangsu, Anhui and Zhejiang, lasting 71 days, covering 1,702.7 km (1,064 miles), and reached its destination on October 5! Travelling by foot during the Chinese summer, Lord Bates had to endure scorching heat, mosquito and insect bites, unfamiliar climate conditions, blisters on his feet and massive traffic congestion at a regional level, while covering approximately 40 km (25 miles) per day. In order to prevent the two phones that he kept in his backpack, essential for keeping track of the mileage, from becoming soaked in sweat and 'going on strike', he had to wrap them in a plastic bag. He would set off in the early morning, in high spirits, and continue until sunset, although by that time he would often begin staggering and even collapsed a few times owing to heatstroke. In spite of all this, he kept walking, which moved us deeply. He relied, he said, not only on his physical ability but first and foremost on his firm belief in his great goal and in the need to persevere in pursuing one's cause despite the difficulties. As he wrote in his diary: 'I am not walking, I am using my legs to chase after the objective in my heart.'

Reading Lord Bates's diary, the reader will discover a happy journey described with typical British humour, while the hardships he encountered are rarely mentioned. He crossed the Yellow River and the Yangtze River, he walked along the Grand Canal, the Hongze Lake and Lake Tai, going from the vast plains of northern China to the elegant network of waterways in the Jiangnan area, walking through bustling cities and quiet villages, seeing fruit being collected, fragrant fields, the rising sun of the morning and the setting sun behind the mountains – all of this unfolding like a beautiful painting! The magnificence of nature, offering a different landscape every day, left Lord Bates in profound awe of the beauty of China, and in his journal he used the wonderful words of Jane Austen to describe this experience of beauty.

In Lord Bates's opinion, the Walk for Peace was a pilgrimage through Chinese culture, and many entries in his diary contain exquisite passages discussing the history of Britain and China, as well as comparisons between their cultures. He lingered in the native places of Confucius, Mencius and Mozi, passed through Mount Tai, one of the Five Sacred Mountains, bought an English translation of the Analects of Confucius, and, while in the birthplaces of sages, he reflected on how to apply their thoughts to reality, further fuelling his love for Chinese culture and his interest in its origins.

The Walk for Peace brought Lord Bates up close to the extraordinary history of the Chinese people's War of Resistance against Japan. In the key battlefield of Tai'erzhuang. Where the flames of war had once raged, he diligently copied the commentary he found in the memorial hall. He visited the Huanghua banks, which once were the general headquarters of the New Fourth Army of the Republic of China, and now host a memorial hall dedicated to the Chinese who perished during the Nanjing massacre, and the former residence of John Rabe, perfectly preserved, and he talked with a 95-year-old veteran of the War of Resistance … The heroism of the Chinese people, who put up vigorous resistance and made enormous sacrifices during World War II, greatly contributing to the victory of China, moved Lord Bates and gained his deep admiration.

The Walk took Lord Bates deep into inner China, where he sowed the idea of peace and friendship between China and the UK, all the while looking for the real China of the past and of the future, her sufferings and her splendour, as well as her people and their hopes and dreams. He met hardworking people carrying out road maintenance works, owners of jujube orchards, old shepherds, young students full of energy, as well as the accompanying Red Cross volunteers and the people who are silently dedicated to work in the Red Cross's 'Homes of Hope', and the enthusiastic grassroots officials leading the way towards reform and opening up, in search of development ... He made a point of respectfully memorizing their faces and names, and recorded them all in his diary. The industriousness and authenticity of the Chinese people, their honesty and kind-heartedness, the diversity of popular local customs and their bustling lives, the amazing 'Suqian speed', their pride in the great successes of the last 30 years and their longing for the 'Chinese dream of a better future all left a profound impression on Lord Bates. In his eyes, this is the story behind the Chinese miracle, the workers and the groups operating in all professional fields who are the backbone of the nation, enabling the miracle of millions and millions of people breaking out of poverty, thanks to the spirit of struggle that is quite difficult to understand for a Westerner. However weary he was, he persevered with writing his journal every day, and would stay up at night with his wife and the volunteer team to translate it into Chinese, to transmit the experiences and impressions of his journey while they were still fresh, revealing to the world the real China he saw with his own eyes.

The Chinese Red Cross's noble mission of pursuing world peace and protecting human dignity was willingly put at the service of Lord Bates. Waves of Red Cross volunteers accompanied and escorted him all along the way, ranging from workers, farmers, teachers, students and housewives to rescue team members, surgeons and professional painters; the oldest was over 60 and the youngest only 17. On the road, they acted as guides, medical personnel and consultants enabling Lord Bates to understand the local situation. During rest breaks, Michael Bates liked to sit down and talk to everybody, and they received a morale boost and encouragement by walking alongside him. In his diary Lord Bates expresses his gratitude to them: 'Thanks to each and every Red Cross employee and volunteer who worked hard for this walk; your passion and dedication to your work have encouraged me every day to set out on my journey on schedule and to reach my objective … I was only able to continue on this walk thanks to you, and the ultimate success represents a victory for our entire team.'

'Now I love China even more, because I understand her!' These were Lord Bates's final words to us upon ending his trip. After returning to the UK, he published several articles about China, and gave many speeches about his experiences, including in the British Parliament. 'You cannot look at China and comment on China from the outside,' he says. You have to experience it in person before you can really understand her.' In his diary he wrote: 'This wonderful experience will forever be in my heart, and I will continue to tell the world my Chinese story: the story of a real China, a beautiful China.' In his speech in Parliament during his visit to the UK in October 2015, President Xi Jinping praised Lord Bates as an ambassador for Sino–British friendship. In October 2016, Lord Bates was appointed Minister of State at the Department for International Development. It is our heartfelt hope that he will come on more visits to China, and that he will continue to present new stories about China to the world.

Just as this book was going to press, we learned the impressive news that Lord Bates and his wife had completed another 'Walk for the Olympic Truce', on the occasion of the 2016 Rio Olympics! This time the walk started in April in the Argentine capital, Buenos Aires: without any local support, they trekked for 115 days through remote and desolate South American wastelands, jungles and mountains. Thanks to his exceptional willpower and the support of his wife Xuelin throughout the journey, Michael Bates reached his destination, the statue of Christ the Redeemer at the top of Mount Corcovado in Rio de Janeiro, Brazil, having covered 3,025 km (1,890 miles). Less than a year after their walk through China, they had set a new record! Their indomitable spirit, their relentless ambition to pursue their cause and their wonderful selflessness are distilled in a power that boosts people's morale, as more and more followers are starting to call for a truce, for world peace.

Although the Walk for Peace from Beijing to Nanjing and Hangzhou has ended, the great idea of peace for mankind will forever be in our hearts, and its light will inevitably illuminate the whole world.

ZHANG Ming
Former Chinese Red Cross External Liaison Department Director
October 2016

Introduction

'A journey of 1000 miles begins with a single step.' Laozi (c. 600 BC)

For me, that single step will begin informally early in the morning of Monday 27 July 2015 outside the iconic Beijing 'Birds Nest' Olympic Stadium and formally at the Temple of Heaven at 2PM. They will be the first steps on a solo walk, which will cover half the length of China, reaching Hangzhou via Nanjing and taking at least two months to complete.

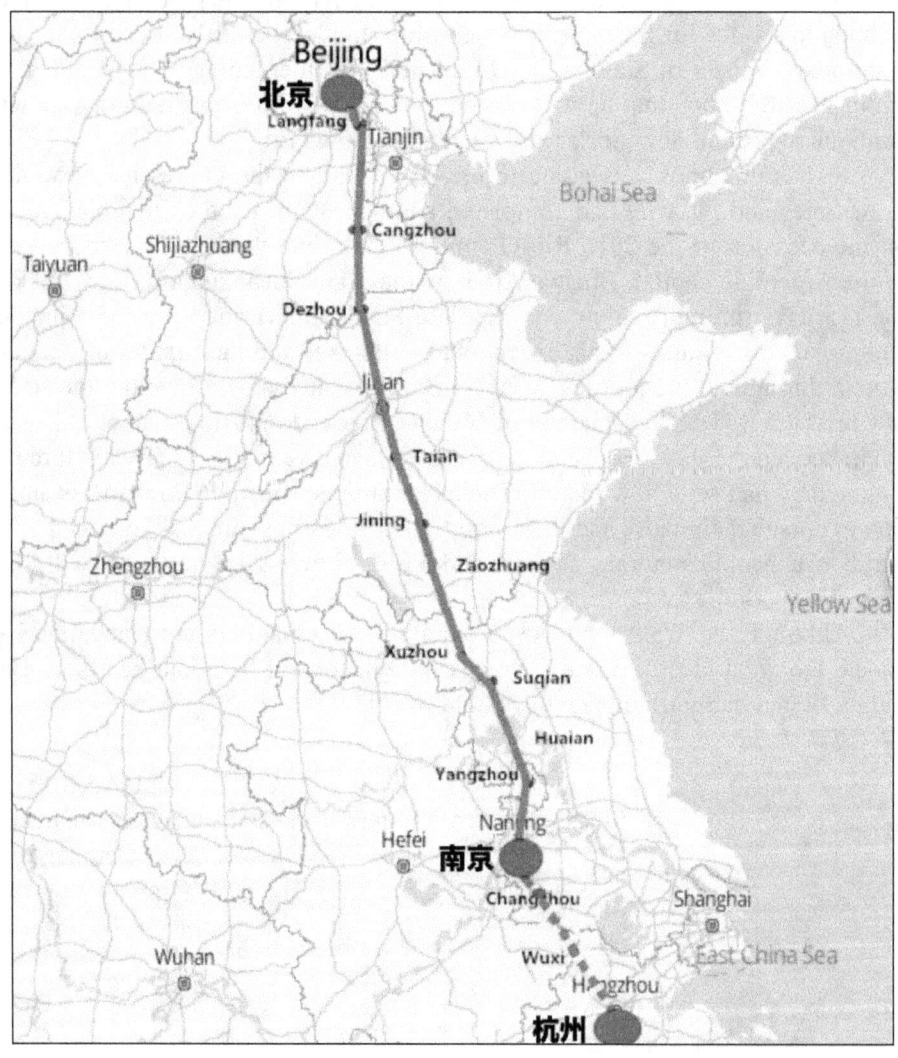

There are four main motivations for the walk. First, this is designated the first UK – China Year of Cultural Exchange and there is a rich calendar of events showcasing the best of Chinese culture in the UK and UK culture in China. My wife is Chinese and we both respect and delight in our respective adopted cultures. Culture connects us as human beings like nothing else: music, film, poetry, art, dance, literature, education, sport, cuisine, religion, language, social traditions, appreciation of the beauty and wonder of nature and sport. These are humanity's lowest common denominator and its highest value. The more we emphasize what we have in common, the more relations grow – in fact, the Latin and French roots of the word 'culture' are all connected with nurturing growth. See http://www.britishcouncil.cn/en/programmes/arts/2015YOCE

Second, 2015 is the 70th anniversary of the end of the World War II, in which Britain and China were allies from 1941 to the conclusion of the war. For China, the war began in 1937, two years before Britain's engagement. At the conclusion of the war, China, along with the United States, Britain, France and the then Soviet Union were founder members of the United Nations and became Permanent Members of the United Nations Security Council. China paid a very heavy price during the war, losing an estimated 14 million lives through hostilities and famine. Cold War politics were probably responsible for the lack of attention to this alliance. It is right to remember the alliance then and the costs of war on all sides and the absolute necessity that we continue to work together through the international community to stop such needless waste of life from ever happening again.

Third, 27 July is the third anniversary of the Opening Ceremony of the London 2012 Olympic and Paralympic Games. London memorably took on the mantle of Olympic host city from Beijing. While both Games were distinctive, taking inspiration from a rich culture and history, they also celebrated the Olympic ideal. It was that ideal, in the form of the Olympic Truce or Peace, that transcended the Ancient Games and which inspired me to first step out on long-distance walks. On that occasion, it was a ten-month, 2,914-mile solo walk from Olympia, Greece, to London. See www.walkfortruce.org. On the first anniversary of the Games in 2013, I set off from London on a 518-mile walk to Londonderry, Northern Ireland, to raise funds for Save the Children's work in Syria (see www.walforsyriaschildren.org), and last year, the 100th anniversary of the outbreak of the First World War, I undertook a 1,054-mile walk from London to Berlin. See www.walkforpeace.eu

Fourth, I am walking to raise funds to support the work of the Red Cross in China. The Red Cross was founded to bring humanity and compassion into the theatre of war and barbarism. I am sickened by the effects of war, terrorism and violence that are streamed into our lives through our 24-hour news networks and presented as entertainment in movies and computer games. We humans seem unable to kick this primaeval tribal instinct, unique to our species, to attain meaning and purpose in our own lives by celebrating the taking or maiming the lives of those who we delude ourselves into believing are morally, theologically or racially inferior to our tribe. In ages past, the young men would disappear off to some distant field outside their homes to slug it out. Today, war has come into the heart of the city, and it is the innocent, the women, the children, the sick and the elderly, who have been placed on its front line. One of my destinations, Nanjing, emphasizes that point, being the scene of the Nanking Massacre in 1937, when over 200,000 of its citizens were systematically slaughtered. H. G. Wells put it succinctly when we said, 'If we don't end war, then war will end us', and the history of the twentieth century shows that humanity came damn close to that end.

So I will set off on another walk, supported as always by my wife Xuelin, who faithfully goes ahead to prepare the way and stays behind to pick up the bills. I am a 54-year-old grandfather, overweight and not fit. My sons remind me I am certainly more 'beer and grills' than Bear Grylls. Walking 20 miles a day in 35–40 degrees of heat will be a challenge. This will be my seventh but by far my most challenging walk so far, and I will talk about it more en route via www.walkfor-peace.eu. That said, if you have a reason for doing something, you can put up with anything it throws at you. So we will do so in the hope that these steps may celebrate what connects the UK and China through culture and history. That they will raise funds to support the work of those who seek to bring peace and comfort in a world of conflict and pain. That we will demonstrate that we are not powerless in the face of suffering but powerful beyond measure. That idealism, passion and dreams are not the sole property of the young. That we do not need to live out our lives under the dark shadows, low expectations or cynicism of others. That in the great Games of Life, we are none of us spectators and all of us have a vital role to play to make this a better world. This is the true meaning of life.

Preparations

July 25

Countdown to the start – departure from the UK

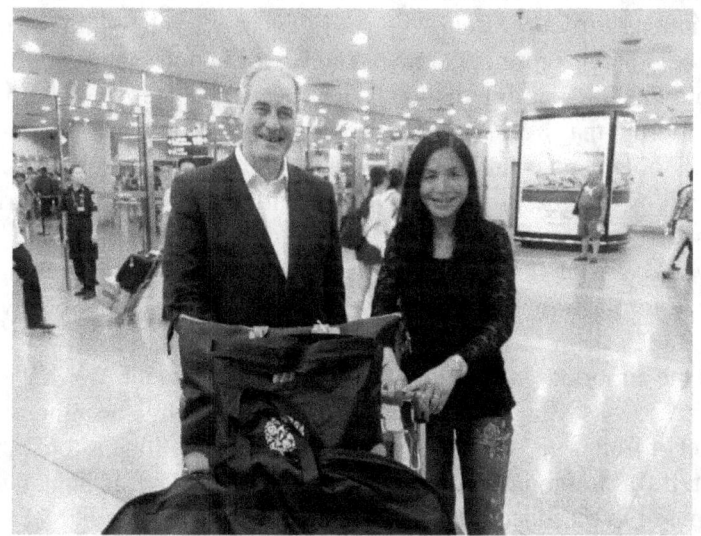

Lord and Lady Bates in Beijing Capital International Airport.

China Eastern Airlines is an excellent air carrier but not even they could control the rains and wind that lashed the coastal city of Shanghai, delaying our arrival and connecting flight to Beijing. I wondered whether the storms were an omen of what lay ahead for the walk.

The ancient civilizations believed natural phenomena were messages from the gods expressing either approval or disapproval. Explaining to the ancients that a typhoon simply happened because of warm sea surfaces interacting with high humidity, causing instability in the middle levels of the troposphere, would be to them as mad as us believing that they were a message from the gods.

That said, we might reflect on the base conduct of young Western tourists on Mt Kinabalu in Sabah, Malaysia, who allegedly angered the mountain gods and undoubtedly angered their parents. They say culture connects. That is indeed one of the key themes of my walk, but sometimes when not respected cultures can collide, creating equally damaging moral typhoons.

The British are often misunderstood abroad. When we ask 'How are you?', we don't expect you to tell us. For us, a queue is not a frustrating inconvenience but a national hobby and a test of social order and patience. If someone robbed a bank, the severity of the punishment would reflect not the amount of money he stole but how long the queue was he jumped to get it. For the British, the rule in life is simply to avoid making a fuss, about anything, and that definitely includes a five-hour flight delay.

I guess this must be my thirteenth or fourteenth visit to China. My first was as a business school student in Oxford in 1998, when I was undertaking research into the operation of the Chinese labour law in Nike footwear factories in Qing-doa in Shandong Province. Being typical students, we rolled into town not quite understanding that this former German colony was famous above all for its Tsing-tao beer and the Qingdao International Beer Festival. I feel we did more cultural diplomacy during that week than has been done before or since. It didn't damage the research too much, as I managed to get a 'Highly Commended' for my disser-tation, which owed more to the refreshment of the beer than to the brilliance of our analysis.

So we arrived in Beijing in the early hours of Saturday morning. We had called ahead to our host, Madame Zhang from the Red Cross Society of China in Beijing, to tell them of our delay and let them know that there was no need to meet us at the airport, as we would just get a taxi to the hotel. When we arrived at 12.30 am, there was Ming Zhang was waiting for us with a beaming smile and a huge basket of fruit. This was Chinese social culture – nothing is too much trouble for a guest. It was humbling. I cannot speak for the whole of Britain, but I think if I was supposed to be collecting someone at Heathrow at 7pm and they arrived at 12:30am, I would probably have left money for the taxi and a polite note saying we would call by the hotel in the morning to check they were OK (Xuelin adds, 'Speak for yourself').

We arrived at the hotel 30 hours after leaving Westminster in London. It was an exhausting trip, but the welcome by Madame Zhang had made me begin to for-get it. We checked in to the hotel with the wonderfully named receptionist, Fancy Ye, evoking lots of silly Geordie schoolboy humour (from me). 'Ye' means 'you' in the Geordie dialect.

As I drifted off to sleep, I reflected that 25 hours from one side of the world to the other was nothing. The great tea races of the mid-nineteenth century, in which great sailing ships would race back from Shanghai to London to deliver the first fresh green tea of the season, would take 67 days to complete. It would take me about the same to walk from Beijing to Hangzhou. I mentioned this profound thought to Xuelin, who replied, 'What a shame we will waste the return section of the Shanghai air ticket'. The rumbling sound of cultures colliding can be heard in the distance, but still, mustn't make a fuss.

URL http://www.walkforpeace.eu/day-2-countdown-to-start-25-july-2015/

July 25

Countdown to the Start – a busy day in Beijing

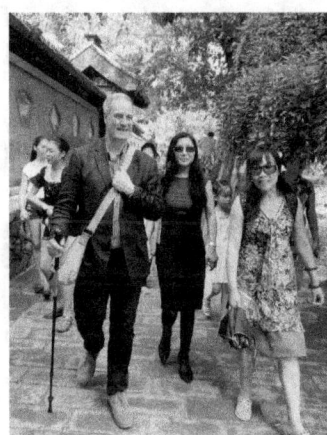 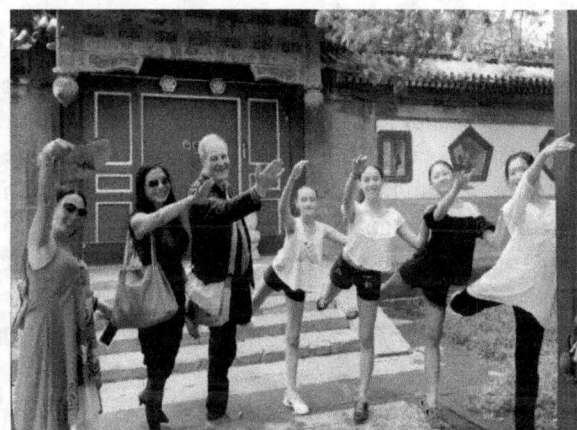

Left: Visiting the Summer Palace. Right: Lord and Lady Bates, and children from the UK
and China, dance at a summer camp in the Summer Palace.

'Even God can't change the past. No matter how many tears I've cried,' sang
Charlotte Church. The past is fixed. It is why we feel so powerless when held to
account for it. It can't be changed as much as we would wish it could. We were
reminded of this by the trial in Germany of Oskar Gröning, a 93-year-old who
was a bookkeeper at the notorious Nazi Auschwitz-Birkenau concentration camp.
He expressed remorse for his actions and laid flowers for the 1.1 million victims
of the camp. He asked for forgiveness, but the crimes were so great a scar on the
conscience of humanity that forgiveness was denied and he was committed to
prison, probably for the rest of his natural life.

What has this to do with a 'Walk for Peace' in China? Well, this: In the af-
ternoon we took a trip to the site of the Emperor's Summer Palace in north-west
Beijing. When it was built, it was one of the wonders of the world, such was its
architectural beauty and the magnificence of the surrounding lake and mountains.
The origins of the Summer Palace date back to 1153, before Magna Carta and the
establishment of the first British parliament. Yet both the old palace, Yuánmíng
Yuán, and the new were destroyed by British and French forces during the Second
Opium War.

There have been volumes written on the origins of the Opium Wars, which
I cannot begin to repeat but essentially it boiled down to tea. The Emperor had
stipulated that tea could only be sold in exchange for silver. The British thought
that silver was too high a price and insisted that they would pay in opium, which
was cheaply produced in the colonies in India, especially Bengal, and then easily
collected on the route from England to China. The Emperor saw the moral decay

resulting from the spread of British opium and tried to stop the trade. The British violently objected to this and started a war, in fact. two wars. to show the Chinese who was boss. The First Opium War was ended only by the Treaty of Nanjing, which extracted humiliating damages for the war from the Chinese Emperor and the granting of British sovereignty over Hong Kong. This was the beginning of what the Chinese now refer to as the Century of Humiliation, first at the hands of the British, French and Germans and then by the Japanese.

As I wandered through the ruins and the rebuilt sections of the old and new Summer Palaces, I felt ashamed that first we, the British, should have peddled drugs in exchange for tea, but second, and more importantly, that we should have destroyed such a magnificent architectural masterpiece. It is like a thief breaking into your home to steal a camera and then burning your treasured family photographs on the way out.

I am very proud of my country. I believe that during the 'Pax Britannica', Britain displayed the same motivation as the Romans in seeking to build institutions, establish peace and order and exchange culture and trade. They came not to destroy but to build. Yet history reminds us of uncomfortable truths, as in 1860, when Lord Elgin with 11,000 troops under his command systematically destroyed these two royal palaces, leaving not one stone on top of another.

Imagine how differently we might have viewed the Roman invasion of Britain if they had destroyed Stonehenge and given us drugs, rather than law, sanitation and roads. I believe this was out of character for the British – though the Americans might chip in unhelpfully by pointing out that in 1812 the British burnt down the White House and both houses of Congress. All we can say now is that it was wrong and it has soured relations for too long. Today, much of the Summer Palace has been rebuilt to its former glory and so, more slowly perhaps, are relations between our two countries.

Xuelin and I went to the Summer Palace to meet a group of UK Chinese dance and culture exchange students. The teacher, Connie Alexander, had brought a group of British Chinese students to China on a six-week dance course. This was exactly what the UK–China Year of Culture Exchange is all about: learning more about our respective culture and histories. God may not be able to change the past but through our actions today we can shape a different future. This is what the British Chinese students were doing through dance and I was setting out to do by undertaking a walk.

URL http://www.walkforpeace.eu/day-1-countdown-to-start-26-july-2015/

July 26

HM Government of the UK and
Red Cross Society of China

Preparations for the walk have been quietly underway for months in both China and the UK. First there was the uncertainty of the General Election. Clearly, the outcome of the election on 7 May would indicate whether I might have more or less time to walk. If the Conservatives won, then I would need to support their legislation as it went through the House of Lords. Also, if we won, then there was a possibility that David Cameron as Prime Minister might ask me to continue to be a minister in the government, or he might decide to promote someone new into the role – and if that happened, then the demands on my time would not be as great, so the walk could be longer.

I have been a member of the Conservative Party since I was 18, in 1979. I owe it so much for the opportunities that the successive leaders of the Party, from Margaret Thatcher to David Cameron, have offered me. When it came to this election, I wanted the Party to win, not just for the Party but for the country. I believed passionately that we had turned the country round since 2010. I worked exceedingly hard for the election – as hard as I ever worked when I was a candidate in the election in 1987, 1991, 1992 and 1997. My wife, Xuelin, and I were sitting at the phones in Campaign HQ urging voters to go out to vote when the exit poll came out predicting we had won. The euphoria I felt at that moment was as great as I have ever felt in any election.

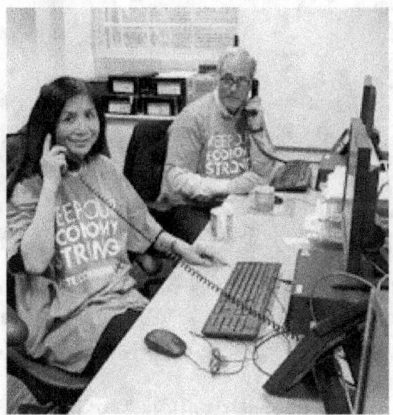

Lord and Lady Bates canvass for votes at Conservative Party headquarters
on the night of the British general election in 2015.

If we had lost and Labour had won, then I would have probably put aside trying to realize my childhood dream of walking around the world for the next five years, but they didn't, and I was honoured and humbled when David Cameron called me and asked me to stay on at the Home Office, as he promoted me to Minister of State. As soon as the election was out of the way, I began the gentle process of seeking permission to undertake another walk for charity, this time in China.

In the UK parliamentary system we get very long summer breaks – normally two and a half months – so that members of the House of Commons can spend a long time in their constituencies listening to the concerns of the people they represent. In the House of Lords we are not elected but appointed by the Queen on advice from the Prime Minister, so for us the summer recess is literally a long holiday, or, for the many members of the House of Lords who have very demanding jobs, an opportunity to focus on these, rather than having to come to the House of Lords to vote each day. I don't have an outside job. Politics is my job. So, since 2009 I have used my summer to undertake a walk for a charity or cause I believed in.

After two months. I finally got word that the Home Secretary (my direct boss), the Foreign Office and Number 10 (on behalf of the prime minister – my ultimate boss) had all agreed to my undertaking the walk, providing arrangements could be put in place to allow important decisions and actions to be taken by colleagues in my absence. It was very generous of them to agree, but the fact that it was the first UK–China Year of Cultural Exchange with the Chinese premier due to make a state visit to the UK in October were undoubtedly important considerations in the approval process.

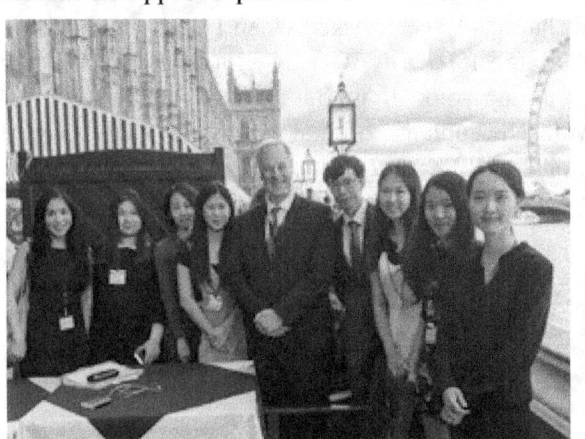 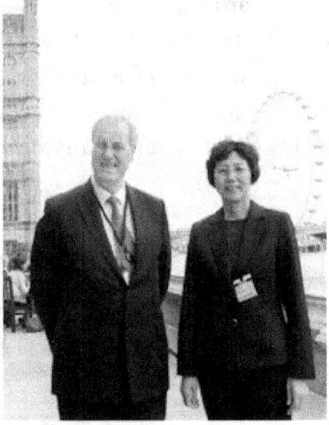

Left: Lord and Lady Bates with Peace Walk volunteers at the House of Lords during a meeting to discuss plans for the walk. Right: Lord Bates and Xu Ke, Executive Vice President of the China Red Cross, in front of the Houses of Parliament.

Xuelin and I work as a team on all walks. My job was to get approval from London. Xuelin's job was to get permission from Beijing. I am not sure whose was the most difficult. Initially, we made the approach to Ambassador Liu Xiaoming in the Chinese Embassy in London. It can sometimes take a bit of time to understand why a politician from one country would want to walk in and raise funds for a charity in another. It sounds crazy. Yet China would not be the first but the eighteenth country I had walked through in the cause of peace. There was a further sensitivity about walking in China, different from any of the European countries I had walked through ...

We were pleased that the Chinese Embassy in London and the Ministry of Foreign Affairs of China were very supportive to our walk in China from the start. To make the logistics of my walk go smoothly, they recommended the Red Cross Society of China to assist us. The Red Cross movement has history dating back 150 years since it was founded on the battlefields of war-torn Europe. Their aim is to save human life and human dignity, irrespective of nationality, and to promote a peaceful and harmonious world. It was a perfect fit with the ethos of our 'Walk for Peace'. The Red Cross has been in China since 1904 and has a long and respected reputation, as it does the world over. It is probably the largest volunteer network anywhere in the world, with over two million volunteers regularly giving their time to delivery of their projects in China.

Xuelin and I were very happy to work with the Chinese Red Cross, with whom Xuelin built up a great relationship. By the time we departed from London, we had not only the permission from China, but also a detailed plan, including the route, daily mileage arrangements, accommodation and other visits along the way that would help me understand the real Chinese history and culture. They wrote a three-page report giving guidance ontravel by foot, weather, traffic and local customs and much else besides. This was our fourth long-distance walk and we had never been so well prepared. It makes me think that having a good plan is halfway to a success.

The final but essential part of the preparations was to build a project team who might work with Xuelin and me in the UK while we were in China. There are a huge number of communications and technology challenges and we felt the need for a larger team of volunteers than on previous walks so that the work did not become so onerous as to interfere with their studies. We were overwhelmed by the responses of outstanding young people who wanted to work with us on trans-lations and social media: Jessie Huang, Jessica Liu, Xiao Xiao, Emily Hu, Liweiqi Ma, Katy Xiao, Violet Ma and Yong Xuan Li. We met for the first time as a team to have tea in Parliament just before we left and expressed our gratitude for their willingness to help the cause.

So, the permissions were agreed in London and Beijing. Support was in place in London and Beijing. We were ready to walk.

URL http://www.walkforpeace.eu/preperations-red-cross-society-of-china-hm-government-of-uk/

Walking

July 27 Day 1

Departure

Route: The Temple of Heaven – Daxing District (South Sixth Ring Road), Beijing
Walked today : 11.50 miles / 18.40 km
Total walked: 11.50 miles / 18.40 km
Donated today: £120.00 and ¥0.00
Total donations: £120.00 and ¥0.00
Note: donations in Sterling and Reminbe are provided as separate amounts

Every journey has its beginning and its ending. The traveller will take great care to ensure that both locations speak to the purpose of endeavour. My first walk began on Holy Island; my second at the Temple of Hera, Olympia, Greece; my third from 10 Downing Street; my fourth from the Tomb of the Unknown Warrior in Westminster Abbey. I had in my mind that, as Monday 27 July was the exact third anniversary of the Opening Ceremony of the London 2012 Games, I would like to start at the Olympic 'Bird's Nest' (National Stadium). The only problem was that the official start ceremony had been set by the Red Cross for 2 pm from the Temple of Heaven. I suggested that I could make a personal start from the Olympic Stadium at 8 am and walk the 10 miles/16 km south to the Temple of Heaven, where we could have the official start. My partners in the Red Cross didn't think this was a good idea, because they didn't want me walking across Beijing by myself when they had been tasked with keeping me safe. More importantly, Xuelin didn't think it was a good idea. I confess to feeling a little stubborn, not wanting to lose control. I was then reminded by Xuelin of an old Chinese saying, 'If you want to go fast, go alone; if you want to go far, go together.' I wasn't the only one investing time and energy in this walk – Xuelin and the Red Cross were too. They were all stakeholders in the collective venture. So we decided jointly that I would start from the Temple of Heaven as planned.

It proved to be exactly the right choice, not least because the temperature was well into the 40s and humidity and air quality in the city were unusually high and low, respectively. We arrived at the Temple of Heaven at the same time as a senior official from Hangzhou, Zhejiang (our destination point). I was amazed that a few senior officials from the Zhejiang Government, including its Foreign Affairs Office Director, Jin Yonghui, would make the equivalent of a flight from Rome to

London just to see me off on a walk. Of course, I shouldn't get too carried away, as the honour was as much for Xuelin as a respected community leader from that city and province as it was for me, but it was a gesture I appreciated for both reasons.

There must have been about 150 people at the ceremony, and we heard excellent speeches from officials talking about what this meant to them. Part of the meaning was hidden in the history of the Temple. I had not appreciated that this sacred site had been used to house British and French forces as they fought the Second Opium War in 1865 and again when they invaded with Germany to put down the Boxer Rebellion in 1900. I guess that we in Britain may have had similar hesitant feelings if the Chinese troops had invaded Britain twice and used St Paul's Cathedral as their military base. Well, the Chinese people were gracious in allowing such a nationally sacred site to be used to send good wishes to a Brit who had come on a different type of mission from some of his predecessors – a mission of peace and friendship.

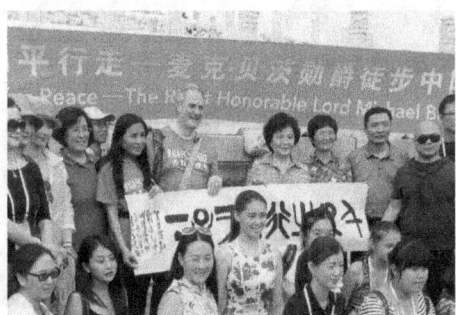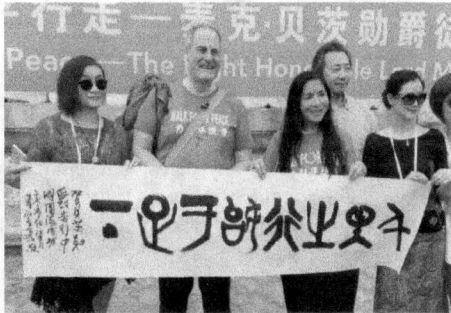

Left: Walk for Peace start ceremony at the Temple of Heaven. Vice President of the Chinese Red Cross, Hao Linna (on Xuelin's right) hosted the event and delivered a speech. Qiu Yuanping, Director of the Overseas Chinese Affairs Office of the State Council (on Michael's left), formally launched the walk. Right: Lord and Lady Bates being presented with a calligraphy scroll

Two things went through my mind as I stood in front of the distinguished audience of well-wishers. The first was a real fear that I could barely stand up in this heat, never mind walk 20 miles. Could I actually do this? Was I just too unfit? I was worried that the praise for my endeavour might be a bit too soon. I could imagine myself collapsing under the heat and humidity at the gate to the Temple of Heaven. My confidence was reduced a bit further when two young and athletic walkers from chinawalking.net joined me to say they were going to walk part of the way with me.

I was getting the feeling like being a tightrope walker who shows up at Niagara Falls to walk across. He takes one look down to the pounding waters of the falls and certain death if he falls and then another behind him to the cheering crowds urging him on. Which is more important to him, his fears or the cheers? Ultimately, if he is to safely cross the falls, it is because he closes his mind to the fears and the cheers and concentrates only on getting the first step right.

My second thought was an appreciation for the generosity of the Chinese people. I walked in the Temple to the ceremony and was given flowers; a renowned Chinese calligrapher turned up with a scroll on which he had written in Chinese, 'The journey of a thousand miles begins with a single step.' Another attached some Buddhist prayer bells to my rucksack to keep me safe along the journey. Minister Qiu Yuanping from the State Council Chinese Overseas Affairs Office walked with me as far as the river, a courtesy that was extended to honoured guests, although perhaps it might have been as much to ensure I was on the right road as to ensure that I wasn't thinking of coming back.

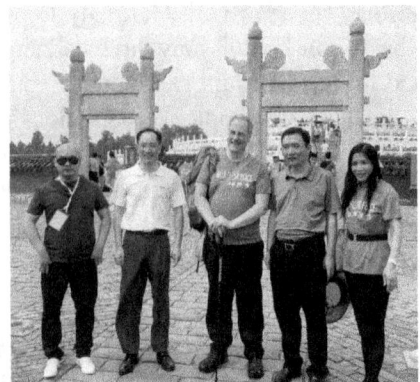 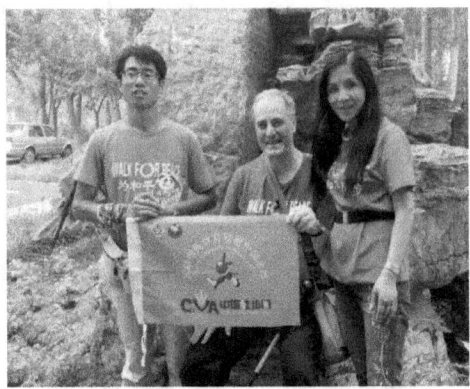

Left: Lord and Lady Bates with senior officials from Zhejiang Government, including Jin Yonghui, Foreign Affairs Office Director (between Michael and Xuelin).
Right: Lord and Lady Bates with a walker from *chinawalking.net*.

Gradually, the crowd of well-wishers reduced, but Madam Linna Hao, Vice President of the Red Cross, stayed with me to the fifth ring road. Madam Hao had studied in Cardiff and spoke excellent English, and we spoke about a range of themes, particularly social mobility and wealth and the growing number of *fu'erdai*, literally 'rich in the second generation'. Here were a Conservative and a Communist agreeing on a central aspect of economic and social policy, namely that 'wealth without work' is a social problem because it stifles creativity and risk-taking and creates a culture of entitlement.

Beijing is configured by a series of ring roads in much the same way as London is defined by the M25 and the North and South Circular roads. The difference is that Beijing used to have two but now it has six, and there are even plans for a seventh and an eighth – such is the unrelenting growth of infrastructure to support the growing population.

By 6 pm I had been reduced to a pool of sweat by the heat, and after 11.5 miles I saw signs for what I referred to as the 'Ring of the Sixth Happiness' after one of my favourite movies of all time, *The Inn of the Sixth Happiness*, starring Ingrid Bergman. I began to explain the plot of the movie, but felt my head going faint and my eyes beginning to roll. I decided to leave that story for another day and counted my many blessings for a good start.

URL http://www.walkforpeace.eu/day-1-temple-of-heaven-to-the-ring-of-the-sixth-happiness/

July 28 Day 2

In the Suburbs of Beijing

Route: Daxing District, Beijing
Walked today: 26.30 miles / 42.30 km
Total walked: 38.60 miles / 60.70 km
Donated today: £185.88 and ¥0.00
Total donations: £305.88 and ¥0.00

I have long admired great travel writers – Paul Theroux, Colin Thubron, Rory Stewart, Patrick Leigh Fermor and Marco Polo, to mention but a few. They have an extraordinary gift that makes them great – the ability to transport the reader to the place they are writing about. It is a gift, but not one I possess.

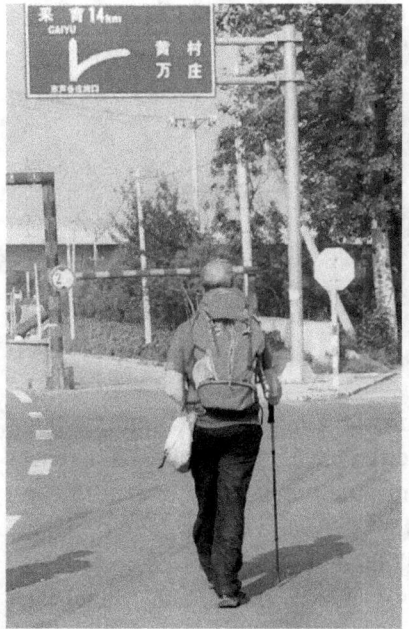
Walking along the roadside.

I have been writing about my travels on foot since 2009. I guess I must have written about 500 blog entries totalling around 350,000 words – enough to fill three or four books – but I have been unable to reach the heights of my literary heroes. Of course, the purpose of writing, as of life, is not to copy someone else's style but to develop your own.

I might wish to play the piano like Lang Lang, sing like Michael Buble, kick a football like David Beckham, run like Usain Bolt. I can't. But I can walk. I can communicate some random thoughts I have when I am walking. I can take a decent picture with an iPhone. If we choose to waste our lives being disappointed about what we can't do, then we will never have the joy of discovering and sharing what we can.

Good days walking are often followed by bad days. Each day of walking has a unique set of challenges that are presented for us to try and overcome. I hadn't managed to reach our designated hotel at the end of Day 1, so we had to drive back to the place we stopped. I was dropped with Wang, my guide, at a junction that looked like the place we had stopped but wasn't. I thought it was a few hundred metres back up the road, but it was nearer 2.5 kilometres. We arrived back at the starting point and my heart sank as I realized we now needed to walk back all that way for no gain.

Just then, Zhang Ming, Head of Communications for the Red Cross, turned up in our support vehicle. Ming has a wonderful 'no nonsense' style, being a highly efficient lady who had played a key role in the Beijing Olympic Organizing Committee. She had seen what had happened and said, 'Jump in! You don't need to waste time walking that stretch twice.' And with that, like Dorothy in the Yellow Brick Road, we were whisked back through time to the point at which we had been dropped.

My legs were suffering from cramps on account of the loss of fluid on Day 1 and insufficient salt, and as Day 2 went on, far from vanishing, they intensified. I took some ibuprofen, which helped or made me think it helped.

At this point, we were still in the suburbs of Beijing and walking along the roadside. There is a smell in the air in heavily populated and polluted cities and it is like the smell of a room that has had some building work done on it. It is really the taste of dust in the air. You can get used to it as you do on particularly hot and humid days in London, but it is not comfortable. In fact, the experience of walking in 40 degree temperatures and high humidity along roadsides is a bit like walking on a treadmill for ten hours in a sauna. But what was the place like?

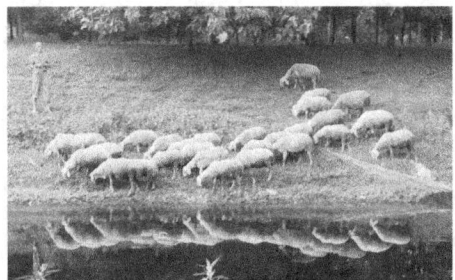 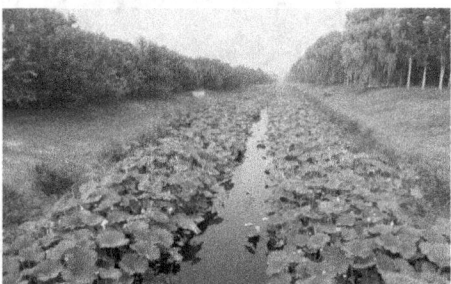

Left: A flock of sheep on the riverside. Right: Lotus flowers in bloom.

Sorry, I'm failing to describe the place again. In many ways, Beijing's outer suburbs are no different from any other major city I have been through. There was perhaps a less sharp distinction between poverty and prosperity. For example, we passed dozens of huge new apartment blocks on the outskirts of the city, where a two-bedroom apartment costs around £100,000 – in other words, comparable to the suburbs of many English cities such as Leeds, Birmingham, Manchester and Newcastle. The difference is, of course, that China has a per-capita GDP of around US$7,900, whereas the figure in the UK is around US$43,700 (2015 figures from the World Bank). The point is that there are large parts of China that are at least as affluent as the UK, in other words 'first world', and correspondingly very large parts that are still 'second' and 'third world'.

This could make for a highly volatile social mix, but that is less evident here. There seems to be no embarrassment or tension on either side, such that at the gates to the apartment blocks there spring up instant markets selling all types of foods, and the well-dressed young professionals will wander round among the bare-topped male farmers sitting displaying their produce on the back of rusty tricycles.

Another thing I noticed was that I walked for an entire day and never saw another Westerner – or any other racial group for that matter. I realized that I was deeply privileged to be able to wander down these roads. Then, suddenly, as I had stepped into a different world, the tall buildings were reduced to trees and the people replaced by sheep and the smells were the fragrance of the lotus flowers in full blossom. Men lined the riverbanks tending flocks of sheep and fishing. It was an image of peace and tranquillity. Was this the real China I had hoped to discover?

URL http://www.walkforpeace.eu/day-2-sixth-ring-road-to-hebei/

July 29 Day 3

Misunderstandings

Route: Daxing, Beijing – Anci District, Langfang, Hebei Province
Walked today: 21.10 miles / 59.70 km
Total walked: 34.00 miles / 94.70 km
Donated today: £100.00 and ¥0.00
Total donations: £405.88 and ¥0.00

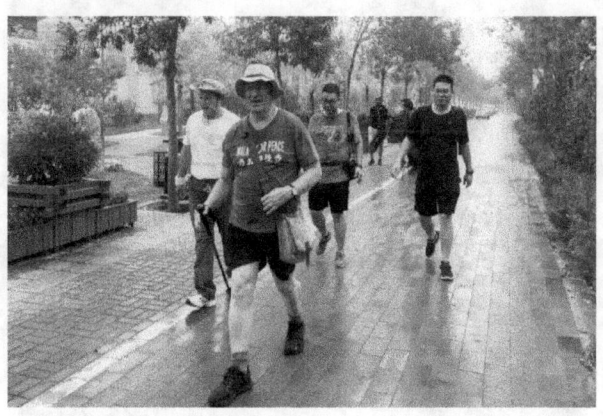

Walking into Langfang City, Hebei Province.

Police officers have a universal effect on our behaviours. In China, as in the UK when passing a police car, motorists slow down to a crawl, keep their eyes straight ahead and never toot their horn. I suppose I had a pre-conditioned response when one young police officer (they all look young to me at my age; even judges look young at my age) started shouting at me – pointing at my stick. I kept moving. He followed, still talking. I was trying to think what I could have 'possibly done wrong' with my stick. Is it against the law to carry a stick in China? Or was it that golf swing I used when we last stopped to whack a peach stone into the hedge? All sorts of things were going through my mind, but only one thing was going through his. The problem was I didn't know what it was.

Never far behind, my guide, who spoke a bit of English, caught up with me to explain that the police officer felt that I shouldn't be using a stick. 'Why?' I asked, expecting some obscure clause in highway law to be quoted. His response surprised me. He said, 'The police officer said your walking technique is wrong – you shouldn't walk with just one stick – it was better for you to swing your arms, or, if you must, use two sticks.' Never in a million years would I have guessed that the police officer was speaking about my walking style.

I thanked the police officer in my basic Chinese and he smiled. He started to walk along the road with me, throwing out random English phrases. I responded with random Mandarin phrases. We both laughed. Just as we were getting along well, a black VW Passat (used by senior police officers) pulled alongside and the tinted glass window was lowered. There was a tirade directed at the young police officer, and I am guessing that he wasn't being offered advice on his walking technique, for he ran off like an Olympic sprinter to the next junction.

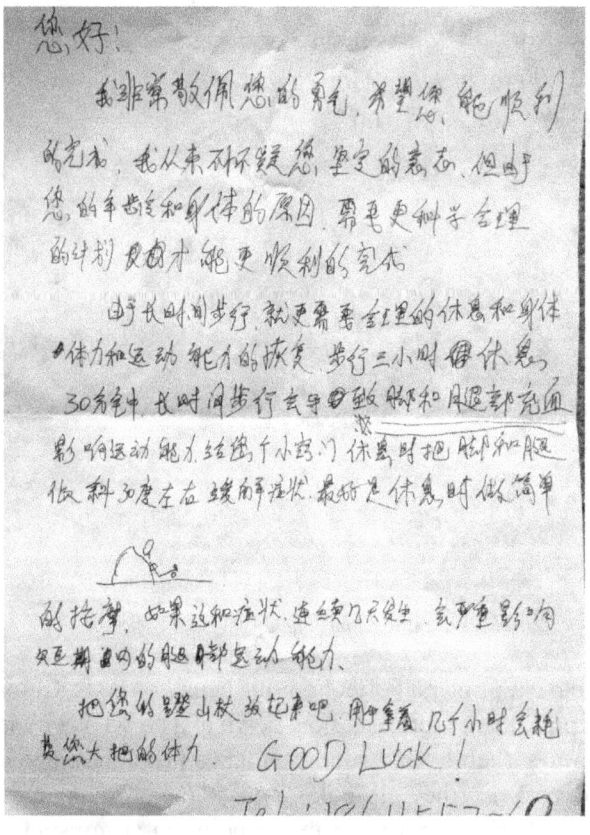

The letter from a young policeman to Lord Bates.

Later in the morning we took a rest break, and as we sat at the roadside drinking iced tea, the same young policeman appeared again, looking nervous. I could see him checking to see that there weren't any VW Passats in the neighbourhood. Then he jogged towards me and handed me a folded piece of white paper. I was a bit confused. When a police officer hands you a piece of white paper in the UK, that means you are in serious trouble. He left and I opened it. It was beautifully handwritten. I put it in my bag and showed it to Xuelin that night. When she read it, I was so touched.

He had written: 'I really admire your spirit and determination to walk. The problem is that because of your age, size and fitness, I really worry you won't be able to complete your journey. If you don't mind, I would like to offer some advice.' He then went on to advise me to stop every three hours and rest for 30 minutes. When I rested, I should raise my legs 30 degrees and massage my knees, etc., to stop using my walking stick…

I reflected that this was more than a lesson in walking; it was a lesson in life. Virtually all arguments, rows and even wars begin with misunderstandings. One person simply misunderstood what the other person intended. Sadly, in many cases those misunderstandings are never resolved until it is too late and more damage is done. Had I not had my guide, then I might have gone away thinking the police officer was trying to be rude and bossy instead of being caring and helpful. Our instinct is always to interpret things we don't understand as hostile rather than helpful. A great teacher, St Francis of Assisi, said a daily prayer: 'O Divine Master, grant that we may not so much seek to be understood as to understand.'

We might remember that next time someone does something we don't quite understand at first.

URL http://www.walkforpeace.eu/day-3-the-laughing-policeman/

July 30 Day 4

Tourist (Human) Potential

Langfang, Hebei Province
A Day Off
Donated today: £0.00 and ¥0.00
Total donations: £405.88 and ¥0.00

Those clever Chinese people, they think of everything: At breakfast I was served a slice of bread with the jam already swirled into it. This not only saved time, but also avoided a mess of jam pots, messy knives and sticky fingers. Brilliant! Why didn't we think of that?

It was a good start to a day off, in which the local Red Cross volunteers were taking me to see Grand Epoch City, a replica of the centre of Beijing, including temples, Tian'anmen Square and the Forbidden City. I had visions of LEGO-LAND Windsor on a slightly bigger scale (and I love LEGOLAND!). When we arrived, I was amazed that they had rebuilt the centre of the city on a 1:1 scale. Not with plastic bricks but with clay bricks – just like the original. Extraordinary!

The idea for the Epoch City was to develop tourism in Langfang, as visitors would be able to experience all the wonder of the ancient centre of Beijing without having to pay enormous hotel bills and fight their way through the traffic to get there. They had actually built hotel rooms into the inside of the city walls (how cool, literally, is that), and the quality of the craftsmanship was impressive.

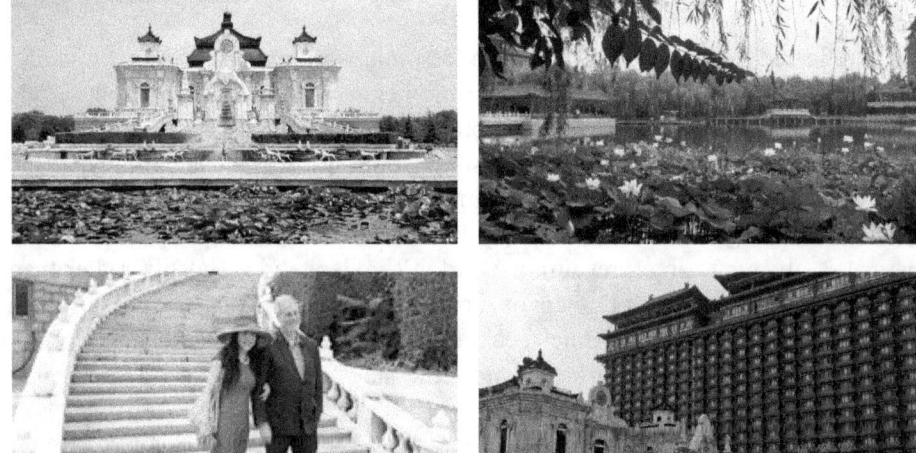

Top left: Replica of the Dashuifa from the Old Summer Palace.
Top right: One of the beautiful lakes in Grand Epoch City.
Bottom left: Visiting Grand Epoch City. Bottom right: A glimpse of Fu'angong Hotel.

As impressive as man's creations are, I have to say that nature beats them every time, and the highlight of the visit was when Xuelin and I were taken to the lakes, which were overflowing with lotus plants in full bloom – and there is nothing quite as radiant and fragrant as a lotus.

Lily, our guide for the visit, took us round, explaining the history and dimensions of the Epoch City. They had built a huge, five-star Fu'an'gong Hotel with over 1,000 rooms using traditional materials in ten months. In Britain, it would take at least two years just to get the outline planning consents. This is not to say Britain is not good at development, it is, which is why so many foreign investors want to come there. It is simply a question of land ownership and permissions. In China, the state owns the land and grants the permissions; then, when it decides what it wants in a particular place, it will happen very quickly. In Britain, you may be dealing with a hundred small private owners who might be affected by the development. They all have property rights that must be considered before permissions are granted. As private ownership expands in China, the ability of the state to make big infrastructure decisions will be reduced, which is why they are so very smart to do them now.

The final part of our tour was a visit to the Buddhist Temple, with its grand statues and incense burning. I am a spiritual person in the sense that I believe that religion is as much a necessary part of our human lives as love, family and meaningful work. However, it wasn't the grand statues that caught my attention but a prayer tree in the corner of the temple on which thousands of visitors had hung messages and prayers. Xuelin and I spent ten minutes just reading through the messages. One seemed to capture them all: 'Wish the whole family peace and good health. Pray for good work. Pray that they have a happy marriage. Pray that their child will study hard and be well-behaved.'

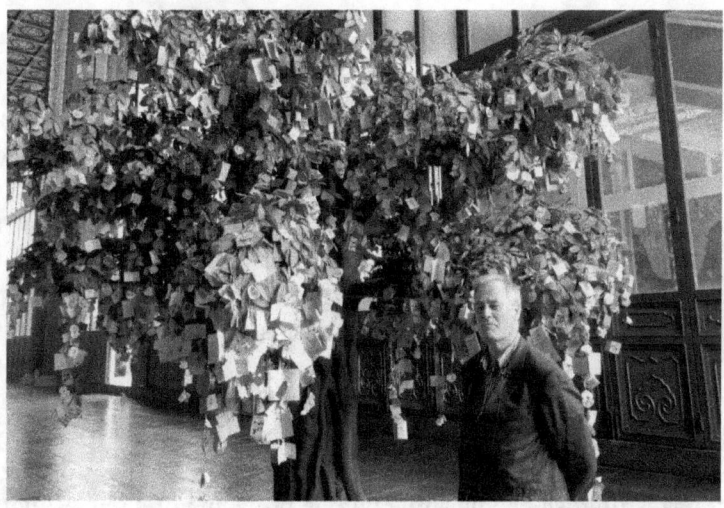

Lord Bates by the prayer tree in the Buddhist Temple.

You could have found a similar prayer card in most cathedrals, mosques, synagogues or other places of worship and spiritual significance in the world. It reminded me of some work we undertook when I was Deputy Chairman of the Conservative Party, in which, instead of the usual opinion poll technique of trying to categorize people into certain social groups by education, wealth or family background, we simply asked people to describe themselves from a list of statements. The statement that, by a very long way, represented how most people identified themselves was: 'Ordinary hardworking people just trying to build a better life for themselves and their families'. My guess is that if we asked the same question in China, the same kind of statement would probably top the poll again. It is a universal prayer, a universal dream and a universal duty on all political leaders to do their very best to help them achieve.

I have wandered off the point of tourism, but I still have 60 days to go, so I have plenty of time to return to it later.

URL http://www.walkforpeace.eu/day-4-tourist-human-potential/

July 31 Day 5

Winter Olympics and Personal Best

Route: Anci District – Bazhou, Langfang
Walked today: 31.00 miles / 49.90 km
Total walked: 90.70 miles / 144.60 km
Donated today: £0.00 and ¥0.00
Total donations: £405.88 and ¥0.00

Xuelin had been up until 3 am supervising the translation of my blogs into Chinese and waking me occasionally to explain phrases and terms, which I tried to do with good grace. The problem for the Chinese, and indeed most languages, is that in English we tend to use a lot of idioms: 'to coin a phrase', 'to pull your leg', etc., which cause deep confusion and frustration. The Chinese are also frustrated by the English habit of 'beating around the bush' – sorry, not being direct. In English we use a lot of conjunctive adverbs, euphemisms and 'padding' around what we want to say. In Chinese, where each word has a character of its own, the language is much more direct, as demonstrated by the Chinese restaurant sign that read:

'All you can eat buffet. Not mean all day buffet. You no come stay 4 hour. You eat. You go home.'

That makes English people smile but the prefacing of a request with, 'Sorry to trouble you. Is there any chance you might happen to know how one might find a shop that might sell various types of bread?' instead of 'Where is the bakery?' leaves Chinese smiling too.

Madam Zhang Ming, our project manager for the walk, is like Xuelin in her astonishing capacity for work. Each day, Madam Ming would bring down a new set of detailed revised plans for the walk, which reflected where we got to the previous night, and the ripple effect of the changes would have been communicated down the line. The attention to detail was staggering. They even marked out where the public WCs are on the route, which kind of had me thinking, 'What are hedgerows for?' Only joking. On one such visit, I discovered an important bit of information in this regard. Most WCs in China do not supply toilet paper. You are expected to carry your own. Not sure why. There are just some things you don't want to ask your host. Anyway, it is a fact I now know. I am also slowly adjusting to the absence of a seat. Sorry, let's change the subject ....

We set out from Langfang City, heading south for Dacheng. The temperature unexpectedly cooled to around 30 degrees and there was a gentle breeze. In addition, I was refreshed by my rest day. This had all the makings of a very good walking day and I was determined that we should make the most of it. We set off at 7.30 am sharp and by lunchtime we had already done nearly 20 miles. What was more, I felt good about it.

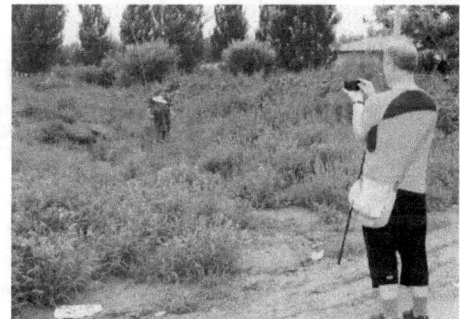 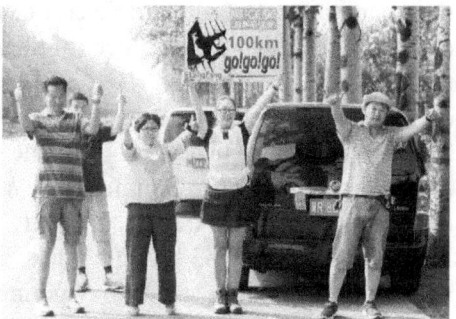

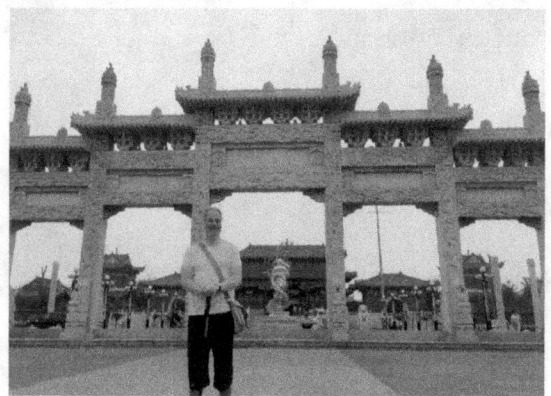

Left: Encounters on the road. Right: Milestone marking the first 100 km of the walk.
Bottom: Lord Bates in Langfang.

Most of the time, I am not on the new highways, as pedestrians would not be allowed, so we take a less direct route. The quality of the infrastructure in China is extraordinarily good. The walking paths, roads and cycle paths are as good as anything I have experienced in Europe and better than anywhere else except Germany. The roads are tree-lined to provide some shelter from the sun. While the quality of the infrastructure is world-class, the same cannot be said for the vehicles using them. Vast numbers of heavy trucks and buses share the space with hundreds of small motorized tricycles, and weaving in between them at speed are the modern executive cars – Mercedes, BMW, Range Rover and VW being the most popular. This is a nation, it seems, constantly on the move. Travellers on foot are extremely rare. Communication therefore is vital and this is done by horns; the trucks and buses that have horns that seem to reverberate through your entire body. Still, in what seems like chaos on the roads, I have not witnessed any accidents.

I pressed on and reached our hotel in Shengfang, having completed 31 miles. When I arrived, Madam Zhang was in a celebratory mood, and I thought that it might be for me completing over 30 miles but it was because it had just been announced that Beijing had won the 2022 Winter Olympic Games. It was fantastic news, and as we sat in the cafeteria of the hotel, all attention was of those wonderful scenes when the president of the International Olympic Committee opened the envelope and declared 'Beijing.' This meant a great deal to China. They had done a fantastic job of hosting the Olympics and Paralympics in 2008 and Madam Zhang was part of that team. This meant that Beijing would be the first city in history to host both the Summer and Winter Games. I was caught up in the celebration as the iced tea flowed. Our only concern about the announcement was that Madam Zhang may be brought back to Beijing to start work on the Games and without her we might still be navigating our way around the outskirts of Nanjing in 2022. A good day all round.

URL http://www.walkforpeace.eu/day-5/

August 1 Day 6

The Kindness of Strangers

Route: Bazhou – Dachengxian, Langfang
Walked today: 30.20 miles / 48.70 km
Total walked: 120.90 miles / 193.30 km
Donated today: £0.00 and ¥0.00
Total donations: £405.88 and ¥0.00

Owing to a slightly wrinkled sock, I had developed a painful blister on the little toe of my right foot. It seemed nothing, but I know from painful experience that small problems become big problems if they are not treated. I spent three days in northern France unable to walk because a small blister became infected. I was blessed to have Xuelin with me on this walk. This was the fourth major walk we had done together and most of the problems of health or logistics had been encountered before; and like all good teams, we work well together. Xuelin has the tough end of the deal because she has become a specialist in foot care. This time she produced some foot-repair cream from the Dead Sea, which my nephew

Daniel had brought back from a visit to Israel over a year ago – Xuelin had kept it and added it to her tool kit. It worked a treat and the next morning I was fully repaired and ready to go.

Another part of Xuelin's role is that she deals with the bills. We have been very fortunate because the Red Cross team has managed to identify great budget hotels with wi-fi, shower and a bed, which is all you need. There have been some great chains that we have been able to stay in for 200–300 yuan per night (£20–£30), including breakfast for both of us. The hotels are just as good as any Premier Inn, Travelodge or Ibis that you would find in Europe, and yet at least half the price, which makes a very big difference for us when we will be here for 70 nights. Once you reach the big cities, then the prices rise, as you would expect, but even in Beijing you would be able to get a good standard hotel for £50–£70 per night.

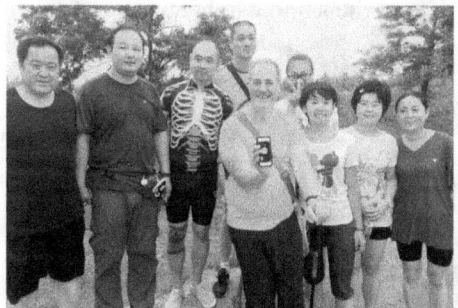
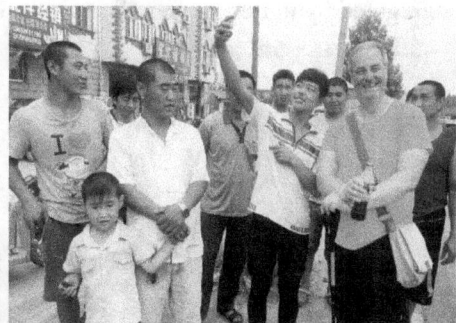
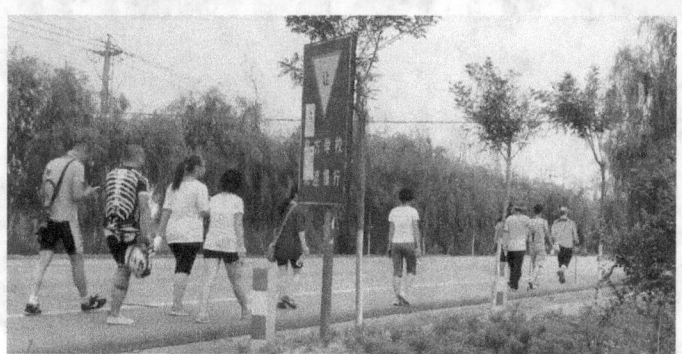

Left: Lord Bates sharing his progress. Right: In Langfang. Bottom: Walking in Langfang.

This does raise the question: why has foreign tourism to China not taken off in recent years in the same way as foreign tourism from China has? The number of Chinese tourists coming to the UK has doubled in recent years from 150,000 to over 300,000 and yet UK tourist visits to China number in the low tens of thousands. It could be that what Brits are looking for is sun, sea and booze, and those three things aren't as readily associated with China as the Mediterranean resorts. Still, for those seeking an experience, different from the norm, and at the price of a package holiday to the Med, they really should consider China more seriously.

Older tourists will find the Confucian culture of respect for age and wisdom refreshingly different from the youth-obsessed Western culture. I have also found the food, with its emphasis on fresh vegetables, rice and tea, a good change from beer, a burger and a bun at home. One of the biggest differences I find is the inter-generational nature of society here. Xuelin and I will often go out for a walk at night when we are in a larger town and city. You will invariably hear music coming from a park, and it will be from the dance groups who come out to perform group dance activities in the evening. All ages will be there – teenagers, grandparents and grandchildren, all just enjoying the fun of doing dance moves together. It is the absence of alcohol that changes the culture and allows people, children and the old, to feel unthreatened by the young men. I have seen this before in some Muslim countries where coffee and tobacco are staples, but their societies are segregated by male and female, so you don't get the same whole community feel.

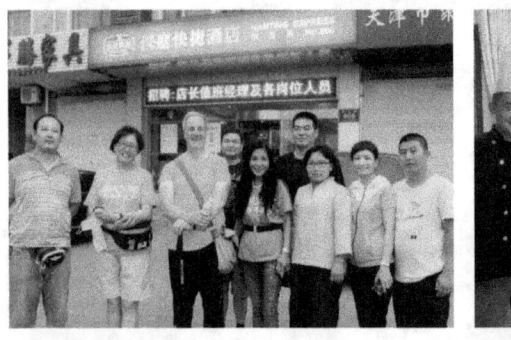 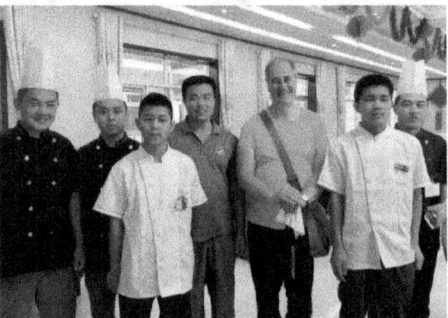
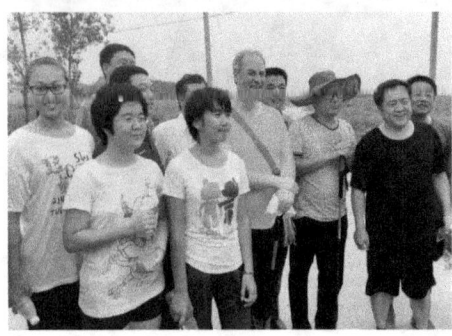 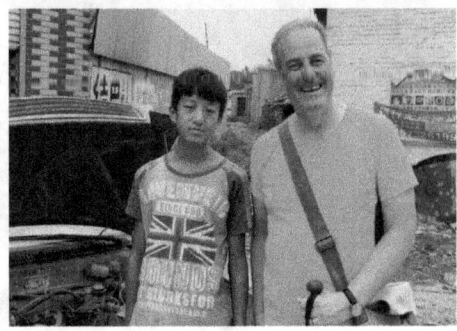

Top left: Lord and Lady Bates in front of their hotel in Langfang.
Top right: Lord Bates and the staff of a restaurant in Langfang.
Bottom left; Lord Bates posing with a group of locals. Bottom right: Making friends on the road.

It is something that every nationality says about themselves but few who say it have had much experience of anything to compare it with: 'The people are so friendly here.' Having walked through 18 countries, I have to say that, with the exception of the Republic of Ireland, there is very little difference between the friendliness of any particular nationality and any other. You smile – people smile back – but most of the time we simply don't connect unless we are buying or selling. I am not quite sure why, but China is currently proving to be closer to the exception of Ireland than the norm of everywhere else.

It could be that I have been walking for four days and I have never seen another foreigner, never mind another Westerner, so I stand out as a novelty and people want to take pictures of me and with me because of your round eyes, big nose, white skin and the fact that you are walking (with a stick) in the middle of the day! They ask in such a friendly way that you cannot say no, even when you are 25 miles into a challenging walk.

One test, which is not scientific but is interesting, is spontaneous generosity. What I mean is that I have walked thousands of miles and only twice have people offered me food for free (many, many have come along the roadside to try and sell). The first was in Albania, where a melon seller asked for a photo with me and gave me a large slice of melon. The second was in Duisburg, Germany, where a Starbucks barista asked me what I was writing and insisted on buying me a latte coffee. But yesterday, a young man ran across the road with an ice-cold bottle of water, which he gave me, and then a few hours later a young lady pulled ahead of us in a car and opened up the boot to show a tray of bottled water, which she offered to me and members of our team. So, I have been walking for seven years and there have been four occasions of this spontaneous generosity, two of which happened yesterday on Day 6 of the walk in China. I hesitate to mention these thoughtful acts because we don't want to encourage them – we want people to be generous to the Red Cross, whom we are here to support, and not to us – but it is just meant as an interesting observation about the real China or, more precisely, the real Chinese people.

URL http://www.walkforpeace.eu/day-6-the-kindness-of-strangers/

August 2 Day 7

Travelling Together

Route: Dachengxian, Langfang – Qingxian, Cangzhou
Walked today: 20.70 miles / 32.70 km
Total walked: 141.60 miles / 226.00 km
Donated today: £525.00 and ¥0.00
Total donations: £930.88 and ¥0.00

There is a Chinese saying, 'If you want to go fast, travel alone. If you want to go far, travel together.' On all my walks up until now I have walked alone. I am not fit. I am old. If you walk with other people, they might want to stop when you don't and vice versa. They will always walk at a very slightly different pace, which over the course of a long day can make a huge difference as you have either had to slow down or speed up from your original pace. Also, people want to talk – fair enough, but in this heat and at my age I barely have enough energy to walk, never mind talk. Sure, if you are going for a five-mile wander through a forest or along the coast, it is great to have conversation and company, but not when you have to do 30 miles in 40 degree temperatures. So, taking people with me seems like carrying unnecessary baggage – why would you do it? Today would provide an answer.

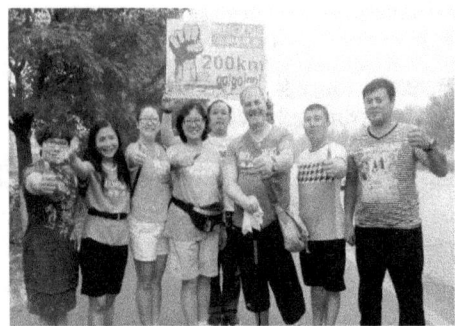
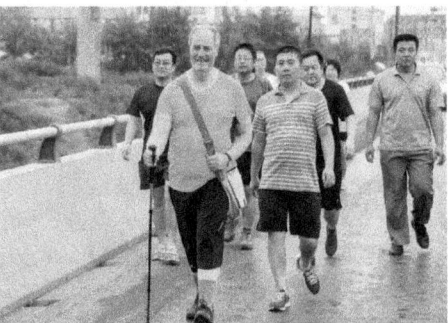
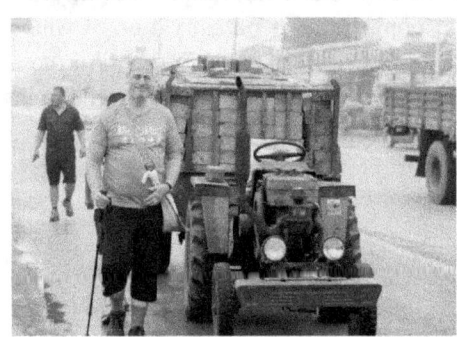
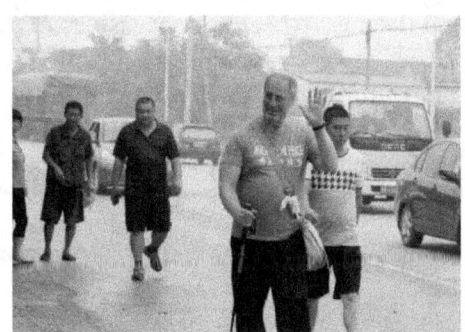

Top left: Milestone marking 200 km of the walk.
Top right: Because it was the weekend, more people joined the ranks of the walkers.
Bottom left: Walking in Langfang City. Bottom right: The group grows larger.

We made an early start on the walk to try and get the cool of the day. I noticed that there were more Red Cross volunteers than the previous day, all looking wonderful in their 'Walk for Peace' T-shirts. About eight were walking in all. We gathered for the ancient Chinese custom of taking smartphone pictures, first the group shots, then one brave soul (normally female) would step forward and ask for an individual picture, then everyone else would want an individual one. Everyone was laughing. It was fun. All of a sudden I, being old, forgot those aches and pains from yesterday and started to look forward to the day ahead. Then, with our collective loud *Jia you!* (Come on!), we set off.

One of the few instincts that I have developed to a high level through walking is a sense of direction. I sense this through the sun and even my shadow on the road. I sensed that rather than travelling south, we were actually travelling west. I thought it might be a short distance but it must have been for an hour. Eventually, I mentioned this to Madam Zhang and she explained that, first, the local volunteers were trying to avoid some of the busier roads and, second, the provincial border with Tianjin and Hebei was at this point and the local volunteers wanted to keep within their province. Fair enough.

Just then, another family group arrived – I thought to take a picture. It was the Deputy Secretary General of Langfang City, who had shown us very kind hospitality with the Deputy Mayor when we had visited the Epoch City a couple of days before. I was without a translator and so the Secretary General's daughter stepped forward and said, 'This is my father. He met you yesterday. We are his family. He would like to walk with you.' I replied, 'Yes, of course,' and mentioned a few rules for safety about walking alongside the busy roads in what was now a group of around 14.

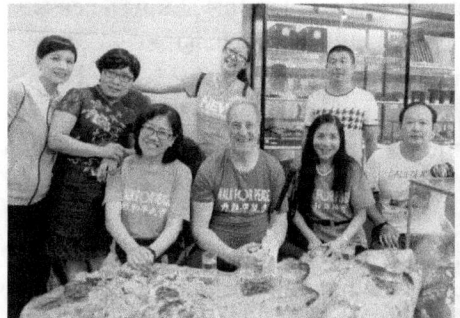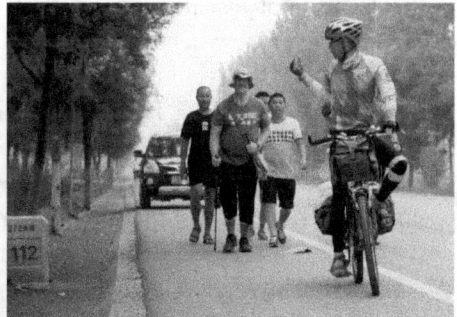

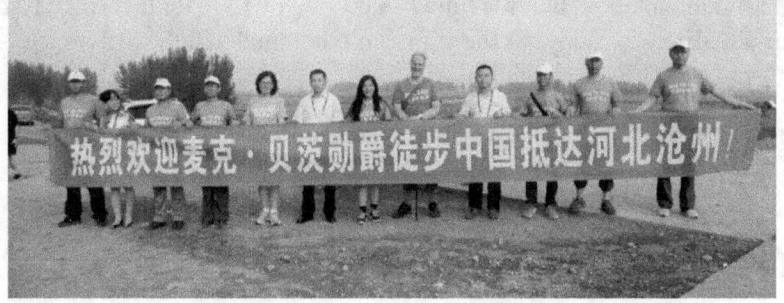

Left: Lord and Lady Bates enjoy some tea with Madame Zhang and other volunteers.
Right: A cyclist showing support. Bottom: Arrival in Cangzhou.

I was walking out in front, struggling as usual with the humidity, but from the outset I heard numerous conversations going on in the group behind. They were sometimes laughing and joking. Sometimes you could hear deep debate. The Red Cross volunteers went to great efforts to make sure that when we stopped for a water break there were enough cool drinks to go around. I thought that perhaps the Secretary General might stay for a few miles and then be whisked away in a black limo, but he was still with us at lunch and we had a good talk.

After lunch we passed some cyclists in full cycling gear, who wouldn't have looked out of place on the Tour de France. Initially they paused for pictures. They then said that they had heard of my walk through a social media group for outdoor pursuits and wanted to know if they could join us. 'Of course,' I said, and so they followed on. The group was now growing and people were not leaving. As we walked through the small towns and villages, we were creating quite an impact because there were so many of us walking. This in turn meant many more stops for photos, but it was fun.

As we arrived at our stopping point for that evening, we had done almost 30 miles. It has become a bit of a tradition that when we finish the day Madam Zhang Ming gets everyone together to cheer the final few steps, and I always feel as if I have just completed a marathon (which in distance terms I often have). This time the crowd was a lot larger than usual because of the people we picked up along the way. But that sense of collective achievement was very real. It also meant more in that it was not just me but us being cheered across the line. Experiences are diminished in value when they are exclusive and multiplied when they are shared.

I reflected on my son Matt's favourite saying when he was a young basketball coach, 'There is no "I" in a team.' I felt that almost spiritual transformation from being a selfish individual to becoming a selfless part of something much bigger. What is more, I was happy about it. Thomas Merton, the great spiritual teacher, talked about just this feeling when he wrote: 'True happiness is found in unselfish love, a love which increases in portion as it is shared …'.

We ended the day with that ancient Chinese custom of taking smartphone photos, first of the team and then one person (usually a female) would step forward to ask for an individual picture, but this time I said, Meiyou (no), for this wasn't a day for the individual; it was a day for the team, and that made all the difference.

URL http://www.walkforpeace.eu/day-7-travelling-together/

August 3 Day 8

Hospitals and the Press

Cangzhou, Hebei Province
A Day Off
Donated today: £20.00 and ¥1,000.00
Total donations: £950.88 and ¥1,000.00

Today was a day off. Well, let me qualify that: it was a day off from walking but not a day off from working. There were the blogs to be written. Xuelin is a brilliant manager. She always starts with the bar very low – 'just one blog … even just a few lines would be great' and by the time the day is done we have four blogs and 2,500 words. Not that the work stops there. The blog is then sent back to the ever-patient team in London, who carefully translate it into Mandarin Chinese.

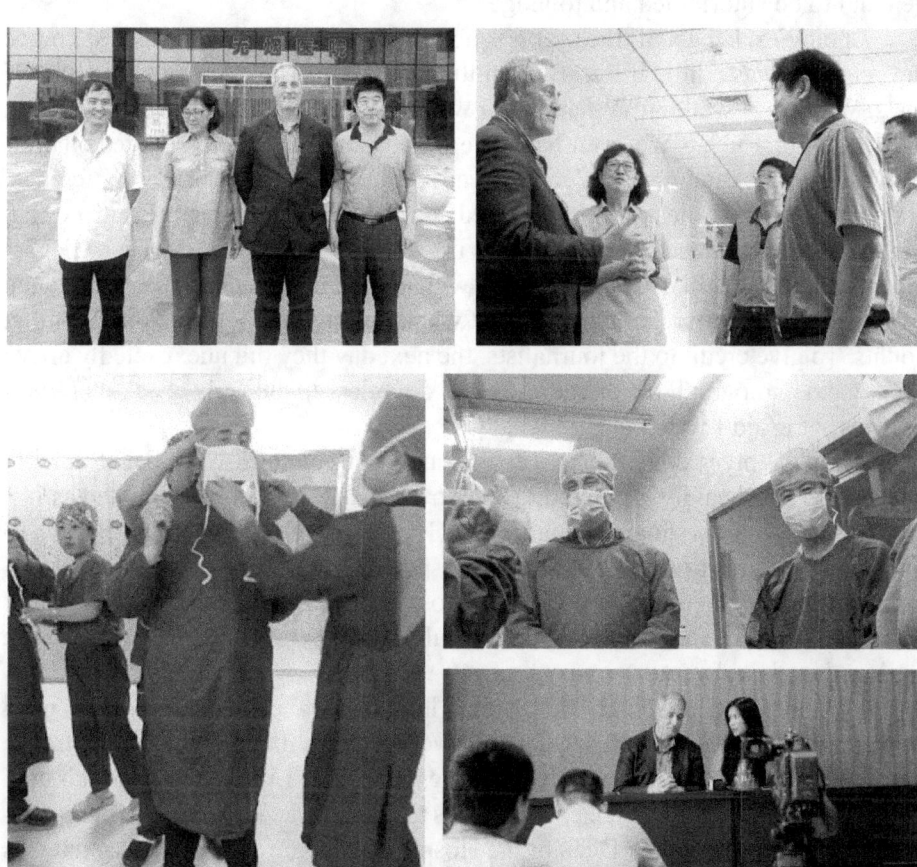

Top left: Lord Bates in front of Qing Xian People's Hospital with Madame Zhang, the President of the Local Red Cross, and Li Shuyan, the Dean of the hospital.
Top right: Discussing healthcare in China with Dean Li Shuyan.
Left and middle right: Lord Bates in Qing Xian People's Hospital, Cangzhou City.
Bottom right: Lord and Lady Bates at the press conference in Cangzhou.

In between the second and third blog, we had a press conference with the press and media of Hebei Province and Cangzhou City. I have done a few press conferences in my time back in the UK and the questions are invariably not about the story, but in search of an angle that might give the journalist a unique take. Now, of course the media in the UK are free from any political constraint, but they operate under the often greater limitation of the need to sell or get viewers. In the UK media marketplace, that can lead to a journalism that sensationalizes, shocks and trivializes, focusing on images rather than messages. This is not their fault. It is ours, the reader and the viewer whose attention span has been reduced to 140 characters plus pictures. Sadly, most stories are way more complex than this, but in our superfast world we don't have the time or inclination to understand, only a demand to be entertained and to judge.

Apologies, I'll get off the soapbox now, and just say that the press conference in Cangzhou was a little different from those at home. The questions were on the facts: Why was I walking? Where was I walking? Who was I walking with? What did I think of Hebei? We even had time to exchange Confucius quotes on welcoming strangers and walking. Xuelin was my translator for the press conference, and if I strayed off-message or indicated something controversial, I noticed that her translations seemed to take longer as if to she was interpreting, 'What Michael meant to say ...'. Still, I was very happy with this, because communication is such a critical part of culture and it is not just what you say but the way you say it that counts. To give credit to the journalists, the next day they did unexpectedly arrive to film and photograph me on the walk and doubtless to dutifully check that I was doing what I said I was doing.

After the press conference, a few of us went out for a walk but it quickly came on to rain heavily. I pointed to an extraordinary building that looked as if it were either a luxury shopping mall or the HQ of Google or Goldman Sachs. To my astonishment, it turned out to be a hospital: Qing Xian People's Hospital. I was with the President of the local Red Cross, who was a doctor, and he said that he knew the Dean and he was sure he would be happy to show me round. I was intrigued, so I said yes.

Normally in China visits are planned long in advance and permissions need to be secured, but this was spontaneous. We went into the marble-lined entrance hall of the hospital and within a few minutes the Dean, Li Shuyan, was with us. I thought, 'Wow! In the UK it can sometimes take a couple days to get to see a doctor and here I was with the Dean of the Hospital in 3.5 minutes.' The hospital was new, opened only a few months ago, and it had 1,000 beds. The only comparison I had in mind was with the Royal Victoria Infirmary in Newcastle, which I had visited just a few months earlier, and it had around 600–700 beds and was one of the largest in the country. This hospital had free car parking and even its own park to aid the process of recovery. I have always viewed the National Health Service as being one of the greatest components of our civilisation, and it was very clear from the outset that Chinese doctors and administrators held the British NHS in very high esteem and it was the model they were aiming to replicate, albeit for a country 20 times the size. Walking along the wide corridors, I sensed there was an order and calm about the place, which was not accidental but built into the design to reduce anxiety and give people space.

One difference I picked up on was the banks of cashiers at the back of the hospital: China may be moving towards a National Health Service model but at the moment it is still insurance-based. The state insurance covers 80% of the costs of treatment and the remaining 20% is either a patient contribution or can be claimed back from the local government. What, I asked, was the situation if someone had no insurance and could not afford the 20%? The answer was that they would be treated first and then they would discuss how to pay the bill – at this point the local Red Cross Society would also step in to help.

We then went up to the operating theatres and needed to be scrubbed and gowned and wear a mask just to look around. There were 16 operating theatres, each equipped with the very latest in medical technology; most of the machines were made by Philips. As we made our way back to the reception, I asked the Dean what the words over the entrance meant. He said, 'The first qualification for a doctor is that he or she should be kind-hearted. The second qualification is that he or she should give all patients – young, old, rich, poor, powerful or weak – the same level of attention and care.'

Our hosts were rightly proud of their hospital. I believe that the quality of our hospitals, schools and infrastructure – 'public goods', if you will – are the hall-mark of a healthy society. On the basis of this quick check-up, Cangzhou certainly passed the test.

URL http://www.walkforpeace.eu/day-8-hospitals-the-press/

August 4 Day 9

Human First

Route: Qingxian – Cangxian, Cangzhou
Walked today: 26.90 miles / 43.30 km
Total walked: 168.50 miles / 269.30 km
Donated today: £50.00 and ¥1,000.00
Total donations: £1,000.88 and ¥1,000.00

As I prepared to leave the hotel, I received a social media notification from the International Federation of Red Cross Societies, reminding us that August 6 marked the 70th anniversary of the dropping of the atomic bomb on the Japanese city of Hiroshima, followed by a second bomb on Nagasaki three days later, on August 9. The social media post from the Red Cross reminded us that, 70 years on, thousands of people still require long-term medical care because of illnesses that had their beginnings on those fateful days in 1945.

The war having ended in Europe, the allies – the United States, China and the UK – met at Potsdam and on July 26 issued a demand for Japanese unconditional surrender, warning of 'prompt and utter destruction' if they did not comply. They did not comply. So, on August 6, an atomic bomb was dropped on Hiroshima, destroying in an instant five square miles of the city. Between 90,000 and 166,000 died, mostly civilians – half incinerated at the point of implosion and half dying agonizing deaths through burns and radiation over the following few months. Over 90% of the doctors and nurses in the city had been killed and all hospitals and clinics were flattened, so there was no medical care available for survivors.

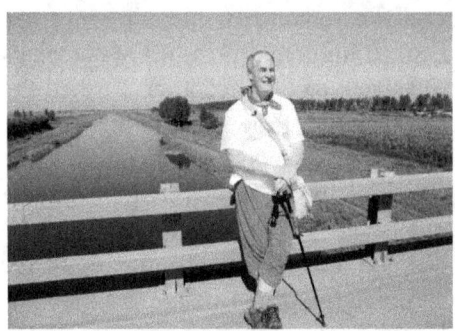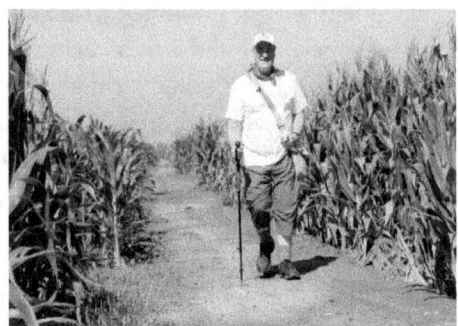
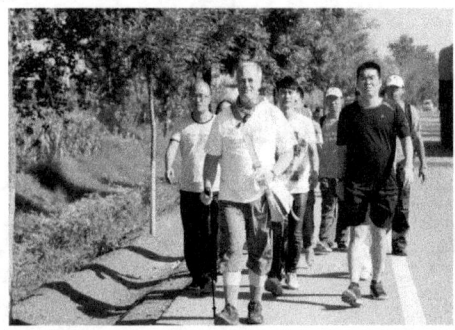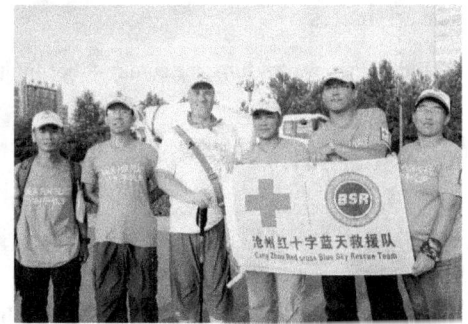

Top left: Taking a short break for pictures. Top right: Walking in the Chinese countryside.
Bottom left: Lord Bates walking with volunteers in Cangzhou.
Bottom right: Lord Bates with the Blue Sky Rescue Team

Water supplies were poisoned with radiation. There was no food. Disease set in. A few days later a second bomb was dropped on Nagasaki, where between 39,000 and 80,000 were killed in the same way. On August 15 Japan surrendered. These remain the only two occasions when atomic weapons have been used.

These are very sensitive issues to write about, especially in China, which was the subject of an unprovoked attack and brutal treatment by Japanese occupying forces in World War II, especially the bombing of Chongqing and the 'Rape of Nanking'. In Britain too, we retain a deep resentment for the sadistic treatment of British prisoners of war by their Japanese captors. Does this mean that we should be immune to the sufferings on the other side? I don't think so. Does showing empathy for the sufferings of enemies undermine a clear moral view backed by international law as to who was right and who was wrong? I don't think so. We can't change the past but if we are to change the future, we must do so from a perspective of our shared humanity rather than enmity.

On this day on my Walk for Peace, I chose to remember the innocent fellow human beings who suffered and are suffering because of the horrific events of this day in 1945 in Hiroshima. That is not being unpatriotic or undiplomatic: it is just remembering we are all human first.

URL http://www.walkforpeace.eu/day-9-human-first/

August 5 Day 10

Milestones: Miles and Kilometers

Route: Cangxian – Nanpixian, Cangzhou
Walked today: 21.90 miles / 36.40 km
Total walked: 190.40 miles / 305.70 km
Donated today: £50.00 and ¥2,100.00
Total donations: £1,000.88 and ¥3,100.00

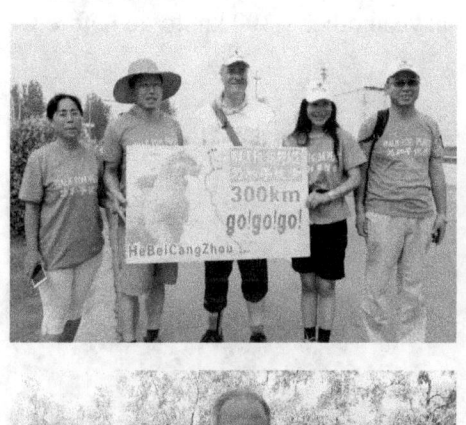
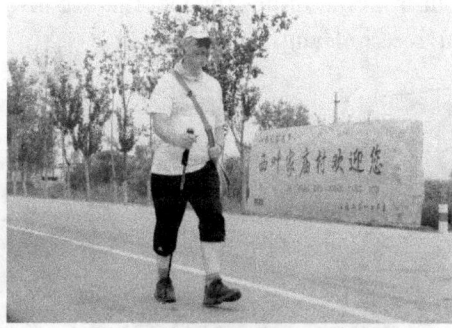
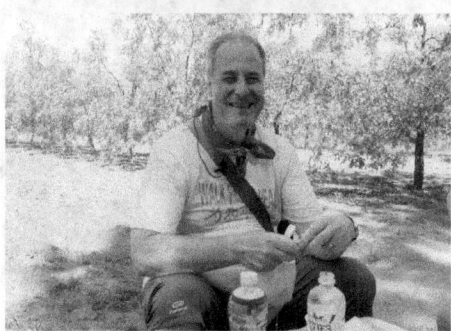
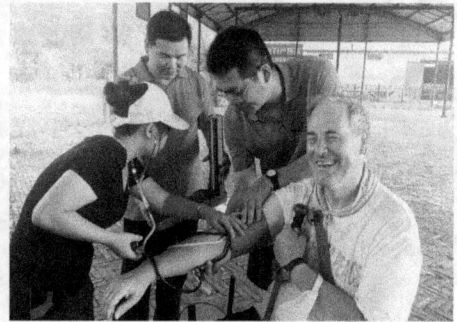

Top left: Milestone marking 300 km of the walk.
Top right: Lord Bates shows his satisfaction at reaching a new milestone.
Bottom left: resting in the jujube garden. Bottom right: concern for the health of the Lord!

Milestones were invented by the Romans to allow their armies to know how far they were from the next garrison. The Roman Mile was 1,000 paces, comprising two steps to a pace. Being a good Roman colony, the British kept the system for over 1,000 years but updated in the 16th century. The kilometre (1,000 metres) is much more recent, a 1790 invention of the French, which explains why the British didn't adopt the kilometre and the French said 'non' to the mile. A kilometre is equivalent to 0.621 miles. A Chinese mile is 500 metres, but road distances are always given in kilometres.

All of this is perhaps of passing interest, because without doubt the greatest benefit the mile-marker gives is to improve travellers' morale by letting them know how far they have travelled and confirm that they are on the right road, heading in the right direction. So, when I was greeted early in the day with a great fanfare of supporters proclaiming 300 km, I found myself forgetting my loyalty to the British mile and embraced this 'milestone' (of course 'kilometre stone' would never catch on).

We took a break with the local Red Cross volunteers for pictures next to a field of date trees – dates are a local speciality of this area. They are smaller and sweeter than their rivals. We took pleasure in making it this far and managed to put from our minds the fact that we might have another 1,300 km to go before we arrived in Hangzhou.

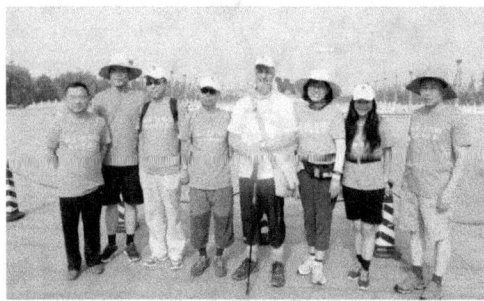
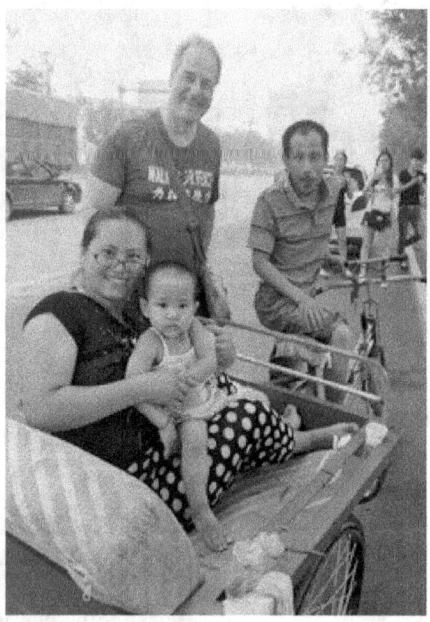
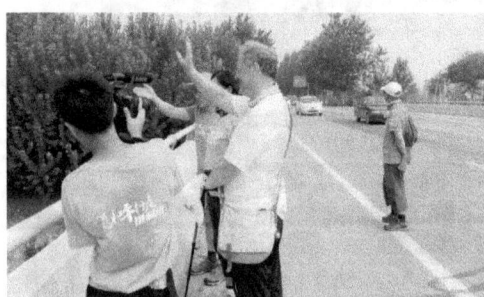

Top left: Lord and Lady Bates with Red Cross volunteers.
Bottom left: Shooting a video in Cangzhou.
Right: Meeting a family.

The skies had cleared that day and the sun was very strong: I only realised how strong when I reached the hotel that evening and discovered the extent of the sunburn to the back of my neck and my calf muscles. Most of the time on the walk so far, there has been heavy cloud, added to by dust, so seeing and feeling the sun accurately has not been possible. That is a problem for confirming a rough sense of direction. I know that if it is in the morning and I feel the sun on the lefthand side of my face, then I am heading south and if it is the afternoon, then I will be travelling south if I feel the sun on the righthand side of my face. Shadow length will give a good indication as to time of day – the shorter your shadow the nearer you are to midday. Why is this important?

Well, on this day I began to feel the sun on the front of my face in the morning so I knew that I was travelling east. The problem was that I wanted to be heading south. I mentioned this to Madam Zhang, who was able to provide an instant explanation in the form of the map drawn for my route by local officials. The overriding concern of the local volunteers was to keep me safe, and so they had sacrificed directness for safety. We had taken a route that had gone south, then east and at one stage north-east, in order to keep on the best roads. Had it not been for the sun and blue skies, I would probably never have realized, but this also explained why my iPhone map was showing 130 miles direct to Beijing and yet I had walked close to 190 miles. We talked that evening about routes, and I said that I was very happy to take my chances on some of the less good roads in order to make progress.

It is in the Chinese nature to do everything in their power to make the guest welcome and meet their wishes, so they went away and came back with a more direct route, which we embarked on the next day. I felt a little guilty because they were only trying to care for me and they worked so hard to make sure every detail was correct. That said, they are friends and I think they understood the reasons, namely that I am on such a tight schedule to make it to Hangzhou before the beginning of October. They did explain an interesting challenge, though, and that was that the network of what we might call country roads is not as great in China as elsewhere, because if a road is to be built between two villages, both the villages need to agree. If they can't agree, then the road simply goes around both, and it was along many of these roads we had travelled.

URL http://www.walkforpeace.eu/day-10-milestones/

August 6 Day 11

'Up the Workers'

Route: Nanpixian, Cangzhou, Hebei Province – Ningjinxian, Dezhou, Shandong Province
Walked today: 24.60 miles / 39.60 km
Total walked: 215.00 miles / 345.30 km
Donated today: £0.00 and ¥0.00
Total donations: £1,000.88 and ¥3,100.00

> This is the true joy in life, the being used for a purpose recognized by yourself as a mighty one; the being a force of nature instead of a feverish, selfish little clod of ailments and grievances complaining that the world will not devote itself to making you happy.
>
> I am of the opinion that my life belongs to the whole community, and as long as I live it is my privilege to do for it whatever I can. I want to be thoroughly used up when I die, for the harder I work the more I live. I rejoice in life for its own sake.
>
> Life is no "brief candle" for me. It is a sort of splendid torch which I have got hold of for the moment, and I want to make it burn as brightly as possible before handing it on to future generations.
>
> **George Bernard Shaw**

It can only have been as a result of my small-family business upbringing that I have always had a huge respect for those who work hard and take risks. There is nobility about work. It is the antidote to the idle musings on why life hasn't served up all that you think you deserved. It is about doing something worthwhile. Have a purpose in life. Have the satisfaction of a job well done. It is about doing something for others and in that way gaining benefit for yourself. For this reason I find it personally difficult to relate to the idle poor and even less to the idle rich – though I realize that these are very broad generalizations and there will be exceptional individuals in both categories.

The success of the Chinese economy is not accidental. Education is the most important thing you can give to a child, and this is every parent's passion for his or her child. Children are affirmed and instilled with self-belief. On that solid foundation is built an almost religious belief in hard work. There is then the savings culture – Chinese people are always saving for something and distrust the easy option of borrowing from a bank. They respect wisdom, especially from the elderly. The final layer is an entrepreneurial spirit – the vast majority of Chinese people want one day to be their own boss. Put those six – affirmation, education, hard work, saving, wisdom and enterprise – together in any country or culture and it will produce a world beater.

As I walk along, I meet many people who are following just this path in life – sweating away in the fields or selling produce in a market. I connect with them in a particular way, as I too am sweating away in the middle of the day and they seem to somehow respect that.

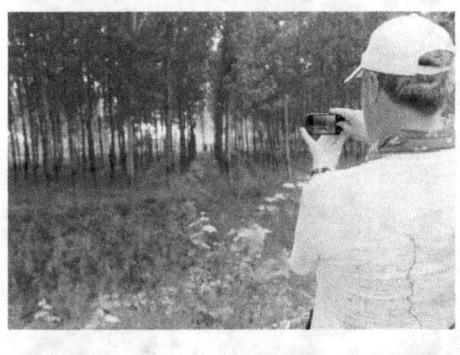
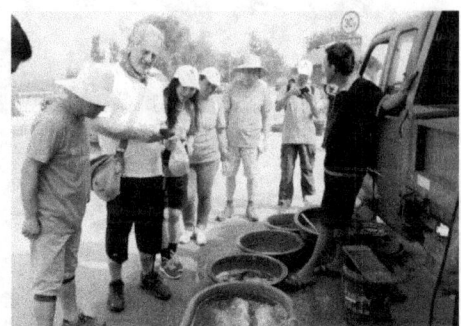
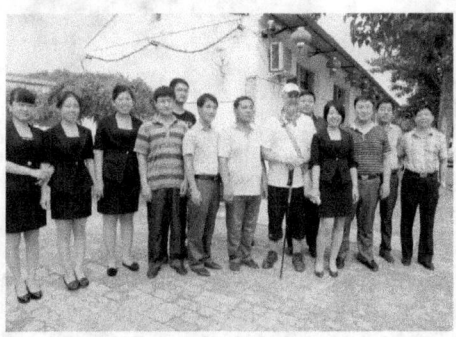
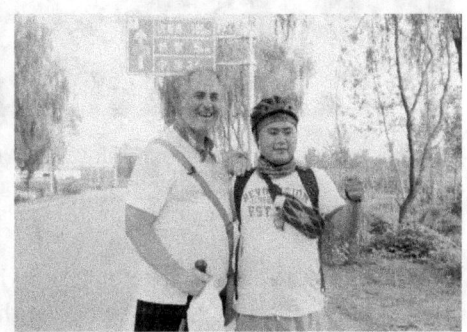

Top left; Lord Bates taking pictures of the scenery. Top right: Talking with a local fish vendor.
Bottom left: Lord Bates and a group of supporters in Dezhou, Shandong Province.
Bottom right: Lord Bates posing with a supporter.

I meet a date farmer and his wife gently pruning the date bushes while waiting nervously for the harvest of their 11 acres in September in time for the Moon Festival, when the best prices are achieved. They express concerns familiar to farmers the world over. Will heavy rains and storms come and damage their crops? Will there be too big a harvest of dates, which will reduce the prices?

Further down the road, a farmer who keeps geese, all free range, comes out to meet me, thinking I am a Russian. Russians are very important because they buy a great deal of Chinese meat. He then took me to his pig farm next door, which he was planning to expand further because of export demand.

Later we had planned a packed lunch by the roadside but the manager of a water treatment works invited us into his fan-cooled office to shelter from the sun. It was as if I was adopted into an honorary fellowship of workers.

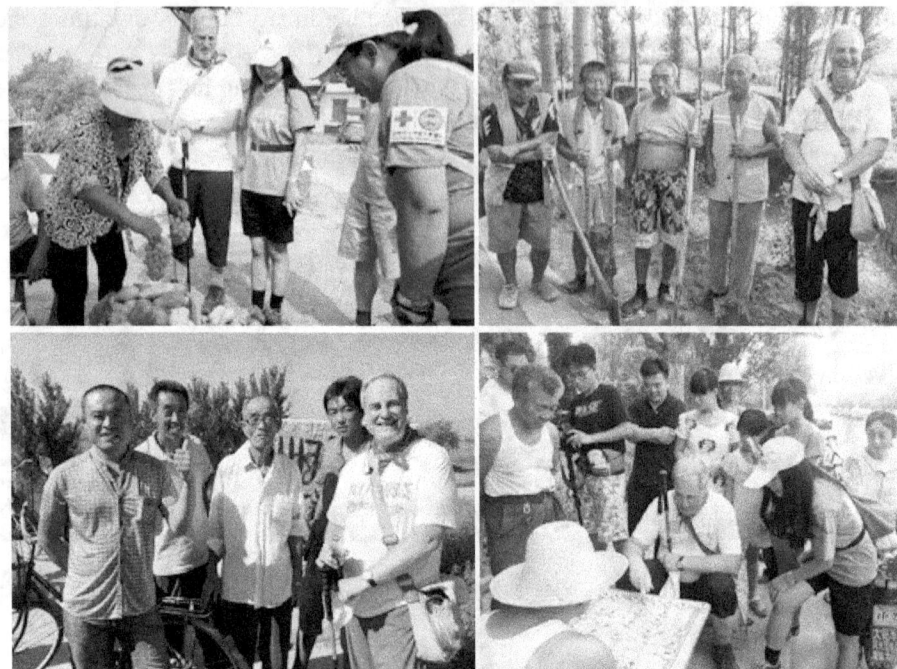

Top left: August 6 – talking with fruit vendors at the roadside. Top right: with the hardworking road maintenance men. Bottom left: with villagers on the way to Dezhou, Shandong Province. Bottom right: August 7 – invited to play Chinese chess at Ninjin New Town.

This leads me to my final reflection, which was confirmed by the noble image of an elderly man I met on a bridge at the end of the day. He must have been 85 years old at least but he still had a rake in his hand and was clearing a roadside bank. In the West we have undermined a great deal of human value because people retire too early. I work in the House of Lords, where some of the most dedicated members and sharpest brains are in their 90s. I am 54 years old. In some professions they would be starting to mutter that I might start thinking of early retirement. I simply cannot think of anything worse. I want to work till I drop, and if at 85 I am found on a grassy bank in Shandong Province in the heat of the day with a rake in my hand, then I would consider my life to have been one of noble endeavour and reward.

URL http://www.walkforpeace.eu/day-11-up-the-workers/

August 7 Day 12

Healthy Living

Dezhou, Shandong Province
A Day Off
Donated today: £0.00 and ¥0.00
Total donations: £1,000.88 and ¥3,100.00

The Red Cross volunteers are carers and first responders. I have been particularly well looked after from a health point of view. I guess they took one look at me at the Temple of Heaven and thought, 'This guy won't be able to make 1,000 steps, never mind a 1,000 miles.' They even prepared an oxygen pillow and insisted on taking my pulse and blood pressure at the end of the day. My pulse was 82 and the blood pressure was around 100, because my arms are so fat they couldn't get the vessel to fully stick when the band was inflated, so we were never quite sure.

I confess that I have never taken my health terribly seriously on my walks – if I am still standing at the end of the day, then I must be okay according to my standards, but for Chinese people healthy living is the most important thing, apart from breathing. Food is not consumed for enjoyment but as a medicine for nutrition.

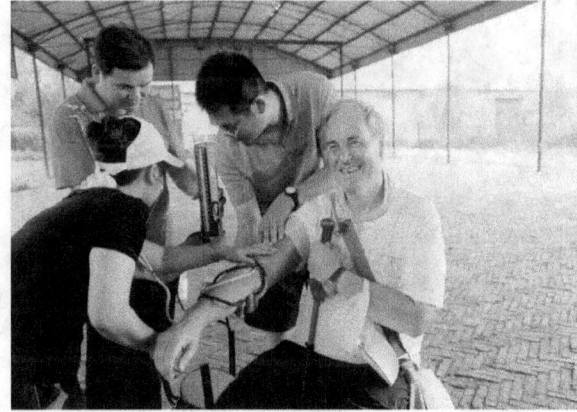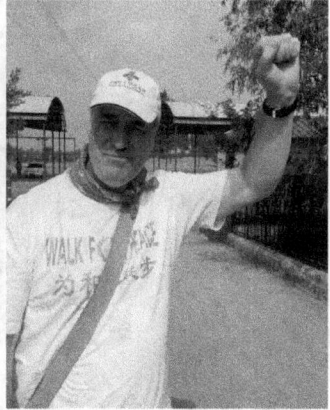

Left: Red Cross volunteers measuring Lord Bates's blood pressure.
Right: Gathering energy during the day off.

I remember when we were first married, Xuelin wanted me to drink turtle soup and stand on my head for 10 minutes each day. I can barely stand on my feet, I told her, and as for 'turtle soup', my kids were brought up on the *Teenage Mutant Ninja Turtle* TV series, and if I were to actually eat or even be rude to one of Leonardo or Donatello's brothers or sisters, I am sure they would never speak to me again.

I came in one day from work and saw Xuelin grimacing as she ate some grey, thin, meaty-type food. 'What is that?' I asked. She replied, 'Donkey skin!' 'Why?' I asked. 'It is supposed to be good for blood circulation!' I began to worry. Had I married Hannibal Lecter's little sister? If someone told me I could live to 250 if I ate donkey skin, I would still probably push it to the side of the plate and carry on eating the fish and chips.

Yesterday, when the temperatures were very high and even I was feeling a bit unsteady on my feet, Madam Zhang appeared with a 'wonder cure for heat exhaustion'. They were little brown plastic bottles of medicine. I didn't look keen. I was even less sure when I was given the name of the medicine, 'Huoxiangzhengqishui'. What's the matter with aspirin or Lemsip? These are short names you can trust! I feel a good rule is I should never take anything if I can pronounce fewer than three syllables of the name.

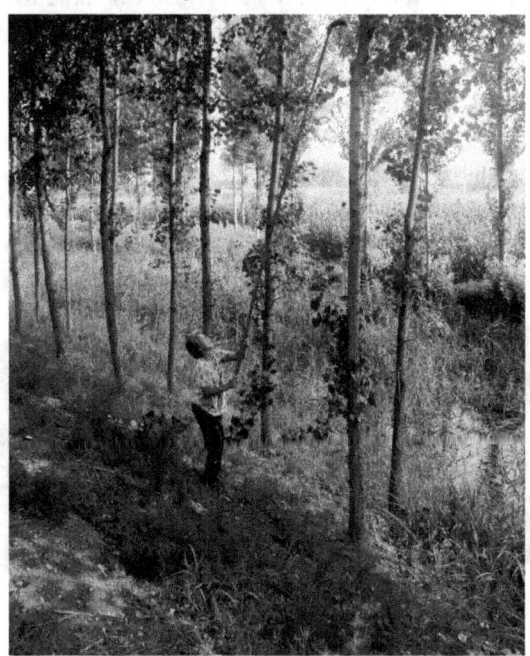

An elderly woman in Dezhou, Shandong Province.

Madam Zhang thought I was being childish, refusing to take something that was good for me, so she took the top off one of the bottles and drank the whole thing in one gulp … she then burst out coughing; I feared she was going to choke to death, which would have been an extreme way of reducing the risks of heat exhaustion. I took another cool bottle of Diet Coke from the ice box and felt much better.

URL http://www.walkforpeace.eu/day-12-rest-reflection-day/

August 8 Day 13

The Good Manager

Route: Ningjinxian – Lingcheng, Dezhou
Walked today: 23.50 miles / 37.80 km
Total walked: 238.50 miles / 383.10 km
Donated today: £100.00 and ¥0.00
Total donations: £1,100.88 and ¥3,100.00

The first 11 days have been punishing because of the heat, humidity and, with all due respect to our wonderful hosts, air quality. I don't think there is any way I could have done over 200 miles in 10 days without the unstinting support of the local Red Cross volunteers. It is their enthusiasm that I feed off in the morning and their sense of achievement that inspires me at the end of the day.

The fact that these teams of volunteers come together at county, town and provincial level and then perform to such high levels, instantly picking up the baton from the previous team, is thanks to their leader, Madam Zhang. We had a major change of team today, with the sore team from Hebei handing over the Shandong team.

It was great to be back in Shandong Province, which was the first place I ever visited in China, back in 1997. It is a vast province with huge economic power and a population of 117 million – that is almost the population of the UK and France combined (not a happy thought).

With regard to the teams – if I am the worst manager of people that I know (and I probably am), then Madam Zhang is fast becoming the best, in my opinion. Xuelin and I reflect on how we both have similar faults when it comes to managing. We are both productive and efficient individuals. We like things done to a high standard and in the quickest time possible. We both love work and somehow resent having to share it, so we don't delegate. We instinctively think 'It would take longer to explain what I want than it would take to do it ourselves.' So we carry on, on our own, missing out on the multiplier effect that comes from successful management of teams.

Madam Zhang, like us, is highly efficient and productive. Unlike us, she realizes that teams are a critical part of delivering major projects successfully. It was not by accident that someone with those qualities should play such a key role in the Beijing 2008 Games. Xuelin and I are keen to learn and we discuss Madam Zhang's approach.

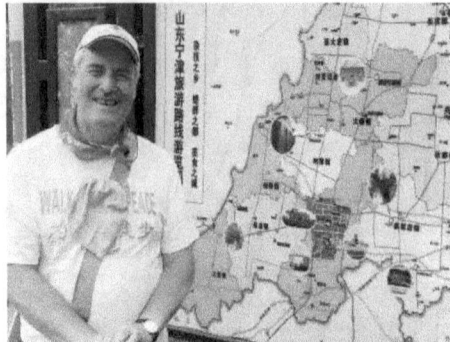 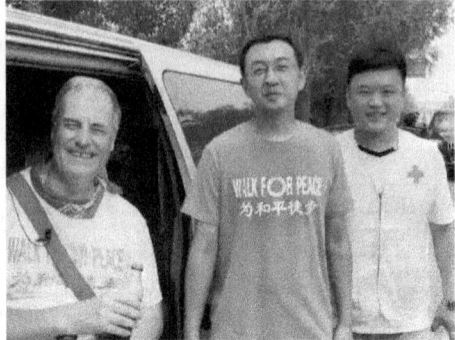

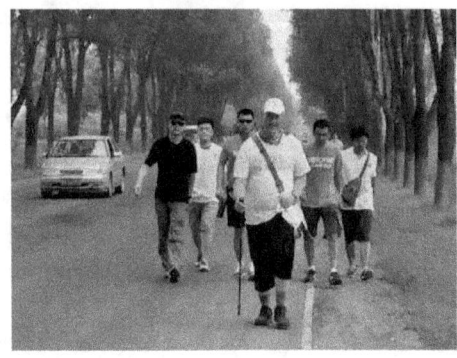 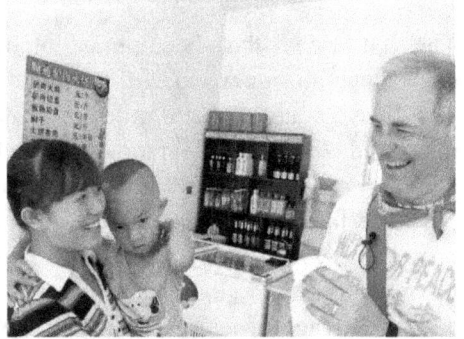

Top left: Lord Bates in front of a map of Ningjin County, Shandong Province.
Top right: Lord Bates and Red Cross volunteers.
Bottom left: Supporters in Ningjinxian. Bottom right: Talking with the owner of a restaurant.

So what are the key ingredients of good team leadership that we have observed in Madam Zhang and we would recommend to others?

Personal security is one. People who are insecure in their roles and knowledge of themselves are hopeless leaders of people, because people feel that insecurity. Insecure leaders personalize criticism, taking it as criticism of themselves rather than of the task. Insecure people need too much praise and so tend not to give praise to others. They manage upwards constantly, trying to please their boss and neglecting their team. Such people will instinctively take every bit of credit meant for the team for themselves and pass on every bit of criticism meant for themselves.

Encouragement is another. A phrase popular in my native north-east of England was, 'You get more by tickling than scratching.' The point is people respond better to being told they are doing a good job, although you may have a few ideas as to how they might be able to do a great job, rather than being given a dressing down. It is the easiest thing in the world to knock someone down, but it requires great skill to pick someone up and enable them to make a contribution.

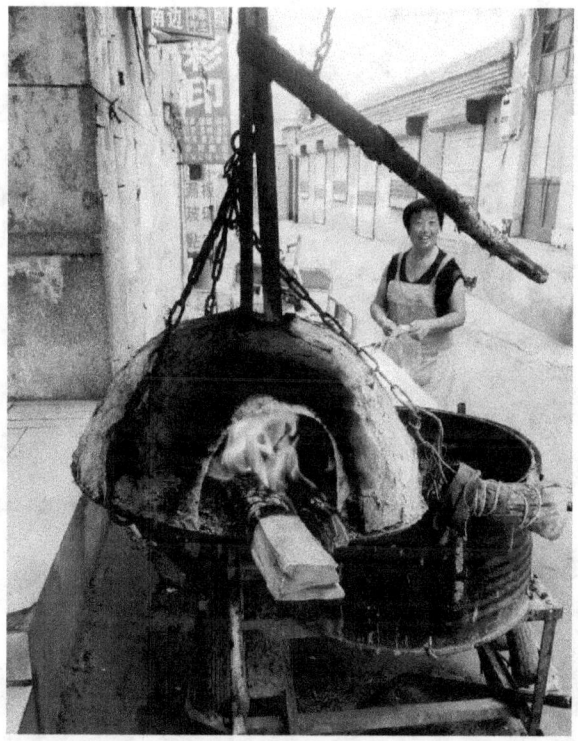

A traditional oven .

Listening is a third ingredient. How long do you spend transmitting instructions to your team and how long do you spend listening to feedback? I would suggest that the good team leaders are good listeners. They are eager to hear suggestions as to how performance could be improved, and the best source of that is from the people who are doing the job. This needn't take a long time: One of the most transformative management books of all time is the *One Minute Manager* by Ken Blanchard – it has sold 13 million copies so far. The basic premise of the book is that good management need only take a few minutes but bad management can cost you months or even years in lost production.

Being quick to praise and slow to criticise is vital for the reasons already stated but most of all because a basic human need is for people to feel they are appreciated. Think of the last job you left; the chances are that it wasn't that you didn't like the firm or the department, but that you felt underappreciated by your line manager – that is what endless business school surveys tell us. Appreciation is spelt R-E-S-P-E-C-T.

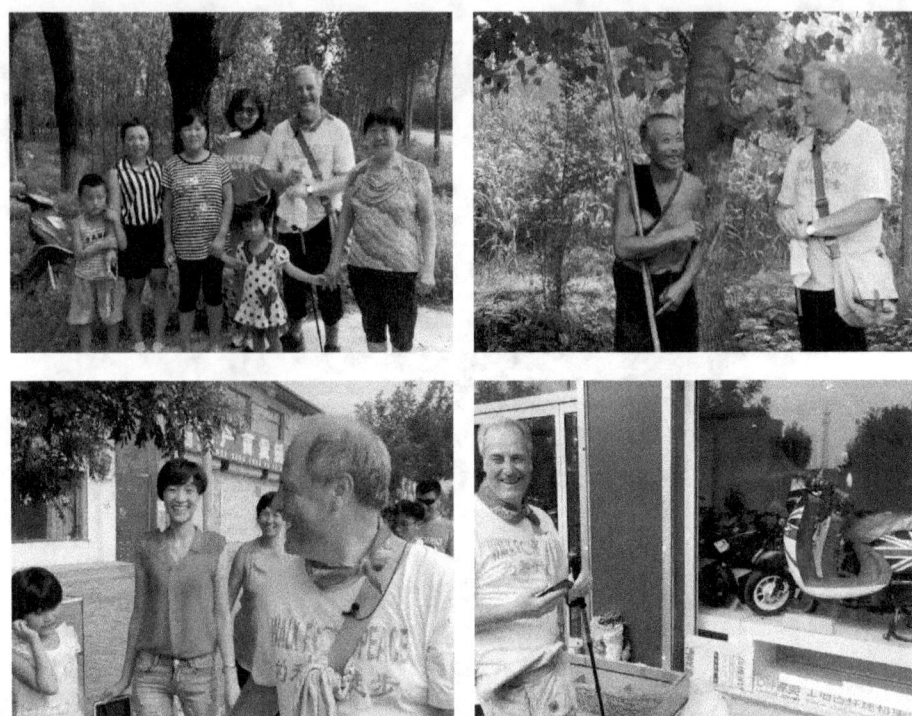

Top left: Lord Bates, Madame Zhang and different generations of supporters.
Top right: Talking to an elderly man.
Bottom left: Meeting local people. Bottom right: An interesting find.

Seeing the big picture is another characteristic. Most failing managers will look at a team and see only its inadequacies. Most successful managers look at the same team and see only its potentials. I love football and often see a team with some gifted players failing to deliver the performances on the pitch that they should. Then there is a change in manager, not the players, and all of a sudden the same players are world-beaters. Part of the reason for that is the vision that is instilled in them by their manager. One day a wise manager visiting a major construction site asked one of the workers what was he doing. The worker responded, 'I am just baking bricks.' 'No,' said the manager. 'You are building a great cathedral.' Focus the team on the big picture, not the small task.

Good leaders have a gift for spotting talent.. Building a good team is like putting together a jigsaw puzzle. You know what you want it to look like because you have a picture on the cover of the box, but inside all you have are 1,000 odd-shaped pieces. I think the best managers are the ones who recognize first that every piece is different but is of equal value, that they all have a place and their task is to find a space where they fit in and contribute to the overall beauty of the picture.

Be calm. Things will go wrong. That is life. The question is not why did it go wrong but what is the wise thing to do in the situation now to try and put it right or minimize the damage? The qualities of a cool head and a warm heart are perhaps the most important of all.

The poem *If* by Rudyard Kipling, which I won't translate into Chinese because much of it is word-play in English, to me captures the essence of the good manager and the qualities we have observed in Madam Zhang:

> If you can keep your head when all about you
> Are losing theirs and blaming it on you;
> If you can trust yourself when all men doubt you,
> But make allowance for their doubting too;
> If you can wait and not be tired by waiting,
> Or, being lied about, don't deal in lies,
> Or, being hated, don't give way to hating,
> And yet don't look too good, nor talk too wise;
>
> If you can dream – and not make dreams your master;
> If you can think – and not make thoughts your aim,
> If you can meet with Triumph and Disaster
> And treat those two impostors just the same;
> If you can bear to hear the truth you've spoken
> Twisted by knaves to make a trap for fools,
> Or watch the things you gave your life to, broken,
> And stoop and build 'em up with worn-out tools;
>
> If you can make one heap of all your winnings
> And risk it on one turn of pitch-and-toss,
> And lose, and start again at your beginnings,
> And never breathe a word about your loss;
> If you can force your heart and nerve and sinew
> To serve your turn long after they are gone,
> And so hold on when there is nothing in you
> Except the Will which says to them: "Hold on!"
>
> If you can talk with crowds and keep your virtue,
> Or walk with Kings – nor lose the common touch,
> If neither foes nor loving friends can hurt you,
> If all men count with you, but none too much;
> If you can fill the unforgiving minute
> With sixty seconds' worth of distance run,
> Yours is the Earth and everything that's in it,
> And – which is more – you'll be a Man, my son!

URL http://www.walkforpeace.eu/day-13-the-good-manager/

August 9 Day 14

Shandong Highway and Dual Language Signs

Route: Lingcheng – Linyi, Dezhou
Walked today: 25.40 miles / 40.90 km
Total walked: 263.90 miles / 424.00 km
Donated today: £0.00 and ¥0.00
Total donations: £1,100.88 and ¥3,100.00

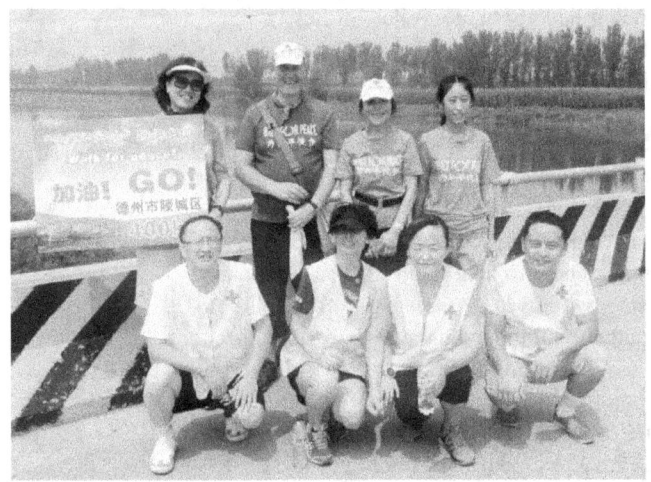

Milestone marking 300 km of the walk.

The Shandong Highway and I have grown very close over the past few days. I have travelled its length since crossing over from Hebei Province. It offers the great comfort of not only providing kilometre markers but breaking it down into 100 metre intervals. This is a huge help in pacing myself.

The landscape is a picture of China's economic progress. Shepherds with their flocks travel along the road and riverside, impervious to the heavy traffic and the occasional walker. Then there are the bustling villages and towns, all with roadside markets as well as shops. It is in the villages and towns that people have the greater confidence to wave, shout 'Hello' or 'Welcome to China' and then ask for a photo. It adds to the time of the walk and breaks the stride, but this is the purpose of the walk, to connect with the real China.

Villages are mostly located off the Shandong Highway and will have ornamental gates and a sign showing the village name, often in English as well as Chinese. The villages are normally about 500 metres or so from the highway. At the junction of the village lane and the highway there is normally a traffic police officer standing smartly to attention. Often we are invited to come to the village to take shelter from the heat of the sun or for some food. Other times young people will wait at the end of their village lane and offer water or even, on one occasion today, an ice-cream.

It all adds up to an interesting study in communications in rural China, because news of the 'foreigner walking' is sent through social media WeChat, QQ or Weibo. WeChat is the Chinese WhatsApp or Twitter and Weibo is more a micro blogging site. They both have about 500 million users. QQ is an instant messenger for China and has over 800 million users, the same number as WhatsApp globally. To place those numbers in some sort of context: Twitter would have 330 million active accounts but Facebook remains way out in front with 1.4 billion. We witness the power of social media in China every day as pictures taken from one village motivate some member of the next village to join in.

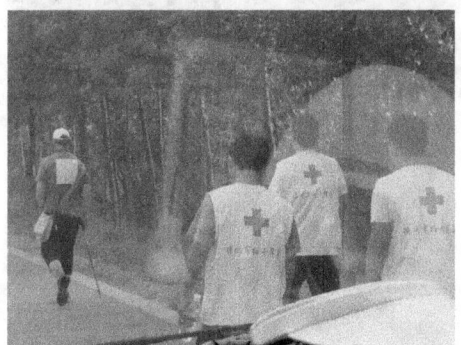 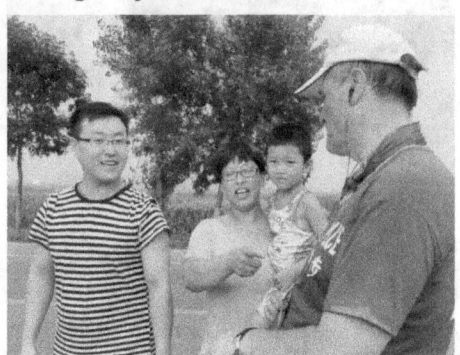

Left: The local team of Red Cross volunteers. Right: Villagers engaging with Lord Bates.

Some suggest that the Chinese government is worried that currently blocked US social media firms Facebook, What's App and Twitter will otherwise dominate the market in China. This may be so, but there is an equal possibility that Chinese social media giants QQ and WeChat will take a chunk out of the US market share when they become global brands and platforms.

We stop to talk to people along the Shandong Highway – mostly when Xuelin arrives and we can engage in conversation. We hear time and again how advances in farm machinery and technology mean that they don't need to have two people looking after the land, so normally the female will go and work in the new factory making clothing or some other produce, usually for export markets. With the two incomes, they are able to get clothes and a motorized tricycle and send their child to school. Soon the villages are embraced by the cities and so the villagers are trading their traditional village homes for flats in modern high-rise blocks with electricity, gas and water and schools and hospitals nearby. For some of the older villagers, the offer of a brand new flat for their final years lacks the appeal of the village and home they have known their whole lives and those of previous generations. It is exactly the same pattern of industrialization that has gone on through time the world over.

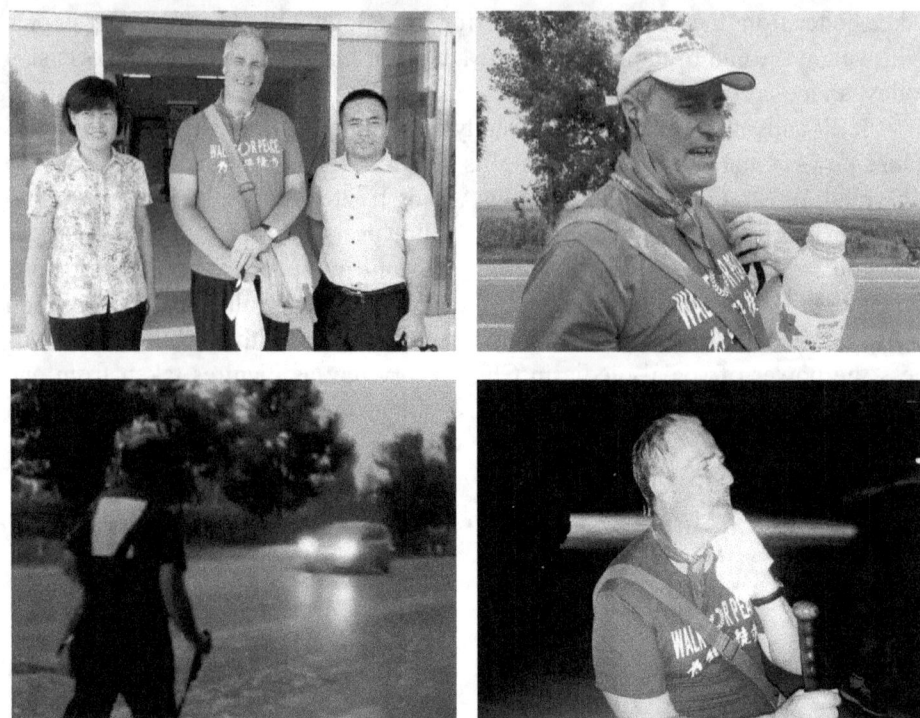

Top left: Lord Bates with two locals. Top right: Getting some refreshment.
Bottom left: Walking in the heavy rain. Bottom right: Recovering from the rain.

Of course, they will soon reach such as level of prosperity that, having cars, they won't want to be cramped into blocks of flats and will start to build new homes back in the countryside. My point is there is nothing that I have yet seen in China which from an economic point of view has not happened in every other industrializing economy. It is classical industrialization. This may give some comfort to the Chinese leadership but soon they will see new social challenges taking over from the old economic ones with the growth of a highly educated, entrepreneurial and confident middle class.

URL http://www.walkforpeace.eu/day-14-shandong-highway/

August 10 Day 15

Back in Beijing & Yao Chen

Beijing

A Day Off

Donated today: £1007.25 and ¥200.00

Total donations: £2,108.13 and ¥3,300.00

Day 14 turned out to be one of the toughest days of walking I have ever undertaken, owing to the heat and humidity. I felt the symptoms of heat exhaustion coming down to cover me like a heavy cloud. The Red Cross team and Xuelin, ever mindful of my health, managed to arrange for a local council office which was open on a Sunday to allow me to lie down in a cool room during the heat of the day. Otherwise, things could have been a whole lot worse. We set off walking again at 4 pm and finished at 7.30 pm, when it was getting dark and the busy roads offered a different type of challenge.

The two-day trip back to Beijing that Xuelin had arranged could not have come at a better time to aid my recovery. We left from the high-speed rail terminal at Dezhou East and were in Beijing just 90 minutes later. Travelling at speeds of over 300 km, it made quick work of what had taken me two weeks to walk. I love rail travel. I grew up close to the main East Coast line and my earliest memories are of rushing down the bank to the bridge over the railway line to catch a sight of trains like the Flying Scotsman. I have always tried to live close to railway stations: Durham and now Victoria. There is an elegance about train travel. If I lived in China, I would love to live beside any of these spectacular high-speed rail stations. So, the experience of the rail journey lifted my spirits. Just as we left the train, a staff worker came along and changed all the seats around to face the forward direction – I thought this was brilliant. I hate travelling with my back to the direction of travel, and yet again Chinese people had come up with an elegant solution.

Xuelin and I arrived in Beijing and were met by representatives of *China Daily*. We were in town to help launch a smartphone photo competition called 'Amazing China' at its headquarters. *China Daily* is a true global publication – it is readily available alongside *Metro* and *City AM* on the London Underground. What is more, as many print publications are in decline, *China Daily* is increasing its reach. It is clearly positioning itself in the *FT* and *International Herald Tribune* space and such is the thirst for insights on China from within China that it has a very strong future.

From the moment we arrived at HQ, we were shuttled from interview to interview by *China Daily*'s London Bureau Chief, who had flown in for the launch event. Given that this is a business publication, there was great interest in Xuelin's views and it was good to participate together. After the interviews by print, TV and online journalists, it was off to meet Kang Bing, who is Vice President of the China Daily Media Group. It was fascinating to get his insights on the global media industry. After the high-speed rail journey, this was high-speed business.

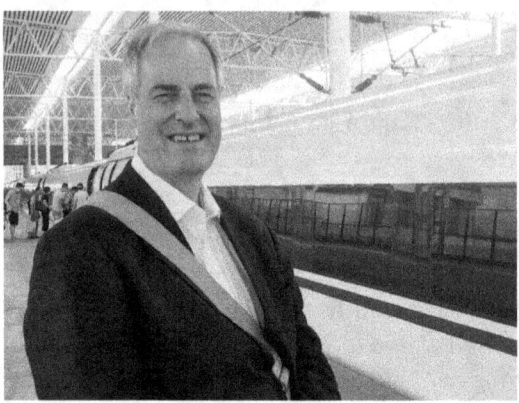

Travelling for the first time on the legendary high-speed railway.

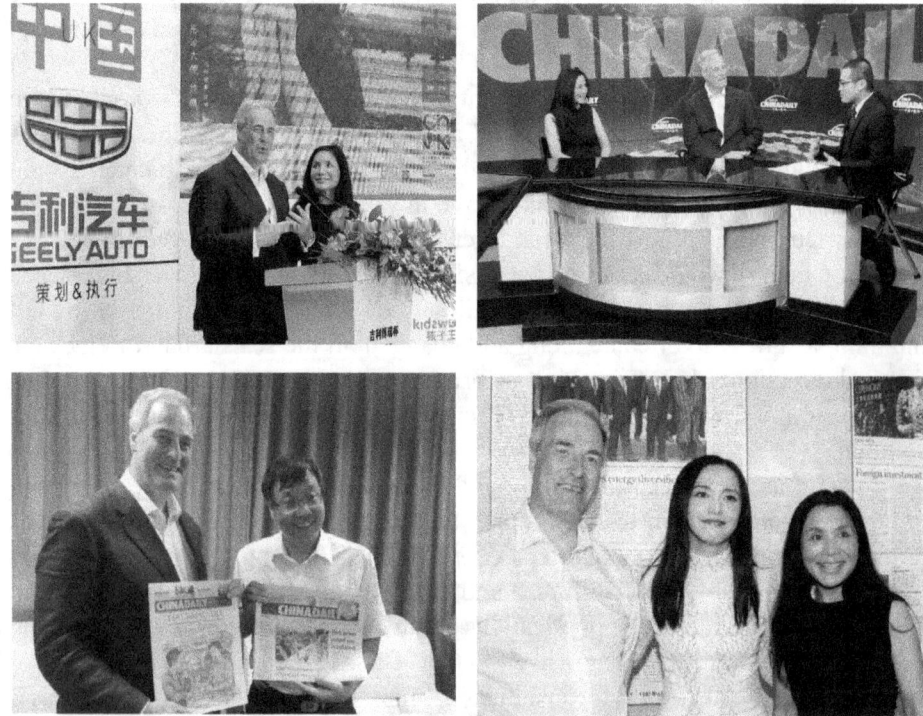

Top left: Attending the launch of the 'Amazing China' smartphone photo competition.
Top right: The *China Daily* interview. Bottom left: Lord Bates and Kang Bing, Vice President of the China Daily Media Group. Bottom right: Lord and Lady Bates with the actress Yao Chen.

At precisely 1.55 pm we were ushered to the lift and taken down to the large auditorium which had been set up for the launch. We arrived out of the lift and there must have been a hundred young people with smartphones raised waiting with anticipation. When I walked out of the lift, there was an almost audible sigh of collective disappointment – it is something you get used to as a British politician. But just then there were screams as they rushed across to the next elevator and this time they weren't disappointed. The reason? The actress Yao Chen, China's Angelina Jolie!

What is it about celebrity? Yao Chen just lit the auditorium up with her presence. I wanted to grab my iPhone and go across to film her arrival too, but Xuelin held me back. Here were a collection of some of the most powerful figures in media and business and politics in China, but we were all willingly made spectators at the Yao Chen show. As so often, behind a very successful image, a hugely intelligent person knows how to present her brand their brand. Her micro blog has 78 million followers, mine has about 78, on a good day – well, on a day when I am mentioning Yao Chen in it. No wonder *Time* magazine named her in its list of the top 30 global figures on the Internet. Amazing China!

URL http://www.walkforpeace.eu/day-15-back-in-beijing-yao-chen/

August 11 Day 16

Cultural Exchanges in Beijing

Beijing
A Day Off
Donated today: £600.00 / ¥1,000.00
Donated today: £600.00 and ¥1,000.00
Total donations: £2,708.13 and ¥4,300.00

We were very grateful for the invitation while in Beijing to meet our (British) new ambassador, Barbara Woodward. In the Beijing traffic you can either be half an hour early or half an hour late. We prefer to be either an hour early or on time. We arrived at the Ambassador's residence half an hour early and were kindly allowed in and served a cup of tea. It was a hugely busy time for the ambassador, as the British Foreign Secretary arrived the next day on a regional tour from Tokyo and Seoul with very complex issues on the agenda.

Barbara Woodward was a gracious host and was very interested in the walk. She had just been appointed to the role of ambassador in February this year and had begun her working life in China as a teacher and therefore was fluent in Mandarin. What is more, she understood the culture very well having lived and worked here. In China, culture is even more useful than language. More misunderstandings happen through lack of respect and understanding for the culture than misinterpretation of the language.

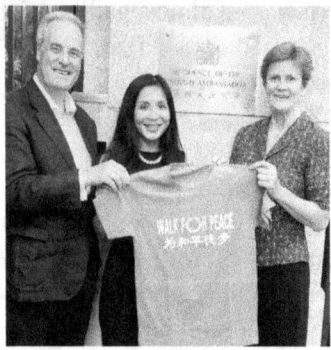 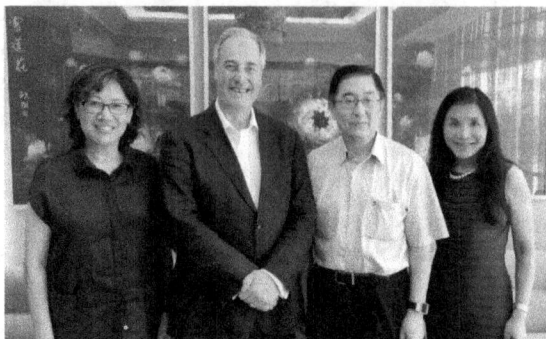

Left: An exchange with the British ambassador to China.
Right: Madame Zhang, Lord Bates, Qiao Wei and Lady Bates.

One of the greatest challenges facing British diplomats in China is that power does not always come conveniently dressed up in a way in which is easy to spot – a fine-cut suit, fine-cut accent, impressive title, confidently dropping the right names and the right cultural experiences. Britain still retains many of the characteristics of a class-based social system, especially at elite metropolitan levels, although it is being weakened through education and social mobility. China is a bureaucracy.

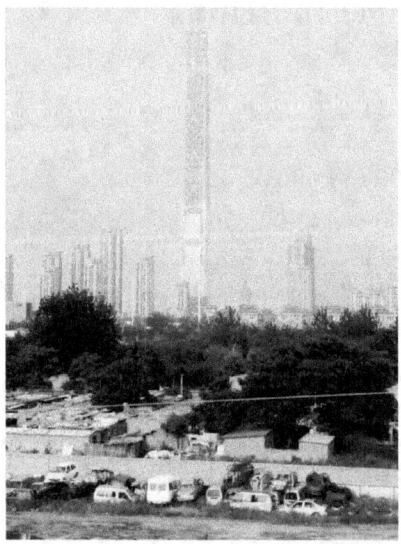

Two sides of Beijing.

We had just had lunch with one of the most unassuming and humble Chinese officials you could ever meet – Qiao Wei, a friend of Xuelin, who is Deputy Chairman of the Chinese All Federation of Returned Chinese, but as Vice Minister a highly influential figure in Beijing. This reminded me of one of the first visits I had made to China with Xuelin, when there was a British business reception in Shanghai and Xuelin was present as a board member of the UK–China Business Association. The guest of honour was HRH Prince Andrew, who was hugely respected for the work he had personally done in promoting UK–China trade.

One of the problems was that a major UK investor was being frustrated by delays to his application. The CEO had flown in to try and unblock the delays. A senior British diplomat navigated the VIPs around the reception room in search of titles and fine suits, etc., brushing aside anyone who didn't 'look the part'. Xuelin happened to spot a casually dressed guy in the corner of the room. She was intrigued as to why he would be here and started talking to him in Mandarin. She was able to establish that he was in fact the local official who had the investment application on his desk but had some legitimate questions about the detail of the proposal, which he was hoping to have a chance to discuss with the CEO. However, in conformity with Chinese culture he didn't want to push himself forward when there were other more senior figures in the room. Xuelin put the two of them together, helped with translation, and within a few days the investment was agreed. Welcome to China.

URL http://www.walkforpeace.eu/day-16-dialogue-and-the-ambassador/

August 12 Day 17

Back on the Road in Shandong

Route: Linyi, Dezhou – Jinan
Walked today: 24.70 miles / 39.80 km
Total walked: 288.60 miles / 463.80 km
Donated today: £0.00 and ¥500.00
Total donations: £2,708.13 and ¥4,800.00

It had been a packed two days in Beijing. We concluded with a visit to CCTV's studios to record an edition of *Dialogue*, which happens to be one of my favourite programme formats on the English-version CCTV Channel – as to whether it will remain that after our appearance I don't know. Questions ranged vary widely from British education to World War II, sport and how Xuelin and I met. Xuelin was keen to extract every possible opportunity from the visit, which even included an interview with the Xinhua News Agency in Beijing station while waiting for the train back. We arrived back in Dezhou East late and had an early start the next day.

The seven-km section of the Shandong Highway we were travelling along was blocked by major roadworks, so it required some detour to get to the starting place. We had good guides from the local Red Cross, who at one point took me over a huge mound of earth and through a narrow gap in a fence to make it on to the road where the resurfacing was taking place. Following the direct original route rather than the detour because of the roadworks would have saved a day in walking, and that meant that as far as I was concerned it was a risk worth taking.

It was a hard walk and the dust was thick in the air from the road repairs, but just as we ended I was guided over another mound and into a police station in Linyi. I thought I must be in trouble again, but the local police chief had heard of the walk and wanted to show his hospitality. It was a welcome stop in a cool, air-conditioned office and an opportunity to look at maps of the next section of the walk. The target for the end of the day was to reach a river crossing, which was the boundary between Dezhou and Jinan, so there was to be a small ceremony to mark another handover. That was a good clear aim.

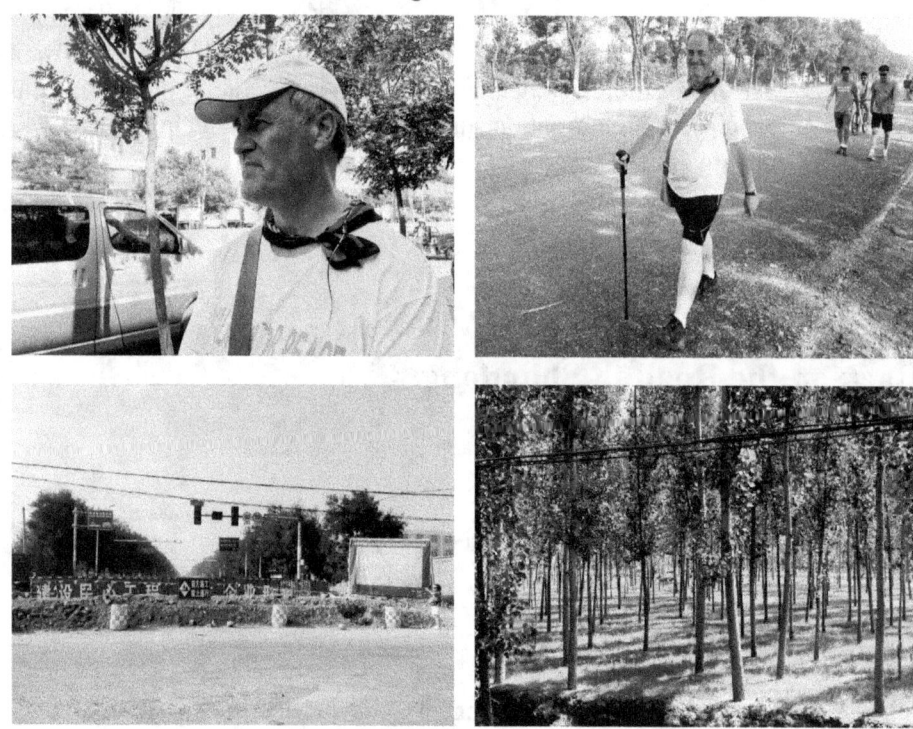

Top left: Leaving Dezhou. Top right: Arriving in Jinan.
Bottom left: Road construction site in Jinan. Bottom right: Roadside scenery.

After two days off, I felt fantastic: I was pushing a near six km per hour pace. I felt so good I didn't want to rest for lunch but instead to keep going to complete the day's walk as early as possible and then to get to the hotel and rest. I was walking mostly through rural communities with occasional intrusions of urbanization. As usual, people were very friendly and curious. I wish that I had more time to talk to them and find out more about their lives and to explain what I am doing and why.

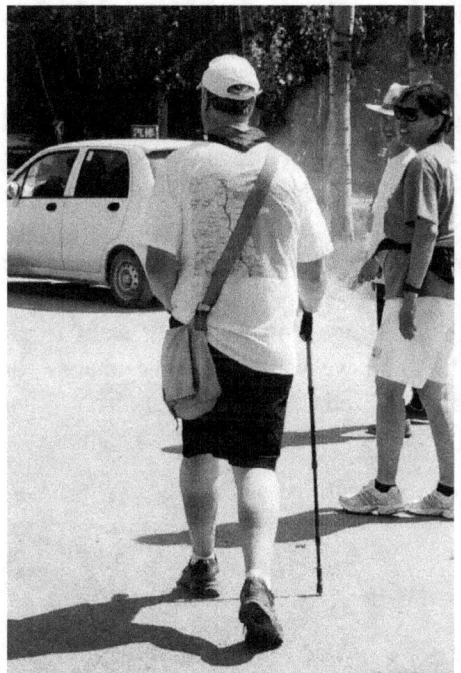
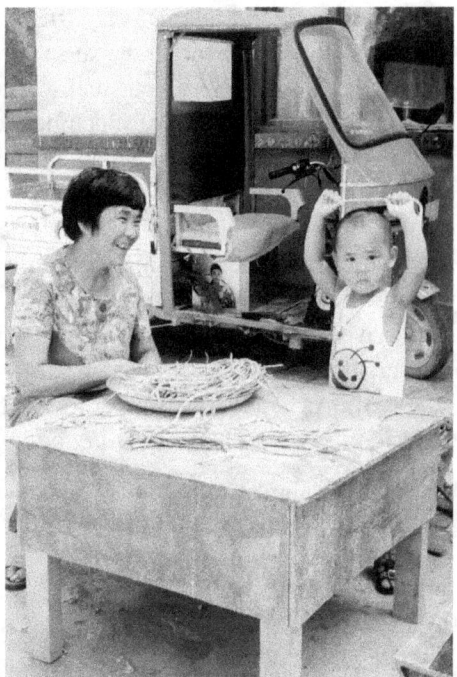
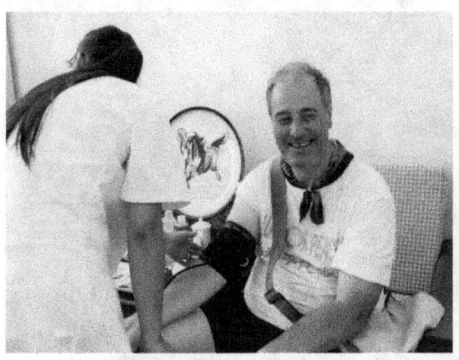
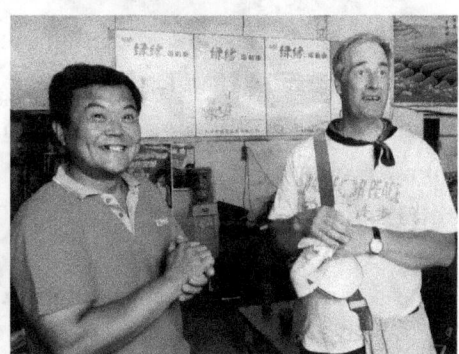

Top left: Walking towards Jinan. Top right: A woman with her young grandchild.
Bottom left: Another health check. Bottom right: Lord Bates and a motorcycle repair shop owner.

Some people I did have the chance to speak to were a hospital dean, who invited me in for some tea and to cool down and of course to have my blood pressure taken. One of the advantages and disadvantages of walking with the Red Cross volunteers is that they take such a concern over my health. I seem only to have to sneeze and a packet of some medicine is produced, only to be politely declined, but such attentiveness on their part would come into its own the next day.

In one of the final communities we passed through, a man with the most wonderful smile came out to greet us. He ran a motorcycle repair shop. He was very busy but had time to show me around his garage, which was piled with spare parts and motorcycles in various states of repair. He had the look of the type of man whom I would instinctively trust with my motorcycle repairs if I had one. I enjoyed being in his garage because it reminded me of the sight and smell of my grandfather's shed. He was a steel worker but had a part-time fascination and talent for repairing all sorts of machines, even his grandson's bicycle. As a child it was less of a shed, more of a magical cave where broken things went in and came out fully restored. In the West, we have become a throwaway society and moved from a 'make do and mend' to a 'buy new and spend' culture – this has left a legacy of consumer debt. China would do well to avoid our mistakes and keep the motorcycle repair man in business.

We arrived at the bridge and toyed with the suggestion we might want to go further, but no, we had put in a good shift and we would save the energy for tomorrow. As usual, it was great to meet the new Red Cross volunteers from Jinan and sad to say goodbye and *Gan de hao* (great job) to the team from Dezhou.

URL http://www.walkforpeace.eu/day-17-back-on-the-road-in-shandong/

August 13 Day 18

Thoughts with Tianjin and Red Cross Rescue

Route: Jiyangxian – Huanghe Bridge, Jinan
Walked today: 23.80 miles / 38.30 km
Total walked: 312.40 miles / 502.10 km
Donated today: £600.00 / ¥3,000.00
Total donations: £3,308.13 and ¥7,800.00

It was a familiar start: from the bridge where we had finished the nightt. Our aim for the day this time was the bridge over the Yellow River and into Jinan City. At our starting point, a bustling roadside market had sprung up. By the time we got there at 8 am the market had already been going for three hours. There was such an incredible selection of fresh fruit and vegetables bursting with colour. In Chinese culture, great value is placed on fresh food, and in many areas there is no refrigeration, so the tradition of daily shopping is alive and well. I asked how the prices were at the market – the chilli seller said that his price had fallen over the past year from 1.5 yuan to 1 yuan, whereas the garlic seller had seen the value of garlic almost double over the same period. I love small markets because there is no manipulation with cross subsidies and promotional offerings, and pricing is straightforward supply and demand (and open to negotiation).

Around lunchtime, Madam Zhang and some of the Red Cross team were evidently receiving bad news. There had been an explosion at a chemical plant in the port area at Tianjin. Early reports indicated that there may have been over

100 casualties. This was a major incident for the Red Cross because they are first responders in emergencies like this, including in Tianjin the week before. To know that many of the Red Cross teams who walked with us would now be engaged in conducting search and rescue operations amidst the rubble of the former factory and operating blood donation centres for the victims personalized the tragedy for us. It also strengthened our determination to raise funds for the Red Cross Society in China so that it could continue to provide this wonderful emergency service at times of crisis and disaster. I was also encouraged that British Foreign Secretary, Philip Hammond, who had been in Tianjin that morning, had responded to the disaster with a pledge to support the rescue efforts with specialist teams from the UK.

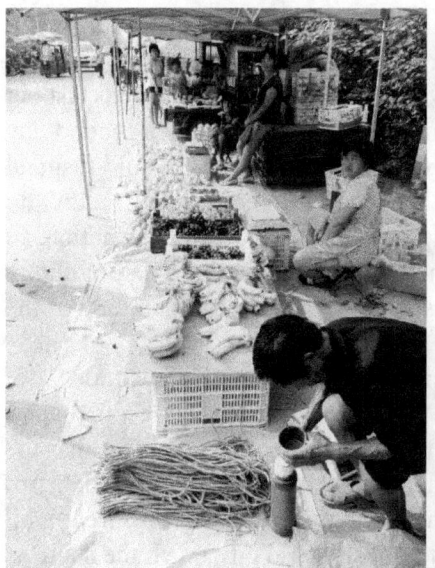
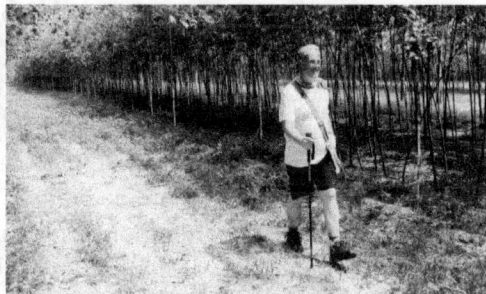
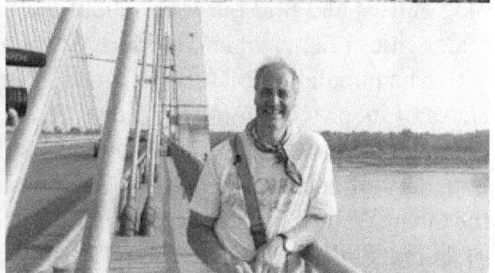

Left: Fruit vendors at the side of the road.
Top right: Looking for some shade. Bottom right: On the Yellow River bridge.

Perhaps it was the general low mood that persisted during the afternoon as more reports came in from Tianjin and the very high temperatures that made the last 15 km some of the hardest I had ever walked. To complicate matters I had had an upset stomach (sounds pathetic even to mention it on such a day), which meant that I had lost my appetite for food. This then led to stomach cramps. I made it across the Yellow River bridge, but only just, and then needed to get back to the hotel to rest. I began to worry whether I would be able to walk at all the next day, even though that would knock us off schedule, having already taken two days out to go to Beijing. That said, not taking a day off might knock us off schedule later for longer. The decision was taken not to walk the next day, and I think the Red Cross team accepted that, perhaps with some relief, as their thoughts remained with their colleagues in Tianjin.

URL http://www.walkforpeace.eu/day-18-thoughts-with-tianjin/

August 14 Day 19

Return to Jinan City

Jinan, Shandong Province

A Day Off

Donated today: £10.00 / ¥2,000.00

Total donations: £3,318.13 and ¥9,800.00

I slept for almost twelve hours, waking at 7 am. I felt very weak. It seemed as if it took all my energy to brush my teeth, never mind walk 40 km. I was grateful we had taken the decision to cancel the day's walking. I went down for breakfast but couldn't face the prospect of eating anything again. This was now a second day without proper food. Not a good sign. Henry Kissinger, I am told, would respond to any piece of bad news with the phrase, 'What can I do now that I couldn't do before?' It is a very good tool for turning negative events into positive action. In answer to the same rhetorical question, I thought I could get up to date with my blog entries and find out more about the history and culture of Jinan, one of the major cities of ancient and modern China.

The population of Jinan is around 7 million (about the size of London). Because of its proximity to the Yellow River, it has abundant natural resources, including lakes and 72 fresh water springs. It is sometimes easy to forget that the boundary of ancient China ran across Shandong and Jinan. In fact, remnants of the Great Wall of Qi built in 500 BC remain. It is a predecessor of the Great Wall of China, built in 250 BC. Today, Jinan is a typical global city much the same as many others, with its high-rise buildings and high-speed rail, but its long history is what sets it apart.

I was honoured to be visited at the hotel by the Deputy Governor of Shandong Province before breakfast. Shandong Province has a population roughly twice that of the UK, so her kindness in visiting this traveller was particularly appreciated. As we walked in to the hastily set-out meeting room with marked seats for all those attending and UK and China flags, I was greeted at the entrance by the Deputy Governor. Normally, introductions with officials and visiting guests have a certain predictability but when the translator enquired, 'How is your diarrhoea this morning?', I was a little wrong-footed. Not wishing to protest that it was a stomach ache, rather than diarrhoea, I simply replied, 'Much better, thank you.'

The Deputy Mayor had been well briefed, noting that my first visit to China in 1998 had indeed been to Shandong Province. She explained the long history and natural beauty of Shandong Province and how it suffered under Japanese occupation. Then conversation turned to life in the UK, about which she seemed to be particularly knowledgeable. She later explained that her daughter is currently studying at university at Loughborough. It reminded me that, of all the possible aspects of cultural diplomacy possible, education is the greatest. Shandong retains a special memory for me because I undertook my business degree research project here in 1998. The UK was a special place to the Deputy Governor because her daughter was being educated there now.

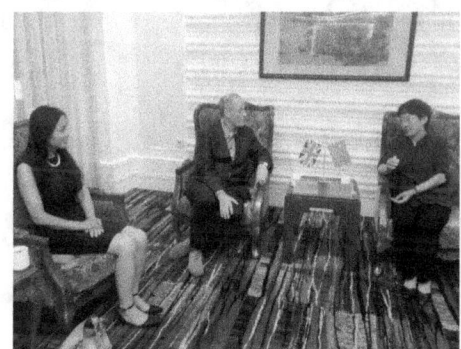 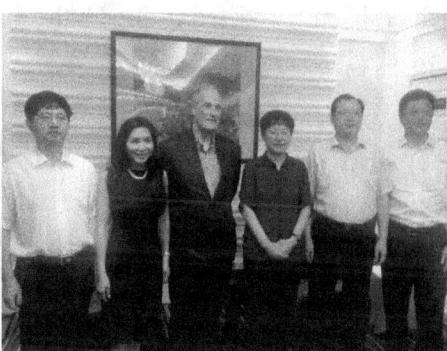

Lord and Lady Bates with the Deputy Governor of Shandong Province.
Lord and Lady Bates with the Deputy Governor and her staff.

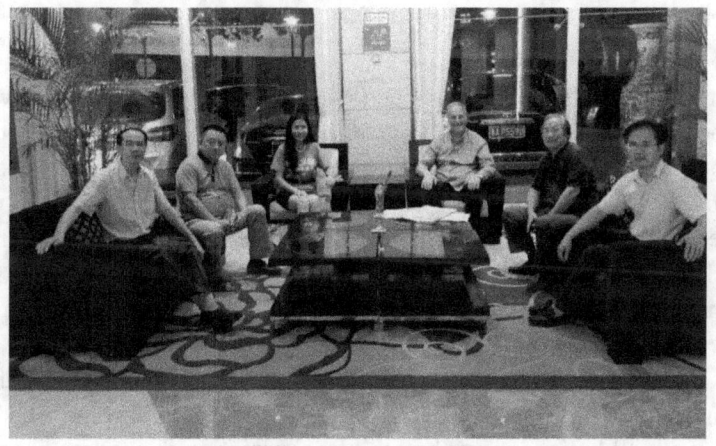

Lord and Lady Bates meeting of the Zhejiang University alumni association in Jinan.

Education links were the theme of the day, Xuelin having arranged a meeting with members of the Zhejiang alumni association in Jinan. Zhejiang University is one of the top universities in China, and it had two major points of significance for this walk. First, Xuelin attended the university and is now President of the Zhejiang alumni branch in the UK. Second, my plan is to walk through the Zhejiang University campus in Hangzhou on the final few kilometres of the walk. They were very supportive, although I was particularly interested in one of the alumni because he had been a classmate of Xuelin's, and I wanted to try and get him to share some stories about Xuelin from her student days. I was surprised that, after a long and obviously funny set of comments in Chinese, his remarks were translated simply as 'Xuelin was a hard-working student.' The translator, of course, was Xuelin!

By the end of the day I was almost up to date with my blog entries and e-mails and had some very interesting meetings but the loss of appetite and stomach problems persisted… though the diarrhoea was now fine!

URL http://www.walkforpeace.eu/day-19-rest-day-jinan-city/

August 15 Day 20

Across Jinan and Fellow Walkers

Route: Huanghe Bridge – Licheng District, Jinan
Walked today: 25.90 miles / 41.70 km
Total walked: 338.30 miles / 543.80 km
Donated today: £0.00 / ¥0.00
Total donations: £3,318.13 and ¥9,800.00

I couldn't face breakfast but I was keen to get back on the road. This was going to be a special day – I would reach the 500 km marker. It was also a Saturday, so the number of those joining the walk increased. Xuelin and I have been deeply touched by the number of people who have come along to walk with us. There is a large number of followers of the walk on WeChat, which Xuelin and the team back in London ensure is regularly updated, so for those in the area it is not too difficult to estimate where we will be and when, and if not then WeChat messenger can get a direct response.

It is one of my regrets that I don't get more time to speak with those who come along to join in. I apologize that I am so old and unfit that it takes all my energy to walk 40 km and every breath of conversation is one less breath available to take a step. Early on in the walk, I saw that wonderful sign '500 km' in the distance being waved. It always puts a spring in my step.

Among those joining the walk today was Vice President Wang Rupeng of the Red Cross Society in Beijing. Wang is a very senior and respected figure in the Red Cross, having steered through a number of important reforms. That said, for me the greatest thing was that he had organised a walk from Hong Kong to Beijing (3,000 km), which took six months and raised £2 million for the Red Cross – respect!

He had also brought his 13-year-old daughter with him, who was very keen to walk, having walked similar distances in the past. I always reflect on my first 'big walk' was when I was 14. It was a 25-km circular route centred on Wylam in

Northumberland. I could only manage 15 km before I stopped to bathe my blistered feet in the cool River Tyne, and I needed to get a car ride to the finish point. I am therefore full of admiration for younger walkers who come along and keep the pace.

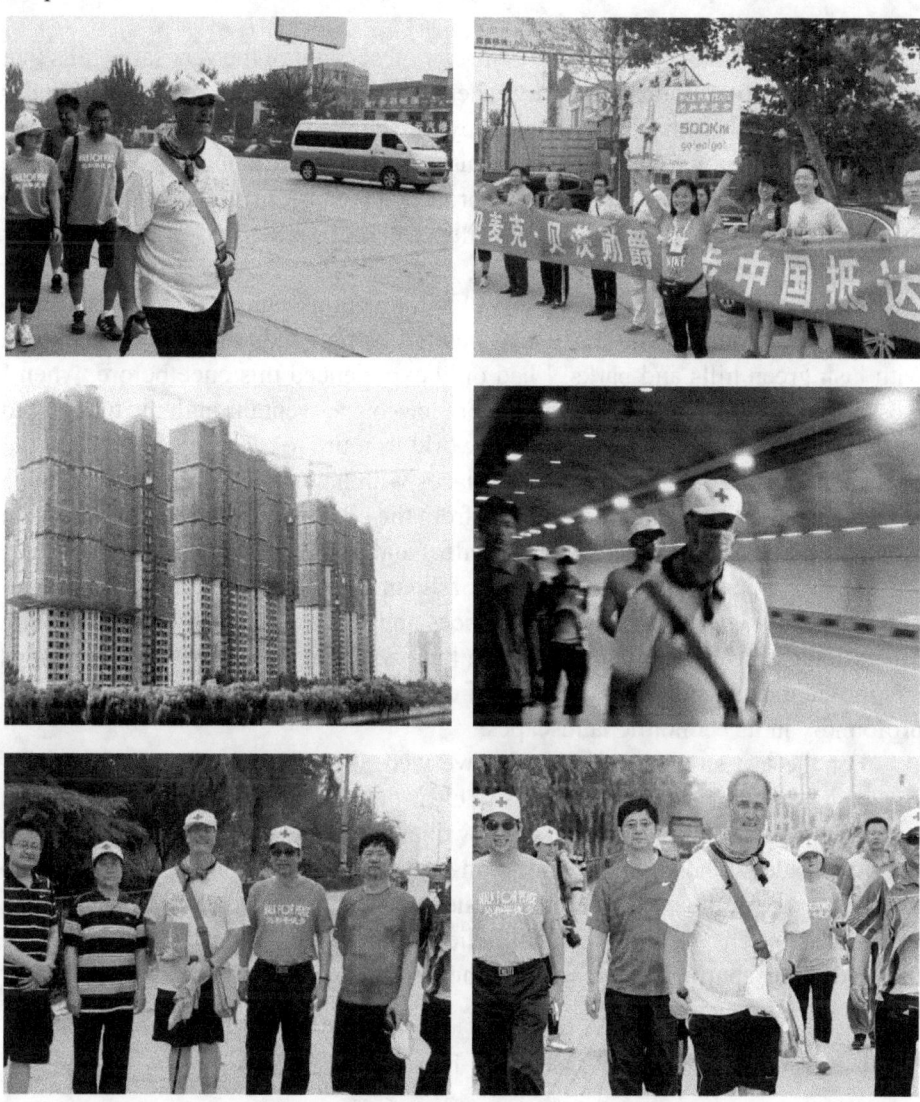

Top left: Walking towards the '500 km' sign. Top right: Milestone marking 500 km of the walk. Middle left: Jinan City, Shandong Province. Middle right: Passing through the tunnel under the mountain. Bottom left; Lord Bates with Wang Rupeng, Vice President of the Red Cross Society in Beijing, together with his daughter and other volunteers. Bottom right: On the Yellow River bridge.

As we passed through the centre of Jinan, we could see a major road and public transport junction beneath flyovers towering overhead. Underneath where we walked were hundreds, perhaps thousands of men seeking work. They would normally be from the country districts and come here each day, waiting to be picked up for occasional work, most often on construction sites. It was an unusual scene in China, as people are not usually waiting for work, but rather doing work, any work.

We took an unusual route out of the city on account of the very large hills that surround the city. I understood why when we came to a large road tunnel under a mountain. I am always more than happy to take the risk of walking through the tunnel, rather than walking over the mountain. Of course, being supported by the Red Cross volunteers meant that we approached the task in a far less relaxed way than I had done before, with high-visibility jackets, torches and even face masks to protect us from the fumes.

The tunnel must have been about 3 km long but we emerged into a completely different landscape. The dusty city was left behind and the place was covered with lush green hills and parks. I had only experienced this once before, when I crossed the Golden Gate Bridge in San Francisco and went through the tunnel into Mill Valley (still my No.1 place in the world to retire to). The green hills had an added purpose, being deeply spiritual places with names like 'Thousand Buddha Mountain'. You could imagine pilgrims from the city of Jinan travelling across the mountains we had just come under to reflect and pray.

This prosperous southern suburb of Jinan City, high up among the mountains, was populated with financial services and IT firms. Smartly dressed young professionals drove German cars to the huge shopping malls with luxury shops and movie theatres. China is a nation of contrasts in natural landscapes but more profoundly in its economic landscapes.

For the last stretch on the G104, we were joined by the Deputy Mayor of Jinan City and welcomed rain clouds to clear the air. I am a politician and I think I understand the political mindset fairly well, and I have been so impressed by the political leaders who have joined me on my walk. The reason is that there is no press coverage of the walk, so when President Wang or the Deputy Mayor of Jinan walks, it is purely out of a personal belief in the values of peace and friendship that underlie its purpose, which makes their company all the more special, as their motive is the same as mine.

URL http://www.walkforpeace.eu/day-20-across-jinan-and-fellow-walkers/

August 16 Day 21

There Will Be Days like This

Route: Jingong Villa, Jinan – Tai'an
Walked today: 17.50 miles / 28.60 km
Total walked: 355.80 miles / 572.40 km
Donated today: £50.00 / ¥0.00
Total donations: £3,368.13 and ¥9,800.00

There is a wonderful song by Van Morrison called *Days like This*. I have it on my iPhone and play it often when I walk, especially on good days. The opening lines are:

> When it's not always raining, there'll be days like this. When there's no-one complaining, there'll be days like this. When everything falls into place like the flick of a switch. Well, my mama told me, 'There'll be days like this'.

After some very tough days on the walk because of the weather and my illness, I rose from our accommodation on the edge of the Taishan Mountains. It was Sunday, with a clear blue sky above and green trees and running rivers all around. This was the best day I had experienced so far. I wished more of those who had struggled with us alongside the busy highways and cities could have been with us for this day, as we began a steady climb into the mountain foothills, passing through small villages along the way. As the town gave way to the country, so the friendliness of people who had time for one another and for strangers returned too.

One village in particular was to leave a deep impression on me because of the warmth of their welcome – Xingjiatun. The leader of the village came to meet me off the road with Madam Zhang and invited me to come and see the centrepiece of the town, a 500-year-old tree. Although I was not ready for a break, I was in the mood for learning more about the area I was walking through. I sat in the shade of the tree along with 20 or 30 villagers in a scene that would not have changed for 5,000, never mind 500 years.

Next to the tree was a 700-year-old well. I have never used a working well before, but sending down an empty bucket and drawing up a bucket of pure, clear, cool water must be one of the greatest experiences there is. You could almost taste the purity of the water. The villagers hastily prepared some seats and a table under the shade of the tree to serve tea, while the village speciality, watermelon, which had been cooled in the well overnight, was prepared, as it is a delicacy for special occasions and visitors.

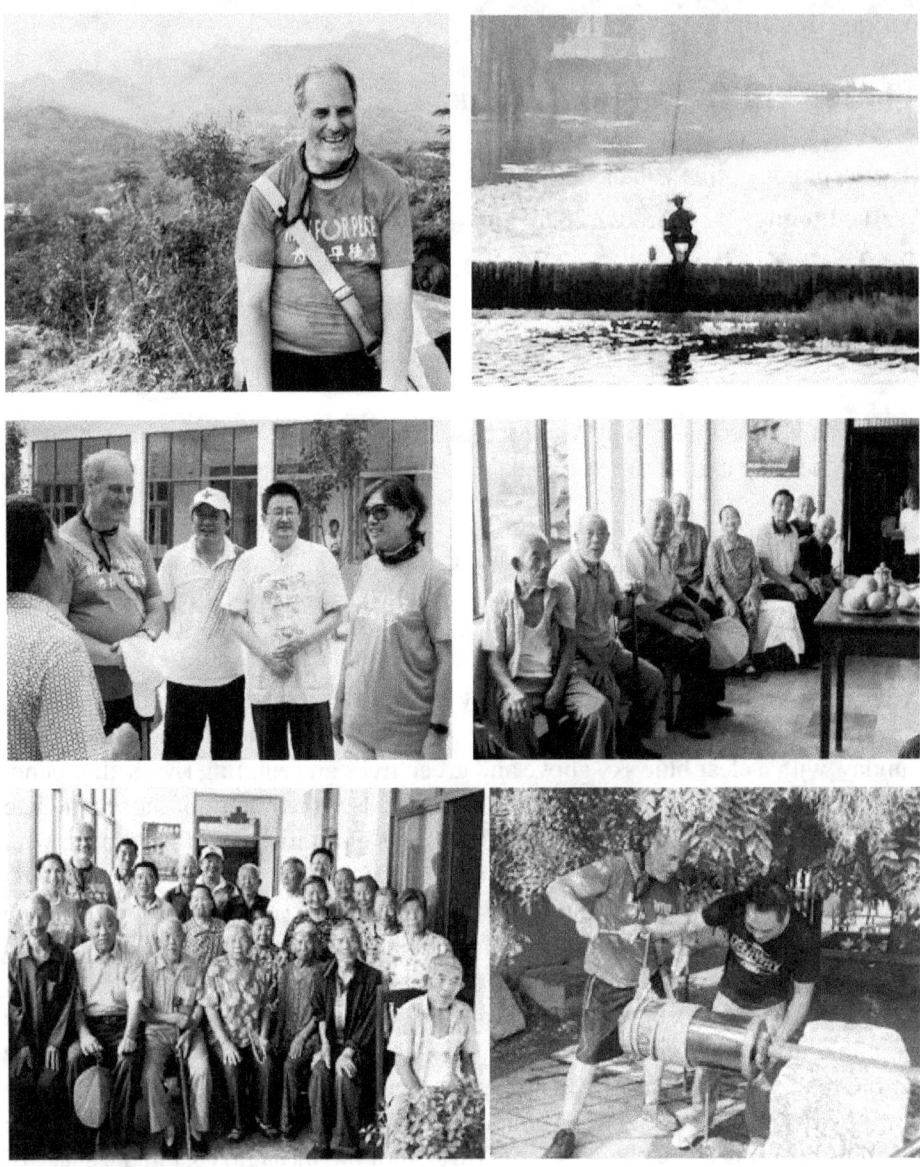

Top left: Taking a break and enjoying the scenery. Top right: A lone fisherman.
Middle left: Meeting in front of the Happiness Court in Gao'er Town. Middle right: Guests of
the Happiness Court. Bottom left: At the Red Cross's Happiness Court in Gao'er Town.
Bottom right: On the way to Tai'an, paying a visit to Xingjiatun, which has a 700-year-old well
full of pure clear water

They seemed keen for me to talk to them, so I talked about the tree. When that
tree had just been planted in Europe, Christopher Columbus was setting sail to
discover America (I then hesitated because it is very likely that the Han Chinese
people crossed the Bering Strait to Alaska a thousand years before and were the

forebears of what are now called Native Americans). When this tree was planted, the people of Europe still believed that the sun and the stars orbited the Earth, until Galileo put us right.

I began to run out of examples, so, being a good politician, I changed the topic. 'Do you have many Westerners visiting this village?' The villagers started looking at each other and then shaking their heads, 'No. You are the first.' I was surprised by the answer and checked again. The answer came back the same. Then they said they would go and get the oldest man in the village who would be able to tell. A tall, distinguished-looking man in what looked like a military shirt came across the square and sat down next to me. I asked how old he was. He replied he wasn't very sure but about 95. The villagers then asked if he could remember any foreigner ever visiting Xingjiatun before. He thought, then shook his head and said, 'No.'

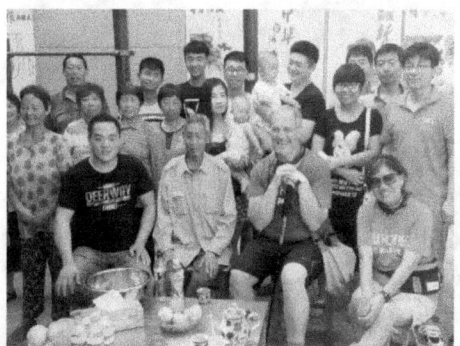 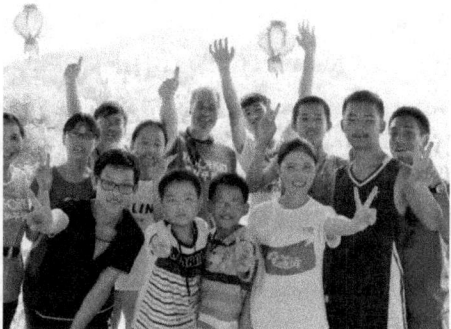

Left: Lord Bates and the villagers of Gao'er.
Right: Lord Bates and some of the young walkers met in a café.

We sat together under the shade of the tree and engaged in conversation through Madam Zhang as the villagers stood all around and watched. The old man told how he had joined the army in 1943 to go to attack the Japanese, who had occupied nearby Jinan City. I asked him what he thought was the secret of his long life and he replied, 'Work.' He said he still worked and that was what kept him healthy. I told him that my grandfather had just turned 100. He was impressed. I then said that the highlight of reaching 100 in England is to get a personal birthday card from the Queen. He seemed even more impressed. I then suggested that when he reached 100, he might get a card from President Xi Jinping. 'Good idea.' They all laughed. The leader of the village said he would send him a card but it didn't seem to quite match the high expectations I had built up.

I carried on walking up the mountain and reflecting that I may go down in Xingjiatun history as the first foreigner to visit the village. We stopped for lunch at a fantastic cafe with wonderful views. Soon we were joined by about 30 to 40 young people from all across China, aged 12_16. They had just completed a 32-km walk as part of a summer camp activity. They were keen to talk and share experiences from the road. Most of all, I was struck by the immense sense of personal achievement that the simple act of walking had given these young people and the closeness of the friendships they had made along the way. I shouldn't have been surprised, because it has given me all of that and so much more, especially on 'Days like This'.

URL http://www.walkforpeace.eu/day-21-there-will-be-days-like-this/

August 17 Day 22

Charity Appeal

Tai'an, Shandong Province
A Day Off
Donated today: £61.95 / ¥0.00
Total donations: £3,430.08 and ¥9,800.00

After the exertions in the Taishan Mountains the day before, it was good to relax in Tai'an for a day and take stock of the walk to date.

The walk was going well – 355 miles was slightly ahead of where I needed to be to finish in Hangzhou according to schedule in early October. The illness I experienced in Jinan was gradually working its way through the system (no more detail necessary, I think!).

Through the walk we had managed to communicate the message of Walk for Peace that 'We are all human first' and that should unite us. Our nationality, culture, language and religion are all 'add-ons', 'apps', if you like, downloaded onto the basic human system, and most are tribal and a complete accident of birth. If we choose to focus on that 95% we share with our fellow humans rather than the 5% of 'add-ones' that are different, then we can create a more peaceful and harmonious world. During the three weeks of the walk Xuelin and I have been able to share that idea with hundreds of people who have either joined us on the walk or come along to support it.

There is, however, a third purpose to the walk, and it is sometimes the most difficult to talk about because it involves money. We set out with the aim of raising £50,000, or 500,000 yuan, to support the work of the Red Cross Society in the UK but more especially here in China. Xuelin and I have seen personally the incredible work the Red Cross does, whether it is being a first responder to disasters such as that at the recent Tianjin chemical plant, caring for the young and the elderly, collecting blood donations, training millions in first aid or providing hardship loans to those who are ill and in need of medical care.

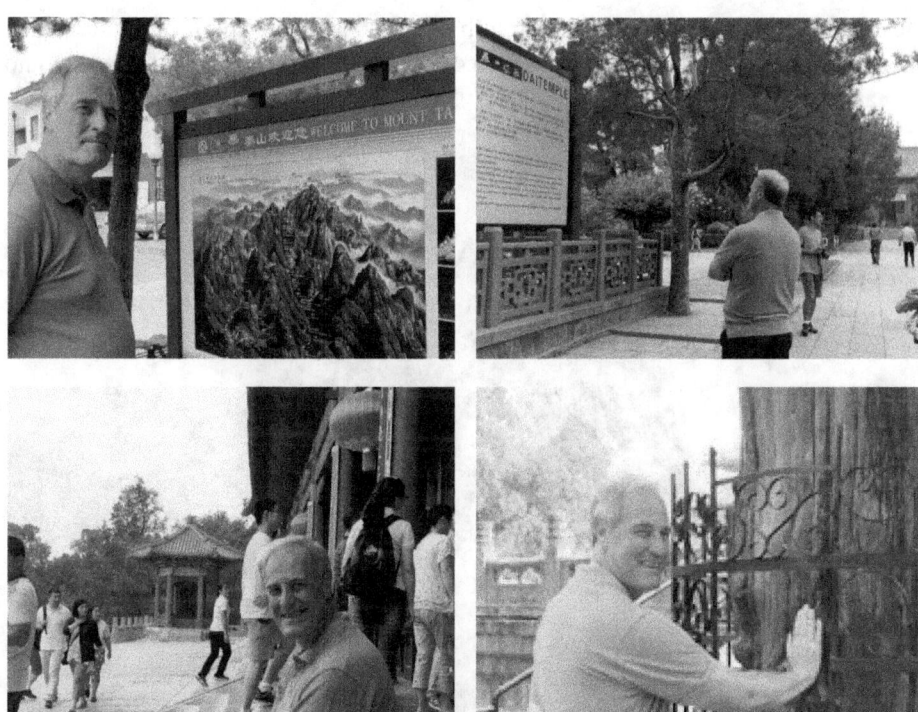

Top left: Overlooking the Taishan Mountains. Top right: A visit to the Dai Temple.
Bottom left: A busy day at the temple.
Bottom right: A visit to Dai temple on a relaxing day off.

So far we have raised £3,500 through our Just Giving website in the UK and £2,000 in direct donations to the Red Cross here in China. That is a total of £5,500, which is only around 10% of the target. (Xuelin and I are, of course, paying all our own travel and accommodation, so all donations go to the cause for which they are intended). This is not the first charity walk that Xuelin and I have undertaken, but the fifth. Xuelin is an amazing fundraiser and we are blessed with some very generous friends. Previously at this stage of the walk we might have hoped to have raised about half of the target funds (£25,000), so we are well short of that.

Xuelin and I have a long discussion about why things might be different this time round. We identify that, of course, this walk is taking place in China, and many people who previously supported us back in the UK might not even yet be aware of it. We also talk about a culture difference between the UK and China in attitudes to charity and Xuelin thinks this might be something worth exploring in a blog.

The history of charitable giving in the UK stretches back the beginnings of our Judaeo–Christian roots. The Bible proposes a tithe (10%) of income to be given to the church or charitable causes. With the establishment of Christianity as the official religion of Britain in the ninth century AD came an official tithe which was paid to the local church for the upkeep and building of places of worship and monasteries.

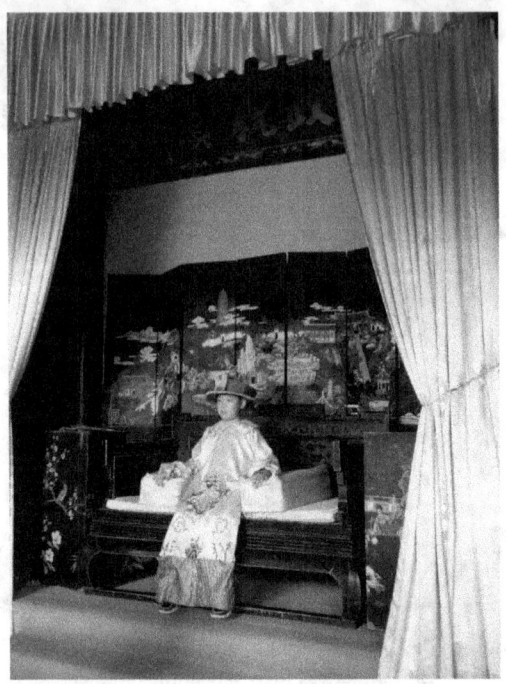

Child in the temple.

So, the concept of giving a proportion of your earnings away to the church was well established, but it really wasn't until the British Industrial Revolution that charitable giving began to expand. The reason was that there was a large new wealthy middle class who had made great fortunes from very humble beginnings. They were from poor communities, so they knew the problems that they faced and felt an obligation to put something back. Thus it became normal for the wealthy middle class to put money into establishing schools, hospitals and homes for those who could not otherwise afford them.

As more and more people became wealthy by their standards, they sought to follow the example of the wealthy industrialists of Victorian England and voluntarily support local charities caring for the poor, animals, the elderly or those with specific diseases such as cancer. It came to be seen as part of being a good society that it was not, and should not be, just left to the state to do everything – everyone has a contribution to make.

In the Bible, Jesus is quoted as saying, 'It is more blessed to give than to receive.' This is not to suggest for a minute that Christianity has a monopoly on charity. All major world religions encourage followers to give a proportion of what they earn to the poor (and, of course, to the religious organisations that encourage them to give it). The point is that when we give, we implicitly acknowledge that we have been blessed with so much more than we deserve and there are others, through no fault of their own, to whom fortune has been far less kind. This is our opportunity to balance the scales in their favour, not because the law demands it but because our hearts inspire us to. That can make us feel good about doing good. Charity is 'twice blessed', as Shakespeare would put it, for its benefits fall both on the giver and the receiver alike.

URL http://www.walkforpeace.eu/day-22-charity-appeal/

August 18 Day 23

Through Tai'an

Route: Daiyue District – Ningyangxian, Tai'an
Walked today: 29.70 miles / 47.80 km
Total walked: 385.50 miles / 620.20 km
Donated today: £0.00 / ¥10,000.00
Total donations: £3,430.08 and ¥19,800.00

It was early as we made our way back up the S243 mountain road to the point where we had stopped two days before. The day was warm, even at 7.30 am, and so the coolness of the mountain breeze and the occasional shade of the trees were much appreciated. We were joined by a new group of Red Cross volunteers with wonderful bright orange jackets. I wrote yesterday about the benefits of giving money to charity, but giving time is an even greater commitment, and in the case of the Red Cross in China, just over two million people do that regularly.

The road from the mountain was mostly downhill, but it would have turns as it sloped down to cross a river and then there was a tough pull to make it up the other side. This variation of pace is interesting but physically challenging. The previous day we had visited Dai Temple, which I found to be a deeply spiritual experience. It had almost persuaded me to make the journey up the 5,000-foot Taishan Mountains. There is a strong element of spirituality associated with struggle, and the ideas of pilgrimage are key parts of most faiths. We assume that our spiritual enlightenment will be stronger having climbed for four hours to the mountain top than if we had just paid 5 yuan to light a candle in the temple. It is probably true, but as usual the experience owes less to the place and more to the motivation it evokes in us.

Back down on the ground it was hot, very hot. Conveniently, our route, took us past our hotel, so we were able to delay check-out for a little longer and stop for the last few bits of food from the buffet breakfast. Then back out into the heat and what seemed like an endless detour around the top end of Tai'an before cutting through the western edge of the city. This route offered an additional benefit in that we were able to call in to the city department of health, in which the local Red Cross team is also located, and enjoy some free hospitality and good conversation. I wasn't rushing to leave, as it was hot outside, so after the usual round of photos I passed my camera across to the team and asked them to take some extra – another five minutes in the cool was worth it.

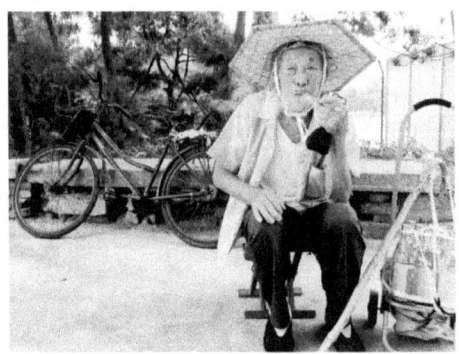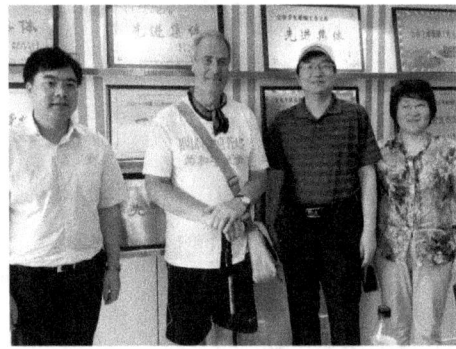

Left: An elderly vendor in Tai'an. Right: The local Red Cross team in Tai'an.

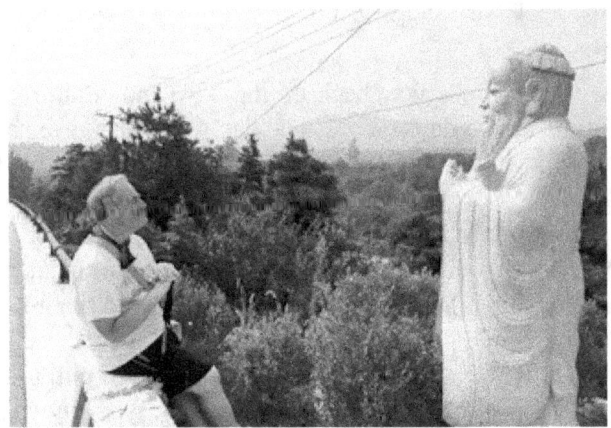

On the way from Tai'an to Ningyang, he stopped in front of the statue of Confucius. The fellow asked the Lord, "Are you talking to Confucius?" He answered, "no, I'm listening."

We followed the route of the G104 out of Tai'an and into the southern suburbs, which were full of partially completed blocks of flats. Judging distances was proving a challenge on the day. We were all very tired on account of the sun. The map was giving us one reading to the junction with the G3 expressway, but the Sat Nav and support car were giving us different readings. It was a bit like walking over huge sand dunes in the desert and at the top of each one you were expecting to see an oasis and fresh spring water below, only to be disappointed – well, so we found it with each turn of the G104 searching for the G3. As it got dark and even the bright orange jackets of the volunteers were growing dim, we decided to stop after 47 km, only to find once we were in the car that the junction was just 500 metres away around the next bend. Such is life on the road. The 500 metres would be still there in the morning, but after a long hard day I was not sure I would be, so it was the right decision.

URL http://www.walkforpeace.eu/day-23-through-taian/

August 19 Day 24

Feast of Friendship in Ningyang County

Route: Ningyang, Tai'an – Jining
Walked today: 23.50 miles / 37.80 km
Total walked: 409.00 miles / 658.00 km
Donated today: £0.00 / ¥0.00
Total donations: £3,430.08 and ¥19,800.00

We arrived late into the hotel the previous night and the only place open was a Western-style fast-food bar about to close, so Xuelin and I quickly shared a bowl of chips, ice-cream and orange squash. If our hosts from the Red Cross were to hear of this, they would be shocked. It is a huge part of Chinese culture to be welcoming and hospitable to guests from afar – as no less than Confucius stated in the opening of his *Analects* over 2,500 years ago.

On this walk, it is food that has often proved to be the trickiest area of cultural difference. For instance, at mealtimes the Chinese tradition is to have up to a dozen different dishes on a revolving glass plate. Each guest takes what he or she wants, but the host will often show how honoured he is to welcome the chief guest by serving food onto the guest's plate. This comes as a shock for Westerners – the last person to serve food onto my plate was my mum when I was about four and a half! To refuse is to refuse the act of thoughtfulness and insult the host. I confess I have made this mistake sometimes.

For the Westerner, eating is a formal and solitary occasion. You ask for what you want. You add your own seasoning. You take more if you want it. I won't get started on the toasting with drinks, as that is worthy of a blog on its own, and my point is to show sometimes how cultural misunderstandings arise.

To take another example, at breakfast one day they were serving eggs. Eggs are a great food for starting the day but less so when fried, so I asked if they could do poached. After Xuelin explained a little what this meant, they came out with two great poached eggs. I told them how wonderful they were. Without saying another word, the next day at a different hotel I came down for the breakfast buffet and there were two poached eggs, and each day thereafter at different hotels for a week – until I was unwell and unable to eat them, when they disappeared as quickly as they had come.

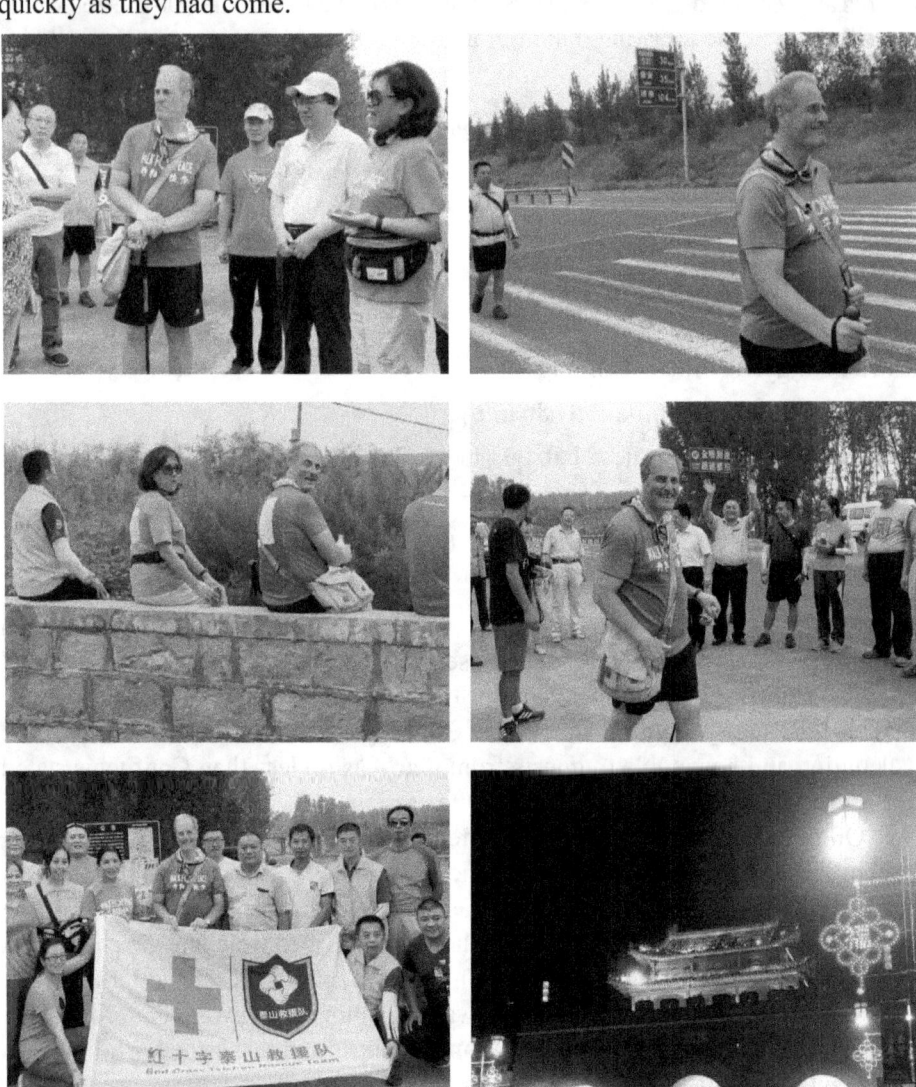

Top left: Meeting the local officials in Ningyang County.
Top right: Walking through Ningyang County.
Middle left: Taking a break. Middle right: Supporters in Ningyang County.
Bottom left: The Red Cross team in Taishan. Bottom right: Jining City, Shandong Province.

When I was unwell, I came down for breakfast and the only thing I could face was a plain jam sandwich on white bread and some green tea. Again no comment was made, but the next day I came down and there was white sliced bread and jam/

marmalade and a cup of green tea, but this time I was feeling a bit better so had some fruit – orange and melon. Again, nothing further was said.

We then undertook our day's walk and arrived in Ningyang County, where Madam Zhang informed me that we had been invited to join local officials for lunch. My heart sank, as I really couldn't face a big meal, as I had a long way to walk and everything I ate at lunch would need to be carried for the next 20 km in my stomach.

We arrived at the offices of the county and were shown upstairs, where a buffet had been prepared. I confess I felt just a little irritated at the thought of having to resist well-meaning attempts to fill my plate and questions as to why I wasn't eating enough. However, rather than sitting me at the large table, they showed me into a small side room, and on the table set for Xuelin and me was a fresh loaf of sliced bread, marmalade, green tea and some fruit. I was so touched by this thoughtfulness of our hosts and ashamed of my own thoughts that preceded it.

The dining table can indeed be a place of cultural mystery and misunderstanding, but once we fully understand the motivations of those who host and prepare it, it becomes transformed into a feast of friendship.

URL http://www.walkforpeace.eu/day-24-feast-of-friendship-in-ningyang-county/

August 20 Day 25

In the Footsteps of Confucius – Part I

Jining, Shandong Province
A Day Off
Donated today: £0.00 / ¥0.00
Total donations: £3,430.08 and ¥19,800.00

- Before you embark on a journey of revenge, dig two graves.
- Forget injuries, never forget kindnesses.
- I hear and I forget. I see and I remember. I do and I understand.
- It does not matter how slowly you go so long as you do not stop.
- Our greatest glory is not in never falling, but in getting up every time we do.
- What you do not wish for yourself, do not do to others.

Many of us in the West have grown up on Confucian wisdom quotes, often not appreciating their origin. Arriving in Qufu, the home of Confucius, has brought these quotes to life in a special way and placed them in a physical context to which I can relate.

Let me acknowledge first that I have just arrived in the town and hundreds of books and thousands of lives have been devoted to explaining the life and times of

Confucius, so this is a very basic attempt to place the life in some kind of context for those, like me, who may know very little but are open to learning a little more.

Confucius was born here in 551 BC. His father was in the military in Lu State and died when Confucius was only three. He was not from a noble family and these were feudal times in China. Power and wealth rested in the hands of three aristocratic families, and each family was headed by a viscount and over them was the Duke of Lu.

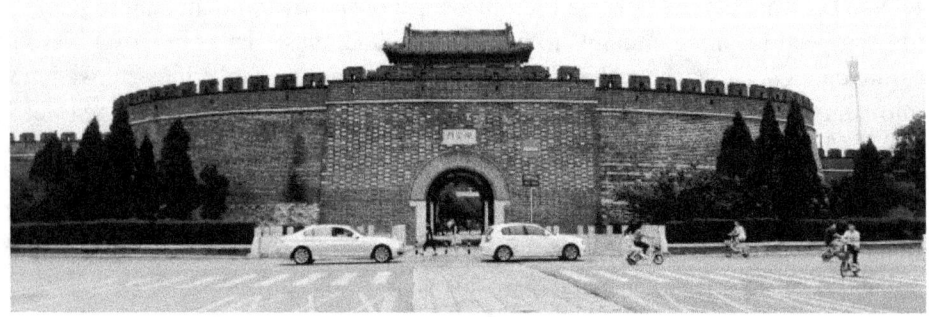

The Temple of Confucius in Jining.

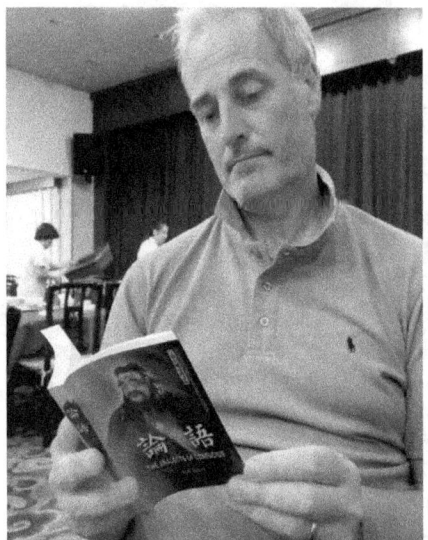

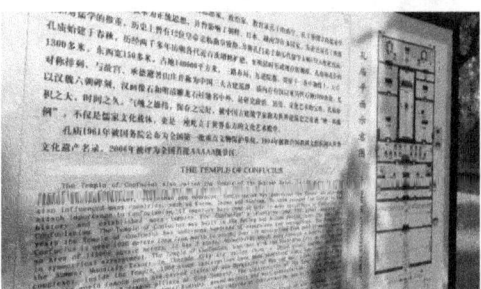

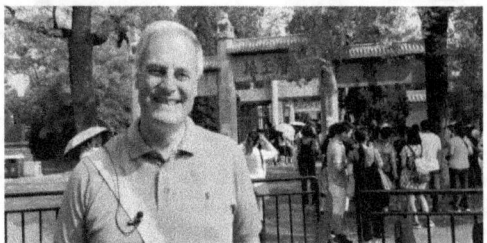

Left: Reading *The Analects* Top right: A description of the temple.
Bottom right: Lord Bates in the temple precinct.

During his political career, Confucius became respected as a teacher of high ethical standards who abhorred corruption and injustice, especially by the powerful against the powerless. He did not seek to challenge the feudal system but rather to make it work more efficiently and justly so it would survive and flourish. He did not advocate that everyone was equal. He served in relatively lowly positions, a governor of a small town being one, but when the Duke of Lu fell short of the standards Confucius expected, he resigned and set off on a journey around the small kingdoms of northeast and central China at the age of 54.

Disillusioned by the conduct of the Duke of Lu, whom he had faithfully served for so many years, Confucius began to practise less and teach more about good government, hoping to inspire the next generation. He toured many courts but few of his ideas took hold. He returned home to Qufu at the age of 68 and devoted himself to study and teaching.

His central teaching was that good political leadership begins with the leader developing good habits and practices starting in the home (filial) – you can't hope to become a great leader in public if you are not first a great son, brother, father or husband in private. Virtuous leaders will earn respect and inspire example among those they lead. It is the complete antithesis to the approach advocated by Niccolo Machiavelli in feudal Italy and recorded down in his book, *The Prince* – and is refreshing for that reason.

One of his great themes, which resonated with me on my Walk for Peace through his hometown, was the idea of the Mandate of Heaven: a belief that there could be an end to the chaos and warring between states and they could peacefully co-exist under an ordered, harmonious, moral-based legal system, where truth and honesty were the most revered virtues and those who embodied those virtues most would rise to the ruling class. It is a big idea that has been distilled by great minds for 2,500 years, but its beginnings are in our personal conduct and small unseen daily acts. What I have read and experienced so far makes me want to enquire more. The day after tomorrow I will visit his home, temple and tomb, which will be a good opportunity to reflect more on this.

URL http://www.walkforpeace.eu/day-25-in-the-footsteps-of-confucius-part-i/

August 21 Day 26

Walk to Qufu

Route: Ningyang, Tai'an – Qufu, Jining
Walked today: 18.70 miles / 30.20 km
Total walked: 427.70 miles / 688.20 km
Donated today: £143.23 / ¥5,000.00
Total donations: £3,573.31 and ¥24,800.00

We had the luxury of being based at the same hotel for two nights, but this meant a long journey back up the G104 to the border with Tai'an, where we had finished two days before. It normally takes the edge off the satisfaction to have to drive to a hotel at the end of a day's walking, rather than finishing at the place we are staying, but I was very grateful for extra time in Qufu. Qufu is undoubtedly my favourite town visited on the walk so far – I stress town – as Xingjiatun will always be my favourite village. In both cases I stress also 'so far'.

On the map, it didn't look like the most thrilling day of walking – 30 km down the same busy road – but when we arrived at the start point, we were joined by some young students from Qufu First School who had been following the walk on the Weibo group, which is managed by Xuelin. It was great to have some time between stops to talk about the walk to Chen Bodong and Wanyan Junjie, who are both Red Cross volunteers, and to find out about their hopes and dreams.

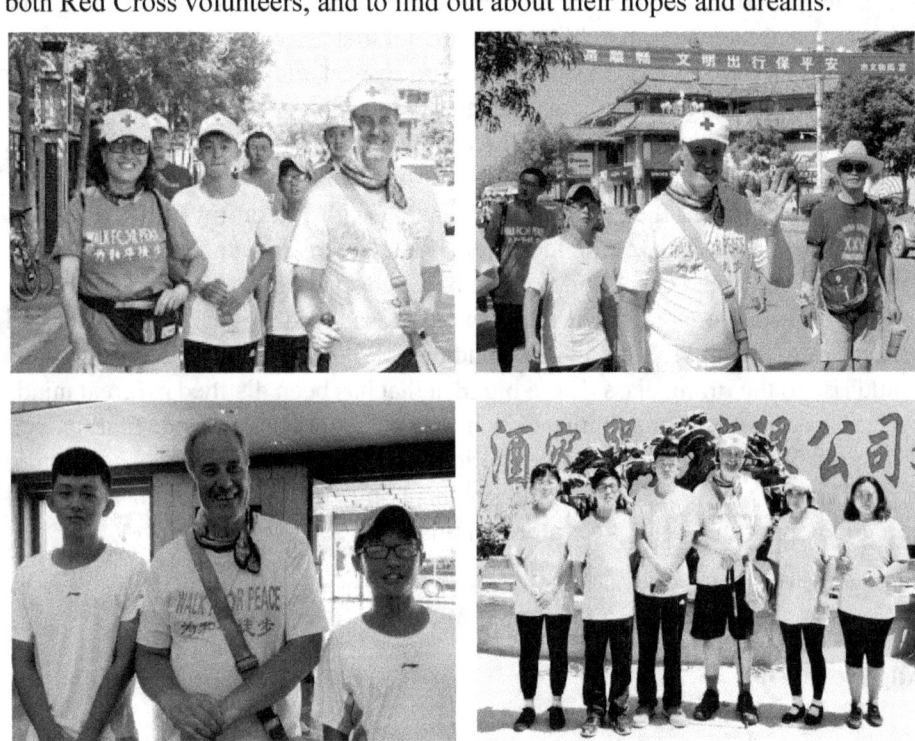

Top left: Arriving in Qufu, the hometown of Confucius. Top right: Walking through Qufu.
Bottom left: Lord Bates with students from Qufu First School.
Bottom right: Visiting the wine container factory of Qufu.

Wanyan wanted to be a doctor. His grandfather was a doctor. I think most young people get inspired by role models, especially their family members. Role models are also vital for raising expectations. My experience of life is that very little of what we achieve is down to natural ability and intelligence; it is more often down to our expectations of what we can do with what we have got.

Eton College, England, is one of the oldest (1440 AD) and most respected private schools in the world. Political, scientific, business and cultural leaders roll off a seemingly endless production line. I was told that one former head teacher used to say to all new students, 'This school has produced 18 British prime ministers [now 19] – we expect you to do better.' This headmaster knew life is about great expectations, not just great talent. It is about what you believe you are capable of achieving, not an endless round of wondering why you haven't been blessed with the same brains, beauty or background as someone else.

Jack Ma of Alibaba, one of China's and the world's richest men, used to be a tour guide in Hangzhou, failed his entrance exam to university three times and didn't encounter a computer for the first time until he was 31, but he believed in himself when others doubted and that was the key factor that brought him success. It is said, 'Whether you think you can or whether you think you can't, you are probably right.'

I guess on a much, much smaller scale, an overweight and unfit minor politician from the UK who hadn't walked more than ten miles in his life before he was 50 can manage to walk 1,000 miles from Beijing to Hangzhou at the age of 54. When my body is creaking and wanting to collapse in an armchair after five miles, it is belief that gets me through the next 20.

In the 1930s, a group of French scientists assessed the bumble bee against the laws of fixed wing aerodynamics and concluded that a bumble bee could not possibly fly because of the surface area of its wings was out of proportion to the size and weight of its body. Fortunately, the bumble bee didn't understand the laws of fixed wing aerodynamics and ignored the doubts of the scientists, so when the jar was opened, he flew straight out of the laboratory window. Hmmm.

Well, the point is that Wanyan is halfway to being a doctor because he has someone who has shown it is possible and, even more importantly, he believes he can.

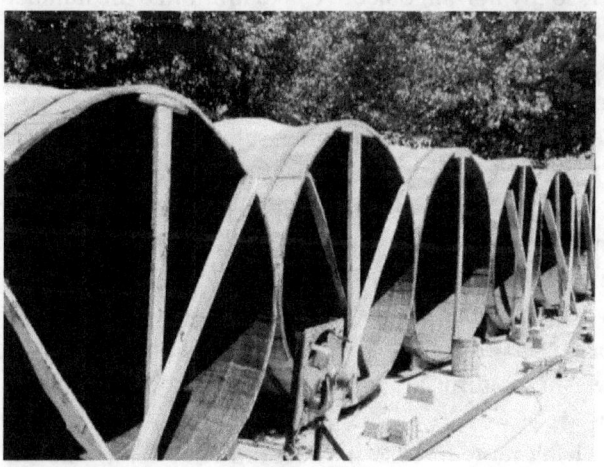

Barrels at the wine container factory in Qufu.

Towards the end of the walk, we passed the Wine Container Factory of Qufu. The owners very kindly let us shelter from the heat under the trees in their courtyard.

While we were there, they told us how they lined the wine vats. They used paper. Not just any paper but the original paper preparation method invented by Cai Lun in 200 AD in Shandong. This was the first paper in the world and revolutionized communication, because previously writing had been done on silk, which was expensive, or bamboo, which was very heavy. The technique moved slowly from East to West, for it was nearly 900 years later before the earliest paper documents were found in Europe and not until 1490 AD did paper production begin in the UK. It was an inspiring end to the day to see an invention and process of almost 2,000 years ago still alive and well in Qufu today. As I left, they kindly presented me with some of these sheets of paper. Perhaps they hadn't appreciated that, albeit 1,200 years after Qufu, paper production had now caught on back home.

URL http://www.walkforpeace.eu/day-26-walk-to-qufu/

August 22 Day 27

Confucius – Part II

Jining, Shandong Province
A Day Off
Donated today: £50.00 / ¥5,288.00
Total donations: £3,623.31 and ¥30,088.00

It was a day off, so my normal objective is to minimize the number of steps I have to take. Sadly, no one had informed Eva. Eva was our tour guide for the Confucius temple, home and tomb and was waiting for us at 8.30 am to begin what turned out to be a very long walk around the historic sites of the city. Eva was very knowledgeable and enthusiastic about her subject. Before we arrived at the first site, I already felt as if I had read the great man's biography.

Our first visit was the Confucius temple. It was very grand, with nine court-yards, each with its own gate drawing you into the temple itself. Numbers are very important to the Chinese people – 8 is the lucky number and 4 is the number you want to avoid – often a hotel will not have a '4th' floor but might have 8a and 8b; 9 was a number reserved for the Emperor. To have nine courtyards, nine pillars or nine steps was to confirm the highest status rarely seen outside the Forbidden City in Beijing.

I must confess I felt more at ease in the Confucius family home, which was on a more modest scale and focused around family living, reading and teaching. It revealed a tension, probably as a result of my lack of knowledge and understanding (despite Eva's best efforts), between Confucius the man and Confucianism the religion. There had been a broad symmetry in human development around the world from primitive religions based on tribal practices worshipping the sun and the moon to sophisticated religions based on more complex early civilizations worshipping human gods or kings in temples and pyramids. Then, after centuries of scholarly religious study and civilization, there appeared at almost the same time Socrates in Athens (470 BC) and Confucius in Qufu (551 BC), who were to create the first human philosophies of life and meaning. Neither wrote a book himself; that was left to their disciples. Yet 2,500 years later, their philosophies, though different, remain at the cornerstone of Western and Eastern civilizations, respectively.

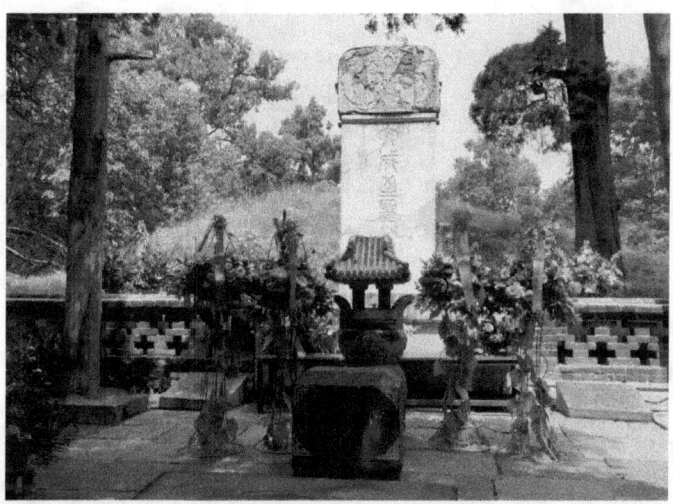

A stele in the temple.

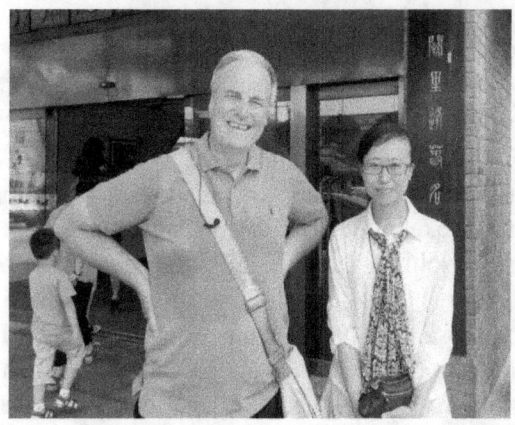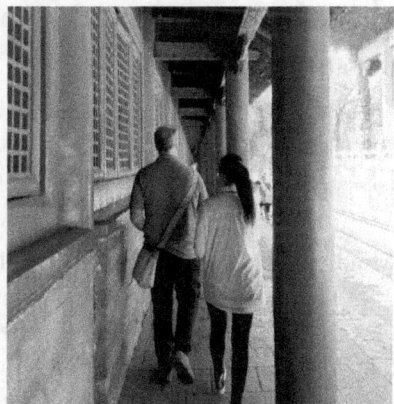

Left: Lord Bates and his guide Eva. Right: In Confucius' family mansion.

So why the tension? Well, it was just that here was undoubtedly a great man, Confucius, who led a good life and sought to raise the standards of ethics in government and officialdom when it was not fashionable to do so. Rather than leave it at that and learn from it, after his death there emerged a range of claims made about his birth and life by his disciples, and these are recorded in the temple and are the basis of the religion. For example, Confucius' mother, Madam Yan, visited a holy mountain before she conceived. Prior to his birth, a unicorn appeared at his home with a book on his horn, making prophetic claims about the new child's life. At his birth, music floated down from the heavens accompanied by the words, 'The Heaven senses a child-sage coming into the world, so it plays music to accompany him.' After his birth, the wise immortals came down to pay tribute to him.

We need religion as we need love. It cannot be rationally explained but we have a heart and we also have a soul. The point I was left reflecting on at the end of the day was that we have a heart and soul, and they have their wonderful place, but we also have a mind capable of astonishing thoughts and insights. It was that great mind of Confucius that I wanted to discover more of in Qufu, but his teaching I had found obscured by their temple.

URL http://www.walkforpeace.eu/day-26-confucius-part-ii/

August 23 Day 28

Zoucheng and Mo Farah

Route: Qufu – Zoucheng, Jining
Walked today: 25.30 miles / 40.80 km
Total walked: 453.00 miles / 729.00 km
Donated today: £0.00 / ¥900.00
Total donations: £3,623.31 and ¥30,988.00

Because our walk had finished at the hotel in Qufu, we were able to set out from there at 7.30 am on a beautiful morning. We rejoined the G104 Shandong Highway, which had become a trusted friend since joining the road 200 km back in Jinan. I had no explanation for it, but I made very hard going of the morning session. In fact, I might not have made an afternoon session had Madam Zhang not insisted that we break between noon and 3 pm from the heat of the sun at our hotel, which was on the way. It was an excellent bit of team management and meant that we were able to finish the day on schedule, which is good for health.

As we crossed the city borderline between Qufu and Zaozhuang, we had to say goodbye to two young students (both 17) from Qufu middle school. I wrote about Wanyan a couple of days ago, but as we parted it was Chen who was to surprise and encourage me. Chen had written a letter – his English handwriting and grammar were better than mine, so it was easy to read the text – but the thoughts behind it showed a maturity beyond his years and gave me hope for a better future. In one section he wrote, 'I think peace is not the kind of affair of one country but also of everyone on earth. All of us are citizens of earth and should make our contribution to world peace.' 'Amen,' I exclaimed when I read it. I pondered this concept during the rest of the day, as it fitted with Confucius' view that there was a 'Mandate of Heaven' for a peaceful and harmonious world.

Over the past few days, Xuelin and I had been enjoying the World Athletics Championships in Beijing. They brought back great memories of the 2008 Olympic and Paralympic Games. The highlight of this evening was the 10,000 metre race, in which Mo Farah was running for Britain. We wanted to see every step of Mo's preparations, but, of course, we were watching CCTV (the Chinese BBC), so the directors were paying more attention to the ladies shot put final, in which Gong Lijiao was looking for Gold, but ended up with a good Silver. Coverage was uninterrupted from the third or fourth lap, as a fascinating tactical struggle took place between the three Kenyan runners and 'our' Mo. I thought at one stage that the American with his long stride might be in with a good chance but in the final laps Mo showed his class. There was one heart-stopping 'Mo'- ment when he appeared to stumble on the final lap but he came home a comfortable winner.

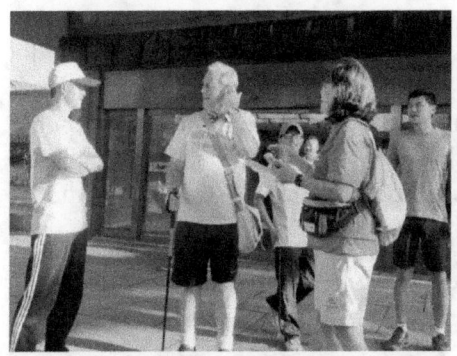
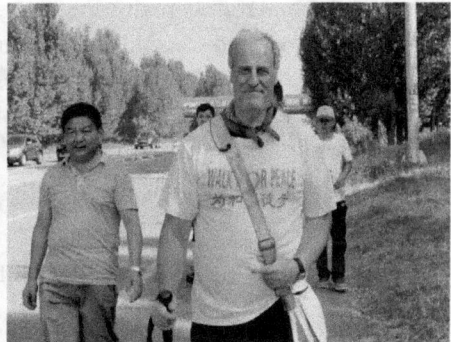
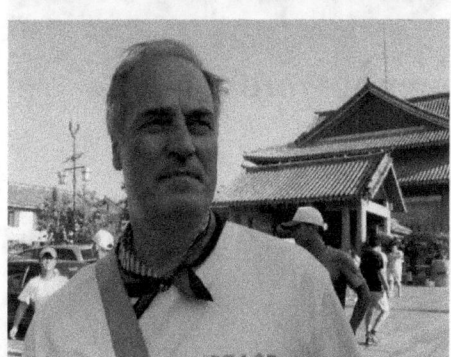
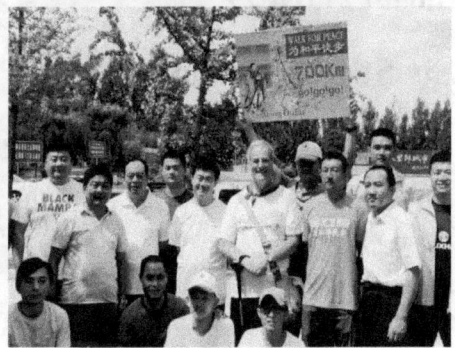

Top left: Saying goodbye to the students from Qufu middle school.
Top right: Crossing the border between Qufu and Zaozhuang.
Bottom left: Lord Bates in Zaozhuang. bottom right: Milestone marking 700 km of the walk.

I love sport. I think if I could have changed anything about my life it would have been to try and excel at any sporting discipline that might get me in with a chance of competing in the Olympics – surely the greatest honour on earth. I recall watching the curling competition at the Winter Olympics and seeing the team members whose job is to brush the way for the stone on the ice and thinking, 'I could do that.' I couldn't, of course, but the dream lives on. The rise of global sporting competition has, in my view, done more than anything apart from the United Nations to reduce war and conflict between nations. It is a human instinct to compete for glory and to challenge rival tribes – this used to be done by warriors using violence, but it is increasingly being achieved through sport. In every human society in history the most revered members of society are its warriors. Through sport, we have managed to create a new 'warrior class' who are also honoured with national pride.

Of course, we are still not at the levels of peace and civilization as in 776 BC when the Olympics were founded. The ancient Olympics were not a celebration of their divided nationality but of their shared humanity. No athlete could carry any emblem or reference of his City State into the arena at Olympia. The athlete left his political identity at the gates of Olympia, and inside that arena and temple he and all his fellow athletes were Olympians only. We are still a very long way from that ideal. I wonder how many spectators would tune in to see one Olympian take on another. How many would shed a tear if it was the Olympic anthem played for every podium finish? How many athletes would drape themselves in the Olympic flag on their victory lap? Not many, is my guess. This is no criticism, of course, but if I love sport, as I say I do, then I should be more than happy to watch the women's shot put final instead of the men's 10,000 metres just don't test me too far, CCTV!

URL http://www.walkforpeace.eu/day-28-zhoucheng-and-mo-farah/

August 24 Day 29

Sir Stephen Redgrave and Power of Words

Route: Zoucheng, Jining – Tengzhou, Zaozhuang
Today walked: 23.30 miles / 37.50 km
Total walked: 476.00 miles / 766.50 km
Donated today: £0.00 / ¥0.00
Total donations: £3,623.31 and ¥30,988.00

Back on the Shandong Highway for another long day, I noticed that I was seldom taking out my iPhone to take pictures whereas in the early weeks I seemed to stop for a 'must take' shot every mile. Was this because there was nothing remarkable along the G104? Was it because I had become used to the sights and sounds of Chinese daily life – I hope not. I still had not reached half way. Sometimes it can be that we don't see the extraordinary because we have stopped looking for it. It is still there, but we wake up thinking it is just another day along the Shandong Highway of life and miss the rich colour and diversity of culture and nature. How can you walk 23 miles in a country like China and not be inspired and challenged by what you see?

On the road through Zoucheng I had been joined by two Red Cross volunteers who were both sports enthusiasts, working, I think, in the local city sports bureau. Our communication was limited because they spoke little English and I, of course, spoke little Chinese. We did have one stop when Madam Zhang was able to translate a little for us because one of the volunteers produced his mobile phone on which he had scores of photos of Sir Stephen Redgrave. Redgrave is Britain's greatest ever Olympian, having won Gold medals at five successive Olympic Games between 1984 and 2000. What was the connection?

Well, my fellow walker today, Zhu Benguo, had been a rower inspired to take up the sport by Stephen Redgrave, who was his sporting hero. The young rower had competed in the Asian games. I thought it was astounding that a rower from Britain could have had such an impact on a young student in Shandong, China. Sometimes we will never know whom we inspired and, sadly, those whom we discouraged. Someone once asked whether, if you received a pound (10 yuan) for every kind word you said and 50p (5 yuan) for every unkind word you said, at the end of your life would you be rich or poor?

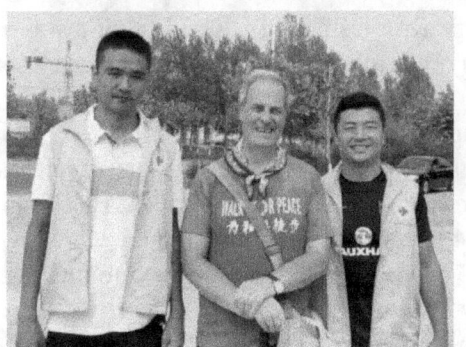 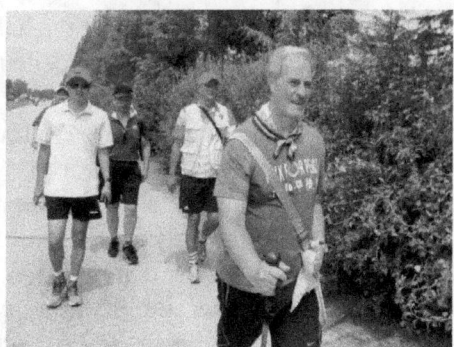

Left: Lord Bates and the two Red Cross volunteers from the local city sports bureau
Right: Walking through Zoucheng with Red Cross volunteers

I recalled one event on the BBC when Steve Redgrave was receiving yet another award, and he dedicated it to Francis Smith of Marlow, England. When asked later why he had done this, he explained that Mr Smith was his English teacher at school and had said to the tall young Redgrave, 'Have you ever tried rowing? I think you would be good at it.' And with those few words of encouragement, he started the career of a great Olympian and, at one remove, inspired a young man in China to take up rowing too. I wanted to know why he wasn't competing: he looked in the peak of physical condition and couldn't have been more than 30, but time didn't allow.

Words are wonderful. They have an ability to build and destroy, to inspire dreams and to crush dreams. It is estimated that we speak 30,000 words per day, but it took only 13 to launch the career of a great Olympic champion and probably the same number to crush the hopes of others. As I write, words are being hurled back and forth across the DMZ between North and South Korea, like missiles spreading fear and despair in the region. Words matter. They matter because we remember them. Choose them wisely.

URL http://www.walkforpeace.eu/day-29-zaozhuang/

August 25 Day 30

500 Miles Walking – a Comparison with Albania

Zaozhuang, Shandong Province
A Day Off
Donated today: £0.00 / ¥6,100.00
Total donations: £3,623.31 and ¥37,088.00

This was not the day I was to hit the halfway milestone of 500 miles but it was a rest day in Tengzhou and so provided an opportunity to reflect on the journey so far:

This has been undoubtedly the toughest walking I have done in the 5,000 miles I have walked so far. The reason is the combination of weather and structure.

I have walked in higher temperatures before. Coming up through Albania in June/July 2011, I regularly encountered 40 degrees and more, but there were two essential differences – on that occasion I had been walking for three months and so was very fit, and second, it was a dry heat, not a heavy, humid heat, which is compounded by the poor air quality of the city areas in China.

The second reason why it is tough (and then I will turn to the many, many positives) is that it is a highly structured walk, where even short breaks have been planned in advance out of great kindness and care by the local Red Cross volunteers. The challenge is that it is often the unknown and the spontaneous moments that have created an excitement in previous walks, for example, to avoid the heat, sometimes starting at 3 am and reaching my new destination by lunchtime. Or I might just not feel like walking at all and want to explore a place of particular historic or natural significance. Or I might change the route at the last minute on the suggestion of a local person. These acts make the walk seem less like a treadmill session at the gym and more like an unfolding adventure.

I feel guilty in mentioning the negative aspects first: This is, after all, not something that Xuelin and I are undertaking just for adventure. If we wanted fun, we might choose to spend our two-month summer break on a beach or on a cruise. There is a serious purpose to this walk, with its messages of peace and cultural exchange and the objective to raise funds for humanitarian projects through the Red Cross. I think Xuelin and I can certainly say that, were it not for this purpose and objectives and the efforts of Madam Zhang, then we probably wouldn't have made it beyond the sixth ring road of Beijing.

Now let me turn to some of the many more positives:

First would be the privilege of getting to know and walk with so many wonderful Red Cross volunteers. We have been stunned that so many busy people have freely given of their time to come along and walk with us or support us. I haven't kept a count, but I would guess there have been a couple of hundred involved so far. They display the finest human qualities of care and commitment, which inspire me to keep going even, when the going gets very tough. It is also through their involvement that the message of Walk for Peace is being spread through their own networks.

Second would be the number of people who have gone to extraordinary lengths to come and join the walk for even a few hours. There are too many to mention all, but a few would be: James Chen, the famous artist who flew from Hunan to walk with us and encourage us; Shelly Hu, who travelled 8.5 hours by train from Xiamen; Wenjun Zhang, who had never done any walking before but came up from Hangzhou; Dean Liu, Siu Lam Li and her colleague Mrs Xue Jianjun, who travelled down from Beijing to Tengzhou; and Zhejiang University alumni at various locations. All of these people have encouraged us with their willingness to identify with the cause.

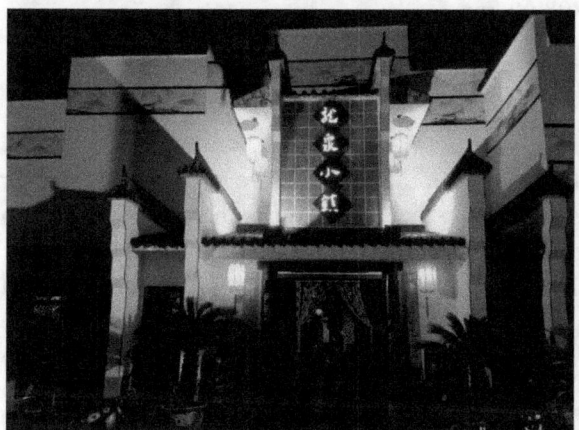 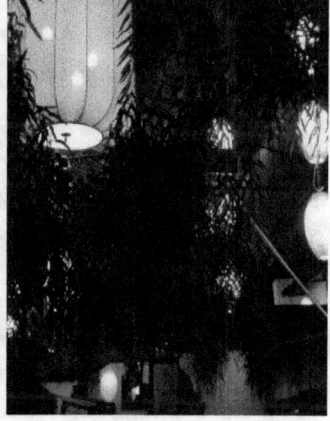

Left: A night view in a small town. Right: Chinese lanterns.

Third would be the chance encounters with ordinary Chinese people along the way. The shepherds tend their flocks by the roadside. The market traders with their stalls stocked in the coolness of the early morning. The young people who shout 'Hello!' or 'How are you?' and capture a picture on their smartphone of this 'crazy foreigner' walking in the heat of the day through their town. The old people gathered under trees around a chess board or a card table. The local traffic police trying to get us across busy roads safely in urban areas. All ages of people doing synchronized dance during the evening in the parks or market squares. The workers sweeping the roadside or working in the fields with whom we exchange a smile and a *Nihao* (hello) as we walk by.

Fourth would be the spectacular beauty of China: I think of the lakes and rivers covered in lotus flowers as we came through Hebei; the majestic splendour of the Taishan Mountains; the fields of fruit-laden trees in Shandong; the Pomegranate Road of Yichang; the history and culture of Qufu; the temples of Tai'an; and the industry, architecture and energy of Beijing and Jinan.

Finally, it would be the over 100 people who have generously given funds to the Red Cross in support of our walk.

Thank you to all. *Jia you!*

URL http://www.walkforpeace.eu/day-30-reflections-on-500-miles-800km/

August 26 Day 31

Mencius and Legge

Route: Tengzhou – Xuecheng District, Zaozhuang
Walked today: 25.80 miles / 41.50 km
Total walked: 501.80 miles / 808.00 km
Donated today: £100.00 / ¥0.00
Total donations: £3,723.31 and ¥37,088.00

There had been a spectacular thunderstorm the night before, so as we set out for this landmark day there was a freshness in the air that made the going easier than usual. As a result, we made good progress before lunch and the added incentive of reaching 500 miles meant that we all felt we could press on with only a short break and try and finish by 4 pm. We did, and finished at a hugely impressive plaza and lake in the centre of the city.

I had had an excellent introduction to the area of Zaozhuang from the Deputy Mayor the evening before, so I knew a reasonable amount about its history and economy. It is a very impressive city and the layout and buildings are on a grand scale. The Deputy Mayor also came out to join me on the walk a couple of days before. I was very grateful to him for taking such an interest in the walk. I have had the honour to be received by about a dozen deputy mayors or deputy governors on my walk so far. In China, these visits are very important to gather official blessing for the walk and the work of the Red Cross in supporting it.

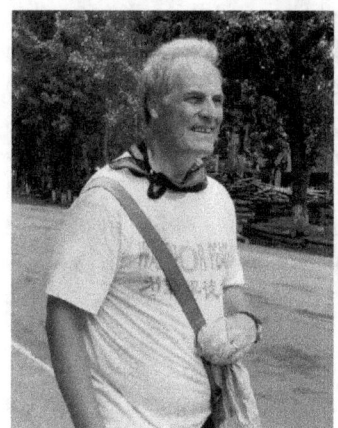 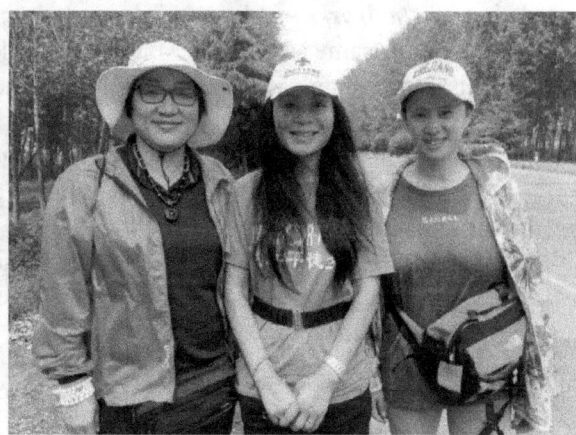

Left: Walking around Zaozhuang. Right: Lady Bates with local officials.

Diplomacy in China is more Confucian than Communist in some respects. It has a very strong 'pecking order' or social hierarchy. Hence, it would be an insult to the guest of a certain rank to have him/her received by someone of a lower rank and an insult to the host to receive a guest of lower rank. Before my arrival, the Ministry of Foreign Affairs in Beijing had been asked to assess my 'rank'. They had concluded it was 'Vice/Deputy Minister' on account of being 'the No. 5 ranked minister at the Home Office' (to be honest, I had no idea that I ranked that high, but Xuelin thought it best not to let on), so it was communicated that I should meet only those officials of similar rank on my journey.

The most revered person in history from Zaozhuang was Mencius – a disciple of Confucius. It is to Mencius that we look to discover the true meaning of much of Confucius' teaching, although he differed in the unquestioning reverence for authority and stated facts in a way that would have perhaps made him more at home with Socrates and Plato in the West. He stated, for instance, 'One who believes all of a book would be better off without books', challenging the blind acceptance of knowledge and even arguing that it was almost the duty of the people to overthrow a leader who ignores the needs of the people and rules harshly, for the king must govern by example to and consent from the people – brave stuff for any philosopher, especially one in the third century BC.

Mencius argued that people have innate goodness and that this sense is sharpened through education. He also stated that ultimately we are only significant for what we give to society, not for what we take. This reminded me of one of the favourite sayings of my grandmother, who would urge us to be 'givers and not takers' in life. That is a high ideal that I struggle to live up to.

Of interest, I am sure, to my grandmother, who was a devout Christian, might also be that the teaching of Mencius came to the wider attention of the West because of a Scottish representative of the London Missionary Society called James Legge. It was Legge who, in 1861 while he was based in Hong Kong, prepared a translation of *The Works of Mencius*. In fact, I noticed from a Wikipedia page that he had visited this same area in 1873 on a journey down from Jinan, through Qufu and the Taishan Mountains and then on through Zaozhuang to the Grand Canal to Shanghai.

I mention this also because I have been ashamed to learn of my country's involvement in the Opium Trade and the destruction of the Old Summer Palace and to learn how arrogant Westerners with commercial or religious ambitions showed little respect for the ancient culture and sophistication of China. James Legge was someone who showed that there was indeed a different view and approach at the time and one that was in the spirit of Mencius.

Legge was a Christian and yet when he visited the Temple of Heaven, where I began my walk, he felt compelled to remove his shoes in holy respect. He was an ardent opponent of the British opium trade with China and was a founding member of the Society for the Suppression of the Opium Trade. He became professor of Chinese Language and Literature at Oxford University in 1876 and devoted his life to the translation of the great works of Chinese literature and poetry contained in the 50-volume *Sacred Books of the East*.

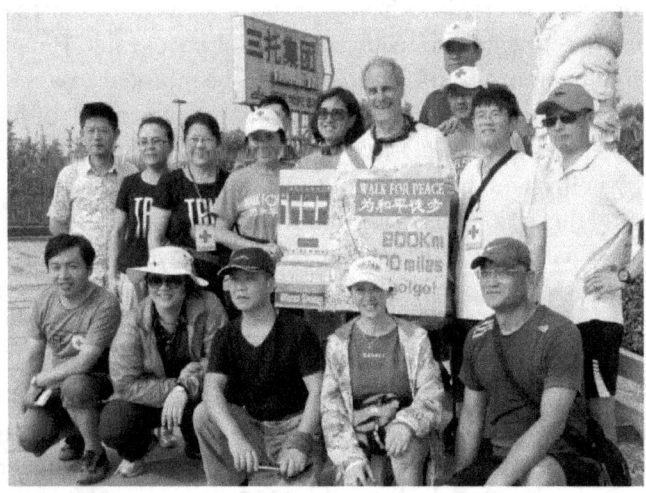

In the Central Square of the beautiful Zaozhuang City, celebrating 800 km on the walk

I think in this first Year of UK–China Cultural Exchange we might understand more about each other if we were to examine the lives and example of Mencius and Legge, who, though separated by 2,000 years of history, were united by their shared love of humanity.

URL http://www.walkforpeace.eu/day-31-halfway-point-zaozhuang-city/

August 27 Day 32

Age of Innocence

Route: Xuecheng District – Yicheng District, Zaozhuang
Walked today: 20.20 miles / 32.60 km
Total walked: 522.00 miles / 840.60 km
Donated today: £50.00 / ¥13,000.00
Total donations: £3,773.31 and ¥50,088.00

Xuelin and I took a bus ride into the city centre last night in search of a cashpoint machine and some food. I was struck again by how civilized and orderly the city centre was compared to the UK. There were large numbers of people out and about shopping at the roadside stalls that continue to trade by electric light, creating a carnival-style atmosphere. Families sat outside one shop that had placed a large screen to show a movie. Further along there was one of several groups of formation dancers. The difference in the atmosphere is, in my view, because of the absence of alcohol and the presence of many generations and both sexes. Alcohol is clearly consumed in Chinese society in large amounts but this happens either in a bar or at home. The streets, meanwhile, are left for families, even until after 10 pm.

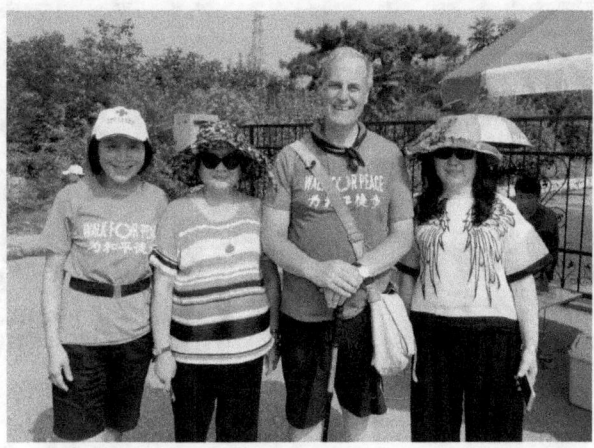

Friends Li Shaolin and Xue Jianjun made a special trip from Beijing to Zaozhuang

The dancers form in lines of between five and ten. The best dancers are placed at the front, so that people can follow their moves. The novices start at the back. Small children are at the very front beside the sound speakers so they can be kept an eye on and also because in Chinese society children are the centre of the

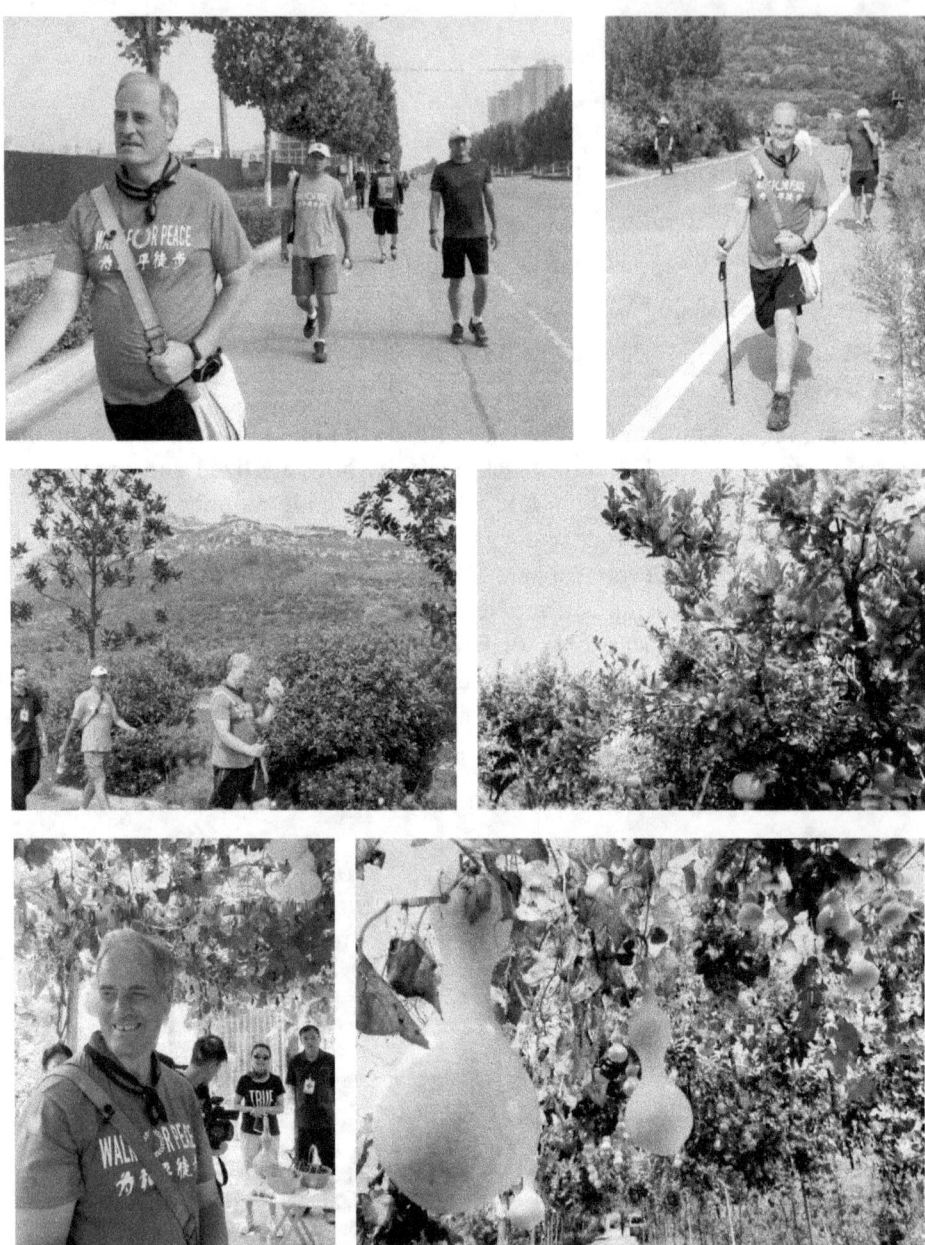

Top left: Leaving Xuecheng behind. Top right: All along the stretch from Xuecheng to Yicheng are endless acres of pomegranate gardens and beautiful rural scenery.
Middle left: The Pomegranate Way to Yicheng. Middle right: Pomegranate trees.
Bottom left: Lunch at Happiness Farm. Bottom right: Hulu fruits.

universe. I need to be very careful as a man how I describe the next point, but the dress and moves of the dancers, male and female, are invariably graceful and modest and not at all sexually suggestive. The focus is on fun and exercise for all the family.

There is laughter but it seems always to be laughter *with* people, rather than, as often in the UK, laughter *at* people. It is like a picture of a village dance hall in rural England in the 1940s or 1950s. It reminds me that we all lose something in the UK when we section off generations. It is why Christmas and other formal occasions retain their appeal because they allow all generations of the family to intermingle as they were intended to. The old were all young once. The young will all be old. It is good to learn to live and laugh together.

The walk this day was one of the most beautiful that we have yet done. It was along a newly created garden or green route G312 through the mountains – it is known as the Pomegranate Way and leads into Yichang. As the name would suggest, the road is lined with pomegranate trees and all kinds of other fruits and flowers. On the mountains there are some spectacular temples. It is idyllic.

We stop for lunch at Happiness Farm, where there are hulu fruit – I am not sure what its name is in English. In fact I haven't seen it before. It grows alongside grape vines and reaches almost melon size. The hulu fruit is considered to bring good luck. It is often allowed to dry out and used as a casket for wine. The owner of the farm invited us to take shelter from the sun under the vines of grapes and hulu and alongside the pomegranate trees – I don't think I had seen a pomegranate tree before either.

Mr Liu Xinyuan, the executive dean of Beijing University, Cyber Security College, Mrs Li Shaolin, Chairman of Wuyishan Hearty Tea Expo Garden Tourism Development Co. Ltd, and Mrs Xue Jianjun, President of Wuyishan Hearty Tea Expo Garden Tourism Development Co. Ltd, had joined us for a day from Beijing. As we sat resting from the walk, drinking green tea and soaking up the beauty of the surroundings, Madam Xue began to sing the most beautiful Chinese song. I asked what it was called and she said it was *The United Song* and it was about peace and harmony. She sang more, accompanied by music from her iPhone. It was blissful. I then played the tune You & Me, which was the theme from the 2008 Beijing Olympic Games – it is in my 'Most Played' list, and I reminded Xuelin that I had downloaded the song three years before we first met because I was so captivated by the performance at the Opening Ceremony for the Beijing Games.

I couldn't help but smile as I thought back to July 20, 2012, when friends and family came back to our home after the service and wedding meal in the Houses of Parliament. There must have been about 80 of our closest family and friends finishing off a very special day with us, and the champagne corks had been popping for some time. Some of Xuelin's friends asked if they could sing a traditional Chinese song in her honour called *What a Beautiful Jasmine Flower*. It was wonderful, and was followed by a couple of others. It was then suggested that the English friends and family might offer a song to the groom – they struggled to respond with any song to which they knew the words, so in the end I got up and sang God *Save our Gracious Queen* followed by *Rule, Britannia!* and the first lines of *Three Lions on My Shirt* (a popular football chorus).

There is an innocence and refinement in Chinese society that we have lost, especially in the popular youth, sex and alcohol cultures of the West. I hope as China opens up and grows up in the modern world, it will not lose this spirit: that the families will still lay first claim to the streets at night; that the children will continue to be the centre of the universe and that all ages on the planet will be welcome to orbit around them; that modesty can be allowed to retain its majesty and mystery and that the melody of *What a Beautiful Jasmine Flower* may still be heard above *Three Lions on My Shirt.*

URL http://www.walkforpeace.eu/day-32-age-of-innocence/

August 28 Day 33

Somewhere in Zaozhuang?

Zaozhuang, Shandong Province
A Day Off
Donated today: £0.00 / ¥200.00
Total donations: £3,773.31 and ¥50,288.00

'I have no idea where I am' might seem an unusual statement for a walker, but it is true. Today was like navigating across the Gobi Desert. I ask if this is Zaozhuang and I am told that is the county, but this is Yicheng – no, says another, that is the district. I turn to my 'Moves app' on my iPhone, which logs every step I take and calculates distance and plots it all on a map. It says I am in Liuyuanzhen – everyone looks blank. After a few minutes, I decided not to waste time debating where I was, I just wanted to get moving. The maps are all in Chinese, so let me just say we spent most of the day walking along the S352 and the S344, crossing the S38 on the way and finishing at a Sinopec Petrol Station next to a small canal.

Map reading is one of the great joys of walking: sitting on a wall or even better in a café or a bar trying to work out where you are and how you might get to where you want to go. Map reading forces you to be observant of your environment, looking for hills, rivers, railways and crossroads. When asking for directions, often people will say, 'Oh, I wouldn't start from here', to which you want to respond, 'Where else I am supposed to start from?'

This is very much like life itself: Often we will feel we have lost direction over our career, our education and our family.

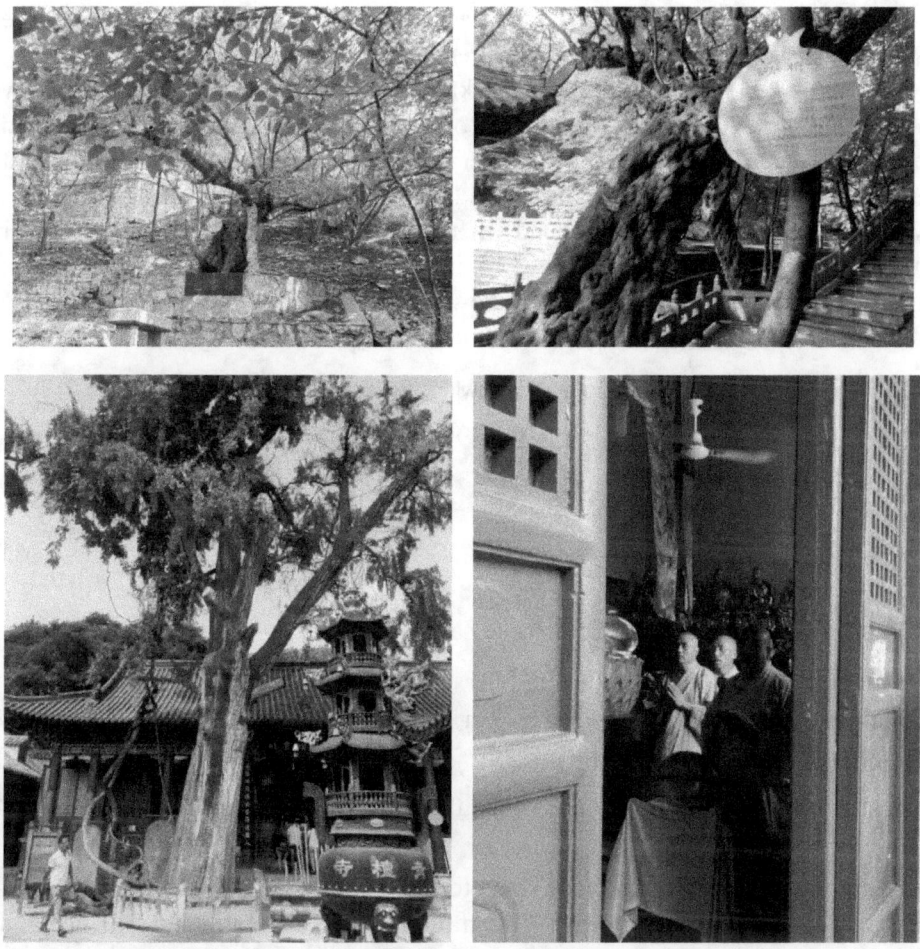

Top left: Wandering around Zaozhuang. Top right: Garden in the temple.
bottom left: A temple in Zaozhuang. Bottom right: Monks praying.

The first question to answer is, 'Where do you want to go?' For me, that is Hangzhou on this walk. For many people who say their lives lack direction, however, it is not because they do know where they are, but because they don't know where they want to go. It was once said, 'If you don't know where you are going, any road will take you there.' This is so true. So, the first rule of navigation in walking and in life is 'be very clear about your destination'.

The second question then comes more into focus: 'Where are you now?' Where you are now is not where you want to be, because if it was then you wouldn't be thinking of going on a journey to get there. Obviously, you can only start from where you are. Often people will say, 'If only I had that qualification. If only I had this or that.' We focus on what we haven't got but don't focus on what we have. The truth is you can only start from where you are with what you have got – it may have been easier if you had started from somewhere else or were someone else, but you didn't and you aren't, so get over it and get on with it.

This should be it, shouldn't it? You know where you want to be and you know where you are. Well, almost, but there is one more golden question, which I would argue will determine more than any other the success of your journey. Why? What is it that you are seeking to achieve and how sure are you that it can be found in your destination and can't be found where you are? Who will benefit from your reaching your destination? Just you or will others benefit as well? Our purpose in life is most clearly revealed not when we say what we want or where we want to go but when we say honestly why we want it and why we want to go there.

URL http://www.walkforpeace.eu/day-32-somewhere-in-zaozhuang/

August 29 Day 34

The Battle of Tai'erzhuang

Route: Yicheng District – Nigouzhen, Zaozhuang
Walked today: 14.30 miles / 23.00 km
Total walked: 536.30 miles / 863.60 km
Donated today: £0.00 / ¥1,200.00
Total donations: £3,773.31 and ¥51,488.00

The Battle of Tai'erzhuang (1938) was to the Chinese people what the Battle of Britain (1940) was to the British – a defining moment of national resilience and courage.

I think my hosts were a little apprehensive about how a 'Walk for Peace' may respond to the famous military victory site. They needn't have been. I have visited many on my walks; in fact, I often design my route to visit them. I find that they are places for deep reverence for the lives of those devoted to their country. All nations honour the courage and sacrifice of its armed forces above all else. There is a sense that, without their sacrifice and service, we would not have our security and identity.

Tai'erzhuang is a place of immense strategic importance, being at the junction of the Jinpu and Longhai railways, the Grand Canal and the border of Jiangsu and Shandong Provinces. It was a walled city of immense historic and cultural importance. It is not difficult to see the significance of such a prize to the invading Imperial Japanese forces. The Japanese forces were much better equipped and trained than the Chinese army and had made swift progress in occupying the country. The Chinese people's morale was low. The victory of a largely peasant army against the formidable Japanese forces at Tai'erzhuang brought a nation on its knees proudly to its feet.

Just as the Battle of Britain was seen as the turning point in the European theatre of war during World War II, as it resulted in the German forces calling off their planned invasion of Britain, so Tai'erzhuang was to China in its efforts to defeat the invading Japanese forces. The significance of this famous victory was all the greater as this was the 70th anniversary of the end of the war. Our first visit via barge on the Grand Canal was to the museum that commemorated the Battle of Tai'erzhuang and contained detailed stories, relics, maps and art from the conflict.

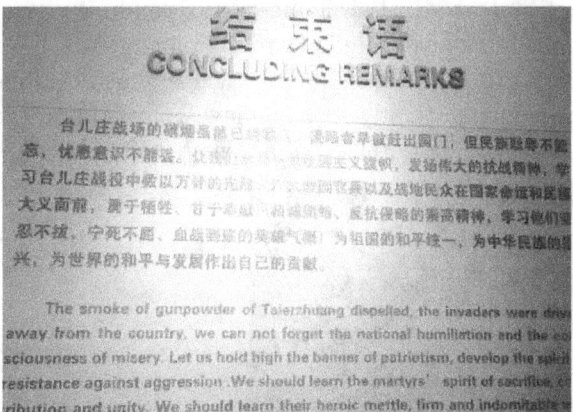
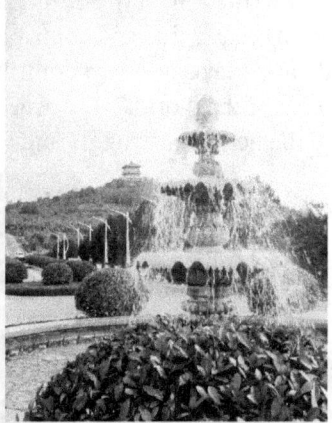
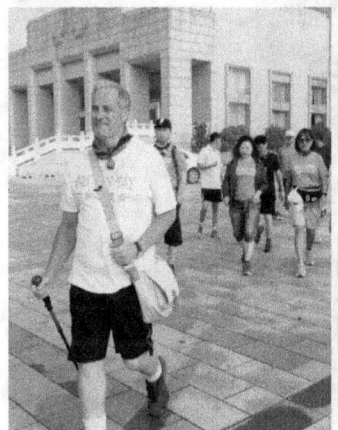
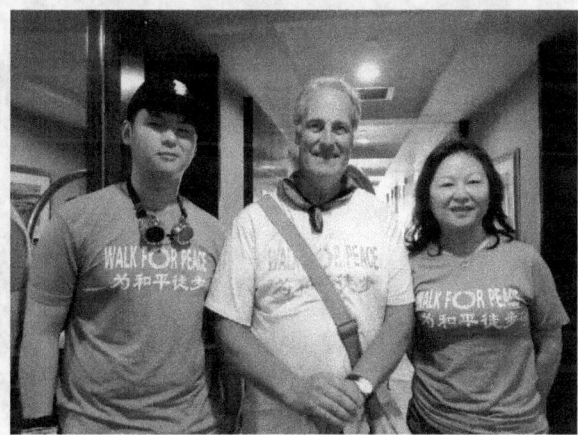

Top left: Learning about the Battle of Tai'erzhuang. Top right: The fountain outside the museum. Bottom left: Leaving Yicheng District. Bottom right: Lord Bates with two volunteers from Zaozhuang.

As we emerged from the exhibition, I was asked by journalists for my reaction. I first expressed my respect and honour for those courageous Chinese armed forces whose lives were lost in pursuit of this strategic victory. Next, I expressed sadness that such a war should have been necessary, as China had not been the aggressor, it had been occupied and in places brutally, so the people of Tai'erzhuang and China should not have suffered in this way.

I then said that, as we celebrate 'victory' in a military context, we needed to be careful that we presented the full picture of the human cost of battle and war, for there were 40,000 sons, husbands and fathers whose lives were cut short here and tens of thousands more who were maimed and suffered horrific injuries.

I said that the finest way in which we honour the sacrifice of our fallen war heroes is to work tirelessly to ensure we do not add to their number. This sentiment was, I felt, best expressed in the closing message of the exhibition, which was written in Chinese and English. It reads, 'We should learn from the martyrs' spirit of sacrifice and contribution to unity. We should learn from their heroic mettle and make our own contributions for the unification of peace and the development of the world.' How true those words! If only we could invest a small fraction of the heroism, struggle and resource into peace as we summon up in times of war!

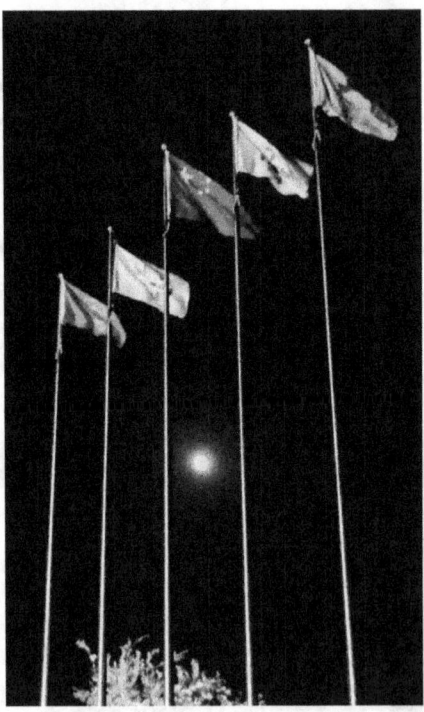

Flags under the moonlight.

The curators of the exhibition had it absolutely right. We should come and honour the example and courage of those who were forced to fight to regain and protect their country. We should leave stirred to play our active part in ensuring that peace so hard won is not lost.

URL http://www.walkforpeace.eu/day-33-the-road-to-taierzhuang/

August 30 Day 35

The Road to Tai'erzhuang

Route: Nigouzhen – Tai'erzhuang, Zaozhuang
Walked today: 10.60 miles / 17.00 km
Total walked: 546.90 miles / 880.60 km
Donated today: £80.00 / ¥2,421.31
Total donations: £3,853.31 and ¥53,909.31

Today was a short walk, a little over 10 miles. The shortness of the walk was because of a few important meetings at the beginning and the end of the day. Xuelin and I were honoured to meet the Vice Chairman of the Standing Committee of the National People's Congress, the President of the Chinese Red Cross, Chen Zhu, and the Executive Vice President of the Chinese Red Cross, Ms Xu Ke, in the early morning. They came down from Beijing late last night and would have to leave immediately after the breakfast meeting to go back for important meetings in the capital. We were humbled that such senior leaders would come down to meet us on Sunday, rather than inviting us to travel to the capital to meet them. Such is Chinese hospitality. We had met Ms Xu Ke in London in the past but this was the first time we had met President Chen Zhu. He was not only a highly respected national leader but also a very accomplished medical doctor. He had studied in France and he is a typical scholarly leader and fluent in several languages, including, fortunately for me, English. He had a gracious and generous temperament. The talk with President Chen Zhu was very encouraging. We talked about my upcoming visit to Tai'erzhuang and its significance in Chinese history. We also talked about his hometown of Jiangsu, which we had walked through on our journey. It was a warm and memorable meeting and Xuelin and I left feeling immensely grateful for the privilege.

Talking of protocol, we almost caused a minor diplomatic incident, as after breakfast, Xuelin went to pay the bill as usual for our food and accommodation. I could see that the accompanying officials were getting restless. Madam Zhang then mentioned to me that our guest had a train to catch. I replied, 'Please tell him to go and catch it.' She then explained that protocol is that he could not leave until we had left. I quickly got Xuelin and we said goodbye, jumped in the car and left. Xuelin had to arrange for someone to go back quietly and finish paying our bill later.

Protocol was much in evidence at the end of the day too. We were hosted by the Vice President of the Shandong Province Red Cross Society for a farewell dinner, as we would be crossing into Jiangsu the next day. We had been in Shandong for nearly four weeks and we had got to know members of the local team very well indeed – Li Nan and Liu were less friends and more family by the time we came to say goodbye.

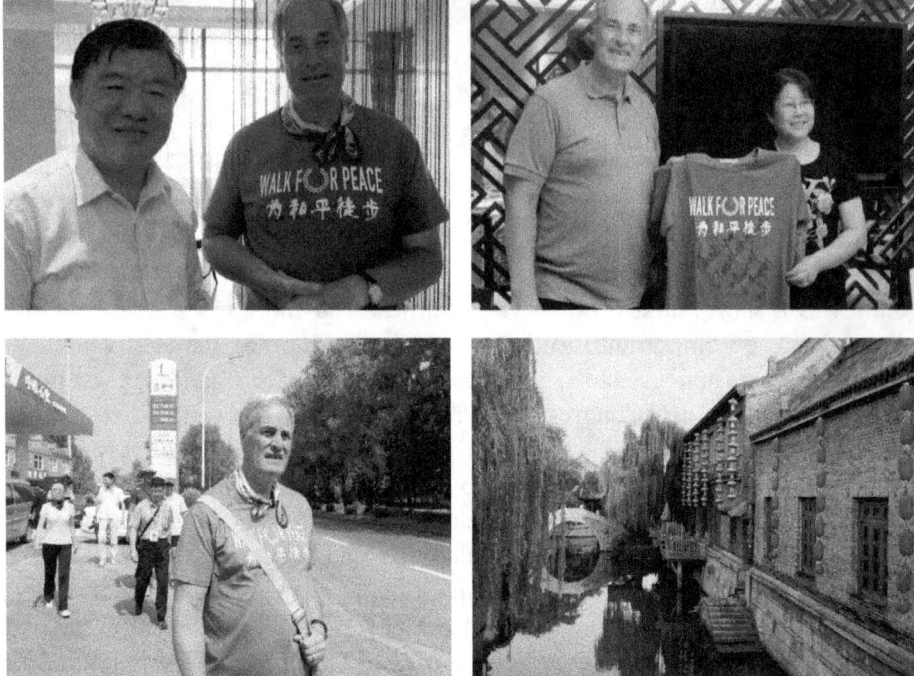

Top left: Lord Bates and Chen Zhu, President of the Chinese Red Cross.
Top right: Lord Bates and the Vice President of the Shandong Province Red Cross Society.
Bottom left: Stop at a gas station on the road to Tai'erzhuang. Bottom right: Tai'erzhuang.

The formalities of the Chinese dinner table are quite sophisticated, compared to the informality that characterizes most meals in the West. The principal host sits at the round table facing the door or the kitchen, so he can direct the waiters and waitresses and see other guests arriving. The most honoured guest sits to his right. The second host sits opposite him and the second most honoured guest sits to his right. The rest of the seats are filled accordingly, with occasional polite and friendly disputes, as a guest may seek to place a fellow guest in a more honoured place at the table.

Once the table seating is concluded, the principal host will make the first of three short toasts. After each toast, the guest will stand and go round to touch glasses with each of the others. Even in this action, status is all-important: the less senior of the two people clinking glasses must touch his or her glass slightly lower than the lip on the more senior person's glass. There is often again a playful polite exchange as people of similar status may try to lower their glass to show greater honour and the other guest will respond likewise.

Every Chinese table has a carousel revolving glass tray on which food is placed. It is acceptable, after a number of toasts, simply to tap the carousel.

After the principal host had given their three toasts, I went to try and respond before getting a familiar stare across the table from Xueli,n saying more eloquently than words ever could, 'Don't you dare!' Later, she explained that if I spoke as the guest and proposed a toast, that would mean that the meal would be finished, but we had hardly started. There were three more toasts, and then, after the sliced melon had been served, Xuelin smiled and raised her glass from across the table and I knew it was time for me to propose a toast, after which there would be the exchange of small gifts and finally photographs.

After navigating the higher points of Chinese protocol from breakfast through to dinner, navigating the traffic and road crossings of the S344 seemed much easier and far less dangerous.

URL http://www.walkforpeace.eu/the-battle-of-taierzhuang/

August 31 Day 36

Jiangsu Province

Route: Tai'erzhuang, Zaozhuang, Shandong Province
– Pizhou, Xuzhou, Jiangsu Province
Walked today: 23.70 miles / 38.20 km
Total walked: 570.60 miles / 918.80 km
Donated today: £0.00 / ¥6,100.00
Total donations: £3,853.31 and ¥60,009.31

This was a multiple landmark day. We crossed the Grand Canal from Tai'erzhuang into Jiangsu Province. It was an emotional time to say goodbye to our Red Cross team from Shandong and the volunteers who had walked with us through Zaozhuang. It was also a time to meet the new team. We had about 30 minutes of farewells/greetings and photographs just across the bridge.

I had slightly held up proceedings because I was captivated by the Grand Canal and especially a shipyard under the bridge, where three new barges were under construction. I come from Tyneside, which used to be known for its shipbuilding prowess, and that sight of welders at work on rusty steel decks is one that resonates with my soul. Shipbuilding is one of those strategic industries that all developing countries try to promote by feeding them subsidized military orders and then by nationalization, but ultimately the jobs go because they can be built much more cheaply elsewhere. In the case of Tyneside, it was the rise of South

Korean shipbuilders that led to our demise, but then we switched to offshore oil rigs and so some of the skills were kept. After the oil rigs came the offshore wind farms – and next …? A quick fact check reveals that most of the world's new ships are built in north-east Asia (41% in South Korea, 29% in Japan and 24% in China – that leaves just 6% shared among the rest of the world).

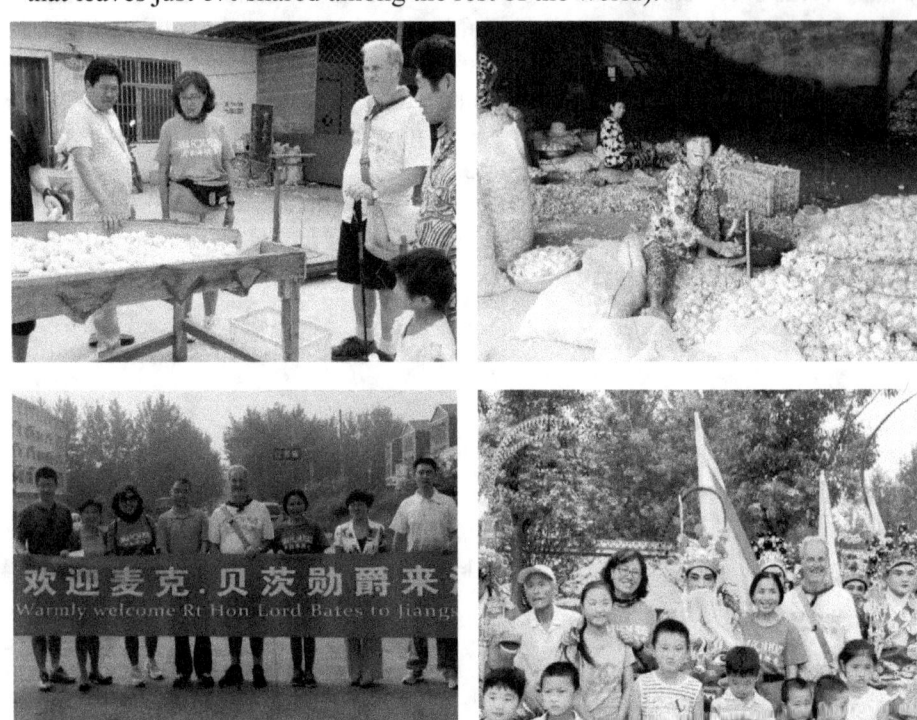

Top left: Discussing garlic farming. Top right: Garlic farmers in Pizhou.
Bottom left: Arriving in Jiangsu. Bottom right: Meeting the performers during the rehearsal.

As we walked along the road towards Pizhou, it was not shipbuilding but farming that again dominated the landscape and the roadside. This area was renowned for the production of garlic, which made for an interesting smell along the road. I was able to talk with some of the farmers and discuss garlic farming and what makes a good garlic, and so on. A top-quality garlic, so I discovered, has an unbroken skin over the segments and has a slight red or purple tinge. It is this colouring that indicates extra flavour and attracts a premium price. Most of the garlic produced at this farm was for export markets, the largest market being Brazil. I know the price of a garlic bulb at our local Sainsbury's on Wilton Road, London, is about 50p (5 yuan). I mentioned this to the farmer, who laughed and collected up ten of his best garlic bulbs and said that was what 5 yuan would get you if you bought from him. It is another interesting comment on globalization that 5p in Pizhou becomes 50p in London. Where does the 45p go? I ask, and the farmer says he has no idea either, but I think he deserves more of it.

Just as we were about to finish the day of walking, there was an extra surprise, as Madam Zhang and Xuelin directed me into a school playground where there was a full dress rehearsal for a traditional folk play. The costumes were spectacular and the music created an atmosphere that you felt had not changed for centuries. Children surrounded the school yard with their parents and were absolutely captivated by the story, which as usual involved goodies and baddies, and after a lot of chasing about, the goodies won in the end. It was wonderful.

This was raw cultural exchange. So much of what happens in culture in the UK has become professionalized, but this was all put on by local garlic farmers to celebrate the end of the harvest. There were no Lottery or local authority grants or sponsorship by local companies. This was just a community coming together to celebrate its history and culture. Every aspect of the play was home-produced. There was a family who had specialized for generations in making costumes, another that had specialized in making the masks, another in painting the masks, and still others were responsible for the music. It seemed that the homemade ingredients added to the sense that this was authentic culture. I loved every single minute of it … this was the real China I had come to see.

URL http://www.walkforpeace.eu/day-36-jiangsu-province/

September 1 Day 37

Hope House – Pizhou

Xuzhou, Jiangsu Province

A Day Off

Donated today: £0.00 / ¥15,827.00

Total donations: £3,853.31 and ¥75,836.31

Today was a day I will never forget. We went to visit Hope House, a school/clinic in Pizhou caring for children with disabilities, both physical and mental (learning difficulties, as we refer to them in the UK). The House has been supported by many organizations including the Red Cross and the Norwegian Agency for Development Cooperation (NORAD). It is not difficult to see why. It is a place of hope and transformation.

To see children with disabilities evokes a special empathy in parents and, in my case, grandparents. These are not remote, distant people, but children, and they could be any of our children. It is quite normal for children to refer to an older man as 'grandpa' in China. But when these children did, my eyes would well up, as I would see my grandson Matthew in their faces.

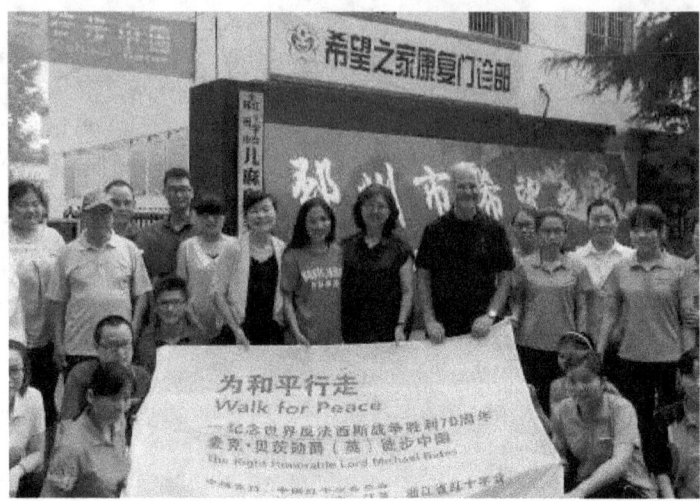

Welcome committee in Pizhou.

Hope House began in the 1990s in response to a flood in the area, which resulted in disease, probably something like typhoid. The result was a large number of children who lost limbs. There was a crisis and a local man decided to provide a solution – Hope House. The founder focused particularly on the benefits of sport for children with disabilities in building health, strength and confidence.

We first visited a treatment room for small children with brain injuries and then rooms where extensive physiotherapy was being performed on small children for 20 minutes at a time. We stood by one girl, aged about two or three, as she had her ankles and knee joints rotated. She looked up and smiled at us as if to say, 'It's okay – it looks worse than it feels.' I was so humbled by her courage.

In the next room was a small stepping machine. One of the boys, about five, was stepping on the machine while facing the wall so he could concentrate. When we all arrived, his face lit up and he wanted to show us how he could do the big steps – he struggled up one side and down the other – and again, and again, and again, and again, each time to loud cheers. His physiotherapist politely suggested we might like to leave, as he simply wouldn't stop while we were there and he really shouldn't do more than one of the big set of steps in each session. What energy for life!

We live in a society that often treats victimhood as a badge of honour. Everybody, it seems, is a victim of something or someone and we are encouraged to respond to that person in relation to the circumstance of which they are a victim. We are encouraged to unearth examples from our own lives in which we might too have been victims of something. The life-limiting message is that your circumstance is not your fault, it is the fault of someone or something else, and so your family and society should devote itself to compensating you for your suffering. Yet here were young children with almost unspeakable disabilities, whose faces were nonetheless full of joy and hope. They may have been victims of circumstance but, rather than wallow in self-pity, for which they would be fully justified, they became victors over those circumstances.

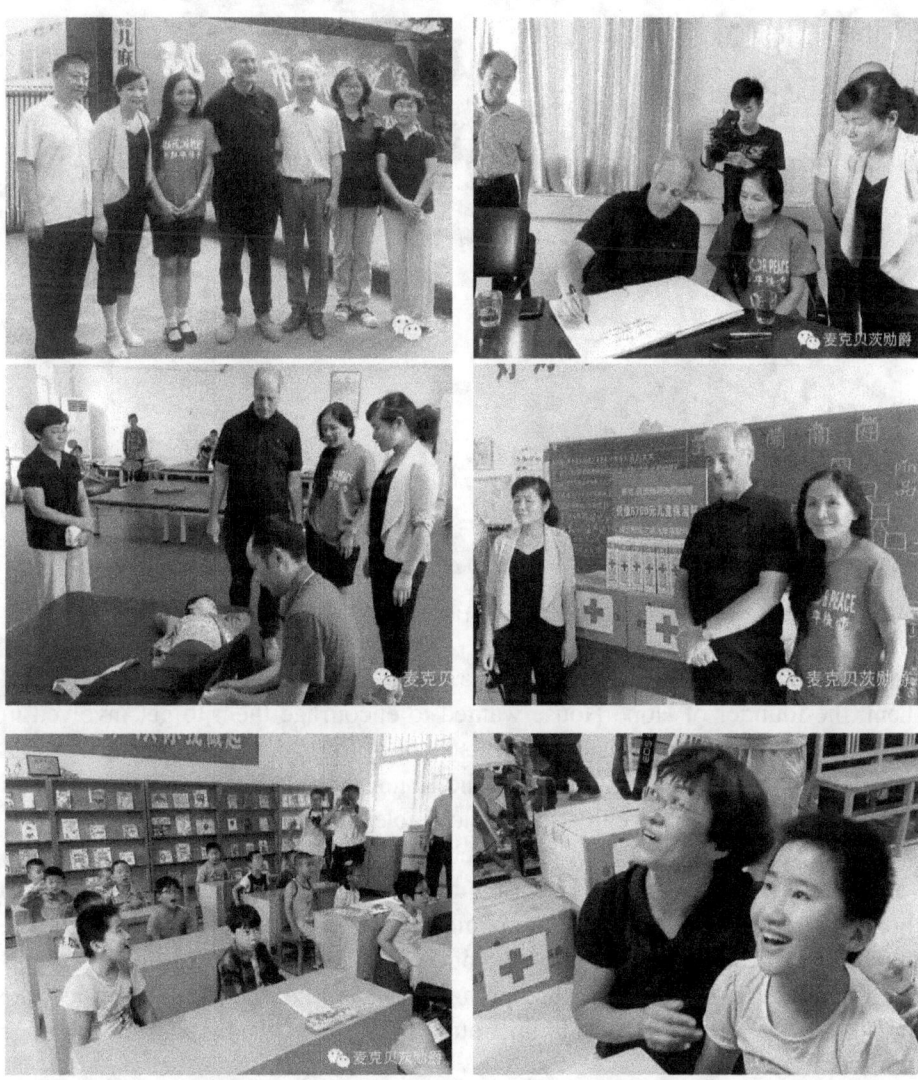

Top left: Meeting the staff of Hope House. Top right: Leaving a message in the guestbook. Middle left: A treatment room. Middle right: Visiting a classroom. Bottom left: The wonderful kids of Hope House. Bottom right: Smiles full of joy and hope.

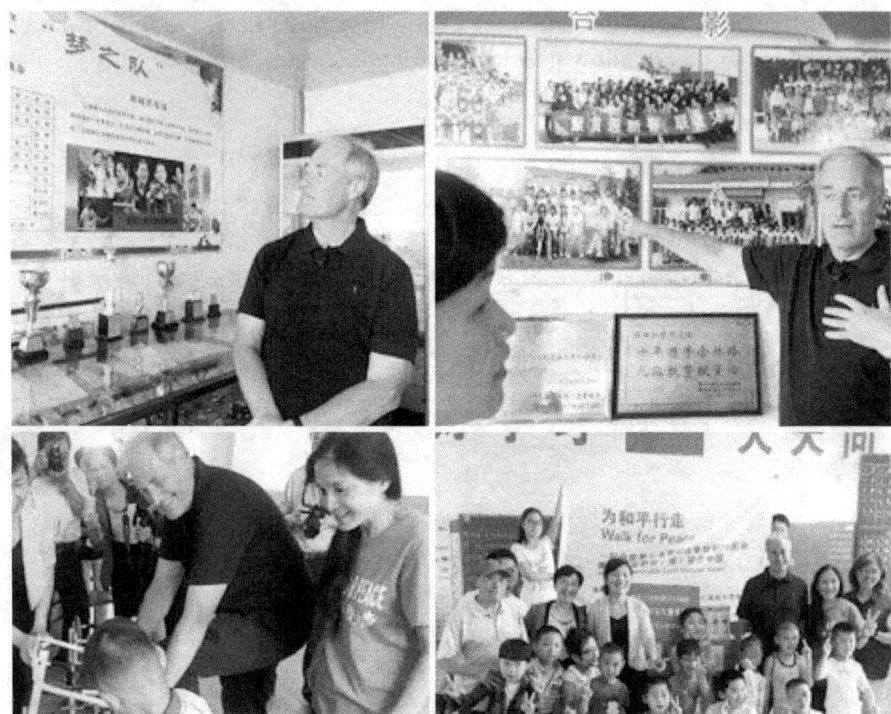

Visiting Red Cross's Hope House in Pizhou.

Sport was a major theme. Rather than wrap the children in cotton wool to protect them, the founder of Hope House wanted to encourage them to get involved in competitive sport. From this one small school in Pizhou, they produced 12 Gold medal and 2 Silver medal winners at the London 2012 Paralympic Games, and they were hoping to do even better in Rio. Table tennis is their speciality.

After a short introduction to the school in the boardroom, I was invited to write a message to the school. I was so moved by what I had seen that I went on to three pages of the record book, but my most heartfelt message was that, while the school had a deserved reputation for producing great sporting champions, everyone I had met that day was a champion, be it the child, the physiotherapist, the parent or grandparent or the administrator. They were 'champions' for the hope they inspired in us all.

Our final visit was to a classroom where we were to present 170 new Thermos flasks from the Red Cross with some of the monies raised so far from the walk – one for each child. When we arrived, a young girl of about five stood up and welcomed us in excellent English. They then sang the traditional Chinese folk song *What a Beautiful Jasmine Flower*, which they had learned especially for us – perhaps because I had let slip earlier in the walk that it was a favourite of Xuelin and mine and had been sung at our wedding. At the end of the song, I was invited to say something and I was just lost for words, or, should I say, any words I said could not have adequately conveyed the feelings I had at that moment.

Hope House has had a profound impact upon us, and Xuelin and I are so grateful for the opportunity to have seen this for ourselves, to witness such courage, such optimism, such devotion, such beauty and such hunger for life. Our desire is that the Spirit of Hope will continue to inspire us and others for many years to come.

URL http://www.walkforpeace.eu/day-37-hope-house-pizhou/

September 2 Day 38

Peace and Sport

Route: Xinhezhen, Pizhou, Xuzhou – Border of Suqian

Walked today: 20.50 miles / 33.10 km

Total walked: 591.10 miles / 951.90 km

Donated today: £0.00 / ¥5,100.00

Total donations: £3,853.31 and ¥80,936.31

It was a quiet day... Xuelin and Madam Zhang had gone back to Beijing for the 70th Anniversary Parade.

We finished the 20.5 mile walk by 5 pm and I took the opportunity to have a relaxed walk in the evening sunshine in Shagou Lake Metasequoia Park, a short walk from our guest house. I have been struck all the way from Beijing by how wonderful the parks are, immaculately maintained. Indeed, that goes not just for the parks but for all the hedgerows and borders alongside the roads. Labour is cheap, I suppose, but the way in which a community maintains its public spaces says something about its values.

As I walked through the park alongside the lake, with its view across to the temple, I noticed a sports area of basketball and badminton courts. The basketball courts were all in full use. I enjoy basketball. My son Matthew was a talented player at college in the USA and later in basketball coaching. I have many happy memories of taking him to games and watching him play and coach.

Watching these games on a Walk for Peace inevitably got me thinking about human nature and the role of sport. Sport in many ways has become as important as commerce in ordering some human societies. It is not difficult to see why.

First, we must accept that human beings are by nature competitive and tribal. Players would arrive from work or college and join a game of basketball. It only seemed to take a few minutes to establish a pecking order in the team and a ranking of the most and least talented. Players seemed a bit lost as they first entered the game but as soon as they could see who was the most talented player, they seemed to relax, accept their position in the team (tribe) and enjoy the camaraderie.

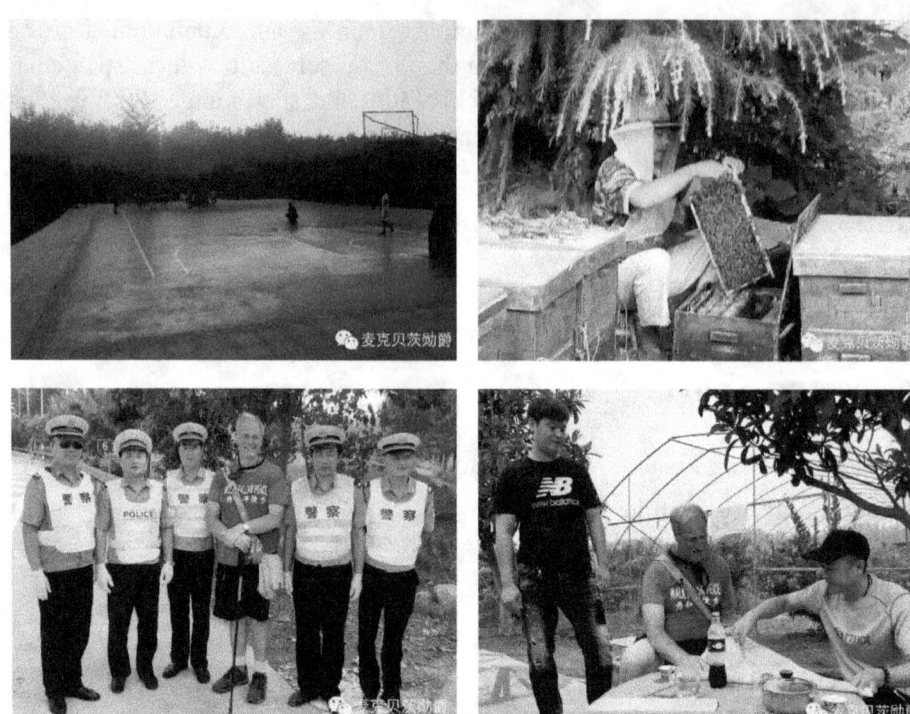

Top left: Basketball court in the park beside Shagou Lake. Top right: A beekeeper in Pizhou.
Bottom left: Lord Bates with a group of policemen in Pizhou.
Bottom right: Consulting the map with local people.

Second, the comradeship of the players was low-key, but when they started to play against another team, it became intense. It was as if the team was a loose association of individuals when playing among themselves but once there was an opposing team, they formed strong bonds, the joking stopped and they seemed able to sacrifice their own ambitions for the greater success of the team. A few minutes ago these individuals had arrived at the court as friends, but once lined up on opposing teams, it was if they were from different countries.

Third, when two very pretty young ladies who had been playing badminton on a neighbouring court finished their game and came across to watch, the effect on the male players was almost instantaneous. Although the players never seemed to look in their direction, the arrival of the girls seemed to dramatically raise the energy and effort levels of both teams. Tackles became a lot more physical and there was a lot more shouting and arguing. It was as if competition and aggression were being used to show dominance in order to secure a mate. That said, the girls didn't look that impressed by it and soon left, allowing the game to return to its original pace.

The more those in world political and military leadership understand this basic hardwiring at work in and between humans, the more aware we will be of the forces that draw us into war, terrorism and acts of violence. The more these instincts can be worked out on the basketball court, the safer the world will be for us all.

URL http://www.walkforpeace.eu/day-38-peace-sport/

September 3 Day 39

The Big Parade

Route: Border of Suqian – Sucheng District, Suqian
Walked today: 22.50 miles / 36.20 km
Total walked: 613.60 miles / 988.10 km
Donated today: £50.00 / ¥2,000.00
Total donations: £3,903.31 and ¥82,936.31

It was quiet on the roads, as today was the day of the 70th Anniversary Parade in Beijing. It was a major national and international event. For many people it was a national holiday, so they could gather with friends and family and watch the Parade on their TV. The tickets for places at the Parade in Beijing were highly prized, and we were honoured that both Xuelin (overseas Chinese representative of the UK) and Madam Zhang (Red Cross Society of China) had been invited.

We had a long walk ahead of us, but I suggested to the team that we start earlier and then break around 10 am for a couple of hours so we could all watch the Parade together. This we did. We were fortunate that the governor of the nearby township of Caiji, Mr Zhu, invited us to join him at his offices and watch the parade on a large projector screen, sustained by endless refills of green tea.

The parade was held in glorious sunshine and blue skies in Tian'anmen Square. We were told that there were 12,000 troops, 500 pieces of military hardware and 200 planes taking part in the parade – it looked more. It was begun with a precision demonstration in marching and drill. The personnel looked like robots (and soon they may be), such was the coordination of every step.

It is the ability of individuals to come together to form multi-skilled units, to willingly sacrifice all personal ambition, identity and even life itself for the advancement of the common mission of the group, which has made the human species such an awesome predator. Ironically, of course, history shows it is a skill that has been and still is used with greatest potency against other members of its own species.

I am a politician and therefore I was impressed by the words of President Xi Jinping at the beginning of the parade, 'Justice will prevail! Peace will prevail! The people will prevail!' I thought that those words could have been uttered by any of the noticeably absent Western leaders and would have won widespread approval.

The subtext of this message was of course that justice, peace and people will only be able to prevail if they have the military strength and organization to deter acts of aggression such as that which was experienced against China by Japan in World War II. This doesn't make China exceptional; it makes China normal. The fact that today we still have wars taking place around the world tells us that being armed to the teeth can deter conflict, but it can also provoke conflict. Moreover, if you place your national security in weapons alone, you begin to see solutions only through that lens, sidelining diplomacy, law and international institutions.

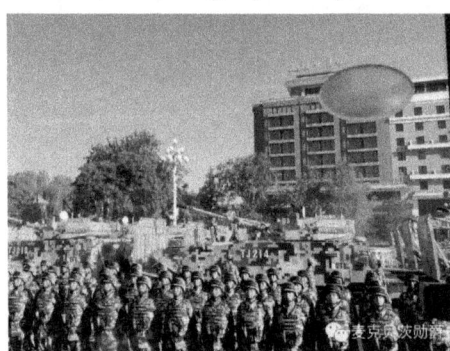 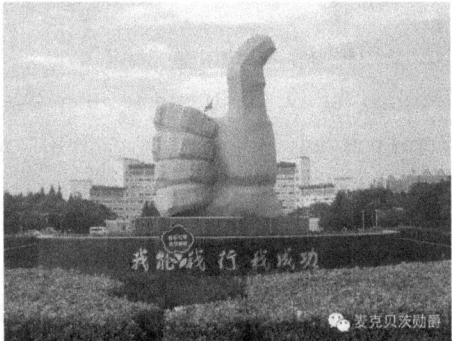

Left: Military parade in Beijing. Right: 'I can make it, I am capable, I will succeed'

The parade proceeded perfectly – not a foot out of place. It was led off by veterans of WWII, and it was right that their contribution was recognized. This was very similar to the Victory over Japan (VJ Day) commemoration that had taken place in London a couple of weeks earlier. The commemoration, rather than celebration, was led by Her Majesty The Queen and focused on expressing national thanks and gratitude to those 71,000 British and Commonwealth casualties in the war against Japan and honouring survivors. There would have been a lot more casualties, of course, had it not been for the courageous action of the Chinese Expeditionary Force in coming to the rescue of the encircled British 1st Burma Division at the Battle of Yenangyaung. All countries have a selective memory when it comes to history. In Britain there was traditional wreath-laying at the Cenotaph in Whitehall. A service of remembrance was held in church, where the focus was on sacrifice and reconciliation. Finally, there was a marching display on Horseguards Parade and a flypast of military aircraft. The expression of gratitude for VJ Day in London and Beijing was different, but it reflected a difference in scale of the experience – Britain had not been brutally occupied for eight long years. A city the size of Birmingham or Manchester had not seen a massacre of 300,000 of its citizens – men, women and children butchered by the occupying forces, as in Nanking/ Nanjing.

The end of the parade brought some greater hope with the release of 70,000 doves and thousands of balloons, and a sense of a new beginning lifted the mood. I took this as an unspoken recognition that times had changed – the Japan of today as a democratic market economy is not the same as the militaristic Imperial Japanese Empire of WWII, just as modern Germany is not the Nazi Germany of WWII, and, to stretch the point a little further, Britain is not the colonial Britain of the Opium Wars. Countries with long histories inevitably have dark chapters they would prefer to forget.

The parade being over, it was time to get back on the road… to Suqian.

URL http://www.walkforpeace.eu/day-39-the-big-parade/

September 4 Day 40

1,000 km in Suqian

Route: Sucheng District – Suyu District, Suqian
Walked today: 26.00 miles / 41.90 km
Total walked: 639.60 miles / 1,030.00 km
Donated today: £0.00 / ¥5,000.00
Total donations: £3,903.31 and ¥87,936.31

Little mysteries continue to be explained on this trip.

Every time Xuelin and I check into a hotel, Xuelin will be on the phone asking reception for the toothbrush and toothpaste. I always find this a little strange. But in China I have discovered that, no matter how basic the guest house or hotel, they always provide toothbrush and toothpaste, a comb and a shower cap.

I mentioned in the first week of this blog that I had encountered more 'random acts of kindness' (bottles of water or food) in the first miles in China than I had in the previous 4,500 miles of walking for peace. This experience leads me to challenge my belief that China was different from all the other 18 countries I had walked through. I reflect that all these examples were in Hebei Province. This is not to ask them to start again, it is simply to say that my thesis, which was, 'People are the same all over the world in their approach to strangers.' I believe this still holds – if you smile, they smile back; if you ask for directions, they do their best to help and if you ask for food or accommodation, then they will ask for money. That is nice and as it should be – it is not being Chinese, British or Greek, it is being human.

Another update is that in my five weeks and 600 miles of walking I have only ever seen one other 'foreigner' – a Western-looking man in our hotel in Jinan 300 miles back up the road. Coming from Britain, which is so cosmopolitan, I find that quite a surprise. Thinking of China's importance to the global economy, I again find that a surprise.

In order to keep in contact with my two sons during the trip, they have both signed up for WeChat, a Chinese social media app like What's App or FaceTime. I think if I were to point to one thing about the modern world that utterly amazes me every time, it would be that I can sit in a hotel lobby in rural China and have 30-minute video call with Matt in Texas. I can ask my grandson Matthew about his first few days at school, and he can show me his work. I can then speak and see my other son Alex in Brazil to discuss the latest transfer signings in the premiership, all in perfect-quality video. And, it's all free! How do they do that?

After a long day on the road, we arrived into the beautiful and highly sophisticated city of Suqian. It is located on the Yangtze River Delta on the edge of Lake Luoma. It has a rich and distinctive culture, being the birthplace of Xiang Yu (born 232 BC), who at the age of 27 became the Conqueror of Western Chu and Qin and who died at the age of 31. His story is similar to that of Alexander the Great, who became head of the army in Macedon (modern Macedonia) at the age of 20 and whose empire extended from Africa to the western reaches of modern China in 320 BC and who died at the age of 32.

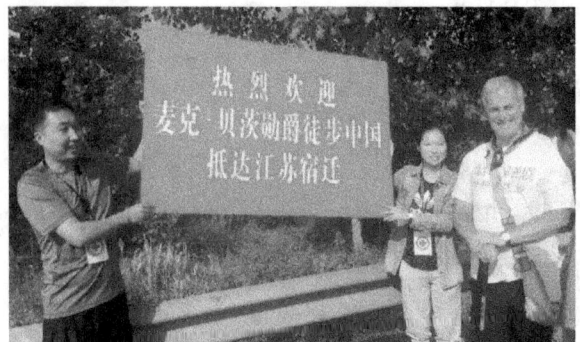 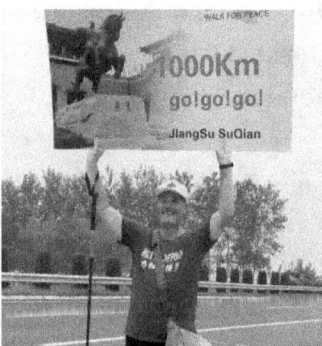

Left: Volunteers welcoming Lord Bates to Suqian, Jiangsu.
Right: Milestone marking 1,000 km of the walk.

Ducks on the lake.

That phrase, 'Only the good die young' – I really never understood where it came from. So many great figures from history did die young: Diana, Princess of Wales, JFK, Joan of Arc, Anne Frank, Martin Luther King, Buddy Holly, Bruce Lee, Mozart and Van Gogh, to name a few. Apparently, it was first put forward by the Greek Herodotus in 442 BC and then made famous by William Wordsworth in his poem *Excursion*: *The good die first, And they whose hearts are dry as summer dust / Burn to the socket* – although Wordsworth himself lived on until he was 80. I can only think that in some ways our preserved memory of these people is of their youthful energy and potential cut short. Anyway, I find that the older I get, the less I want to agree with this…

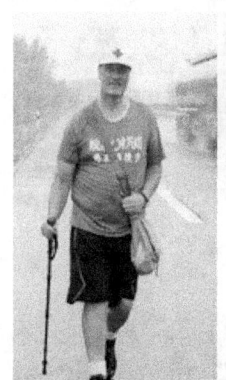 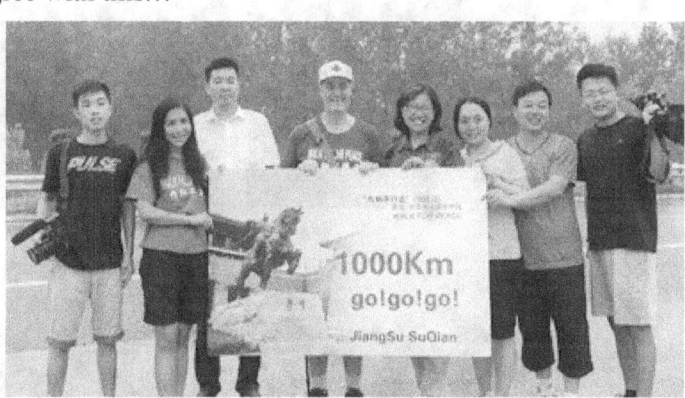

Left: Walking 41.9 km in heavy rain. Right: Celebrating 1,000 km on the walk.

Oh yes, and Xuelin and Madam Zhang arrived back just in time to celebrate 1,000 km on the walk outside a mushroom factory at Dingzuizhen on the S325 to Huai'an.

URL http://www.walkforpeace.eu/day-40-1000km-in-suqian/

September 5 Day 41

International Eco-Quadrathlon Classic

Suqian, Jiangsu Province
A Day Off
Donated today: £0.00 / ¥200.00
Total donations: £3,903.31 and ¥88,136.31

Zhao Kai, the vice president of the Red Cross in Jiangsu Province, had received an invitation for me to take part in the opening of the 2015 Suqian Eco-Quadrathlon being held at Lake Luoma and Santai Hill. I didn't know quite what to expect.

I didn't know what an 'eco-quadrathlon' was, but it was sport and I saw an opportunity to convey the message of peace through sport, so I immediately accepted. Special-event shirts for us to wear at the opening ceremony were dropped off at our hotel the evening before, and I was glad I had lost a few pounds on the walk from Beijing so I could squeeze into it.

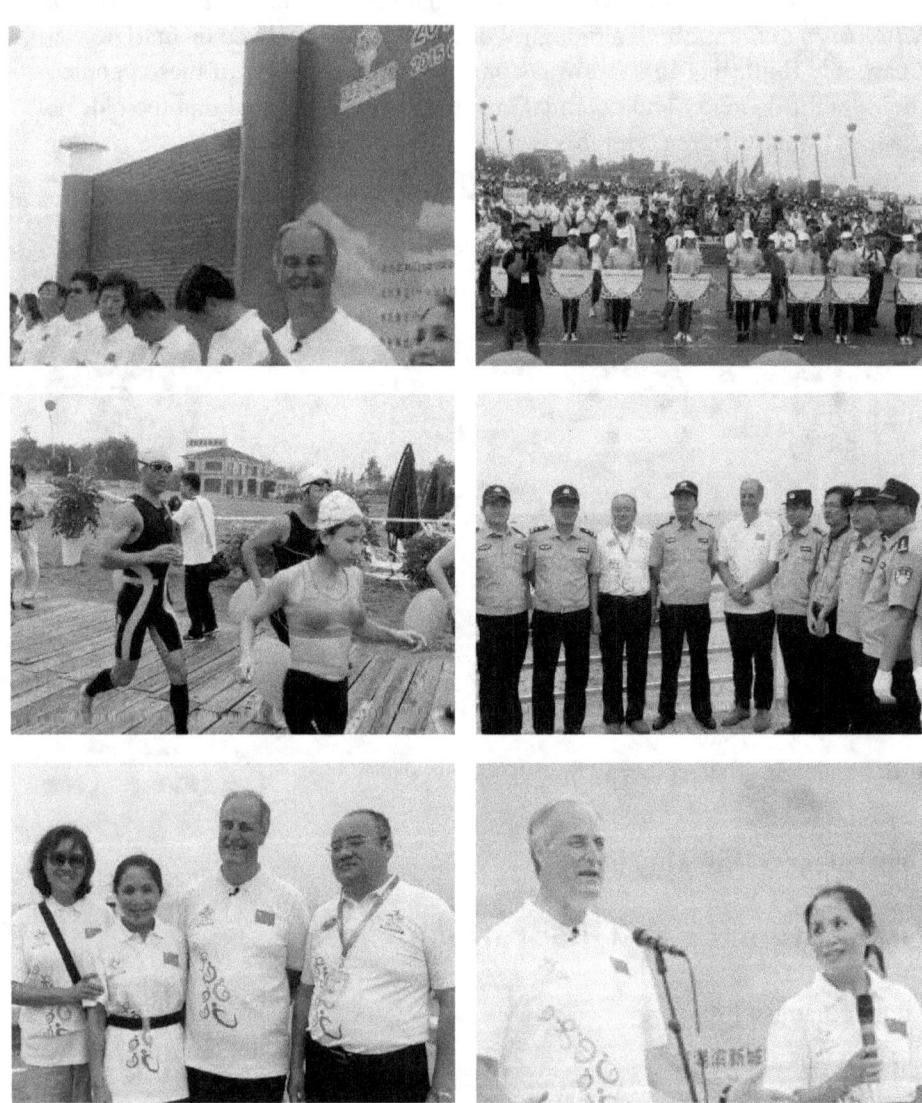

Top left: Lord and Lady Bates attending the Eco-Quadrathlon in Suqian. Top right: Start of the Eco-Quadrathlon. Middle left: Athletes taking part in the Eco-Quadrathlon.
Middle right: Lord Bates with a group of police officers at the ceremony.
Bottom left: Lord and Lady Bates with Madame Zhang and ZHANG Jian, the first Chinese man to cross the English Channel. Bottom right: Lord Bates speaking at the opening ceremony.

We arrived at the edge of Lake Luoma and were quite surprised to see a few thousand competitors and officials gathered on the lakeshore. The Quadrathlon is made up of cross-country running, cycling, swimming and kayaking over a 58-km course. The 'eco' part of the competition was to try and blend competitive sport in with the natural environment. I hadn't really thought about it before, but most sports take part in stadiums, indoor arenas, pools or city centres. There are not many sports that come easily to mind which seek to use the natural environment as the backdrop: race track skiing, fishing, hunting, three-day eventing, rally driving and some cycling stages. The limitation is, of course, not just for competitors, but also access for spectators and providing a route accessible for the media.

The point that the Suqian organisers were trying to make was that sport can play a great role in drawing people to explore outdoor spaces. We often say the world is crowded and yet the entire world population of 7 billion standing shoulder to shoulder would be able to stand in the city of Los Angeles (500 square miles). We have vast open spaces but have chosen, largely for economic reasons, to concentrate human populations in cities. As the global population expands, we are going to need to reverse that industrialization trend, and with the wide availability of IT and super-fast broadband connectivity, there is no reason why we need to be crammed together in expensive congested and polluted cities.

Along with Wei Guoqiang, Secretary of the CPC Committee in Suqian and Wang Tianqi, the Mayor of Suqian, I was invited to speak to the competitors at the opening ceremony. I struggled to think of what to say but landed on the word 'eco', which in the Greek original means 'home'. Ecology is literally the study of our home. So an 'eco' sporting event is a sporting event that seeks in some way to promote or study our common home. Most of the time we look at the world politically. Lines drawn on a map, and often disputed, show the boundaries of 200 or so polities on the planet.

Yet national boundaries are a human and legal construct. If you were to look down on the Earth from the International Space Station, there would be very little evidence during the day that humans actually lived there – the Suez and Panama Canals and the Great Wall of China – so I am told. At night, the cities light up, revealing the concentration of human populations, but there is absolutely no giant sign that states 'United Kingdom', 'United States of America' or 'People's Republic of China' or 'Vanuatu'. All nations, cities, mountains, deserts, rivers and oceans merge into one glorious and beautiful planet called Earth – our home.

Some things nations can do alone, but caring for and maintaining our planet/ our home is something that we can only do together. The care of the environment is not of one nation but of all nations. The responsibility for maintaining our home is not the task of one individual or organization but of all humanity. The 'eco', then, is not about you or me, but about us. The 'eco' will not shape our histories, but our actions today will shape our future. Suqian is onto something very significant here and I hope it continues with it ....

URL http://www.walkforpeace.eu/day-41-international-eco-quadrathlon-classic/

September 6 Day 42

Whatever You Do for the Least …

Suqian, Jiangsu Province
A Day Off
Donated today: £0.00 / ¥1,000.00
Total donations: £3,903.31 and ¥89,136.31

One of the great things about this walk is working with the Red Cross. It is not just the practical support they give us but also the introductions to inspiring people and hear their stories. In my mind I am still thinking about the visit to Hope House in Pizhou, which left a big impression on Xuelin and me. As we arrived into Suqian we were invited to visit the Suqian Welfare Institute, which is similar to Hope House in that they are caring and educating children with severe physical and mental disabilities.

As parents, it makes our heart ache that, through a lottery of life, these children arrive into the world with disabilities. It is natural to look at their disabilities and ask why? But this does not help. Far better to look at their abilities and ask why not? This is the inspiring work taking place each day in Pizhou and Suqian. There is a major difference, though:

Whereas the children in Pizhou were surrounded by families who loved and cared for them and brought them to and from Hope House each day, the children in Suqian were orphans. In some cases, parents had died, and in others, the parents could not cope and placed them in the care of the Welfare Institute. As parents we would not dare judge or criticize another parent whose position we cannot begin to understand. We were at the Institute for an hour but we understood the demands on parents, grandparents and siblings of providing the constant care required.

That said, the effect on the child must be enormous. Not only must they come to terms with their disabilities, but they must do so without the love and support of their family. What overwhelmed us during our visit was that. although these children would have every reason to be resentful and bitter, they were instead overflowing with happiness and love.

It is as if God has looked upon them and given them a larger than normal heart and soul, which radiates warmth and love to all those who are privileged to come into contact with them. Discussions with staff and carers confirmed it was this golden quality in these young lives that kept them going and wanting to give the children the best possible start in life. But they have other tasks too …

In addition to caring for the children, the Institute seeks to find permanent homes for theem. In one area of the Institute's 'Honour Hall', they show photographs of children placed with families all over the world and their life achieve-

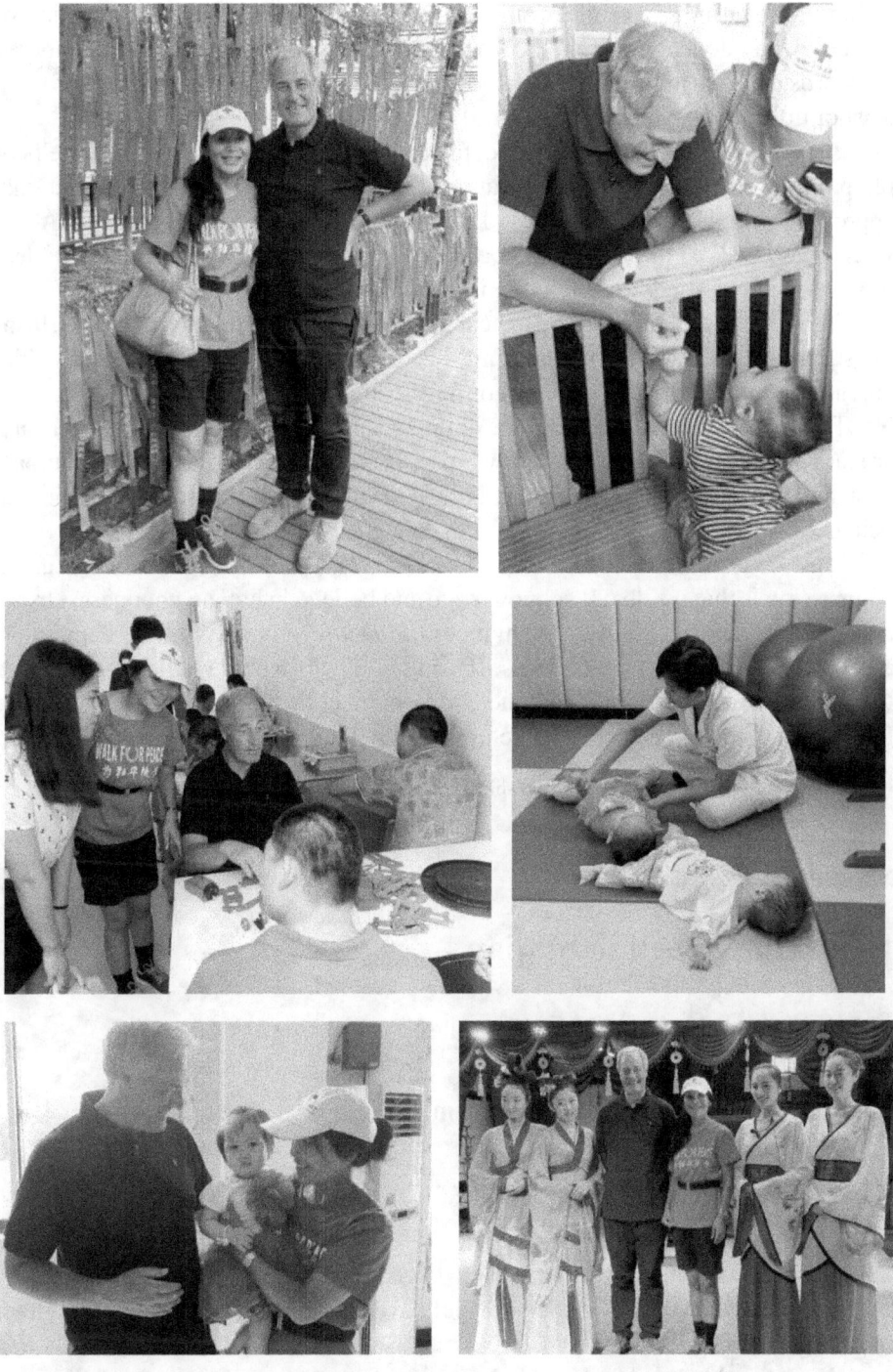

Top left: A backdrop of prayer ribbons. Top right: With a baby at the Child Welfare Institute in Suqian. Middle left: Meeting children at the Suqian Welfare Institute. Middle right: Some of the children and their caretaker. Bottom left: Visiting the Suqian Child Welfare Institute. Bottom Right: Performers in Suqian.

ments – graduating from college or getting married. I so admired these families for what they had done, not for their own child but for someone else's. I remembered the words of Jesus in the Matthew's gospel in the Bible, 'Whatever you did for the least of my brothers [children], you did this also for me.'

I always want to believe that people are basically good, although some people point to our daily news stories and disagree. They say that the only rational approach to life is pure self-interest. I disagree, and I am in good company: A few weeks ago I walked through the hometown of the great teacher Mencius, a student of Confucius; he used the following illustration to explain this concept. If a child falls into a well, will those who are nearby calculate their actions based on self-interest, saying, 'How will this help me if I help?' 'Does the child have wealthy parents who might pay me a reward or powerful parents who might promote me?' No. They rush to the well to help the child because it is in danger and their hearts are moved to want to help. This 'movement of the heart' Mencius called 'compassion' and it was his starting point for believing in the basic goodness of all human beings.

This raises the possibility that the reason why we don't see more of human compassion is that we do not acknowledge and believe in human goodness. On the contrary, our starting point in social media and television news often seems to be a belief in essential human badness. If you feel this, I would challenge you to go to Suqian Welfare Institute, meet the children, meet the carers, meet the adopting families, and it will show you something that will be sure to change your mind.

URL http://www.walkforpeace.eu/day-42-pink-nails/

September 7 Day 43

Lightning Speed in Suqian

Route: Suyu District – Siyangxian, Suqian
Walked today: 25.50 miles / 41.10 km
Total walked: 665.10 miles / 1,071.10 km
Donated today: £0.00 / ¥1,999.00
Total donations: £3,903.31 and ¥91,135.31

Suqian literally means 'overnight'. The 'overnight' refers to the overnight refuge that was used when the Yellow River would overflow, but I was to discover another meaning of the word.

Xuelin and I were honoured to be invited for dinner on Sunday with Suqian's Party Secretary Wei and Mayor Wang, whom we had met at the opening ceremony of the Eco-Quadrathlon the day before. Both Secretary Wei and Mayor Wang were keen walkers, and they were interested in what further measures could be taken to make Suqian a 'walker-friendly' city.

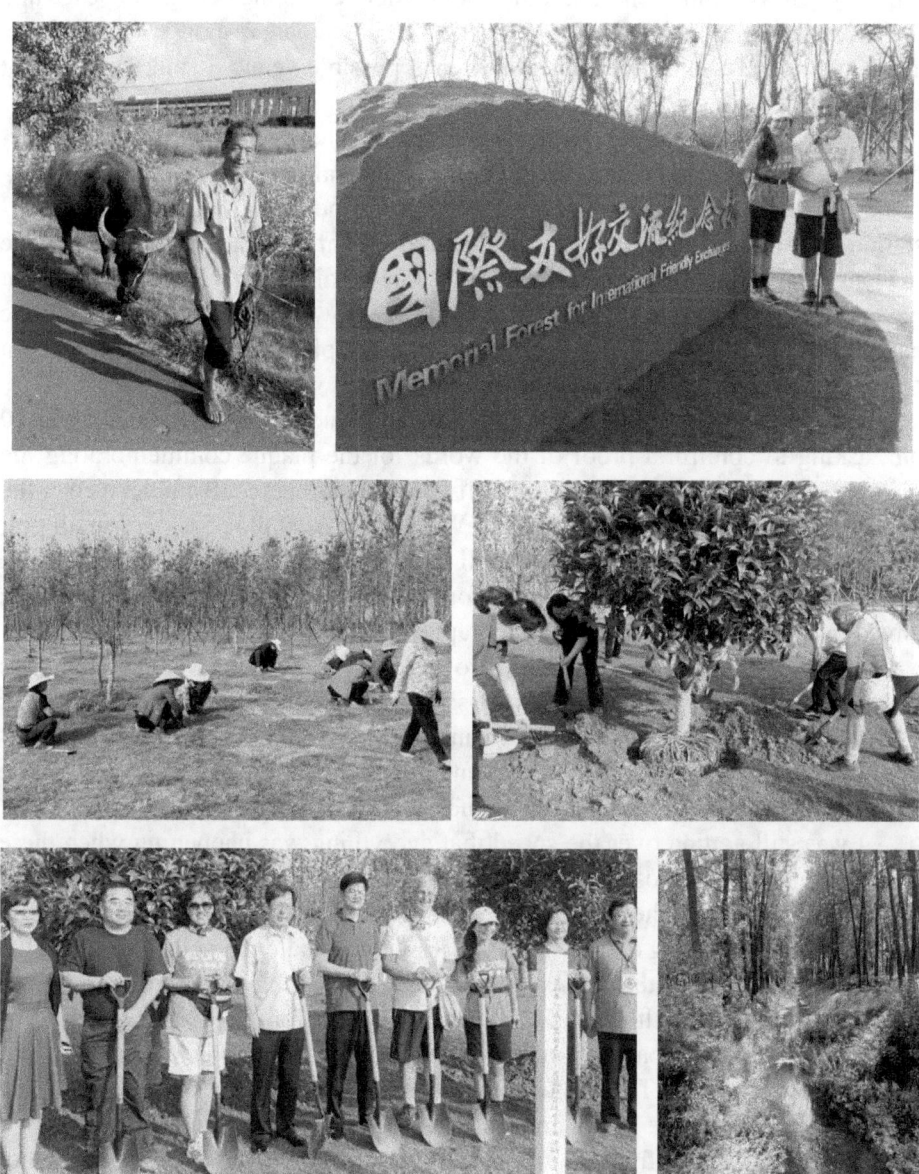

Top left: A farmer and his water buffalo. Top right: Lord and Lady Bates at the Memorial Forest for International Friendly Exchanges. Middle left: Staff of the Memorial Forest. Middle right: Planting a tree. Bottom left: Planting two Osmanthus trees with Wei Guoqiang, Secretary of the CPC Committee in Suqian (third from the left) and Wang Tianqi, the Mayor of Suqian (centre). Bottom right: Scenery in Suqian.

I sensed a good moment to pitch an idea: could Suqian become the first place in the world to hold an annual Walk for Peace? The successful Eco-Quadrathlon event combined sport and the countryside: could they combine peace and the countryside through a Walk for Peace? The immediate response was positive. They mentioned Santai Hill Forest Park as a possible venue. I said that I hadn't seen the park …

There was then a long conversation in Chinese between Xuelin and the Mayor, Party Secretary and Zhao Kai, Secretary General of the Red Cross, the outcome of which was that I could visit the park the next morning at 7.30 before I started my walk out of Suqian towards Huai'an. What is more, they would like me to plant a tree in the Memorial Forest for International Friendly Exchanges. 'What type of tree would I plant?' I smiled. I could see how I might be able to visit the park but how would they manage to organize a tree planting? It was already 8 pm on Sunday. 'This is Suqian,' came the reply.

We were back in our room in the hotel and Xuelin got a message about 10 pm, asking to confirm a proof of the words for the plaque commemorating the planting. On Monday morning we set off from the hotel at 7.30 and arrived at the Forest Park. It was a beautiful morning. Waiting for us at the gate were small golf buggies with a tour guide, who told us all about the park in the five minutes it took us to reach the Memorial Forest. At the forest, the Party Secretary and Mayor were already waiting with a group of photographers.

The Party Secretary pointed to two trees and said these were the trees we were going to plant. They were 'sweet-scented Osmanthus trees, the city tree of Suqian and also of Xuelin's hometown and our destination, Hangzhou', the translator reported. We were handed spades and directed to the spot alongside a plaque marking the occasion in both Chinese and English.

I was still getting over the speed that everything was happening when there were some formal photos and then farewells, and the Party Secretary, Mayor and entourage were gone. The whole event took about five minutes from start to finish.

I was left reflecting on how long this might have taken to organise in the UK. Leaving aside the fact that this was a Sunday evening … there would be planning approvals, tree health checks, wording approvals for the plaque, and the purchase of the trees and spades would need to be put out for public tender following EU procurement rules. Those attending would need to be checked to ensure that they had the appropriate health and safety experience to oversee the planting of a tree. There would be a full risk assessment, first-aid trained individuals on hand, high-visibility jackets, protective gloves, footwear, hats and goggles for participants to wear. There would need to be contingency plans in case it was raining.

In Suqian they 'Just do it.' This is why, when the EU economy grows at 1%, we call it a 'recovery', whereas when China grows at 7%, we call it a 'slowdown'.

URL http://www.walkforpeace.eu/day-43-whatever-you-do-for-the-least/

September 8 Day 44

Red Nails

Route: Siyangxian, Suqian – Huaiyin District, Huai'an
Walked today: 20.60 miles / 33.20 km
Total walked: 685.70 miles / 1,104.30 km
Donated today: £0.00 / ¥10,700.00
Total donations: £3,903.31 and ¥101,835.31

One of the first jokes I can remember telling in the schoolyard at Kells Lane School, aged six or seven, was:

> Q: Why do elephants paint their toenails red?
> A: So they can hide in cherry trees.

Wait for groans …

> Q: Have you ever seen an elephant in a cherry tree? [wait for them to say 'no']
> A: See? It works, then!

I was reminded of this when I sat down to start writing my blog updates today. I confess I don't find the discipline of writing blogs easy – on my days off I just want to sleep. Xuelin thinks sleep is something that happens in the seconds between social media replies on WeChat. The most interesting of all Chinese characteristics to the British is that of being direct, so Xuelin looked up and said, 'Try and make the blog funny. Your blogs are too serious. People don't want to read them.' I replied with my usual ironic, 'Honey, you shouldn't hold back for the sake of my feelings. Tell me what you really think.'

There aren't many laughs in walking 25 miles alongside busy roads day after day in 30 degree-plus heat, but let me try and find something… oh yes.

I have been suffering with a highly embarrassing problem for a man over the past few days – pink fingernails. I know our fingernails are meant to be pinkish but this is pink nail varnish colour. I think that it must have come from some 100 yuan I had in my bag when it was raining. But no matter how much I washed the nails the colour wouldn't come out. Concerned, I did what we all do in such circumstances, namely put 'pink nails' into a search engine. One of the entries suggested that this could be a sign of the early onset of kidney disease and that I should see a doctor. I didn't feel unwell, though.

Next morning, during a drink break, I joked about my nails to Madam Zhang, who said she had exactly the same problem and had cut her nails to remove the pink. Xuelin then said that she had found pink spots the same colour in her hair that morning and was worried that it was some kind of infection. Madam Zhang then said, 'This will be from the launch of the Eco-Quadrathlon … We were all on the stage together and when the Games were officially opened, Chinese fire-crackers went off over our heads. This is the powder from the firecrackers that got into our hair.'

Mystery solved. Now, if only we could find some cherry trees to hide in.

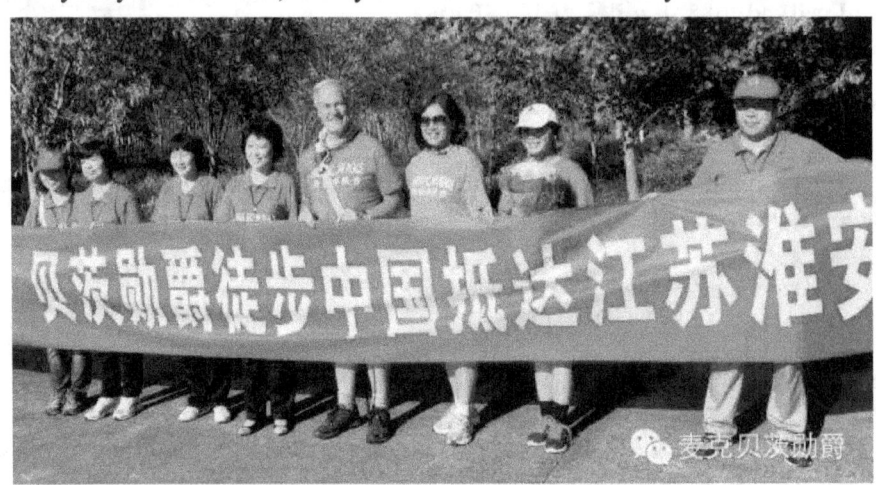

The volunteer team in Huai'an, Jiangsu.

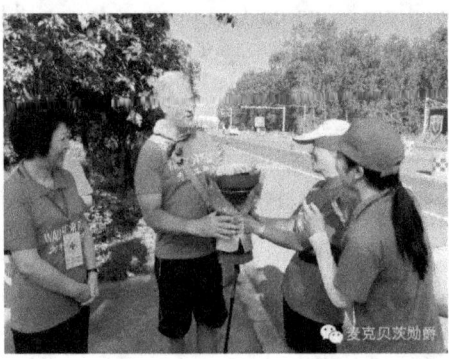 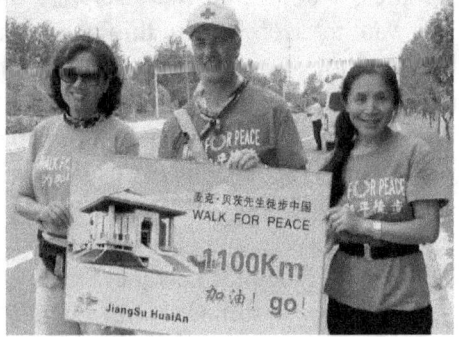

Left: Being greeted in Huai'an.
Right: Lord and Lady Bates and Madame Zhang holding the '1,100 km' sign.

URL http://www.walkforpeace.eu/day-44-lightning-speed-in-suqian/

September 9 Day 45

Huai'an: Zhou Enlai and Billy Graham

Huai'an, Jiangsu Province
A Day Off
Donated today: £0.00 / ¥3,800.00
Total donations: £3,903.31 and ¥105,635.31

Huai'an is a city of around five million people in Jiangsu, standing on the edge of the Grand Canal connecting our start point of Beijing and our destination point of Hangzhou. The canal is a UNESCO World Heritage Site, being the longest (1,104 miles/1,766 km) and one of the earliest canals in the world. The oldest sections of the canal were built in the 5th century BC. I know this because we visited the excellent China Water Transport Museum in Huai'an this afternoon. In fact, I could tell you a whole lot more, from how it was funded (a special levy), to its early uses (military), etc., but I won't, just in case you get the chance to visit the exhibition for yourself.

We crossed the boundary between Suqian and Huai'an yesterday and with it came a now familiar change routine for the Red Cross volunteers who would guide us through their county or city. We must have done around 20 of these handovers by now, and they have developed a ritualistic, almost religious process of thanks and photos to the past team and greetings (and photos) with the new team. Sometimes the teams change so fast we don't get to know everyone's names. These people are the backbone of the walk, and they have been planning and preparing for the few days we might be in their city for months.

Invariably, the first day is a bit tough as we get to know each other. I always thank them and then tell them that I am sure there are many scenic roads in their wonderful city or county, but for me the shortest route is always the most beautiful. I explain that, while Chinese people's generosity, hospitality and care for guests are qualities admired around the world, on this walk we value simplicity highest of all. The longer we have together, the more we all adapt, which is where Xuelin and Madam Zhang play such a crucial role in communication and team building.

Huai'an is a famous city in China because it is the birthplace of Zhou Enlai, premier of the People's Republic of China from 1949 until 1976. Zhou, with his film-star good looks and Western education, was a kind of 'thinking man's revolutionary', a Che Guevara of the East. He served faithfully under Mao Zedong, despite threats from the Red Guards during the Cultural Revolution. I confess I knew very little if anything about Zhou Enlai before I arrived in Huai'an; however, this afternoon we also visited the Zhou Enlai Memorial Hall and Exhibition, and so

I could write a whole lot more, but again this is a place you may get a chance to visit for yourself.

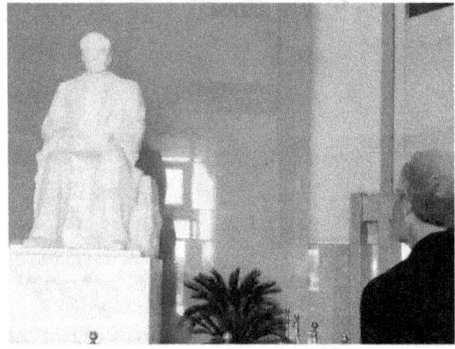
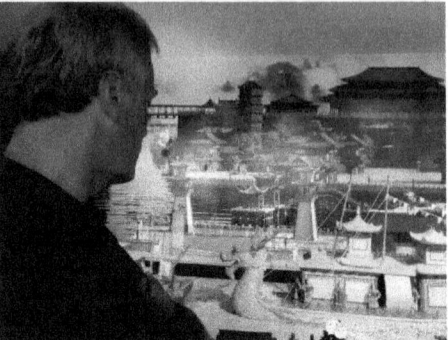
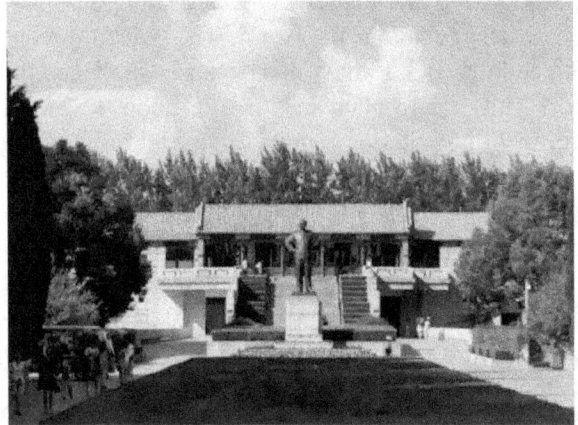
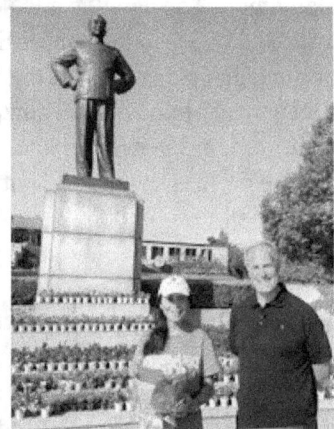
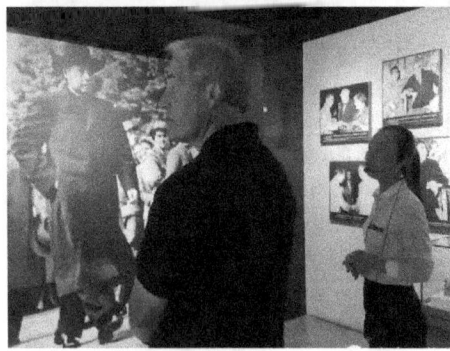
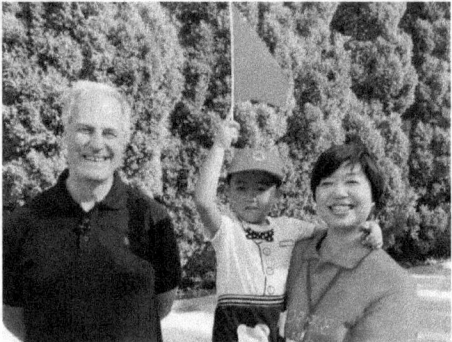

Top left: Visiting the China Water Transport Museum in Huai'an. Top right: Visiting Zhou Enlai Memorial Hall. Middle left: The Zhou Enlai Memorial Hall. Middle right: Statue of Zhou Enlai. Bottom left: Inside the Zhou Enlai Memorial Hall. Bottom right: Lord Bates and a local Red Cross volunteer.

Now here is a good quiz question: What connects Zhou Enlai of the Communist Party of China and Dr Billy Graham, the American Evangelical Christian evangelist and spiritual confidant of successive American presidents since Richard Nixon? The answer is that Huai'an was the birthplace of both Zhou Enlai and Ruth Bell Graham, wife of Dr Graham. Ruth Graham's father was a doctor and medical missionary in the city before they moved to Pyongyang (North Korea), where Ruth attended the same Christian school as Kim Il Sung, founding president of North Korea. Interesting also, isn't it, that Zhou Enlai was to make his international reputation as the person who opened China up to the West by organizing the visit of President Richard Nixon to China in 1972 and the Geneva and Bandung Peace Conferences, which sought to lower Cold War tensions following the Korean War? Billy Graham's greatest diplomatic success was to help facilitate improved relations between North and South Korea in the early 1990s.

It's a small, small world in Huai'an.

URL http://www.walkforpeace.eu/day-45-its-a-small-world-in-huaian/

September 10 Day 46

Secretary of the Party Committee in 'Peacetown'

Route: Huaiyin District – Hongzexian, Huai'an
Walked today: 21.60 miles / 34.70 km
Total walked: 707.30 miles / 1,139.00 km
Donated today: £50.00 / ¥940.00
Total donations: £3,953.31 and ¥106,575.31

Day 46 and back on the S205, this time heading out of Huai'an. Our visit to Huai'an had been fascinating and I was sorry not to be able to spend more time there. As always, it is the schedule that drives us on. We need to be in Nanjing on September 19. The S205 takes us all the way and road signs had started to appear, showing 'Nanjing 215 km' and they were drawing us in.

We were told to expect a VIP visitor who wanted to walk with us, so we stopped for a lunch break in a small town on the S205. A visit to the local shop to get stocked up with some iced green tea, which has now overtaken Coke Zero as the drink of choice on the walk, quickly made us a focus of attention.

English is a compulsory subject in Chinese schools, so it is often children and young people who are most willing to start up a conversation. Two young girls told Xuelin that they had heard that 'There was a foreigner who was walking for peace down their road and they wanted to come and find out more.' Their first question was, 'What did I think of their town?' I guess that would be the most common question on all my walks, as we are all proud of our hometown, but there was a particular reason I would remember this town.

'Welcome to Huai'an, Lord Bates. You have chosen a perfect place to rest. This is Peacetown!' said a tall, elegant man in perfect English, smiling warmly. The person greeting me was Dr Yao Xiaodong, Secretary of the Party committee in Huai'an. It is difficult to convey to a Westerner the importance of the position of Party Secretary in China. Perhaps if you combined the roles of Mayor of London with Commissioner of the Metropolitan Police and added the Bishop of London into the mix for good measure, you might be getting somewhere close. Added to which, Huai'an is a second-tier city with a population of five million.

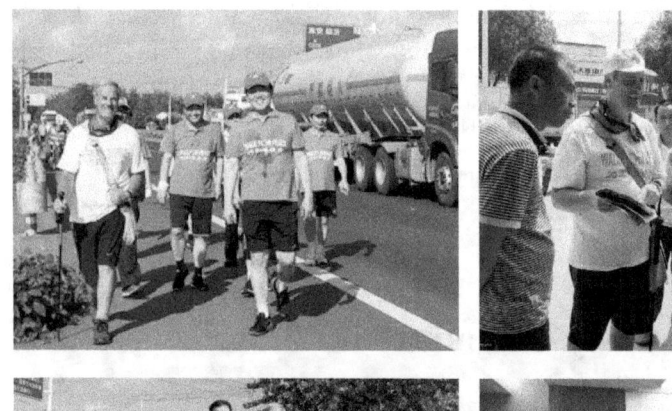
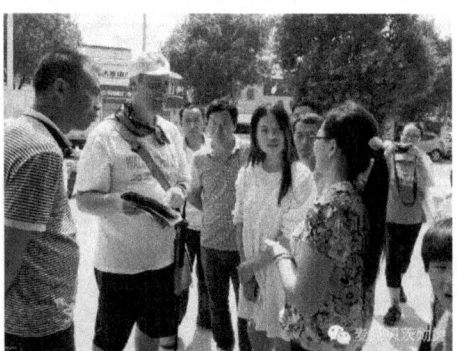
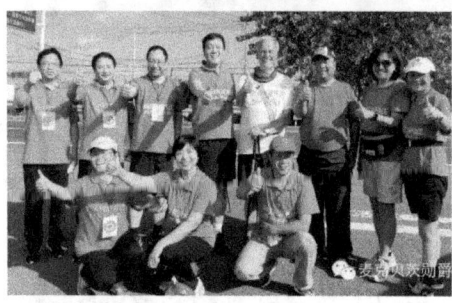
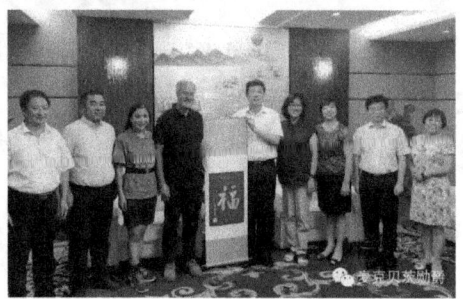

Top left: In Peacetown, Lord Bates walked with Yao Xiaodong, Secretary of the Party Committee in Huai'an. Top right: Lord Bates with local students.
Bottom left: The volunteer team in Huai'an. Bottom right: Meeting the city officials.

So the fact that Huai'an Party Secretary Yao had travelled back from Beijing to meet us and was dressed in a splendid 'Walk for Peace' T-shirt had our local Red Cross volunteers rubbing their eyes to see if this was really happening. We politicians are a predicable lot and I took it that when we were told that a VIP was coming to walk with us, that meant there would be a few steps and a lot of photographs, but Secretary Yao was with us for the remaining 12 km of the walk.

As we walked and talked I discovered that Secretary Yao had not only visited London many times but had actually had lunch in the House of Lords canteen with our mutual friend Lord Wei. The 'small world' of Huai'an just got a lot smaller.

His academic background and early career were in journalism, which was an unusual background for a Party Secretary, as most had worked their way up through administrative roles.

We had a long conversation about the challenges Huai'an was facing in seeking to drive economic growth and at the same time care for the environment. The whole of the Huai'an area is flat and low-lying, with a network of rivers, lakes and canals, which makes it prone to flooding. If you live in Huai'an, understanding rising water levels and changing climate patterns is not a debate about science, but a question of survival. We also spoke about healthcare, and Yao was very keen to learn from the experiences of the National Health Service in the UK, which is as admired in China as it is in the UK.

After our walk and talk he invited us for dinner, where we sampled the local delicacy of crayfish from Hongzehu Lake. I have to confess that the crayfish weren't my favourite memory of Huai'an, but in China they have a phrase that means doing something you don't really want to for a greater good: 'I ate/drank/went/walked, etc. for the Revolution.' Well, I did my bit for the revolution. Xuelin did even more by eating some of my share and discreetly placing some of her left-over shells on my plate.

Secretary Yao, like myself, was an admirer of Professor Joe Nye, the former Dean of the Kennedy School of Government at Harvard University. Professor Nye had famously advocated greater use of 'soft power' to advance strategic aims, soft power being things like culture, education, tourism, sport, business and the arts, as opposed to a focus on the military, trade blocs, and the like, the so-called hard power. We spoke about China's soft power and how it could be deployed in the future.

Soft power is also, of course, what had brought us together, a Communist and a Conservative politician taking time to walk and talk with each other and appreciate each other's culture a little better as a result. It is interesting, of course, that our memories of places are so often not of the things we see but of the people we meet. The people of Huai'an and Peacetown will endure long and happily in the memory, although I hope the crayfish of Hongzehu Lake will endure not quite so long in the stomach.

URL http://www.walkforpeace.eu/day-46-friendship-in-peacetown/

September 11 Day 47

Address to Students in Jinling Middle School

Route: Hongzexian – Xuyixian, Huai'an
Walked today: 23.00 miles / 37.00 km
Total walked: 730.30 miles / 1,176.00 km
Donated today: £0.00 / ¥0.00
Total donations: £3,953.31 and ¥106,575.31

Day 47, still on the S205. Not much to add. I thought I would use this time and space to write a draft for a talk I have been invited to give in Nanjing on the subject of culture and peace.

The theme of my talk is the role of culture in peace-building. A purpose of my walk from Beijing to Nanjing has been to highlight the first Year of UK–China Cultural Exchange: My proposition is that 'Culture Connects'.

To explore this topic adequately, we need to understand what we mean by culture. The origin of the word is similar in English, or I should say Latin, to 'agri' culture or farming, and that gives us a clue. The meaning of the word 'culture' relates to the process of cultivation, literally 'inhabit, till, care for' the mind and soul. Culture, it is argued, is what makes us human, a distinctive species. It is the ability to cultivate that space between the ears and around the heart that sets us apart from other animals.

Inherent in this description of culture as cultivation is an assumption that the ground is fertile for culture to develop, and for thousands, perhaps millions of years that was not so, yet suddenly it seemed to burst onto the scene, expressing itself in cave paintings, music playing, worship, ritual and storytelling. As desperate tribes of nomadic hunter-gathers became cultivators of land and settled into cities, the consolidation of cultures gathered pace.

Today culture touches every part of our lives and world. I have walked 7,000 km (4,375 miles) through 18 countries on walks for peace and I haven't yet come across one that does not have its own very strong culture in food, language, music, dress, art, drama, religion, traditions, stories and special sites, national sporting heroes and so on. With the advent of film, television and the internet, we have seen trends towards a globalization of culture, and many countries struggle to keep their cultural identity intact because it is so important to the notion of identity, be that regional, ethnic or national. Why?

I would suggest that culture gives us roots, a sense of belonging, and answers the question of where we came from. Just as a family home has its own culture – mum's cooking, dad's chair, favourite songs, special photos, favourite clothes, family traditions – they all make us who we are and culture gives us identity.

Of course, we cannot expect every family to have exactly the same culture. But rather than being threatened by difference, we should see that our communities are stronger where cultural difference is allowed to flourish for the benefit of all.

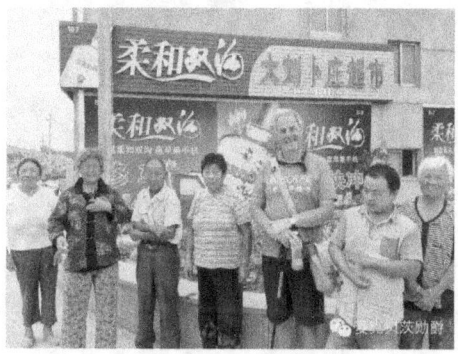 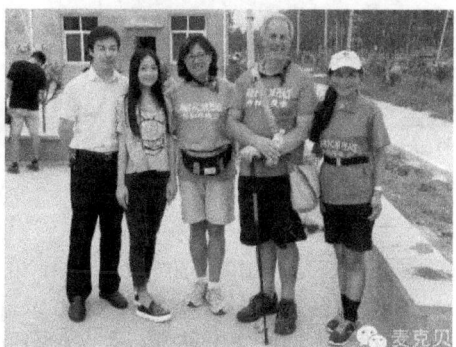

Left: Meeting a group of elderly people.
Right: Lord and Lady Bates, Madame Zhang and two young supporters from Huai'an.

That is not always the case. Our news is filled with wars and conflicts happening all around the world. So what has gone wrong? My suggestion is that disputes begin at a cultural level. They begin by suggesting that one nation's culture is the dominant one and that all others are lesser. On my walks, when I speak to people from different countries, I am struck by how they all believe that their people are the most friendly, their food is the most delicious, their ancient leaders are the most heroic or wise, their music is the most melodic, their fighting men are the most courageous, their religion is the most true, their scenery is the most spectacular and so on.

Culture, as I have said, goes to the heart of our human identity, so when people seek to devalue our culture or replace our culture with their own, they are seeking to devalue or remove our identity, and that provokes a hostile reaction. To illustrate: if you criticize the cooking of your best friend's mother, see how long you will survive as their 'best friend'.

Let me try and explain this another way. We all begin life with the same hardware and operating system, then, through family, culture and education, we gradually load on different programmes. My computer, with all its files, photos, music, emails, programmes and apps, will be unlike any other, but it can connect with any other because the underlying operating system allows it to and encourages it to. Culture is about communicating, and the more we share culture out of mutual respect, the more we communicate. The more we communicate, the less we distrust and the more we respect and understand. The more we have trust and understanding as the basis of human relations, the less likely we are to have conflict. Hence, culture connects and the more we cultivate it, the more we will harvest peace.

URL http://www.walkforpeace.eu/20150911-2/

September 12 Day 48

Wei Shen Mo – Walk for Peace

Huai'an, Jiangsu Province
A Day Off
Donated today: £0.00 / ¥91.00
Total donations: £3,953.31 and ¥106,666.31

As I walk from Beijing to Hangzhou, the most frequent comment I get is *Wei shen mo*? or 'Why?' It is a straightforward question, but the answers quickly exhaust my limited Chinese vocabulary, so let me try to explain in English.

Why walk? When I was a young boy, I had a map on my bedroom wall and I would imagine how I might walk around the world one day. It was a childhood dream, but it wasn't until I was asked by a group of young people in 2009 whom I was encouraging to pursue their dreams why I hadn't pursued mine, that I began to step out. I quickly realized that at the age of nearly fifty, I couldn't walk without a clear and compelling purpose. That is because as you get older your body may be weaker but your mind gets stronger. I decided that my purpose would be peace. I also found that when I walked, we could use that as a means to raise money for charities. I have now undertaken major walks every year since 2011 with the support of my wife, Xuelin, and have covered over 8,000 km (5,000 miles) in 18 countries, raising over £120,000 for charitable causes.

Why peace? There needed to be a strong enough reason for me to walk, and my passion is peace. Our TV news screens and history books are filled with examples of the catastrophic effects when people seek to resolve their differences not through dialogue but through violence. I recall seeing documentary pictures in black and white film of men marching off to war, and I wondered what would it take for men to march for peace instead. What would it be like if young men heroically marched off not to die for their country but to live for the world? I still haven't found answers, but I have found a cause and that cause is peace.

Why China? This is a special year as we mark the 70th anniversary of the end of World War II, the most devastating war in human history. China suffered greatly in that war, and the original plan was to walk from Beijing to Nanjing to recognize that terrible suffering. It is also the first Year of UK–China Cultural Exchange, where we recognize the way in which culture – be it sport, education, fashion or tea – enriches the modern relations between our two countries. Finally, the decision to start the walk in Beijing and end in Hangzhou was because Hangzhou is the home city of Xuelin. As someone observed, 'Michael is walking from Beijing to Nanjing for peace and from Nanjing to Hangzhou for love.' Not a bad summary.

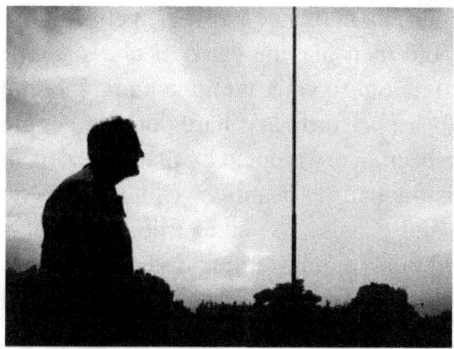
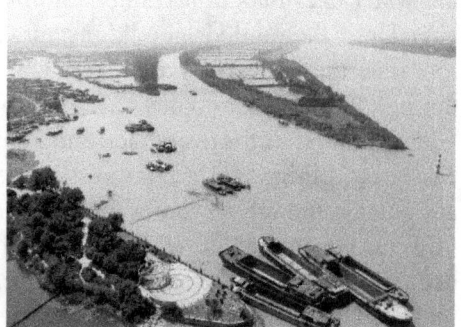
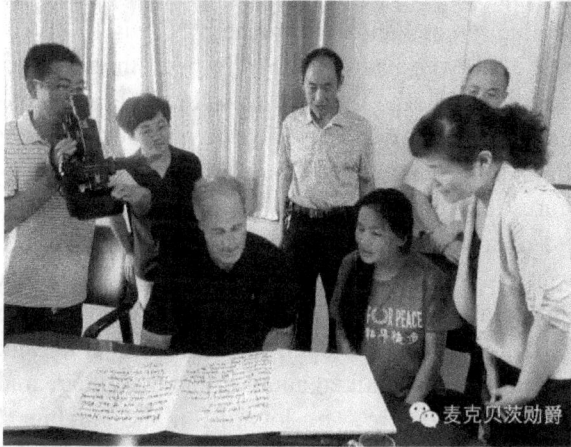
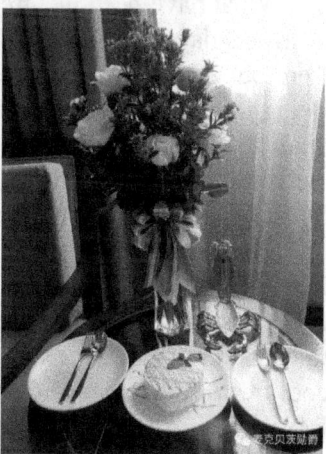

Top left: sunset in Huai'an. Top right: Hongzehu Lake.
Bottom left: Official meeting in Huai'an. Bottom rght: A welcome treat.

Which charity are you supporting this year? Xuelin and I are delighted to be working closely with the Red Cross Society of China. The Red Cross in China is one of the largest volunteer organizations in the world, with over two million people in China who regularly give of their time to support their work, undertaking First Aid training, giving blood donations, helping struggling families financially and providing emergency response to disasters. With the Red Cross, we have identified two projects in Jiangsu Province, which we will be supporting with donations raised on the walk: Hope House school in Pizhou, which provides support for children with physical and mental disabilities, and Suqian Child Welfare Institute, which cares for orphaned children with disabilities. We have visited both schools on the walk and been impressed by the marvellous work they are doing. So far we have raised 160,000 yuan from over 500 donations, and we would love this figure to reach 500,000 yuan by the time we reach Hangzhou on October 6.

What has impressed you most on your walk? First, I have been struck by the warmth and kindness of the Chinese people we have met along the way: shepherds minding their flocks of sheep, small traders selling pomegranates, women harvesting water chestnuts in floating bathtubs, road maintenance workers, petrol pump attendants, the outdoor noodle restaurant, old men playing cards or chess by the roadside, the Red Cross volunteers who come out to walk with me and guide me through their city or county safely. It is invariably ordinary, hardworking people with whom I come into contact, and I have been overwhelmed by that experience. The second thing that has impressed me is the natural beauty of China once you get outside the city. The tree-lined rivers and canals. The lakes filled with lotus flowers. The mountains of Tai'an. The third thing that has impressed me most has been the quality of the surface of the roads. I have walked on a lot of roads, and those in China are as good as or better than any I have walked on in Europe.

What have been the greatest challenges you have faced so far? So far, after nearly 50 days, we have reached Huai'an in Jiangsu Province, which is 1,100 km from our start point. The greatest challenge has undoubtedly been the weather. Being from the UK, I am used to rain but not to the sun. It has been very hot and humid, so much so that on a number of days we simply had to abandon walking and rest in the shade between 11 am and 3 pm. I am 54 years old and not especially fit, so walking in these temperatures just drains every bit of energy I have.

What have been your most memorable experiences? I can think of many in the Taishan Mountains. I walked through a small village called Xingjiatun. There were a group of people sitting around a large old tree and they invited me to come and join them. I sat under a tree that was over 500 years old and drank cool fresh water from a 700-year-old well. We talked about life in the village and I exchanged stories about life in London. There were lots of fun and laughter. I was told that I was the first Westerner to visit their village in living memory by one of the village elders, who was himself 95 years old and a veteran of World War II. We connected through pictures of family and food. Then there was time for photographs and then, as if it was as natural as drawing water up from the old well, villagers opened their smartphones and started scanning WeChat bar codes with us so that we could exchange the pictures online. It was a picture of a truly global village of which we are all part, not by virtue of our nationality but because of our humanity.

URL http://www.walkforpeace.eu/day-48-wei-shern-mo-walk-for-peace/

September 13 Day 49

'In Vogue' Xuyi

Route: Xuyixian, Huai'an, Jiangsu Province
– Tianchang, Chuzhou, Anhui Province
Walked today: 21.50 miles / 34.60 km
Total walked: 751.80 miles / 1,210.60 km
Donated today: £113.64 / ¥0.00
Total donations: £4,066.95 and ¥106,666.31

Vogue means 'style' in French and it is the name of the most famous fashion magazine in the world. It was founded in 1892 in America but now has 26 global editions including *Vogue China*. It has given rise to an idiom in English of being 'in vogue', meaning highly fashionable. Why am I telling you this? Well, today is a day off and I am staying in the Vogue Hotel in Xuyi on the southern edge of Hongzehu Lake and so I am literally 'in Vogue', and my children would add, 'probably for the first and certainly for the last time in my life'.

The Red Cross volunteers, knowing that I had a hard stretch travelling down from Huai'an and needed to recover for the push to Nanjing, found us a perfect hotel with splendid views across the vast lake. The hotel staff could not have been more kind in their care for us. I was astonished how much they knew about my walk from Beijing. This interest seemed to come from a genuine appreciation that someone would come to walk for peace in their country. They didn't want to charge us for our room, but Xuelin patiently explained that we wanted to personally cover all our accommodation and travel costs on the walk; however, they would be welcome to make a contribution to the Red Cross. We were dumbfounded when overnight they decided to raise funds for the projects we are supporting (Hope House, Pizhou and Suqian Institute) and presented Xuelin and me with a cheque to the Red Cross for 20,000 yuan (£2,000).

It is very much part of Chinese culture to 'want to please' – it is drawn deep from their Confucian roots. I can't speak for others from the West, but I find our culture is more about aiming to 'please yourself', rather than going out of your way to 'please others'. An example would be that the chef at the Vogue Hotel wanted to try and find food to serve that his British guest might appreciate – at breakfast, I was served haggis, a traditional Scottish dish made of lamb and oats, and a knife and fork to eat it with, rather than chopsticks. I am not an expert on haggis but this tasted as perfect as any I have had in Scotland.

For some reason, I could never imagine a hotel in Britain serving up Chinese noodles and dumplings with chopsticks for a Chinese walker. The greatest phrase in British hospitality would be to tell the guest where everything is and tell them to help themselves and to 'let them know if there is anything they need'. I have no doubt that many British hotels, if a Chinese guest signed in and said, 'Would there be any chance of having Chinese dumplings with chopsticks?', would do their very best to try and accommodate the request, but they wouldn't initiate the offer for fear of not giving the guest the freedom to choose or, worse still, appearing to presume what the guest would like.

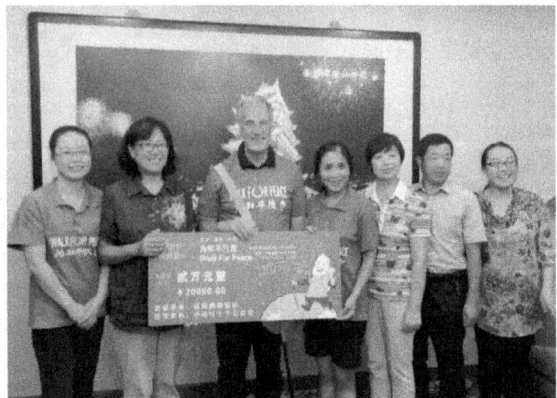
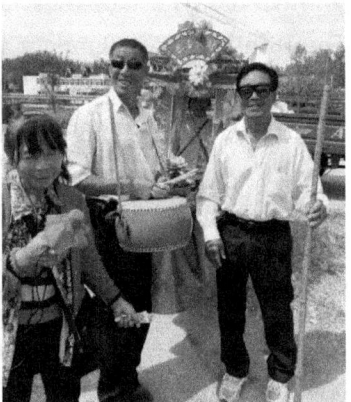
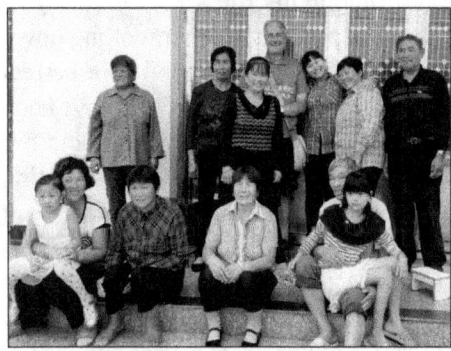
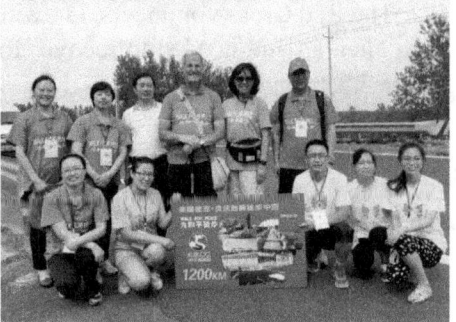

Top left: The hotel staff presenting Lord Bates with a cheque to the Red Cross.
Top right: Meeting performers in Xuyi. Bottom left: Meeting local people in Xuyi.
Bottom right: Milestone marking 1,200 km of the walk.

Xuelin and I discussed the 'haggis' incident quite a bit and she made the point that in Chinese culture it is not totally true to say that they only want to please; it is just that they have found that they get a greater pleasure from putting others first. I then began to think of my mother, who is a wonderful hostess and simply cannot do enough for guests. She will seldom sit at the table and take time to eat, because she will be in the kitchen preparing the next course or washing up. We would often plead with her as a family to sit down and enjoy the meal, to leave the cooking and the washing up to us, but she would say that serving us and guests was something that gives her the greatest pleasure.

Perhaps we are not that far apart after all. Perhaps if we all realized that there is a happiness and satisfaction in giving and serving that can never be attained in taking or helping ourselves, then 'putting others first' might become 'in vogue' and our world might be a better more humane place.

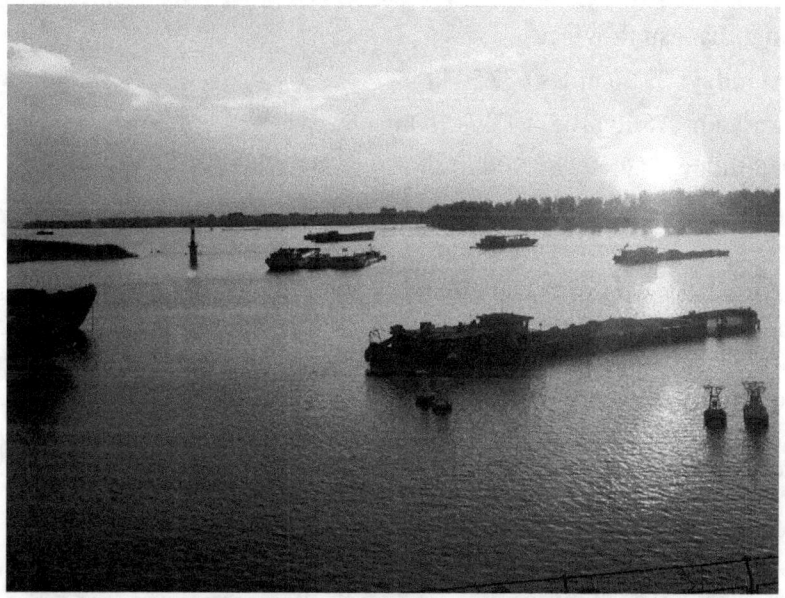

Sunset on Hongzehu Lake.

Thank you again, Vogue Hotel, Xuyi, for your generosity of spirit, which blessed us, and we hope that it will return to bless you twice over.

URL http://www.walkforpeace.eu/day-49-in-vogue-xuyi/

September 14 Day 50

Sinopec, 1,200 km and Jane Austen

Route: G205 Highway, T'ianchang, Anhui Province
– Nanjing, Jiangsu Province
Walked today: 23.30 miles / 37.50 km
Total walked: 775.10 miles / 1,248.10 km
Donated today: £50.00 / ¥0.00
Total donations: £4,116.95 and ¥106,666.31

One very good group of friends we have enjoyed meeting along the long S205 have been the petrol forecourt attendants at the Sinopec petrol stations. They are always such a cheerful group of young people in their smart blue uniforms, who come out to the edge of the forecourt to take pictures of us passing by. It is a strong network, as information quickly passes from one petrol station to the next that we are on our way.

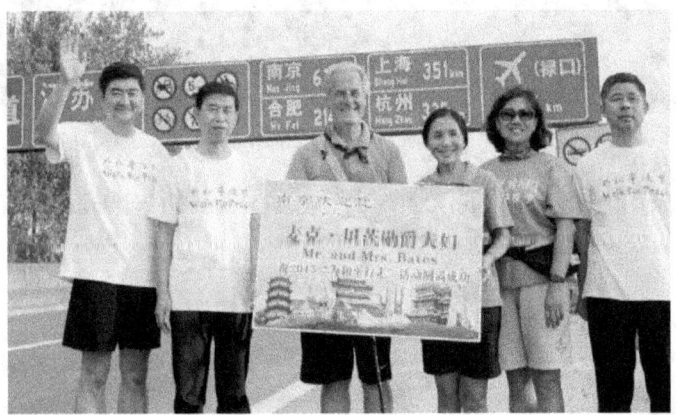

Supporters along the S205.

It is a basic rule of walking never to pass a WC (toilet) without paying a visit. I try to observe this rule on my walks and then feel guilty for using the WC without buying something from the shop, so I go in for some water or iced tea. As a result, I have become a bit of a specialist on petrol station WCs. China is a wonderful place and has so much going for it, but I am still struggling to come to terms with going to the WC in a long communal squat trough. Normally, Xuelin, knowing of my Western sensitivities, will stand guard over the door to give me a bit of space, but today even she wasn't able to hold off about 20 men who arrived off a bus trip. They were all smoking and there was no elbow room. I have said too much. Quickly moving on... as I did...

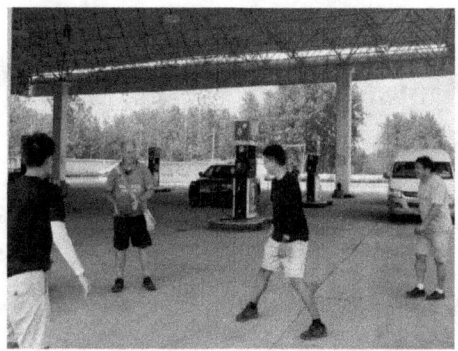 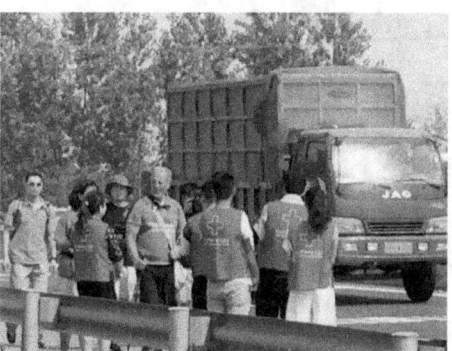

Left: Playing basketball at a gas station. Right: Getting closer to Nanjing.

Today was a very special day for a number of reasons. First, we marked 1,200 km (750 miles) on the walk. Second, we had to say farewell to our volunteers from Huai'an, who had been with us for the past week and done such a great job. Third, it was the 50th day of the walk. Fourth, we crossed our fourth province in China on the walk so far, Anhui, in a day. Fifth, we finished at a sign over the S205 that showed for the first time 'Hangzhou – 335 km', our destination point. Sixth, we arrived into the Nanjing City area and were greeted by our new Red Cross volunteers, who would be with us for the next week.

It is fast approaching two months since we set off from Beijing and over the past few days I have noticed the seasons beginning to change. The crops in the field are less bright green and are turning a mellow yellow. The leaves are beginning to fall from the trees. It is a poetic time of year, a time of reflection on the summer of opportunities past. Yet, with the closing thoughts of the current year, there are just the smallest hints of hopes and dreams for next spring, should we make it through the winter. I love poetry and literature and wish that I could be a poet or an author, but know this is a great talent given to but a favoured few, one of whom is Jane Austen.

Jane Austen (1775–1817) was one of our greatest English novelists, most noted for her classic brooding love stories, *Pride and Prejudice* and *Sense and Sensibility*, but in her first published and lesser-known work, *Persuasion*, she uses the lines below to describe autumn. Having slightly lowered the tone of this blog by delving too deeply into the hidden world of the roadside bog (WC), I will try to conclude on more fragrant terms with an extract from *Persuasion*:

> 'Her pleasure in the walk must arise from the exercise and the day, from the view of the last smiles of the year upon the tawny leaves and withered hedges, and from repeating to herself some few of the thousand poetical descriptions extant of autumn – that season of peculiar and inexhaustible influence on the mind of taste and tenderness – that season which has drawn from every poet worthy of being read some attempt at description, or some lines of feeling.'

URL http://www.walkforpeace.eu/day-50-sinopec-welcome/

September 15 Day 51

Hope, Haircuts and Singing Horses

Nanjing, Jiangsu Province

A Day Off

Donated today: £0.00 / ¥0.00

Total donations: £4,116.95 and ¥106,666.31

It was a rest day in Liuhe, about 40 km north of Nanjing. It has been a busy day with a lot to pack into the blog post, so let me get started.

We have had a documentary team with us since Beijing but today the director visited and wanted to have a substantial sit-down interview with Xuelin and me. We set aside an hour, but it lasted one hour and 30 minutes. The real pressure was on Xuelin, who had to interpret the questions and the answers.

One area that the director was keen to press us on was what happens when 'Walk for Peace' comes up against militarism, be it in a parade or an exhibition? I responded by saying you respect it because wars and warriors are the most honoured and sacred elements of all human tribal societies. Every tribal grouping believes its warriors are the most courageous, fearless and heroic. Every tribal grouping believes its wars and causes are always the most just. Every tribal grouping believes its enemies are evil, a threat to their way of life and utterly unreasonable. I believe that about Britain. I expect they believe that about China. Indeed, I expect all 196 member states of the UN and numerous other military movements will believe that about their warriors and their causes.

This answer doesn't quite seem to satisfy, as the point is well made that China, having been humiliated by the Japanese in World War II, now understandably wishes to make a statement that it is now of a size and power such that it would never allow this to happen again. We agree that when peace goes up against the military, peace will always look weak and cowardly and war will always look strong and courageous. To try and change that, you need to undo millions of years of human tribal hard-wiring that sees violence as the means to resolving conflicts. 'So is walking for peace always going to fail?' 'No,' I answered. 'I have hope ...'

After a heavy interview, I went for a haircut. The hairdresser was just around the corner from the hotel and had started in business a few months earlier. I have written before about my deep affection for those who step out in business on their own, so I wanted to try and help with advice about how to get customers. He wanted to talk with me about how a Chinese hairdresser can do a good haircut for Westerners because their hair is soft and thin (in my case, very thin) but the Chinese found it very difficult to give a good haircut to a Westerner because the hair is thicker and strong.

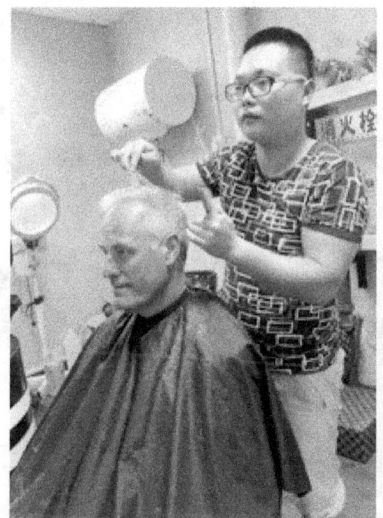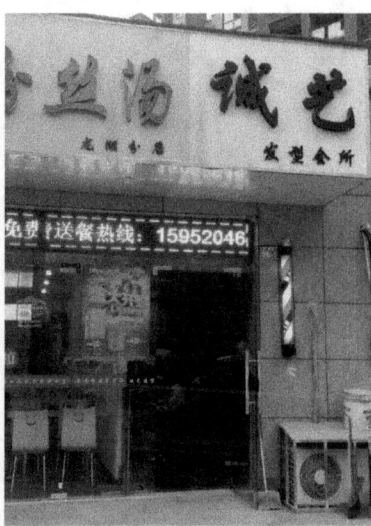

Left: At the barber's. Right: Barber's shop in Liuhe.

I was talking so much (through Xuelin translating again) that I forgot to explain what style I wanted, and what seemed to be taking shape was a kind of Kim Jong-un bouffant. I immediately stopped the business consulting and switched to hair, and we managed to get it back to a Western haircut with Chinese characteristics! Xuelin and female members of the team seemed to like it, so I left him a 50-yuan tip. Xuelin was horrified at my extravagance with the tip and immediately went off the haircut, saying she would expect him to cure my bald patch for that price. Ouch!

Back in the hotel room, on my own, I was pleased to discover the TV had the BBC World Service channel. On screen was an episode of 'Hard Talk', in which Stephen Sackur was interviewing Aref Ali Nayed, the Libyan Ambassador to the United Arab Emirates and a key player in the post-Gaddafi internal conflict negotiations. In that impatient and slightly sneering way in which the British and Americans often interview people for whom English is not their first language, the host quoted back to Aref Ali Nayed his remarks when last on the programme, in which he said in the wake of the Arab Spring that 'Libya was now on a path to peace, prosperity, and democracy …'. Sackur pressed him with 'Why did you get it so wrong?' His reply was, 'I always have hope …'.

The story is told of a prisoner about to be executed who tells the king that he can teach his prize horse to sing for his birthday in nine months' time. Intrigued, the king postpones his execution and the prisoner sets to work. After three months, his cellmate says, 'This is stupid. You know the horse can't sing.' 'Okay,' replies the prisoner, 'but if I didn't say I could do it, I would have been dead three months ago, and who knows, over the next six months, the king may die, the horse may die, or, …'. 'Or what?' asks the cellmate. 'Or the horse might sing.' Hope keeps us alive …

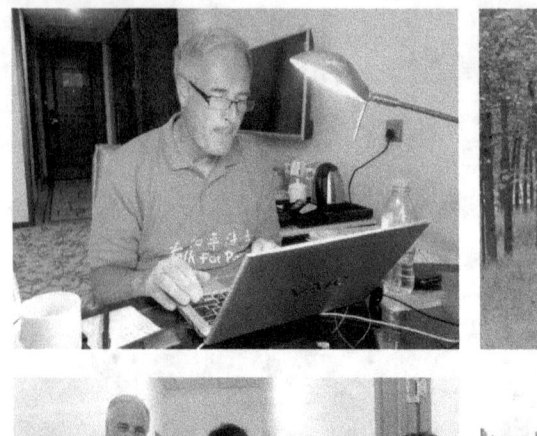
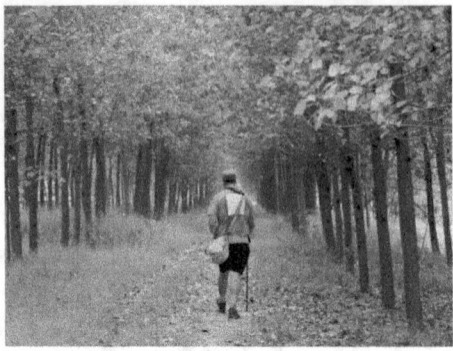
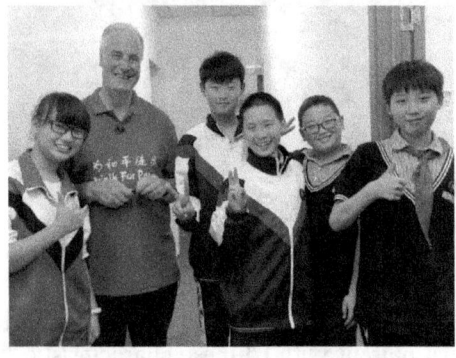
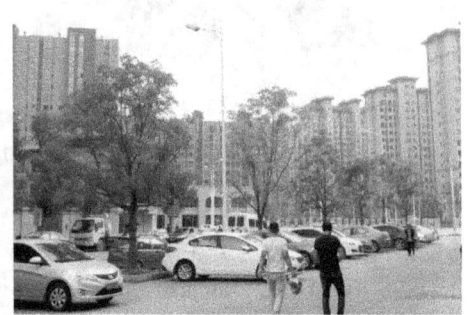

Top left: Lord Bates working on his blog. Top right: Taking a stroll during a rest day.
Bottom left: Lord Bates with students in Liuhe. Bottom right: Residential buildings in Liuhe.

I guess Ambassador Aref Ali Nayed and I are on the same page … so when you are scrolling through your social media news feed and see a phenomenal video from the Libyan desert of a horse singing *Give Peace a Chance*, remember you read it here first.

URL http://www.walkforpeace.eu/day-51-hope-haircuts-and-heroes/

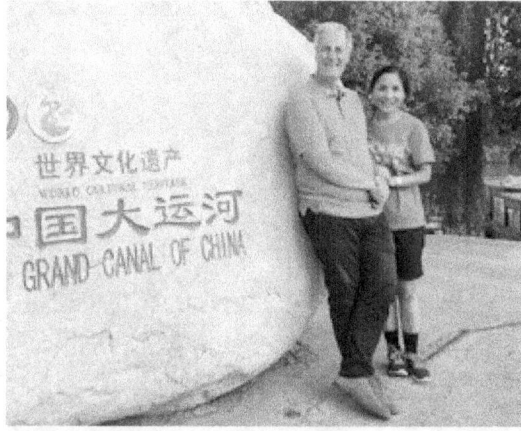
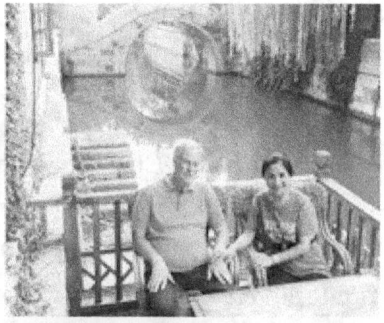
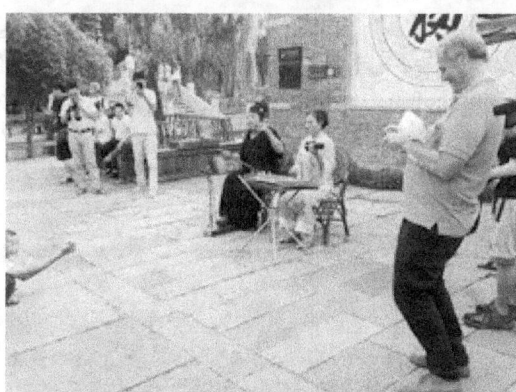
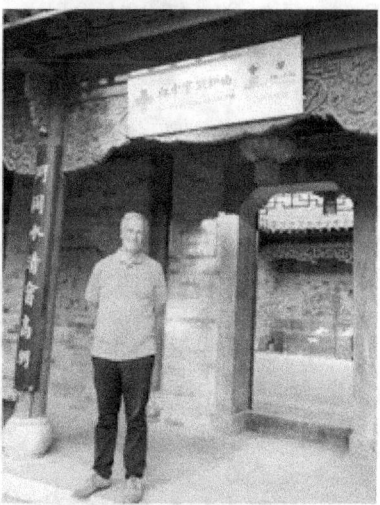
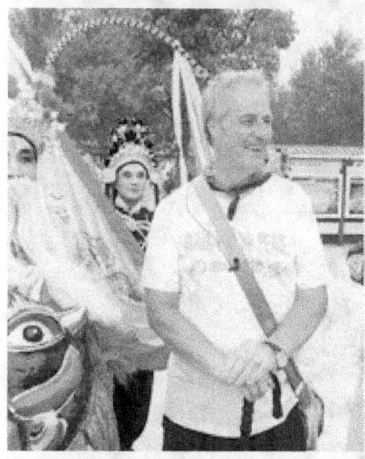
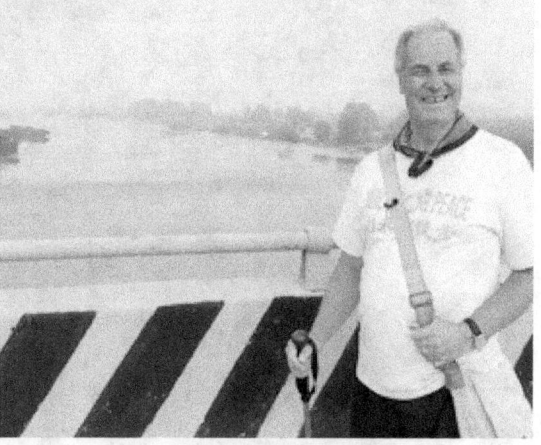

Top left: Lord Bates in the ancient city of Taier, 'Grand Canal';
top right: enjoying the ancient city of beauty at the Grand Canal in China;
centre left: the rich cultural atmosphere of the ancient city;
centre right: there are Red Cross ambulance stations in most of China's scenic spots;
bottom left: an encounter with villagers rehearsing the local folk art bamboo circus;
bottom right: over the canal bridge, bidding farewell to Shandong and departuring to Jiangsu

September 16 Day 52

Nanjing in Sight

Route: Tianchang, Chuzhou, Anhui Province
– Liuhe District, Nanjing, Jiangsu Province
Walked today: 23.60 miles / 37.90 km
Total walked: 798.70 miles / 1,286.00 km
Donated today: £0.00 / ¥0.00
Total donations: £4,116.95 and ¥106,666.31

Back on the road again, but not the S205, which is undergoing repairs, so I was directed to follow the X203. I am so glad we did. It was a beautiful road full of interesting twists and turns, changes in scenery and small towns and villages to walk through. There was a noticeable increase in affluence off the main highway. This was a commuter zone for Nanjing, where families could enjoy gentle hills, lakes and clear blue skies away from the metropolis –if they could afford it, that is.

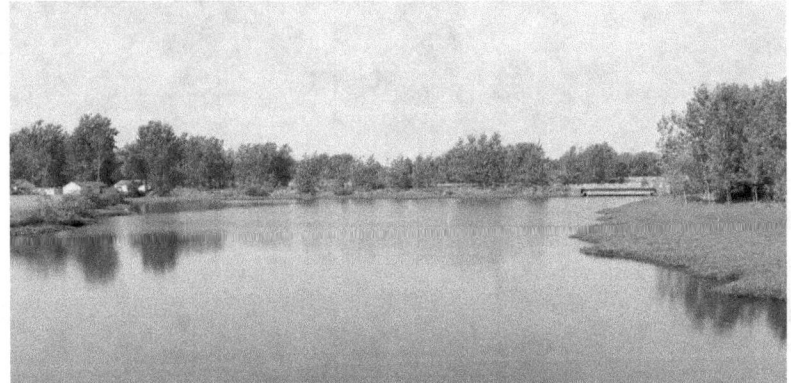

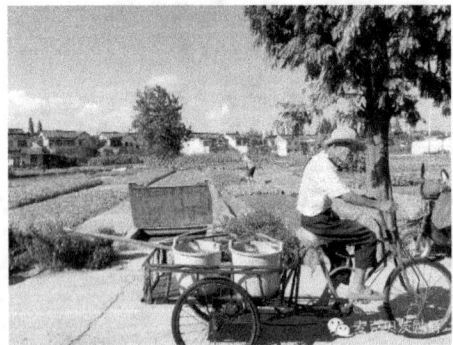
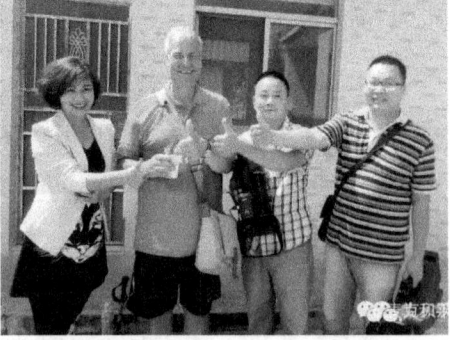

Top: Scenery on the X203. Left: Farmer on his tricycle cart. Right: Lord Bates in Liuhe.

The weather was beginning to turn now. After the summer growth, the crops were being collected in for harvest. It seemed that every available roadside space was spread with wheat being gently raked to dry in the sun before being packed in sacks and sent to market. There is a beauty and simplicity about rural life, especially arable crops. There are obvious seasons. You start at first light and finish when the sun goes down. You work hard in good weather and learn to rest in bad weather. You plant a seed, add sun and water, let nature take its course and then reap a harvest. I am sure that there is more to it than that, but sometimes modern life in the cities can be so complex because we lose sight of what we are doing and why. With modern communications and air-conditioned offices, work is 24/7 and 365 days a year. In return, we seem at times unable to see any evidence of a harvest in return for our labours.

After a serene walk, the best since my walk along the Pomegranate Way, I arrived back at the hotel and opened my email. As usual, a whole wave of complexity flooded into my Inbox from back home. Everything was urgent, decisions needed to be taken in hours. I worked long into the morning to respond and when the last email was sent, I drifted off to sleep, my laptop still open, with envious thoughts of those farmers along the X203.

URL http://www.walkforpeace.eu/day-52-nanjing-in-sight/

September 17 Day 53

'Bridge over the River Yangtze'

Route: Liuhe District – North Yangtze River Bridge, Nanjing
Walked today: 19.80 miles / 31.80 km
Total walked: 818.50 miles / 1,317.80 km
Donated today: £0.00 / ¥51,348.50
Total donations: £4,116.95 and ¥158,014.81

On September 17 (Day 53, Thursday) we set off from Liuhe in the direction of Nanjing. We were not going to cross the Yangtze River today. I was a bit disappointed, as I always get a burst of energy when there is a major city to arrive in. As always, there was a reason for stopping short of the bridge over the River Yangtze: The bridge has a very special significance in Chinese history and we were to cross it at 10 am on Friday, 18 September – not before (for reasons which I will explain tomorrow).

The additional reason to delay was that we were to be joined by Madam Hao (Linna), who is Vice Chairman of the Red Cross Society in China and a great friend and supporter of our walk. Madam Hao was also bringing with her Wang

Jiyan, who is a very famous and successful businessman and founder of Phoenix Satellite TV. It was hinted by Madam Zhang (Ming) that he may have some good news for us on the fundraising side.

Xuelin reminded me over breakfast that I tend to overfocus on the challenge of the walk and forget its wider mission. We are here to raise funds for important causes through the Red Cross, such as Hope House; we are here to spread the message of peace and reconciliation as we mark the 70th anniversary of the end of World War II; we are here to draw attention to the first Year of the UK–China Cultural Exchange.

This wider mission means that we do not always take the most direct route for the walk; that we need to take time to explain our mission to potential donors; that I need to keep my blogs, social media sites up to date; that I need to take time to talk to the journalists and the media and that I need to engage with the young Red Cross Volunteers from each town/city/district who come out and join me for a few hours on the walk as we pass through their area.

I confess that I find the walking itself enough of a challenge at age 54, but I am grateful for Xuelin reminding me that it is not the walk itself but the mission that is the purpose, and the walk is a means to fulfilling that purpose. 'Never lose sight of the mission' was her message. As I walked, I recalled that famous scene from the epic movie, *Bridge over the River Kwai*, directed by David Lean…

The movie is about the use of British prisoners of war by Japanese captors to construct a bridge over a river on the Burma–Siam (Thailand) railway, which is being built to bring supplies and reinforcements to the Japanese front line in the war. The British prisoners are under the 'command' of Lieutenant Colonel Nicholson, played by Alec Guinness. They are being appallingly treated by their captors, dying of disease and malnutrition. In order to secure better treatment and conditions for his men, he agrees to build the best bridge he can.

The British prisoners perform an incredible feat of engineering in building the bridge, earning the respect even of their Japanese captors. The closing scene is of Colonel Nicholson looking with immense pride at the finished bridge and admiring the extraordinary work of his men in creating it. The train whistle blows in the distance as the first Japanese troop train is approaching to cross the new bridge. Then Nicholson notices wires leading to explosives that have been placed there by British and American special forces who have been tasked with destroying the bridge and the train that is about to cross it.

Rather than do his best to support the special forces by concealing their plan to blow the bridge, Nicholson alerts the Japanese guards and tries to stop them. To him, the bridge represents a way of protecting his men from the brutal and inhumane treatment of their captors and maintaining the morale of the prisoners he is responsible for. It has given them purpose and pride in the darkness of their captivity. Yet, in doing so, Nicholson has lost sight of the greater mission – to defeat the enemy.

It is a classic human dilemma, brilliantly exposed by David Lean. In the final scene, Nicholson comes to his senses and, fatally wounded, detonates the explosives on the bridge himself.

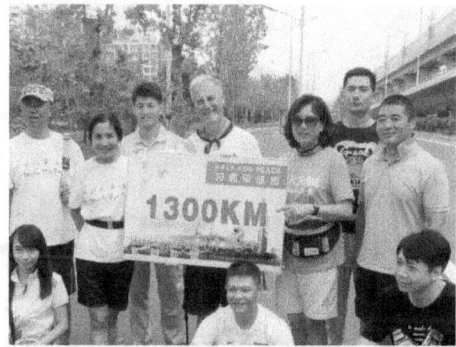
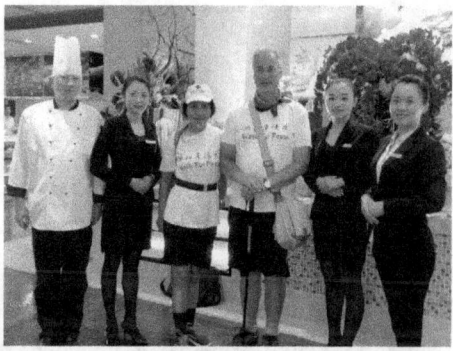
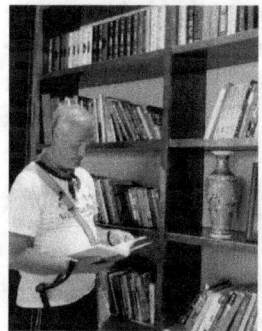
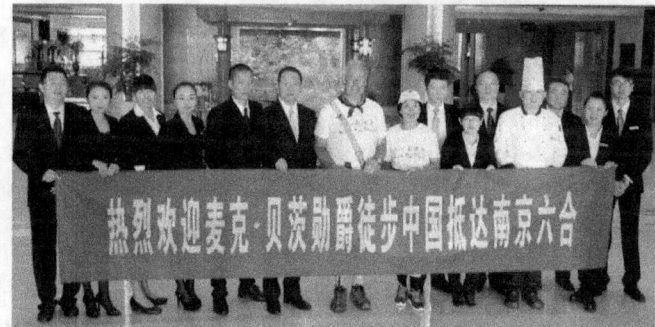

Top left: Milestone marking 1,300 km of the walk.
Top right: Lord and Lady Bates with the staff of the hotel in Liuhe.
Bottom left: Browsing the bookshelves in Liuhe.
Bottom right: Welcoming committee in Liuhe District, Nanjing.

To invoke the memory of the *Bridge over the River Kwai* in order to explain why we delayed our crossing of the bridge over the River Yangtze is, of course, ridiculous, but it is a timely reminder to me that in 'what' we are doing we must never lose sight of 'why' we are doing it.

URL http://www.walkforpeace.eu/day-53-bridge-over-the-river-yangtze/

September 18 Day 54

Crossing a Bridge of History

Route: towards the Yangtze River Bridge, Nanjing
Walked today: 8.80 miles / 14.20 km
Total walked: 827.30 miles / 1,332.00 km
Donated today: £0.00 / ¥1,000.00
Total donations: £4,116.95 and ¥159,014.81

We set off from north Nanjing to walk towards the Yangtze River bridge, revived by my first visit in weeks to a Starbucks coffee shop. There was a much larger group than usual joining us for the crossing of this iconic bridge. Added significance was given to the walk as we timed our departure so that we arrived on the Bridge at 10 am on Friday, 18 September. This is a moment of national reflection, as it marks the anniversary of the Japanese invasion of China in 1931. The bridge is a huge structure carrying cars and also a railway, but the vast natural expanse of the Yangtze River keeps the man-made structure strangely in proportion. The bridge is a symbol of national pride, as it was the first that China built itself. Before that, infrastructure had normally been built and partly funded by the Soviet Union. It was opened in 1968 and Xuelin recalls her father bringing her to see the 'wonder of the modern world' and having her picture taken there when she was eight years old. We try to find the exact spot to recreate the photo.

Enormous 'workers' struggle' sculptures guard the four corners of the bridge. The bridge carries 80,000 vehicles a day but there is also narrow footpath in each direction, which the few pedestrians must share with the many motorscooters. It is not for the faint-hearted – the hand rails on the side of the bridge don't seem that high, and one bump from a passing scooter might send you over the edge. There was, therefore, some relief when the air-raid sirens sound three times to signal the build-up to the 10 am moment of observance, and the traffic stops. We paused for reflection. A few moments later and the horns were sounding again and we were being bumped from side to side of the footpath by the scooters and bikes.

History in China, as elsewhere, is not perfectly coherent. I asked why it was that we were marking 1931 as the start of the Japanese invasion rather than 1937, the year to which other exhibitions and memorials refer. It was explained that the war against the Japanese aggression began in 1937 but the Japanese invasion happened in 1931.

This was still not very clear to me, but I didn't want my hosts to feel un-comfortable and realized that the intervening six years may be a 'missing chunk' from Chinese history. It is a bit like trying to find the chapter in British history textbooks on the abdication of King Edward VIII and his visits to Adolf Hitler as the Duke of Windsor in the 1930s … there's a tendency to say 'Let's not go there', but rather get to Winston Churchill and the Battle of Britain as quickly as possible.

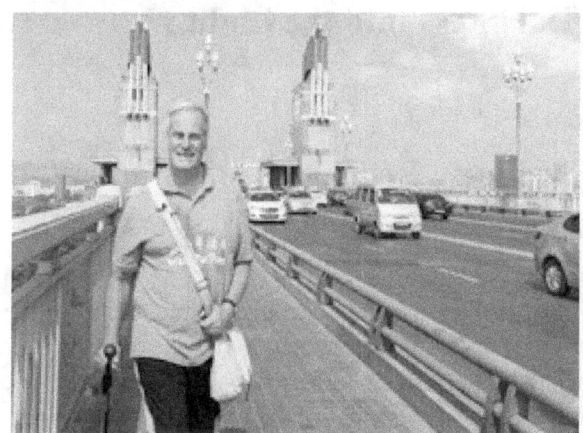 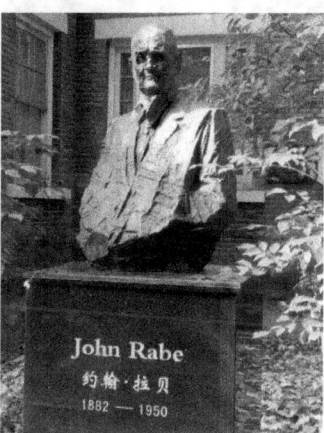

Left: Crossing the Nanjing Yangtze River bridge. Right: Bust of John Rabe.

Later research in history, just for the record, told me that, in the early days of the war, China was a divided country. Chiang Kai-shek had formed a nationalist Government – the Kuomintang (KMT) – but his dictatorial regime was opposed by Mao Zedong's Communists (Communist Party of China, or CPC). Civil War erupted between the Communists and Nationalists – the period of Mao's 'Long March' – after the CPC was expelled from the KMT-led government.

In 1931, Japan, spotting the internal Chinese distraction, made a grab for the northeast region of China called Manchuria. The KMT official strategy was to secure control of China against its internal enemy (CPC) first. This meant the Japanese met virtually no resistance to their invasion and gradually expanded from Manchuria to Shanghai and Taiwan. It wasn't until pressure from Stalin and Western democracies on the KMT and CPC to unite and fight back against Japan, which resulted in the Xi'an Agreement in 1937, that the war against the Japanese occupation began.

The war with Japan ended on VJ Day in 1945, in which the CPC-KMT China were allied with Russia, Britain and America. Not long after the end of WWII and the defeat of Japan, the agreement that had ended the Chinese civil war in 1937 unravelled. The civil war between the KMT and CPC resumed but the now vastly superior strength of the CPC People's Liberation Army led to defeat for the KMT in 1949. The CPC declared the People's Republic of China on October 1, 1949. The KMT was forced to retreat to Taiwan, along with around 2 million of its members. Today, the CPC is a ruling Party in the People's Republic of China and the KMT is the largest part of the ruling government in Taiwan (which they call the Republic of China), which is known as part of China.

URL http://www.walkforpeace.eu/day-54-pause-for-thought-river-yangtze/

September 19 Day 55

Walking through the Darkness into the Light

Nanjing, Jiangsu Province
A Day Off
Donated today: £0.00 / ¥0.00
Total donations: £4,116.95 and ¥159,014.81

It was our first full day in Nanjing. Nanjing is known throughout the world for the atrocities that happened here in what has become known as the 'Rape of Nanking'. Following its capture by invading imperial Japanese troops on December 13, 1937, what can only be described as a mass 'slaughter of the innocents' took place.

In six weeks of madness, Japanese troops butchered about 300,000 unarmed men, women and children, with beheadings, shootings and the burial of people alive in mass graves. In addition, there were at least 20,000 recorded rapes. The horrific accounts are recorded in the Memorial Hall of the Victims of the Nanjing Massacre.

It was right that this memorial to the horror and inhumanity of war should be our first visit on a Walk for Peace. How can you possibly begin to teach about the value of peace until you have examined thoroughly the true cost of war?

The museum was built on a site that contained some of the mass graves. Like other museums of genocide around the world, such as Yad Vashem in Jerusalem, the architects have effectively used dark, subterranean spaces to convey the feeling that you are physically descending into the darkest places of humanity. In the Memorial Hall are etched the names of many of the victims. I looked at the names and thought of them not as iron characters listed on a wall but rather as sons, daughters, mothers, fathers...

This is what happens in war: people lose sight of the human value of a person. Once you cease to see someone as human first, a moral equivalent, then mass slaughter becomes as impersonal as the slaughter of animals in an abattoir. Victor Frankl, a survivor of the holocaust at Auschwitz, would explain that the German guards would strip new arrivals of all clothes, shave their heads, take their identity cards and tattoo a name on their arses. From then on, they were a number, not a name, and the evil became easier to commit.

I don't want to detail the atrocities recorded; suffice to say they were deeply disturbing, and if you wish to find out more of what went on, you can research online or visit for yourself. However, I do want to say something about how I felt. Truthfully angry! How could humans do this to other humans? It seems to me that evil is when we cease to have empathy, to show any feelings for the victims of our actions.

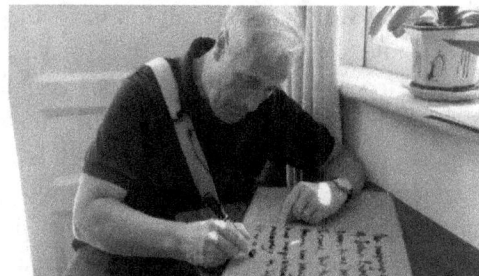

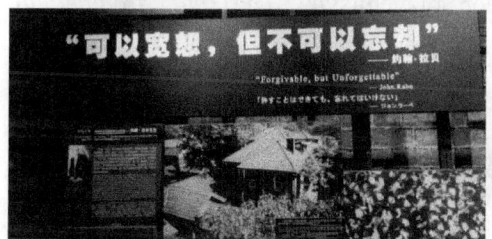

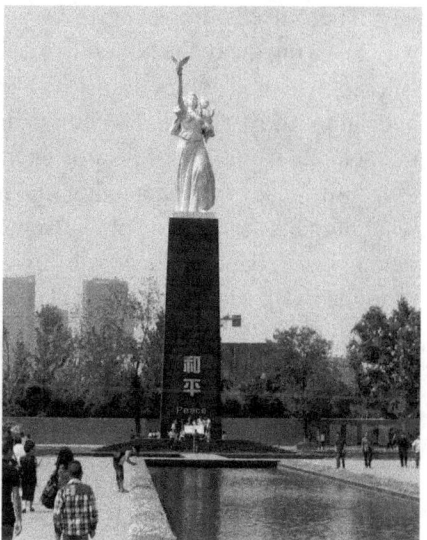

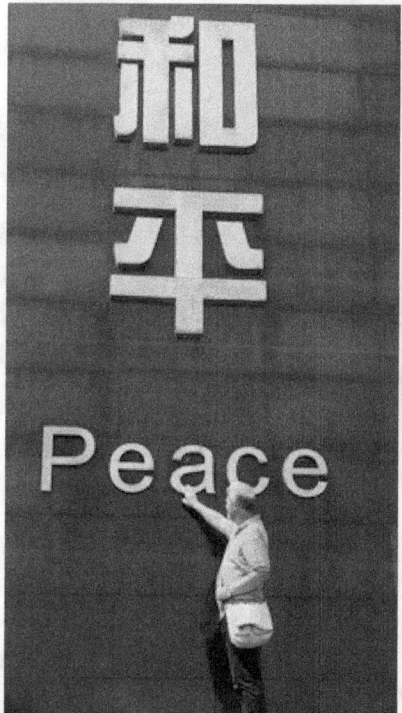

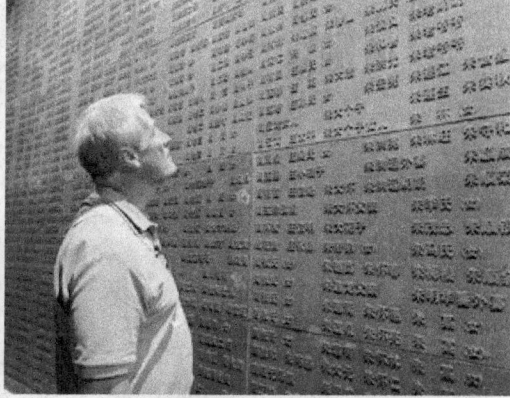

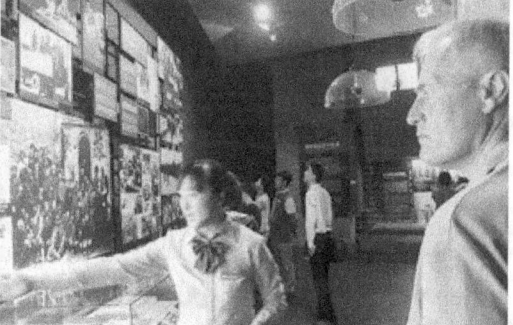

Top left: Lord Bates leaving a message in the visitors' book at the Memorial Hall.
Top right: Monument to Peace outside the Memorial Hall.
Middle left: 'Forgivable, but Unforgettable'
Bottom left and right: Visiting the Memorial Hall of the Victims of the Nanjing Massacre.

There needs, however, to be great care that we do not respond in the same way in taking away the humanity of the perpetrators of these crimes. The Japanese soldiers who had competitions with each other to see how many people they could behead in a day were no less human than those they were slaughtering. To say that this tells us what the soldiers of one nation are capable of is to miss the point and to run the risk of its happening again. The message of the museum is that this is what humans are capable of. Nelson Mandela said, 'When we dehumanize our opponents, we abandon the possibility of peacefully resolving our differences.' I was reminded also of the words of Alexander Solzhenitsyn in *The Gulag Archipelago*:

> 'Gradually it was disclosed to me that the line separating good and evil passes not through states, nor between classes, nor between political parties either – but right through every human heart – and through all human hearts. This line shifts. Inside us, it oscillates with the years. And even within hearts overwhelmed by evil, one small bridgehead of good is retained. And even in the best of all hearts, there remains … an un-uprooted small corner of evil.'

As if to underscore this, I came to one unexpected part of the exhibition dedicated to a German, John Rabe, who was the director of Siemens in China, which was headquartered in Nanjing in 1937, as it was then the capital of China. Seeing and being horrified at the first-hand account of the unfolding massacre in December 1937, Rabe opened his home to refugees – it quickly became home and refuge to 600 people. Then, with others, including American missionaries and academics, they proposed the establishment of an International Safety Zone for refugees in a 4-square-km area of the city.

Why were the Japanese willing even to consider a request from John Rabe? (Reread the Solzhenitsyn quote at this point.) Because, like Oscar Schindler in Poland, who saved thousands of Jews, Rabe was a member of the Nazi Party. Rabe had written to Adolf Hitler personally to draw his attention to what was happening and urge him to put pressure on Japan, a member of the Axis Powers (along with Italy). The Japanese reluctantly agreed to the request, and the Red Cross provided humanitarian aid to some 250,000 people in the Zone. These 250,000 people would have almost certainly been slaughtered along with others had the Zone not existed.

After the war was over, Rabe returned to Germany and was arrested by the British and denounced for his Nazi membership. He lost his permit to work in the British Zone. He then had to undergo an extensive denazification process, during which time he couldn't work and used up all his savings. Rabe and his family lived in a one-room apartment, kept going only by a monthly food parcel sent by the Communist Party officials in Nanjing. He died in poverty in 1950.

I was wrestling with so many different competing thoughts about what I had seen in the exhibition. I needed time to reflect on them, but as I was about to exit the museum, I was led to a table where there was a large, open, red book in which my hosts invited me to record a message. Cameras and dignitaries gathered round to see what I would say. I knew this was sacred ground for the Chinese. It was sacred ground for humanity also. After pausing for a few seconds, I picked up the marker pen and wrote:

'Walk for Peace. To be able to make peace with the present, we must first make peace with the past. This exhibition shows not only what evil humans are capable of but also what good – I am thinking here of John Rabe and the International Safety Zone. In the past, the city of Nanjing has been associated in the mind of the world with an act of unspeakable brutality. My hope and prayer is that in the future it will become known around the world as a place of peace and reconciliation. The journey to that place must take us through the dark corridors of this museum and then out into the light beyond. I have walked this journey with you. Michael Bates 19/9/15'

URL http://www.walkforpeace.eu/day-55-light-in-the-darkness/

September 20 Day 56

Donations Breakthrough

Nanjing, Jiangsu Province
A Day Off
Donated today: £0.00 / ¥4,761.00
Total donations: £4,116.95 and ¥163,775.81

I have mentioned frequently that there were three objectives. First, to complete the walk, and so far we were ahead of schedule in reaching Nanjing with around 300 km to go. Second, to spread the message of Walk for Peace, which is that peace is possible if we work for it and realize that we are all human first – having had the opportunity to share this message with hundreds of young people along the way either directly or indirectly through this blog and social media, I think this objective is being reached. We have still two weeks to go. The final objective has been to raise funds in China and in the UK for projects we have identified with the Red Cross – Xuelin set us an ambitious target of raising £50,000, or 500,000 yuan, and for most of the walk we have been stuck at around the £10,000, or 100,000 yuan, mark.

Xuelin is an outstanding businesswoman, and once she sets an objective she isn't going to miss it. In many ways, this is why we are a good team on these walks. I am a hopeless fundraiser. I hate asking for money. But I can walk, and when I set myself an objective for walking, to this point, I have always hit it or exceeded it, no matter what obstacles are placed in my way. Xuelin is not a great walker but she is a fantastic fundraiser.

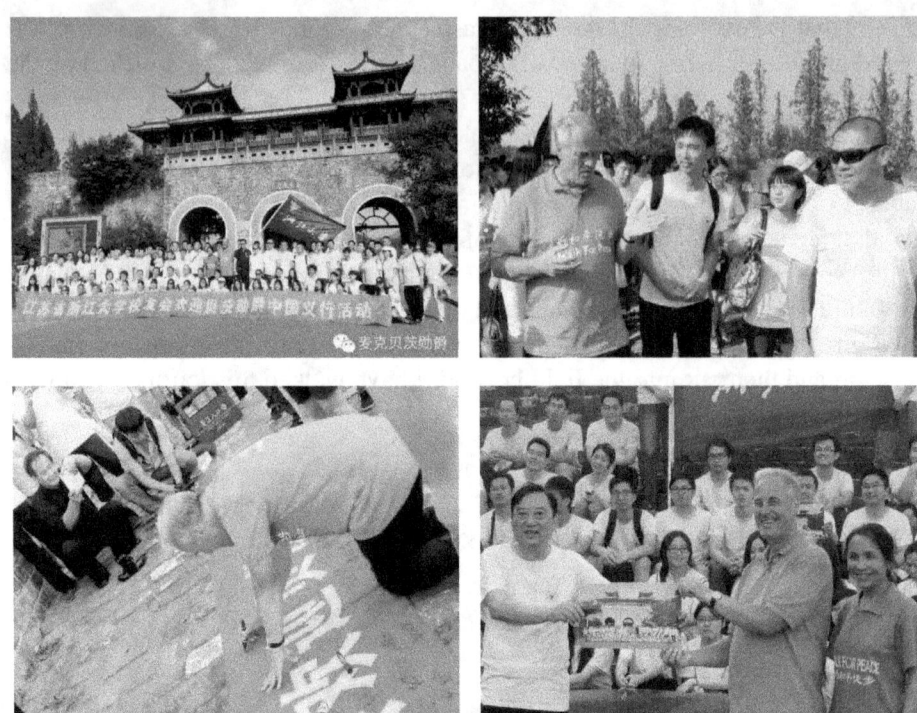

Top left: Group photo with the Zhejiang University alumni. Top right: Deep in conversation with alumni. Bottom left: Signing the banner. Bottom right: The end of a fruitful day.

I suppose the key to good fundraising, like good walking, is to have a clear purpose. Probably at the beginning of the walk, when we were generally raising funds for projects yet to be identified, people felt that they wanted to know where their hard-earned money was going before they parted with it. That is why, when we identified the first two projects, Hope House in Pizhou, which works with children with physical and mental disabilities, and the Suqian Orphanage for Children, we found a more receptive mood for donations.

Xuelin is an active member of the Zhejiang University Alumni, and the alumni have been tremendous supporters of the walk throughout our journey. Today, Zhejiang University and Jiangsu Alumni arranged for over 120 people to come along to support the Walk for Peace and walk with us around the ancient walls of Nanjing. In addition, the alumni created a specific bar code so that alumni in the group could donate via WeChat or mobile phone. This innovation raised 120,000 yuan from 600 people, making donations from 1 yuan to 1,000 yuan.

Xuelin was contacted by a friend in the UK, Julia Wang, who runs a successful international student internship scheme. Julia came up with the idea of getting young people to take part in an 'Apprentice'-style competition to raise funds for the Red Cross projects identified through our walk. Over 200 people applied and Julia selected 30 from Nanjing to undertake the challenge. The young people were divided into six teams, and each team was given 500 yuan and one week to try and increase that amount. It was a fantastic project, and when we met the students at the end of the week-long activity and they presented us with a cheque for 30,000 yuan (£3,000), we were inspired by their commitment and grateful.

Also in Nanjing, we were joined by three local companies who came together through the Red Cross and Wang Jiyan of Phoenix television to present us with a cheque for 150,000 yuan (£15,000).

So far donations have come from over 1,000 people, which is important because, the more people who engage in the walk by walking a few miles with us, donating their money, no matter how much or little, or reading these blogs, the more the message is being spread.

In the UK, there is a website that collects donations in a tax-efficient way for UK taxpayers, and those funds go to the British Red Cross. So far, that site has collected £4,300 (43,000 yuan).

After a slow start to the fundraising, thanks to the efforts of hundreds of people and the work of Xuelin, the total funds raised so far are 460,000 yuan (£46,000), which, when added to the £4,300 in the UK, takes us just over our target for the walk. It is a staggering response, and the funds will make a real difference in many children's lives. Of course, Xuelin, being Xuelin, is not for stopping there, and there is a possibility that we may be able to do even better than this by the time we reach Hangzhou to conclude the walk on October 5.

On behalf of Xuelin and me and the Red Cross in China and Britain, we thank everyone who has contributed to this wonderful result so far.

URL http://www.walkforpeace.eu/day-56-donations-breakthrough/

September 21 Day 57

Nanjing Declaration

Nanjing, Jiangsu Province
A Day Off
Donated today: £300.00 / ¥7,450.00
Total donations: £4,416.95 and ¥171,225.81

It was Monday, September 21, the United Nations International Day of Peace. I was in Nanjing and I wanted to pitch an idea to see if there might be a response.

Preamble: Xuelin and I have been deeply moved by our encounters with young people here in Nanjing. On Saturday we attended an event with around 30 young people who had volunteered for a 'Charity Apprentice' competition to raise funds for Walk for Peace. On Sunday, around 120 young people turned out with Zhejiang University alumni to 'Walk for Peace' around the ancient walls of Nanjing. Today, we were at Jinling Middle School for a talk to around 150 students, followed by a football match. Ever since we left Beijing 57 days ago, we have been accompanied on the walk by different groups of local Red Cross Volunteers. Young people have always energized me with their 'can do' and 'change the world' attitude. It was young people in Newcastle in 2009 who first challenged me to start walking. They continue to be a source of inspiration. So, when asked by some of those young people and a young journalist at this morning's press conference whether Walk for Peace had any plans to leave some kind of legacy organization that could continue to 'walk' and to 'work' for peace, we thought about this very carefully.

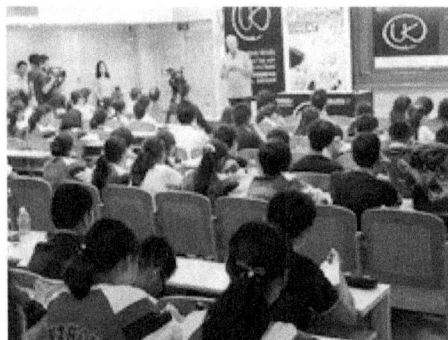 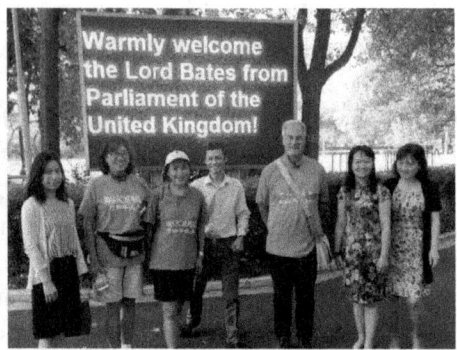

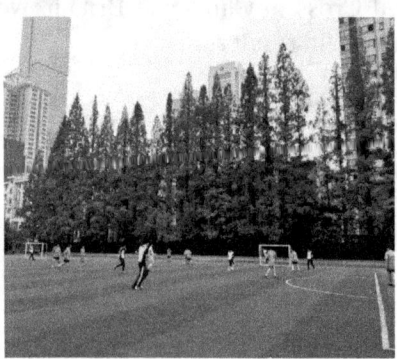 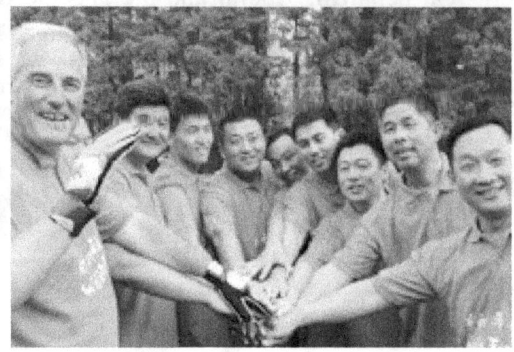

Top left: On the International Day of Peace, Lord Bates delivers a speech on 'The Role of Culture in Constructing Peace', at Jinling Middle School in Nanjing'. Top right: Lord Bates being welcomed by staff of Jinling Middle School. Bottom left: Football match in Jinling Middle School. Bottom right: Lord Bates and the Nanjing Red Cross Society form a Walk for Peace team.

The idea of an organization had not crossed my mind. My thoughts with Xuelin as I finish this walk are turning to the walk in 2016, which we are planning to mark the Olympic Truce for the Rio 2016 Games. I walk alone. Xuelin and I have developed a very efficient mechanism for planning a walk, doing the walk and raising funds for the nominated good cause. Organizations scare me. They are full of committees, bureaucracies, territorial arguments, inflated egos and internal squabbles. I started walking because I wanted to break out of sterile politics and do something direct to make a difference. That said, what if other people share my frustrations and are seeking a vehicle through which they too can make a difference for good? Could we not help them? Should we not help them?

It is late at night. I have a long day of walking out of Nanjing tomorrow but I want to draft an idea on this day in this place for these young people to see if it resonates and, if doesn't, how it could be changed to ensure that it does.

Concept: To create a youth organization that provides a channel for people to explore cultural differences and to think and act about peace and understanding locally, nationally and internationally.

Aim: To build peace through an international public diplomacy network around connecting cultures and enriching individuals' experiences and knowledge.

Idea: A group in Nanjing called PAX (the Latin word for Peace) and representning peace through cultural exchange.

Overarching principles: Enjoyment, excellence, education, respect, service, accessibility and achievement.

Definition: As I observed before, the origin of the word is similar in English, or I should say Latin, to 'agri' culture or farming and means literally 'inhabit, till, care for' the mind and soul. Culture is what makes us human, a distinctive species. For millions of years, culture has expressed itself in cave paintings, music playing, worship, customs, dress, ritual and storytelling. Today, what we mean by culture is education, sport, art, music, drama, religion, dance, philosophy, literature, food, history, film, fashion and language.

Structure:

PAX would be a franchise awarded by the Walk for Peace Foundation, following a bid by a group from a particular city or district that complies with the criteria set out by the Foundation.

Membership would be open to everyone from the age of 16. There could be no discrimination on any grounds.

Members would be encouraged to make activities accessible to those with physical and mental disabilities.

Each city/town level PAX branch would be called a 'Mission'. There could be only one Mission in each city, although it is possible that in very large cities consulates could be opened to cater for particular specialisms and localities.

The Mission would be comprised of members and officers with ranks copied from the diplomatic service and headed by a PAX Ambassador. They would be supported by a Chargé d'affaires, Minister, Minister Counsellor, Counsellor, First Secretary, Second Secretary, Third Secretary, Attaché and Assistant Attaché.

There would be four 'Divisions' of activities, each led by an officer: Arts, Education, Philosophy and Sport. Each Mission would be invited to nominate a particular Division as a 'Major' or a 'Specialism'.

For PAX to work, it must avoid being drawn into the political arena. PAX is about being respectful and seeking to understand and connect with different cultures, not to change them. Each mission must be prepared to respect the host political and legal system that is operating in their area.

To reduce bureaucracy, wherever possible organization and communication should be done through social media.

The purpose of PAX is not to promote one culture as superior to another. It starts from the position that we are all human first. That we are all of equal value. That our cultural identity is a reflection of our particular upbringing, education and experience. Our cultural identity is unique to us. That does not mean it should not be open to question through PAX events, but the questioning must attempt to seek to understand rather than challenge.

Activities:

Each PAX Mission would need to organize events and issue short reports online to give details of activities on:

April 6 – United Nations International Day for Sport Development & Peace

September 21 – United Nations Day for International Peace

The start of the Olympic Truce for both Winter and Summer Games. There would be an annual General Assembly Meeting for each Mission to receive reports on activities, present awards and appoint officers.

There would be an annual Walk for Peace.

In addition …

It would be envisaged that a Mission would be based around activities rather than bureaucracies. In other words, the purpose of the mission is to promote peace through cultural exchange. Examples might include:

Members sharing in a social setting their own unique cultural identity,

Sporting competitions between members and with other groups or organizations;

Learning from the experiences of students who have studied overseas or foreign students or teachers attending local schools or universities;

Visits to historic sites, museums or other locations that might assist in understanding some new aspect of culture;

Attending or organizing concerts with different styles of dance or music;

Lectures on particular aspects of philosophy or other ideas;

Talks by diplomats, officials and businesspeople from other regions or countries;

Marking or exploring major religious festivals or places of worship;

Film nights showing world cinema movies followed by discussion.

Awards:

PAX would promote a system of lifelong service and lifelong learning. The Walk for Peace Foundation will draw up and oversee the judging of award programmes and competitions. Awards will be meritocratic, as will promotion of officers – it's not who you are but what you do that counts.

In today's global world, businesses, organizations and educational institutions are all looking for young people who are culturally aware and sensitive. PAX could provide a means for demonstrating to those organizations a commitment on the part of the member to engage and explore at a cultural level.

How could this be improved to make it more effective in enriching your cultural experience and promoting peace and goodwill to all peoples?

URL http://www.walkforpeace.eu/day-57-nanjing-declaration/

September 22 Day 58

Thoughts on Professor Bates

Route: Gulou District – Jiangning District, Nanjing
Walked today: 25.10 miles / 40.30 km
Total walked: 852.40 miles / 1,372.30 km
Donated today: £28.32 / ¥5,500
Total donations: £4,445.27 and ¥176,725.81

It was a tough start to the walk today. The football match at Jinling Middle School the previous evening had left me feeling aches and pains in muscles I hadn't known existed. All the team members arrived in the hotel foyer at 8 am, limping or trying to stretch out the cramps. Of course, it always hurts more when you lose, and our 3–0 defeat to the young Jinling School was not a fair reflection of the game – it should have been 7–0!

We hobbled our way through the city centre of Nanjing and then out into the prosperous suburbs. In one of those great miracles that I have never experienced before, we arrived at the 20 km mark and a planned stop for lunch, and there was a Starbucks! I feel Starbucks is my spiritual home. My favourite Starbucks is at the junction of 48th and Park Avenue in Manhattan. It was the Starbucks I first called 'home', as it was closest to the office where I frequently worked when in New York with Oxford Analytica, whose HQ was 230 Park Avenue. I even had a special seat where I could see the top of the Chrysler Building. They knew my name and my order and played jazz. Well, Jinling in Nanjing might not be quite there, but they played jazz, so halfway.

As I drank my Grande Skinny Latte and listened to the legend that is John Coltrane, my mind went back to a visit I had made with Xuelin to the home of John Rabe, who was the Siemens manager in Nanjing at the time of the Japanese invasion and who first chaired the International Safety Zone, which saved over 250,000 lives. We visited the home and the museum on our first day in Nanjing but there were too many people with us for the small house with a remarkable history, and so Xuelin arranged for me to go back the following morning for a private visit with Mr Yang Shanyou, who is the Curator of the museum and a member of faculty at Nanjing University, which manages the museum.

Mr Yang was very surprised to see that we had come back again and wanted to show us some displays for Miner Searle Bates, who was a history professor at Nanjing University and had not only worked with John Rabe to establish the International Safety Zone in Nanjing but in 1939 took over its chairmanship. Mr Yang thought that my interest may be because Professor Bates had played such a significant role in the Zone. I was sorry to disappoint him. Professor Bates was an American Christian missionary who came to Nanjing with the YMCA in 1920. He was a graduate of Yale, Oxford and Harvard but felt called by God to serve the people of China, which he did for 30 years until 1950.

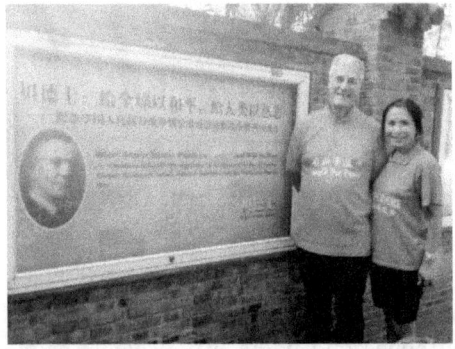 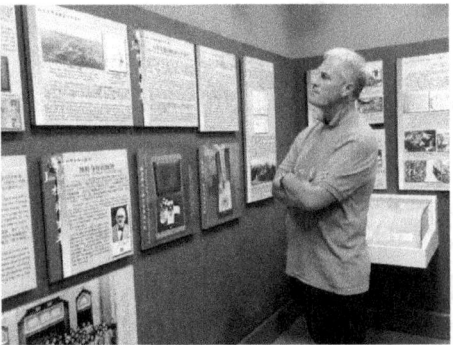

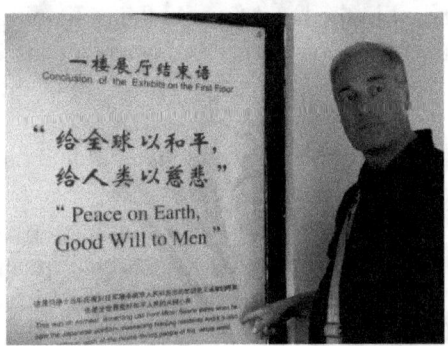 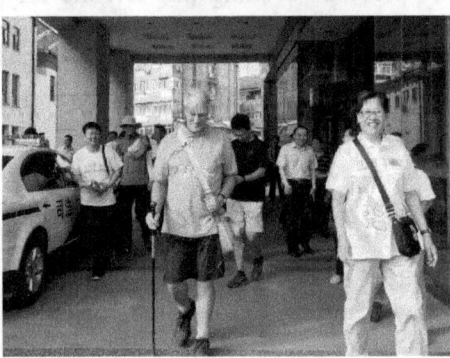

Top left: Learning more about Miner Searle Bates. Top right: A further visit to the John Rabe House. Bottom left: 'Peace on Earth, Good Will to Men.' Bottom right: Walking around the city.

The more I read about him, the more my admiration for him grew. There were many records of him. On more than one occasion, he had pistols pointed at his head as he intervened to protect women who were being molested by occupying troops. There is nothing passive about being a pacifist. Professor Bates documented the atrocities being committed in Nanjing, and his evidence was crucial in bringing the perpetrators to justice in the Tokyo and Nanjing War Trials.

There were two quotes carried in the displays that struck a chord. One was, 'Peace on Earth and Goodwill to All Men' and the second was 'Religious faith is believing that good things are worth doing for their own sake, even in a world that seems overpoweringly evil. I remain assured in hard experience that neither by national guns nor by national gods will mankind be saved, but only by the genuine regard for all members of the human family.'

This second quote had a great effect on me. It is one thing for me, as someone who has never been confronted with the true horrors of war and only had my values of peace tested by the occasional blister rather than the face of death, to express to the belief that we are all human first and encourage people to seek peace and goodwill. Yet here was a man who had had those beliefs tested to the extreme at a time of incredible danger and inhumanity and he upheld their truth and value as a bright light, not through words but through his actions.

Peace heroes, unlike war heroes, seldom merit medals, statues or public adulation, but I was grateful for Siemens, John Rabe House and Nanjing University for keeping these precious memories of John Rabe and Professor Bates alive to demonstrate that 'The light shines in the darkness and the darkness has not overcome it' (John 1:5).

URL http://www.walkforpeace.eu/day-58-thoughts-on-professor-bates/

September 23 Day 59

The Voice of Youth

Route: Jiangning District – Lishuixian, Nanjing
Walked today: 25.70 miles / 41.30 km
Total walked: 878.10 miles / 1,413.60 km
Donated today: £50.00 / ¥12,125.64
Total donations: £4,495.27 and ¥188,851.45

The second day walking out of Nanjing and we were still in the suburbs. Walking through suburbs is a slog. There isn't the excitement of the city/town centres nor the beauty of the countryside and rural life. There isn't a great deal to write about or celebrate, apart from passing the 1,400-km (875 miles) marker.

My thoughts turn back to Nanjing and especially to the young people I met at the Nanjing Memorial Museum who had worked so hard to raise funds for the Red Cross projects. One of the young people spoke for the group as a welcome and Xuelin took a picture of the speech as it was written and delivered in both Chinese and English. Often we are told what young people think or believe, but we don't often get the chance to hear it from them themselves, but here are the words of one young person in China:

Dear Lord Bates, my young friends,

This is the 70th anniversary of the end of the Second World War, which is also an important time when Lord Bates attends the commemorative activity with our young people in the Memorial Hall of the Victims of the Nanjing Massacre. When Lord Bates and his wife travelled tirelessly thousands of miles to China to spread the thought of peace, we shall not forget the bloodshed and humiliation behind this episode in our country's history.

Looking back on those turbulent days we admire the courage of our national heroes who fought and shed blood for our country in battlefields. We also can't forget the spirit of the 56 nationalities united against the enemy as one and we can't forget that over 300,000 compatriots were killed in our homeland. How shocking the past is. They are reminding us not to forget the national humiliation. These shall serve as an alarm bell that reminds us not to forget our national humiliation.

Seventy years have passed; we, the Chinese young people, still inscribe the great dedication of the martyrs who sacrificed themselves for the country and faced death unflinchingly. We bear this history in mind and we cherish peace more than ever. At this moment, we propose to our young friends as follows:

Remember history and don't forget national humiliation. Let's learn that history together, let's remember the precious experience that the tough times taught us, better construct our great country and strive to realize the great dream of the great rejuvenation of China!

Cherish peace, remember our obligations. Peace and development are the themes of this age and also the common wish of people worldwide. The peaceful society where we are currently living is not easily come by. We shall remember our obligations to bravely bear the responsibility of society and country. Do not let history repeat itself; help vulnerable groups, spread justice and ensure that the olive branch of peace never fades.

Live simply, work hard and be eager to learn. The hardship of yesterday makes the prosperity of today. As a Chinese young person, we shall not abandon our traditions, although the material conditions become better and society more stable. We shall be hardworking, thrifty and eager to learn.

Stick to your dreams, be motivated by sincere practice sincerely. Young people shall have dreams and practise sincerely to become a useful person! We dare to dream and we fight with strong minds. Thus, we can get what we want in our old age without regret. We are afraid neither of hardships nor of the long journey because we clearly know we shall see success after these untold hardships and sufferings. In the current society full of the temptations of power and money, we cannot be enslaved. We shall strive for our dreams to lay a foundation for the future.

We wish for you to stick to your dreams and realize your ambitions and get what you truly want. Let's remember history together and cherish peace. Let's put this enthusiasm into action, strive for the development of the Chinese nation and peace in the world and build a beautiful homeland for everyone.

I think it is very important that we let the words of this young person be allowed to stand on their own so that we adults, perhaps from other countries or cultures, might try and understand the sincere thoughts and hopes that lie behind their composition.

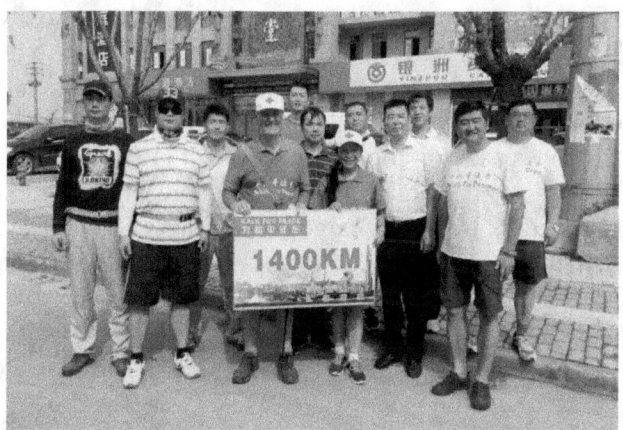

Milestone marking 1,400 km of the walk

URL http://www.walkforpeace.eu/day-59-the-voice-of-youth/

September 24 Day 60

Back to Beijing

Beijing
A Day Off
Donated today: £30.00 / ¥161,320.00
Total donations: £4,525.27 and ¥350,171.45

We found ourselves a few days ahead of schedule on account of having saved time by taking to the S205 route from Huai'an to Nanjing, rather than the eastern side of Gaoyou Lake to Yangzhou. It was a decision greeted by surprise by our friends in the Jiangsu Red Cross, as Yangzhou is an 'amazingly beautiful city' – which I am sure it is – but saving ten miles is an 'amazingly beautiful thought' at this stage of the journey.

Having taken the more direct route and freed up a few extra days, I was looking forward to using them to leisurely get up to date with blogs and emails. No chance. Not when Xuelin is driving the fundraising and activity around the walk. These are three good days to be spent productively. Xuelin arranged an extremely busy round of meetings, interviews and events back in Beijing. When Xuelin told me the programme on the high speed train journey from Lishui station to Beijing, I began to think that the east coast route to Yangzhou didn't seem too bad after all.

Our first meeting off the train was with Lin Jun, head of the All-China Federation of Returned Overseas Chinese. Lin has a very busy job, as he is responsible for more than 50 million overseas Chinese, and it is one that involves seemingly endless travel – he was leaving for Indonesia immediately after our meeting.

The list of places in which overseas Chinese reside makes interesting reading. Many are obvious, such as neighbouring Thailand (9.32 million), Malaysia (6.96 million), Indonesia (2.8 million) and Myanmar (1.6 million), and Singapore, Philippines, Cambodia and Vietnam also have significant populations. During the Chinese Civil War, there were very large movements of the defeated Nationalist government (Kuomintang) to such countries and regions as Singapore, Malaysia, Indonesia and the Philippines, as well of course, as to Taiwan.

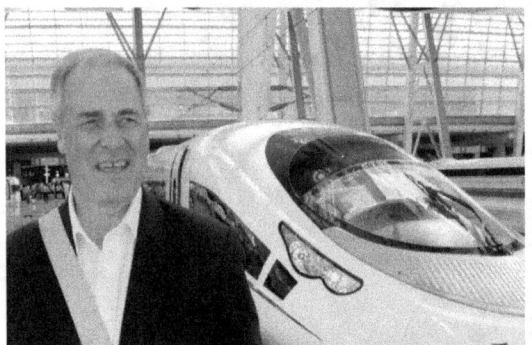
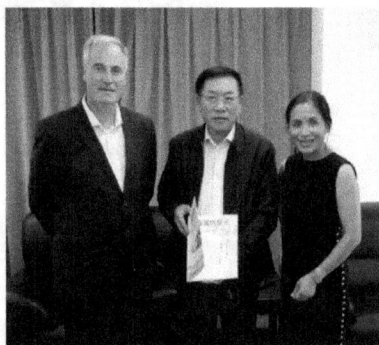
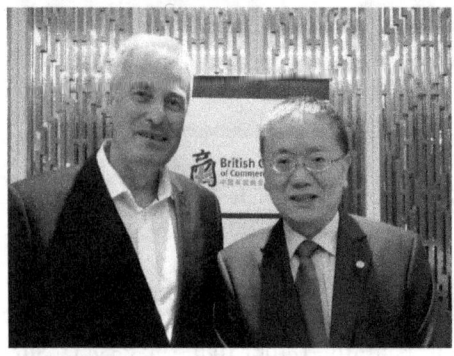
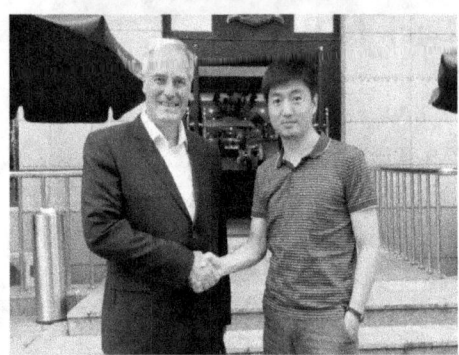

Top left: Heading back to Beijing via high-speed train. Top right: Lord and Lady Bates and Lin Jun, head of the All-China Federation of Returned Overseas Chinese. Bottom left: At a dinner organized by the British Chamber of Commerce/China British Business Council. Bottom right: Lord Bates and CHEN Ying, Journalist of *Beijing Daily*

Some are less obvious – the United States has the third highest number of ethnic Chinese (3.7 million); many travelled there in the 19th century to help build railways and support gold mines. Also, Canada has 1.5 million, many of whom were invited to come following the Hong Kong handover. Peru has 1.3 million ethnic Chinese – I am not sure how or why but would be interested to learn more. In Europe, France has the largest Chinese population (700,000), with the UK second (466,000). The fastest growing overseas Chinese communities are in Africa and in eastern Russia, especially the port city of Vladivostok.

It is good to keep in touch with diasporas because they remind us that great population migrations are nothing new. They have happened down the centuries as a result of wars or famines and will continue to do so, as it is a basic human instinct to move in order to secure food, safety and a better future for people and their families. That is what millions of British people did as they travelled to America, Canada, Australia, New Zealand and southern Africa in centuries past. Australia remains the top destination for British (207,000) emigrating abroad, then the United States (72,000) and Spain (52,000).

As if often the case with very busy people, they have an air of quiet calm about them. It may be very different in the outer office, but Lin is very interested in our walk and the reasons behind it. He is an educated and thoughtful man, I am guessing around 60, skilled in calligraphy and even makes fine teapots – just in case I didn't feel inadequate already. He is wise and broad-minded, as travel often makes one. It was Mark Twain who remarked, 'Travel is fatal to prejudice, bigotry and narrow-mindedness.' In the course of conversation, he offered some advice; in Chinese culture, this is unusual as they don't want to offend the guest, but I think he judged that I, and if not I then certainly our translator (Xuelin) might be open to it. 'You should think of doing shorter walks in more places.' I think this may be a frequent conversation topic between Xuelin and me as we conclude this walk and start to think of the next one.

After some more media interviews, we were invited to a British Chamber of Commerce/China British Business Council dinner for a visiting British parliamentary delegation. This has been a big week in China for the British, as a high-level delegation of government ministers led by the Chancellor of the Exchequer, George Osborne, arrived in China to promote British trade. The Chancellor set the UK the target of becoming China's second largest trading partner after the United States and spoke of a Golden Decade of trade relations. These are exciting times indeed. It is so much more productive for the world when nations trade goods rather than accusations.

The hosts invited me to say a few words about my experiences on my walk to the largely business audience. Peace, hope and walking 1,000 miles for charity perhaps don't come naturally to an audience more concerned with the Shanghai Stock Exchange, so I followed my father's advice on preaching: 'If you don't strike oil after five minutes, stop boring and sit down.' I think I sat down in two minutes, actually, but Xuelin and I had a few very interesting conversations afterwards, one very significant, which just goes to show you should never prejudge people.

URL http://www.walkforpeace.eu/day-60-back-to-beijing/

September 25 Day 61

The Importance of Communication

Beijing

A Day Off

Donated today: £0.00 / ¥50,000.00

Total donations: £4,525.27 and ¥400,171.45

Today was a day set aside purely for interviews, some in our hotel and one that required us to travel to east Beijing and the spectacular new HQ of Phoenix Television near Chaoyang Park. The building looks from the outside like a giant doughnut, but everything about the building is designed for a purpose – the flowing curves of its glass and steel façade capture rainwater, which is recycled for use in the building. The partial arches around the base allow the optimum flow of air through the structure to assist natural cooling.

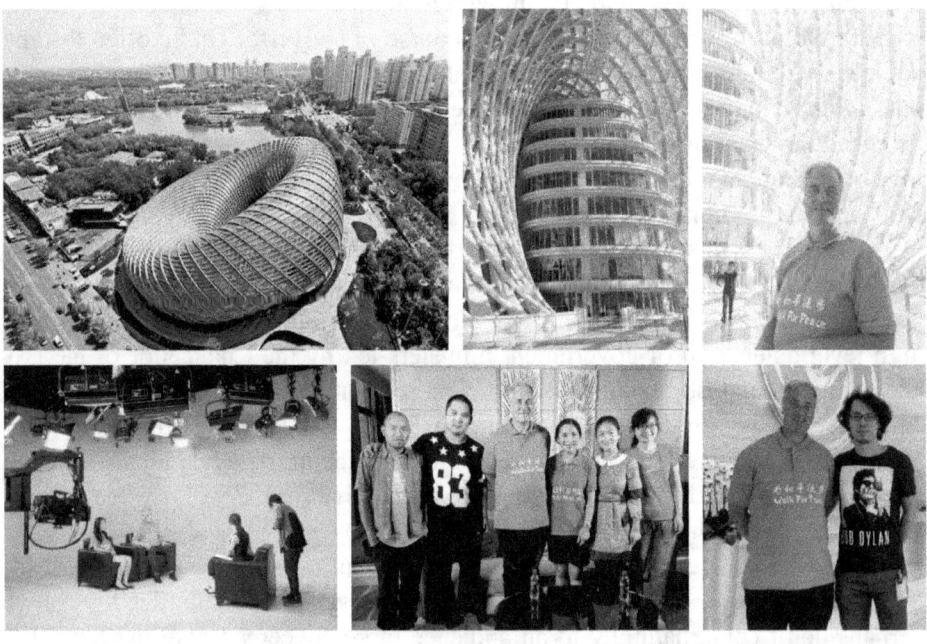

Top left: Aerial view of the Phoenix Television building. Top middle and right: Lord Bates at the new HQ of Phoenix Television. Bottom left: Taping the interview. Bottom middle and right: Meeting the crew and producer of *Charity China* of Phoenix TV.

Xuelin trained as an architect, so this was special treat for her and she had many questions. The original remit or specification to the famous Beijing Institute for Architectural Design was 'Un-forbidden Office', after the Forbidden City of

Beijing. This was to be a building that said to the staff and to the world not 'keep out' but 'come in'. Architecture so often reflects the underlying philosophy and self-confidence of an economy.

In the past, China has made good use of prestigious firms of foreign architects such as Herzog & de Meuron's 'Bird's Nest' stadium' or Norman Foster's Beijing International Airport. The Phoenix media centre is a bit of a statement that 'Hey, we can do this for ourselves' (and at a fraction of the cost). It is a splendid building and we enjoyed exploring its wide open spaces. It was not just for the architecture that we came; it was because Phoenix television had taken a long interest in the walk and in my previous walks through their operations in London. They have a weekly programme called *Charity China* and they were to feature Walk for Peace and our partners on the walk, the Red Cross Society of China.

A key part of any modern charity fundraising activity is the media. It is not that the media drives donations but when the charity has appeared on the media it seems to give authentication to its aims and objectives. This is certainly what Xue-lin has found as she has built up the WeChat and WeiBo platforms, which have helped generate a significant portion of the donations to date. It is very difficult to do this because, of course, there are so many worthy causes and a limited number of media outlets to carry them.

That is why charities increasingly look to celebrities to endorse their activities. One step by Angelina Jolie in the UK or Yao Chen in China in support of a cause can raise more than 1,000 miles taken by an unknown politician. So the very fact that Phoenix, CCTV, *China Daily* and *Beijing Evening Daily* and the *Beijing News* have been so interested in our walk so far is a great encouragement, which is translated each day into real donations for good causes through the Red Cross.

One other benefit of having a series of interviews on days off is that in the past when TV crews have travelled out to walk with us, they have found me absolutely exhausted by the demands simply of walking 40 km, and therefore I am washed out by the end of the day when they want to talk with me. As we take time out to engage with journalists on this trip, Xuelin and I find their line of questions interesting and really helpful in learning not only how to convey what we are doing but why we are doing it. The Latin word for 'communication' is not from a root word about speaking or writing in a didactic (lecturing) way, but from a word that means 'sharing', which suggests that, when good communication takes place, the viewer, interviewer and interviewee should all end up being better informed.

URL http://www.walkforpeace.eu/day-61-the-importance-of-communication/

September 26 Day 62

Rock the Boat

Beijing
A Day Off
Donated today: £0.00 / ¥0.00
Total donations: £4,525.27 and ¥400,171.45

We had an early start to make our way out to Daoxiang Lake on the northern edge of Beijing. It is the new centre for Asian Rowing, being located in a vast area of rivers and lakes sheltered by mountains and two leading Chinese universities, Peking University and Tsinghua University, which supply a steady flow of rowing talent. Asian Rowing has received new impetus since top Chinese entrepreneur Wang Shi took on a leading role.

Wang Shi is something of a legend in China. He is chairman of China's largest real estate development company, China Vanke. Wang is recognized as one of the leading figures in China's economic opening up. He is someone who has also promoted ethical business principles, holding to 'no bribery' and 'no more than 25% profit' policy. He still managed to build a vast business empire. He is a quietly spoken and studious man but one who wants to be judged by his actions rather than his words. He has climbed Qomolongma (aka Mt Everest) twice (breaking the age record for the oldest Chinese mountaineer to reach the summit, at the age of 59 in 2010). He has trekked to the North and South Poles and moves between boardroom and classroom effortlessly, undertaking research studies at Oxford and Harvard.

Needless to say of someone so eminent in so many fields, he didn't have a clue who I was, but fortunately he knew and respected Xuelin. They are members of the same WeChat group. Through the group, he read some of my blog entries and wanted to support us. Following an exchange of emails and late-night telephone calls and in the lightning-fast way that things can happen in China, we were invited to attend the launch of Asian Rowing's new home and take part in a special charity event called 'Rock & Row for Peace' which Wang and his team had organized to promote the Walk for Peace. First there was a little challenge to overcome…

In the flurry of calls and emails, somewhere Xuelin asked me, 'Have you ever rowed?' I replied that I had, of course, thinking of Saltwell Park Lake as a child and a couple of times at Oxford and Durham when studying at university. By rowing, I meant 'sat in a boat with a couple of oars and a couple of beers and ideally a couple of girls'. By rowing, Chairman Wang's team meant one of those eight-man boats you see in the Olympics or the Oxford and Cambridge Boat Race.

We arrived at the launch site, each of us oblivious to the misunderstanding between us – which was about to become apparent.

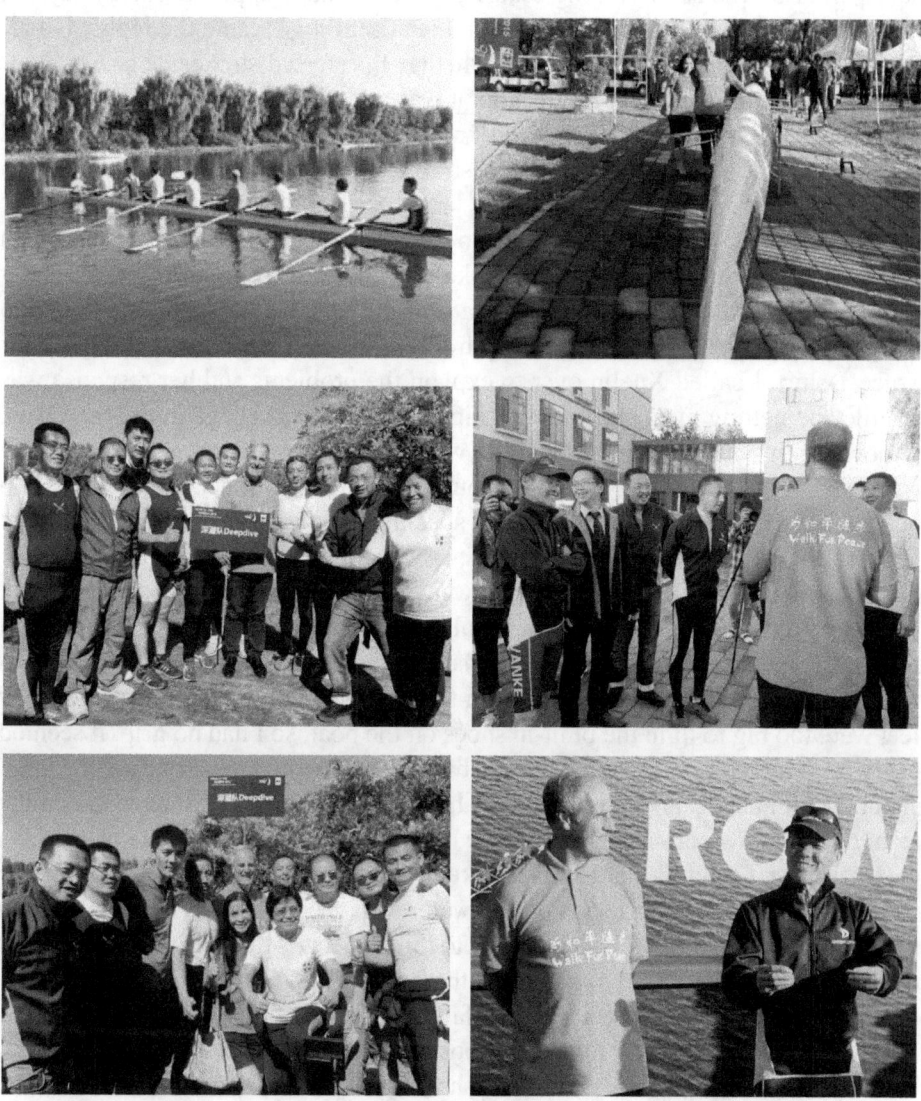

Top left: While attending the 'Rock & Row for Peace' charity event, Lord and Lady Bates were invited to a rowing contest by Wang Shi, chairman of China Vanke. Top right: Lord and Lady Bates with the racing boat. Middle left: Meeting the teammates. Middle right: Arriving at the 'Rock & Row for Peace' event. Bottom left: Lord and Lady Bates and the Deep Dive team. Bottom right: Meeting with top Chinese entrepreneur Wang Shi.

The speeches went well. We cut the ribbon – that went well. I was then introduced to my teammates – from Deep Dive, who had just returned from intensive training in Cambridge, England – which went well, but they did all seem to be half my age, half my weight and ten times fitter. Then we were introduced to the boat. My heart sank. I didn't think I would be able to keep my backside in the boat, never mind on the small sliding seat. I tried to manage expectations by saying, 'I normally row with two oars.' 'Oh, you mean sculling?' came the reply. 'Do I?' I thought to myself. I was then asked whether I preferred strokeside or bowside? They were speaking perfect English but it was a foreign language. 'What number do you want?' asked another, I said '4' with confidence – I had at least figured out by then that there were eight seats, so four would put me somewhere not too obvious in the middle.

The Deep Dive team was going to be racing Wang's team. They stripped down to the rowing kit, all skin tight like a cyclist's, to show off their perfectly defined muscles. I had thought this was a row around a lake, so hadn't bothered to bring any sports kit – I was there in my trousers, black leather shoes and Walk for Truce T-shirt. I called Xuelin over to explain the problems and her response was a smile and getting me a pair of hotel slippers from our baggage in the car. Okay, so now I didn't have leather shoes, but I was still lifting an eight-man boat and we were walking to the river bank. All I could think of was, at what point do I drop out? Knowing that the 'Rock for Peace' special event was to come later, I wanted to show willing and at least try. After all, how difficult could it really be?

I got in or, more accurately, was lowered into the boat; as soon as I landed in P4, I started hearing 'steady the boat' calls. The boat was so narrow and sleek, it felt as if you were sitting on top of the water and the slightest tip would bring water over the side. As we pushed off from the quay, I actually felt quite scared. My feet were too big to fit in the built-in shoes on the boat, so I had no grip. It seemed every time I went to even touch the oar beside me, I would get a 'steady the boat' shout. Teammates who had been saying how thrilled they were to have me on the team on land now out on the water were beginning to utter mutinous murmurings about 'Whose bright idea was this to take this useless sack of potatoes out on the water?' I kept my oar blade flat on the water as it seemed the best way to steady the boat and avoid a Deep Dive. I began to think of a great book title, 'If you want to walk on water, you need to get out of the boat ...'. It seemed as if either I or my teammates were soon going to put that faith to the test.

We set off up the river to take our positions for the race. I tried a few strokes, but they resulted in a 'steady the boat' shout again, so I was told to just stop. We made our way up past the spectators and the press gallery and I could hear Xuelin shouting, 'Why aren't you rowing?' I didn't want to say anything in case I got another 'steady the boat' shout. We got to the head of the river and were joined by a professional umpire on a launch. He wanted to check that I was okay. When I said I thought it might be better if I left the boat and he told me that this would mean climbing onto his launch mid-river, I decided that the safest option was probably to try and stay put. They then decided that if I didn't row and the seat behind me didn't row, then we would keep balance. So we were off. Soon my teammates were happy we were going down the river more quickly with six rowers than with eight. That is the importance of balance in rowing, so I discovered.

We arrived back at the landing platform and I have never been more grateful to see dry land. The fact that we had made it back without sinking covered all the personal embarrassment I felt – well, at least until I made it back to the Club House for a rather quiet breakfast. Chairman Wang was characteristically gracious and philosophical. We then had the 'Rock & Row for Peace' event, which was really fun, showing the progress on a big screen of competing rally teams on rowing machines. It raised a lot of interest in the Walk for Peace, probably mostly around wondering how a man so unfit, who cannot even get into a boat by himself, never mind row, could ever walk 1,000 miles. Well, that, as they say, is another story. which I am still trying to write …

URL http://www.walkforpeace.eu/day-62-rock-the-boat/

September 27 Day 63

Moon Festival

Route: Lishuixian, Nanjing – Liyang, Changzhou
Walked today: 25.30 miles / 40.70 km
Total walked: 903.40 miles / 1,454.30 km
Donated today: £15.00 / ¥0.00
Total donations: £4,540.27 and ¥400,171.45

It had been a punishing and humiliating day out on the river in Beijing. The rowing action is very different from the walking action and therefore I was already seizing up around my shoulders. We arrived back at Lishui Station on Saturday evening, but were met by our wonderful and faithful friends from the Jiangsu Red Cross. We have been together for almost a month now as we travelled across this great province, and their patience and kindness has been a constant inspiration for Xuelin and me.

The way in which the rest-day breaks had fallen meant that we were scheduled to walk on Moon Festival, or the Mid-Autumn Festival, one of the most important family days, according to China's lunar year. It is perhaps not quite Christmas in the Western sense – that would be Chinese New Year – but it is certainly Thanksgiving in the US or perhaps Easter in the UK. We felt very sad for the small core team who were missing their families in order to support us on the walk, but just as we were thinking how we could thank them, they produced a big box of moon cakes for us. It was typical of their generosity of spirit that they would think of us missing our families on Moon Festival, rather than themselves missing theirs.

Moon or Mid-Autumn Festival has been celebrated in China for thousands of years: records go back to 2000 BC but moon worship was common even before then. It is traditionally composed of three elements: gathering of friends, family and, of course, the harvest; thanksgiving for friends, family and harvest; and prayers for partners, babies, good health and a good future. The most famous gift on China's mainland is moon cake, with its moon-shaped lotus-bean centre. Often the cakes are piled in groups of 13 or cut into 13 to symbolize the 13 months of the lunar calendar.

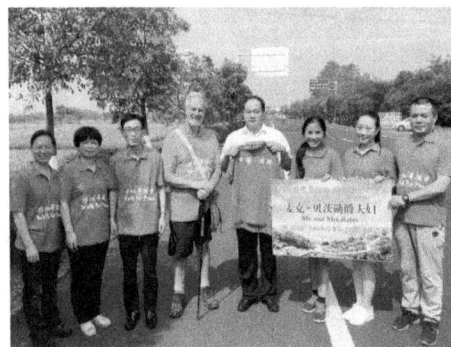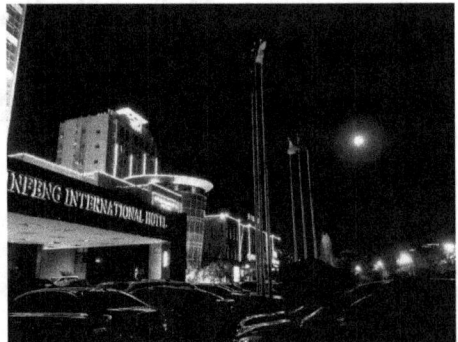

Left: Back in Lishui. Right: Happy Moon Festival!

Next morning, it was moon cake for breakfast and greetings of *Zhong qiu jie kuai le* (Happy Mid-Autumn Festival), which I kept confusing with *Sheng ri kuai le*, which is Happy Birthday. Anyway, no one seemed to mind and we set about the task for the day, which was a long walk from just past Lishui to before Liyang. The road was good, but all my joints were aching from the rowing experience the day before.

One other thing which we had picked up, I suspect from the long (4.5-hour) train journey, was a cold. Xuelin had it worst but it was also building up in me. In the evening, we went in search of pharmacists and different remedies. One thing China has is an infinite variety of medicines or herbal remedies. They are mostly herbal-based. They are all quite cheap, so the approach seems to be to buy a few and see which one works for you. I picked out Bamyl, just because it was made by AstraZeneca, which I had heard of. We went back to our room and mixed various potions before trying to get to sleep.

Normally, I am fairly relaxed about minor illnesses on the grounds that they will just work their way out of the system in time. That was not really an option on the walk. We were now into the last seven days and only had two days for rest. We needed to arrive in Hangzhou on Monday, October 5, and specifically at 5 pm. There was no space for an illness lasting three or four days. I began to regret spending three days in Beijing and cutting our time so close. The news also carried reports that the tail of Typhoon Dujuan would land around where we are on Monday evening. I don't know what we did to offend the Moon but I would now like to officially apologize on behalf of the team. It won't happen again. *Sheng ri kuai le!*

URL http://www.walkforpeace.eu/day-63-moon-festival/

September 28 Day 64

Route Perspectives and Teapots in Yixing

Route: Liyang, Changzhou – Yixing, Wuxi
Walked today: 26.20 miles / 42.20 km
Total walked: 929.60 miles / 1,496.50 km
Donated today: £0.00 / ¥4,010.00
Total donations: £4,540.27 and ¥404,181.45

We continued along the G104 through the south of Jiangsu Province, heading in the direction of the great Taihu Lake. Madam Zhang had been back in Beijing for a few days working on aspects of the final stages of the trip and the mechanics for directing funds to chosen causes. Liyang is on the high-speed rail line, so she was able to return almost direct to the hotel. It was good to have her back with us. Every good team needs a good leader and we are blessed to have Madam Zhang.

Xuelin had been down with a heavy cold, although I have found that in Xuelin's case 'illness' means that she only works for 15 hours a day, rather than the usual 20. Of all the 'medicines' that Xuelin thinks are aiding her recovery, top of the list are 'Hall's Mentholyptus'. I mention that these are British-made candy, not medicine, but she looks at me as if to say, 'So what, if it works?'.

Anyway, we spent about half the day in Liyang and then crossed the border into Yixing for the second half. We were joined by a second television crew who had come from Beijing with Madam Zhang, having secured Red Cross approval to cover the walk for a short promotional video about British–Chinese relations, so I was on my best behaviour (as always, of course).

A new district means a new map. Why is it that when you open a map, you immediately find five men appearing from nowhere who start pointing to different locations on it and arguing? The debates are mostly about competing views of what the route should be: there are those who think safety first and want to stick to wide roads with good cycling/walking lanes; there are those who want the most scenic route, to show me a great temple, museum, battlefield or other place of historic interest. Meanwhile, Xuelin and I observed the debate and simply wanted to find the shortest possible path between where we were and where we needed to get to.

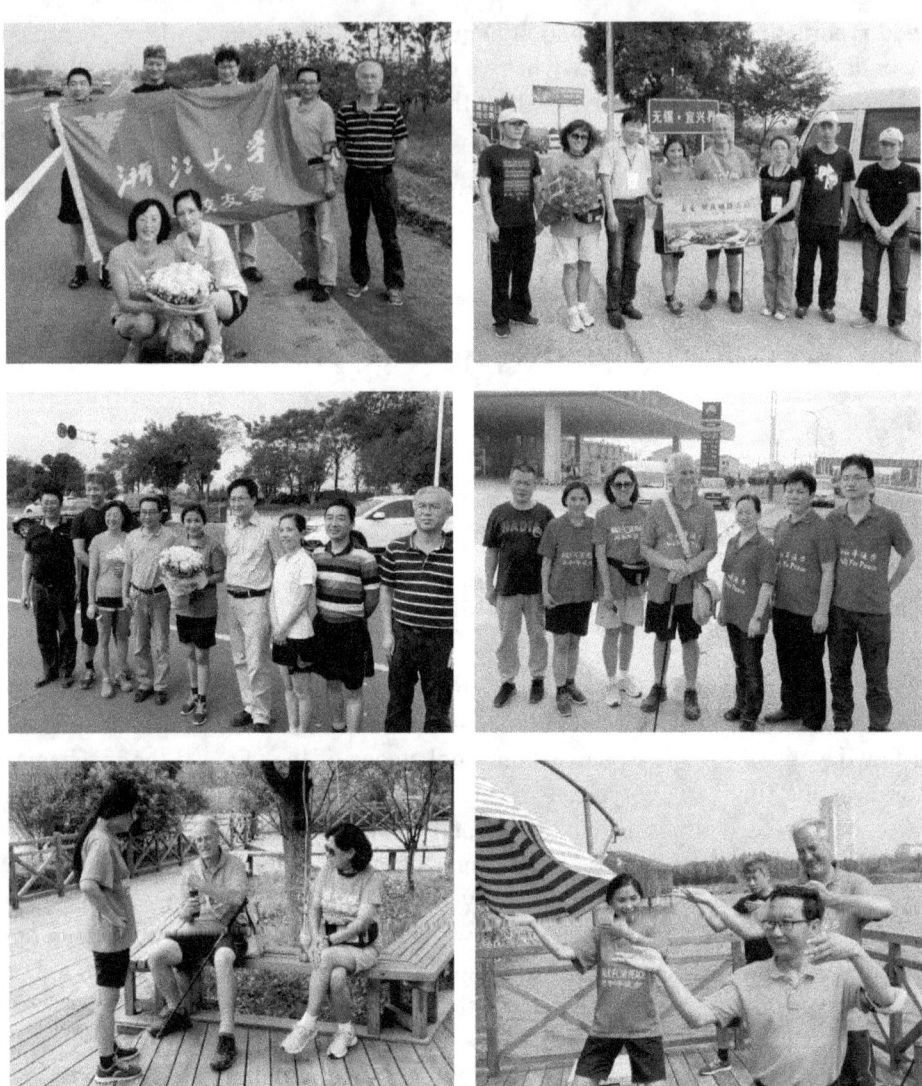

Top left: Another group of Zhejiang University alumni. Top right: Arriving in Yixing, Wuxi. Middle left: The television crew from Beijing. Middle right: Madame Zhang is back from Beijing. Bottom left: Discussing what route to choose. Bottom right: Practising some Tai chi.

Routes are, of course, a question of perspective. If you love your town and city, and most people do, then you want a visitor to see all the wonderful places there are. If you are sitting in a car following the walk, then that scenic route that takes you over a mountain pass via a beautiful temple with spectacular views over a lake sounds just perfect. On the other hand, if you have been walking for 65 days, if every bone and joint in your body is aching and crying out for you to stop, if you have visited 101 'amazing sites' already on your journey, then all you want is to get to the next hotel, shower and get to bed as soon as possible.

If that means walking barefoot over a high-speed rail track or blindfolded through a motorway tunnel, crossing a ravine on a trapeze wire or walking past the main entrance to the Taj Mahal at sunset without missing a step, then you have my current perspective. Madam Zhang arrived at the communal map-reading exercise. 'Ah, Lord, Yixing is very famous for teapots. We can take a detour here and visit the factory of one of the grandmasters of Chinese teapot-making.' I replied, 'Excellent suggestion, Madam Zhang', and doggedly walked on.

URL http://www.walkforpeace.eu/day-64-route-perspectives-in-yixing/

September 29 Day 65

A Tale of Two Dreams

Wuxi, Jiangsu Province
A Day Off
Donated today: £0.00 / ¥0.00
Total donations: £4,540.27 and ¥404,181.45

The term 'Chinese Dream' has become very popular in China since 2013, when it was promoted by President Xi Jinping in a series of speeches on Chinese socialist building. It sounded like the American Dream with which we are more familiar in the West – that ideal that 'All men are created equal and have the right to life, liberty and the pursuit of happiness.'

President Xi said that the Chinese Dream was about 'national rejuvenation, improvement of people's livelihoods, prosperity, the construction of a better society and a strengthened military'. He said that young people should 'dare to dream, work assiduously to fulfil their dreams and contribute to the revitalization of the nation'.

This was interesting background to a deep question that I was asked by an interviewer 'How would you compare the Chinese and the British dreams?' The first problem, which I probably need to return to, was that I wasn't aware that there was a concept of the 'British Dream'. The British culture tends to be very practical, class-based and suspicious of sentimental terms like dreams – in this respect I am not culturally British, as I love the idea of dreams. My life has been shaped by my dreams.

I began my answer by saying that in Britain if you asked young people what their dream was, they might say to be a famous footballer if they were boys or a famous pop singer if they were girls. The problem starts here, because I don't believe that is their dream – it is someone else's. I believe that people have very deep, unique personal dreams for their lives, but they are scared of attracting the ridicule and mockery of their friends by sharing them, so they choose 'social media-acceptable' and ready-made flat-packed dreams instead. It is such a waste of their hidden talent and their personal dreams, which were meant to inspire and illuminate the world.

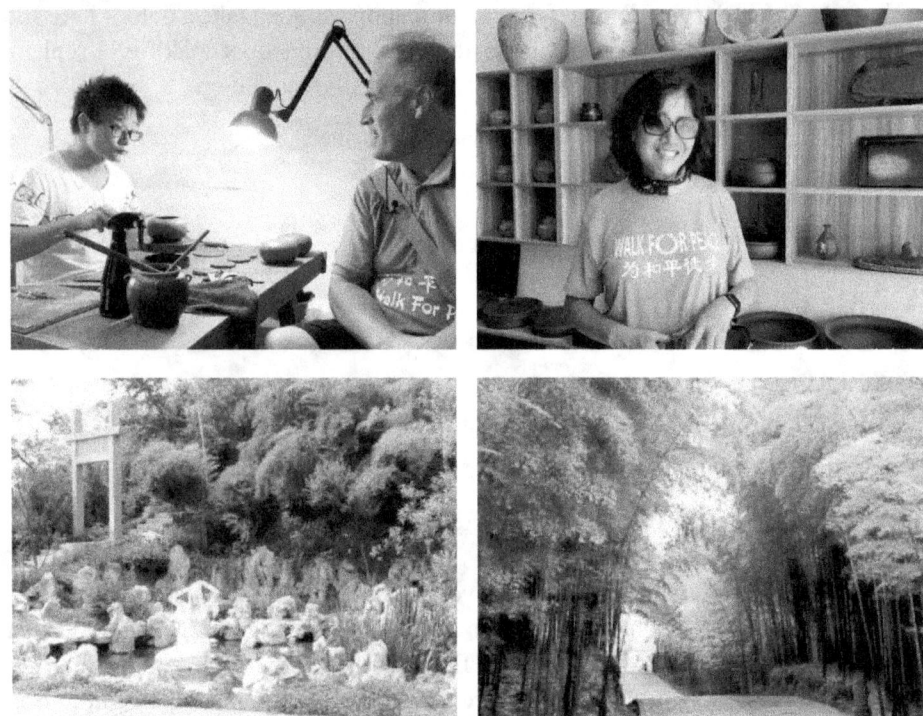

Top left: A pottery master at work. Top right; Madame Zhang in the master's studio.
Bottom left: A stone garden in Wuxi. Bottom right: Bamboo grove in Wuxi.

If there is a weakness in the British or Western dream, then it is perhaps that it is too individualistic and focused on the spin-off benefits of a dream realized, such as fame, money or power. A good society is one that encourages people to discover and develop their unique talents, gifts and dreams, not just for themselves but for benefit of us all.

So how does this compare to the Chinese Dream? The short answer is that I am not very sure. Xuelin would be a better person to ask. That said, here is my best attempt at an answer. In some ways, Chinese young people I meet display similar characteristics to their Western counterparts, in the sense that they may often describe their dream as being something which might win the approval of others, chiefly their parents, such as studying hard and winning a place at a prestigious university. Chinese young people are more collective and less individualistic than their Western counterparts, which is to be expected, given the cultural difference reflected in their history and underlying philosophy. Therefore, instinctively Chinese young people might think not only about what this dream means for them but also what it means for their family and their country. President Xi perfectly captures this thinking in his description of the Chinese Dream mentioned earlier. One final difference between Chinese and British dreams is that failure is a huge source of shame in Chinese culture and can sometimes mean that people don't want to take risks, whereas in America and Britain perhaps the greatest failure would be in not having a go.

I was left thinking that perhaps it is less productive to focus on how Chinese and British dreams might differ and more constructive to think about how they are similar. If the composition of dreams is similar, then I would observe that the reasons why dreams fail are common to both also.

First, people select their dreams too early. In order to discover your unique gifts and talents, you need to have experiences that bring them out. This is a kind of pyramid theory, because you can only build a pyramid as high as the base is wide. The broader the base, the higher you can build. A good piece of advice for a young person is to experience more. Don't just try one sport, try as many as possible before you choose the one you are naturally gifted at. Don't choose one subject to major in but try many to discover where you are strongest. Travel and explore more. Try and have a broader circle of friends who have different interests and passions. Read more. Connect more.

Second, start with the end in mind. Imagine you are looking back at the end of your life. Ask yourself what success looks like. What does life look like once I have achieved my dream?

Third, examine your motivation. Motivation is everything. Ask yourself not only what your dream is but why you want it.

Fourth, build a team of friends around you who are dream-builders, not dream-killers. I am 54 but I have a group of four trusted friends whom I have known for over 25 years. We meet together regularly to offer advice and encourage one another. It is important to have people who will tell you the honest truth, who know you and care for you.

Fifth, don't give your dream to other people to pour cold water on or tell you why it won't work. They should be focused on realising their dream, so don't allow them to undermine yours. Often people are negative about someone else's dream not because they think you might fail but because they fear you might succeed!

Sixth, concentrate on developing your strengths, and don't waste time on your weaknesses. It is normal for us to focus on our weaknesses, what skills we haven't got, and forget to develop the skills we have. We compare our weaknesses to other people's strengths and conclude we are inferior to them. The best way to help minimize your weaknesses is to focus on developing your strengths.

Finally, dreams are not time-limited. As long as we are breathing, then so too the dream within us lives. It is sometimes said that 'education is wasted on the young', by which they mean that the older we get the more we value education and can place it in the context of life experience. So it is with dreams; sometimes they can be wasted on the young, who think success in life is guaranteed and that they will live forever. If they could meet the person who has known the failure of a business, failure in a relationship or ill-health, then they would be different. You can't learn experience in a classroom; it is part of life and needs to lived and learned as we go along. For this reason, it might be that the best people to realize a dream are those who are old. They may be physically weaker but they are emotionally, intellectually and spiritually stronger. You are never too old to be the person you might have been. Why not test this, by starting today?

URL http://www.walkforpeace.eu/day-65-a-tale-of-two-dreams/

September 30 Day 66

China Growing Taller and Getting Deeper

Route: Yixing, Wuxi, Jiangsu Province
– Changxingxian, Huzhou, Zhejiang Province
Walked today: 28.30 miles / 45.50 km
Total walked: 957.90 miles / 1,542.00 km
Donated today: £0.00 / ¥0.00
Total donations: £4,540.27 and ¥404,181.45

Back on the G104 for our final day in Jiangsu Province. I will miss the Red Cross team who have been with us over the last 25 days We have become good friends.

Professionally, I have long taken an interest in trends in events. The argument goes that the world changes gradually and sometimes imperceptibly to our event-obsessed media. Truth is not found in the dot of one event but in the joining together of many dots to observe a trend. All along my journey from Beijing, I discovered lots of dots in the form of new temples being built on mountain tops or prayer towers, parks and pagodas. I think it is a trend that shows a desire to rediscover the deep philosophical and spiritual history of the country.

Those roots have not always been encouraged. Sometimes they have been deliberately torn up, as in the early stages of the Cultural Revolution, but now there is a growing yearning to rediscover the vast wealth of history of the great peoples of China. It is ironic that it was an obsessive adherence to the works of Marx, a German philosopher, that turned the Red Guards against their own history and culture.

The great opening up of China economically has been taking place since 1984, but the deepening of China is something that is seldom written about. However, it is, I believe, something of significance that should be discussed more. I would be as positive about the deepening of Chinese society as I would be about its opening up. Religion and philosophy are part of man's search for meaning. They are what make us human – that desire to see the material world in a spiritual context. Every civilization in the world through history has a religious or philosophical system. Such systems give us our moral codes, our rites of passage, and provide us with a belief about where we came from, why and where we are going to.

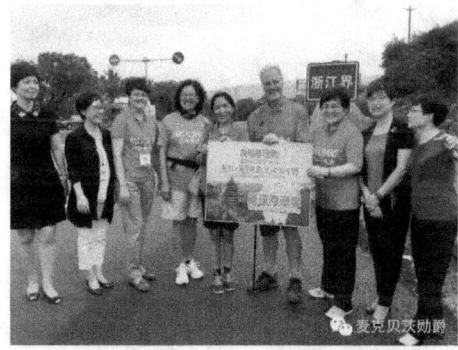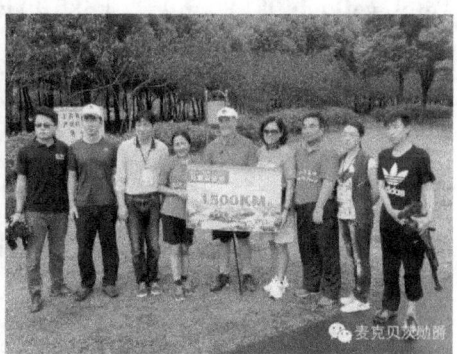
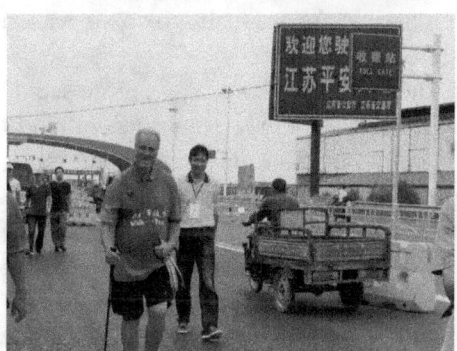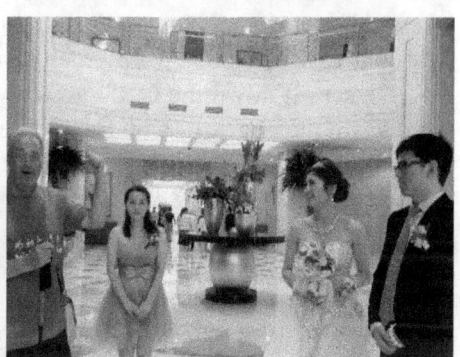

Top left: Reaching Zhejiang Province and meeting local Red Cross employees.
Top right: Lord and Lady Bates holding the '1,500 km' sign. Bottom left: Walking towards Huzhou. Bottom right: Lord Bates meeting a couple of newlyweds.

China has a rich history from which to draw inspiration for the modern soul: Confucianism, Taoism and Legalism, as well as adapted imports such as Zen Buddhism, to name but a few. When the history of 5,000 years of scholarship, literature and architecture was dismissed, the Chinese society was chopping at its own roots. To deny our history and culture is a sign of insecurity; to embrace it is a sign of strength. Now these roots are being rediscovered and invited to take their rightful place in modern China, and the society will be more stable, the branches better nourished and able to produce even better fruit.

URL http://www.walkforpeace.eu/day-66-china-growing-taller-and-getting-deeper/

October 1 Day 67

It's a Small, Small World in Zhejiang

Route: Changxingxian – Downtown, Huzhou
Walked today: 23.90 miles / 38.40 km
Total walked: 981.80 miles / 1,580.40 km
Donated today: £0.00 / ¥0.00
Total donations: £4,540.27 and ¥404,181.45

A spectacular view of the Taihu Lake greeted us from the G104 as we crossed the border from Jiangsu to Zhejiang. Taihu Lake is the third largest freshwater lake in China. It is a good reminder that the natural environment is a key driver in the development of civilization. There is a reason why early civilization flourished on the Yangtze River delta rather than in the Gobi Desert. It is because of the abundance of fresh water, the fertile flat lands for crops and a large network of lakes and rivers connecting to the sea for navigation and trade. It is also the reason why control of the lands was fiercely contested.

We set off down the G104 and it was then suggested we take a more scenic route down the edge of Taihu Lake. The weather wasn't great, blustery with light rain, but the lake still looked majestic. Also, rather than marching along being sprayed by heavy lorries, we were on a glorious cycle path and footpath that ran around the edge of the lake. Everywhere I have been in China I have noticed how extraordinarily well kept the hedges and borders were alongside the road. Along the edge of Taihu Lake, these borders were turned into an art form, absolutely beautiful. I think the 20-km stretch of Taihu Lake down to Huzhou must be the best cycle path in the world, and it is inspiring for walkers too.

I paused for a short break in a bus shelter during a heavy downpour. As I sat drinking my water, a lady wearing a Union Jack T-shirt approached, holding an iPhone. I thought that she might want a picture with this strange Westerner but she was wanting me to look at the phone. I smiled and looked and there was a picture of me on the terrace of the House of Lords with a young man; I didn't recognize him immediately. Madam Zhang appeared and helped translate. This lady was Li Huizi, a well known Huzhou artist. The boy in the photo was Mali Wei Qi, her son, who was studying in London and currently working as part of Xuelin's team translating these blogs into Chinese every day. What a small world!

Li Huizi had put her talents to great use by designing a picture based on our walk, which I had used often without fully appreciating the artist. In addition to the work of Li Huizi and her son, she had also come with a very generous dona-tion to the Red Cross projects we are supporting through the walk. And as if that wasn't a great enough contribution to Walk for Peace from this one family, she then joined me for the remaining 25 km of the day's walk. It is so encouraging to meet such people and to see their commitment to our common cause.

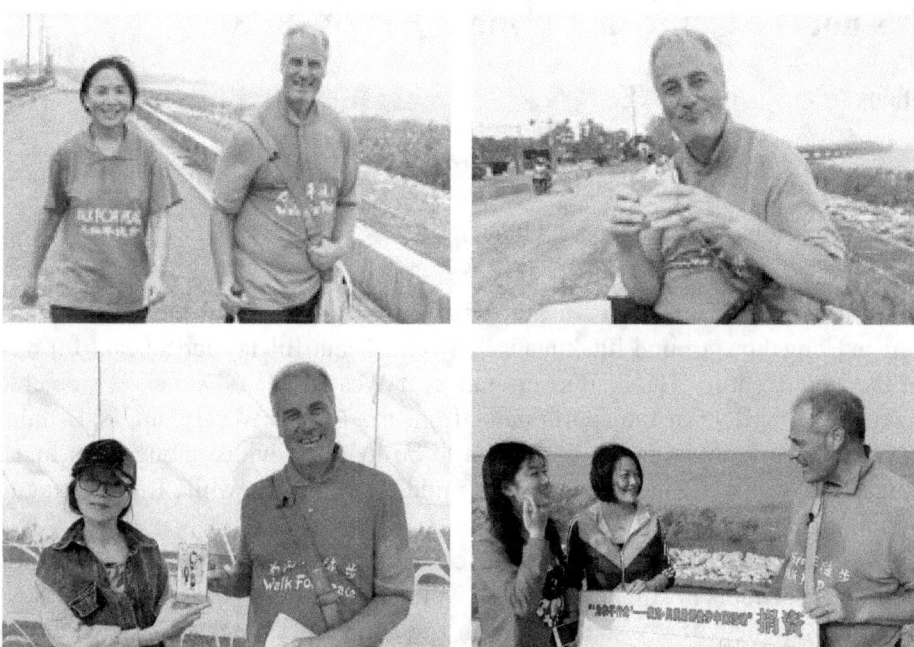

Top left: Walking along Taihu Lake all day. Top right: Lunch at the roadside. Bottom left: Lord Bates and Li Huizi. Bottom right: Lord Bates receives a cheque of 30,000 RMB from a company in Zhejiang Province.

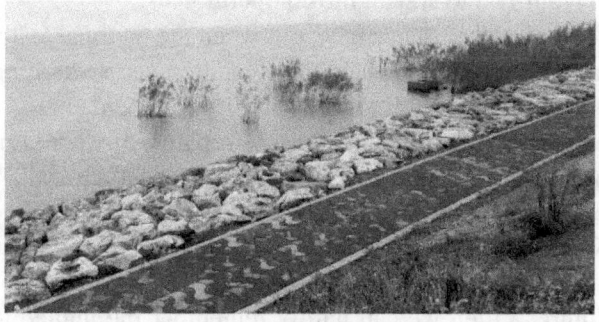

The lake shore.

The meeting also reminded us of the prodigious work being done back in London and here in China every day to take these blogs and translate them into Chinese. I know that my use of some terms often challenges their abilities to the limit, but Xuelin tells me that the quality of their work is absolutely outstanding, and we are so grateful to them.

URL http://www.walkforpeace.eu/day-67-its-a-small-small-world-in-zhejiang/

October 2 Day 68

It's not the Critic that Counts + PS & PPS

Huzhou, Zhejiang Province
A Day Off
Donated today: £520.00 / ¥0.00
Total donations: £5,060.27 and ¥404,181.45

It was a rest day in Huzhou as we prepared for the final three-day push to the finish line in Hangzhou, around 100 km away. It was a beautiful day and a beautiful stay at the New Century Hotel. With its range of Western TV channels, I was able to catch up on lots of the sports news from the Rugby World Cup. In Britain, sport, like so many areas of life, tends to be loosely divided along class lines. Rugby Union-like cricket tends to be a middle-class sport, while Rugby League and football are more working-class.

The division really stems from school, as it tended to be the private schools or the state schools in affluent areas that would play rugby in the winter and cricket in the summer. At my state school in a working class area of Tyneside, they played football in winter, summer and spring and morning, noon and night. Why am I saying this? Well, part as a little cultural exchange, but really because at the moment England is hosting the Rugby Union World Cup, and things aren't going too well. England was defeated by fellow Brits, Wales, and now must win against Australia (the favourites) to stay in the competition.

I follow football rather than rugby, but when the national team is competing, whether it is in the four-man bobsleigh or synchronized swimming, I want them to win and do well. I was watching a string of commentators giving their 'expert analysis' with the benefit of slow-motion replays, of where England is going wrong and what it needs to do to win the game against Australia on Saturday. I don't think there was a member of the England team, including the bus driver and the lady who washes the shorts and irons the shirts, who escaped criticism for their performance against Wales.

Criticism hurts. Often we can hardly remember the numerous encouraging things that are said about us, but we never forget a word of criticism. Why is this? Well, basically it is because we are all a bit insecure and need approval. But the other reason is that, the minute you get off the sofa or out of the stands and set foot on the pitch, you will become a target for criticism. If you can't handle criticism, then your place is back on the sofa with a beer in one hand and the remote control in the other.

Critics know they have power because we are all sensitive to criticism. So, the film critic gives an unfavourable review to a new movie, but he or she has never acted, directed or written a screenplay. The art critic dismisses the latest work of an artist and yet has never painted. The commentator criticizes the actions of officials, but could he or she have done better? Aristotle summed this up perfectly in 350 BC when he wrote: 'Criticism is something we can avoid easily by saying nothing, doing nothing and being nothing.'

Theodore Roosevelt, the 26th President of the United States, who came in for his fair share of criticism said,

> It is not the critic who counts; not the man who points out how the strong man stumbles, or where the doer of deeds could have done them better. The credit belongs to the man who is actually in the arena, whose face is marred by dust and sweat and blood; who strives valiantly; who errs, who comes short again and again, because there is not effort without error and shortcomings; but who does actually strive to do the deeds; who knows the great enthusiasms, the great devotions, who spends himself in a worthy cause, who at the best knows in the end the triumph of high achievement, and who at the worst, if he fails, at least he fails while daring greatly, so that his place shall never be with those cold and timid souls who neither know victory nor defeat.

So, as the England rugby team walk out into the area again in London on Saturday in front of a packed Twickenham with 82,000 spectators after the game, no player will waste a second thinking of the critics. They are there on the pitch, caked in dust, sweat and blood. Which player would swap that spine-tingling opportunity for sitting in the stands with a lukewarm coffee and a soggy sausage roll to commentate on the performance of others? Life is not meant to be a spectator sport. It is meant to be lived out in the centre of the arena, where the voice of the critics is drowned out by the thrill of the game.

Those Chinese friends who have yet to discover the joys of rugby (although there is a Chinese National Rugby team – currently ranked 66th in the world – one place above England – only joking!) should watch the movie *Invictus*, directed by Clint Eastwood and starring Morgan Freeman and Matt Damon. The title of the movie is based on a famous poem by W. E. Henley of the same name. In order to lift the spirits of my home team ahead of the clash against Australia, I will leave you with two short verses from the epic poem:

> In the fell clutch of circumstance
> I have not winced nor cried aloud.
> Under the bludgeonings of chance
> My head is bloody, but unbowed.
>
> It matters not how strait the gate,
> How charged with punishments the scroll,
> I am the master of my fate,
> I am the captain of my soul.

Come on, England!

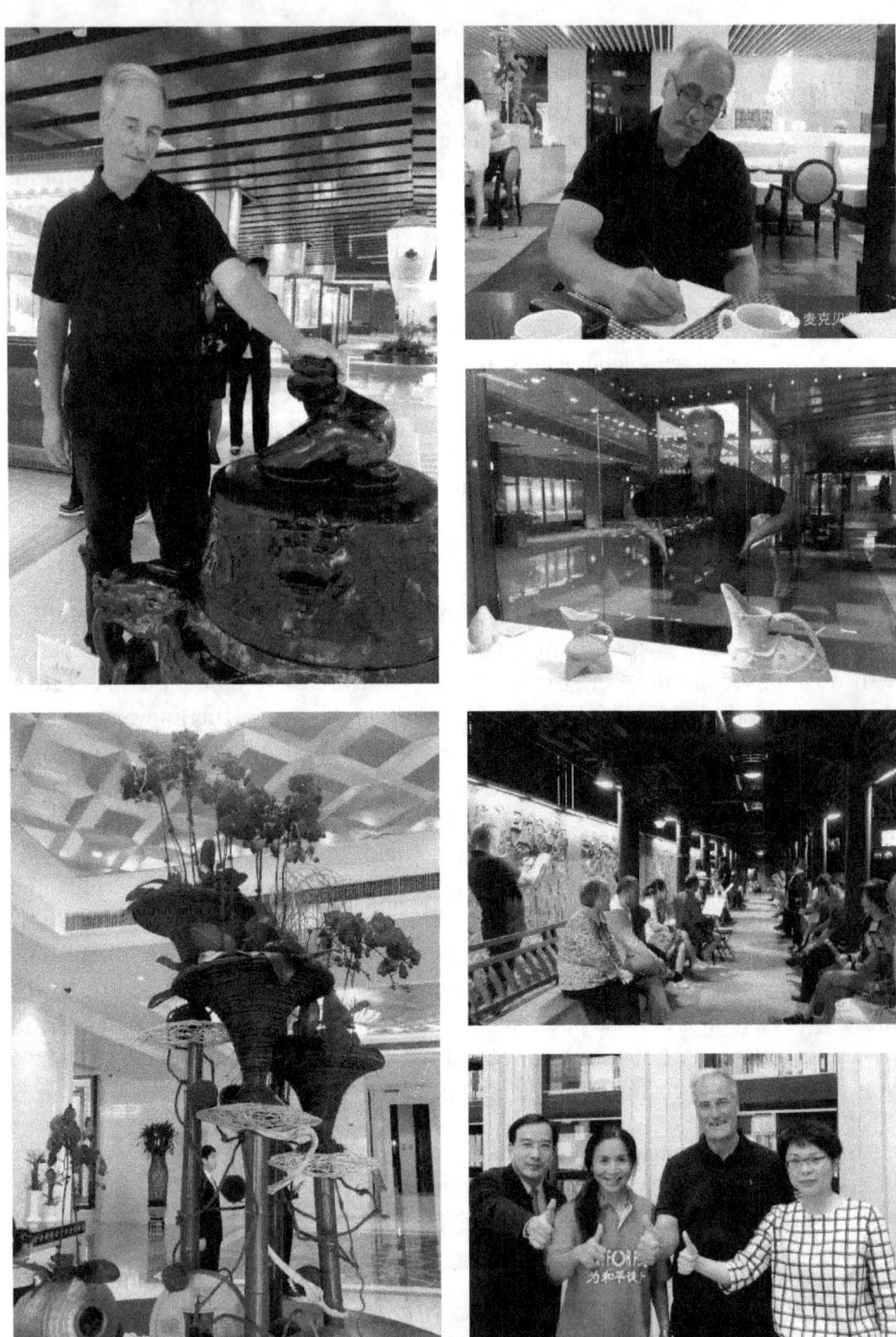

Top left and right: Rest day in Huzhou. Bottom left: Hall of the New Century Hotel.
Bottom right: Meeting supporters in Huzhou.

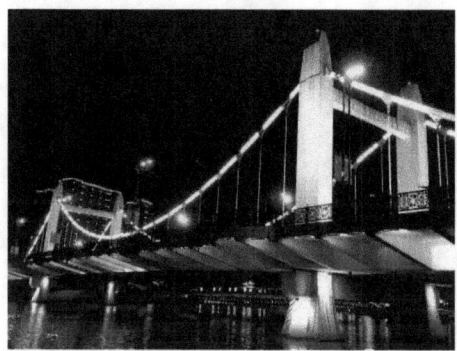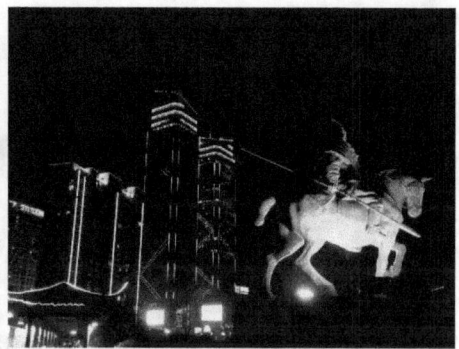

Nighttime in Huzhou.

PS. Postscripts (PS.) are a useful tool when writing about fast-moving events. I am afraid my stirring words did not reach the England rugby dressing room in time, for the team were soundly beaten by Australia, 33 to 13, and are now out of the World Cup, which they are hosting. My point, I think, still holds, in that it is the true joy of life to be out in the arena covered in sweat and mud giving your all, even when you are being thrashed by the Aussies, rather than it is to be a mere spectator or, worse, a commentator.

PPS. Now I am getting confused here: is a PPS a postscript to a PS? Or should this be a new PS? Don't criticize me if I make the wrong choice. The afterthought was that when I had written the blog, Xuelin read it and remarked that in China self-criticism was encouraged and then went on to criticize me for not mentioning it! Xuelin is, of course, right: the best form of criticism is that which comes from within, because you are more likely to act upon it. I should also say that there are some people in this world who will instinctively want the very best for you and will offer selfless advice without any agenda other than your personal happiness – these people are called 'your parents'. Listen to them.

URL http://www.walkforpeace.eu/day-68-its-not-the-critic-that-counts/

October 3 Day 69

Personal Safety?

Route: Downtown – Deqingxian, Huzhou
Walked today: 27.90 miles / 45.00 km
Total walked: 1,009.70 miles / 1,625.40 km
Donated today: £0.00 / ¥0.00
Total donations: £5,060.27 and ¥404,181.45

It was my own fault – I was so excited at seeing a Starbucks across the road from our hotel in Huzhou that I walked out into the road when I thought the traffic had stopped and a motor scooter came around the blind-side of a truck and almost took us both out.

It was a close call but on arrival in the heavenly tranquillity that is Starbucks, I reflected on how rare an instance this had been on my walk in China and how safe I had felt on the journey. I recalled a conversation I had had last year about my proposed journey with someone who had cycled from Qingdao to Beijing. He said that it was dangerous enough being on a bike but on foot on busy roads I just 'wouldn't survive'.

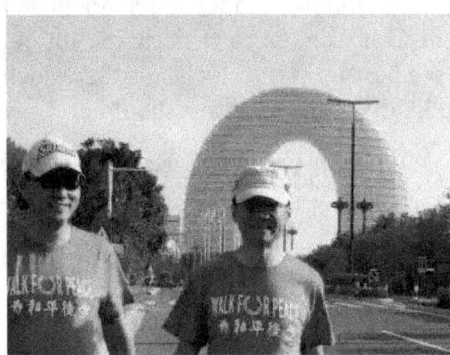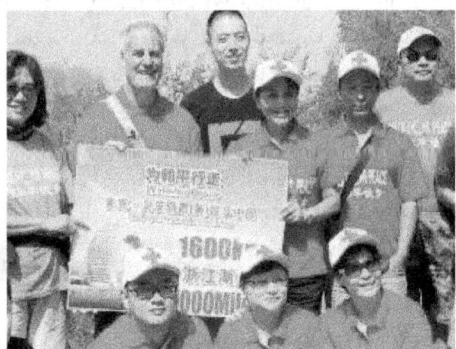

Left: Two members of the local Red Cross team.
Right: The local Red Cross team and the TV crew.

Well, I don't want to tempt fate but so far he is wrong, very wrong. In fact, as I have walked along the roads in the daytime and around the town and village centres in the evening I have felt very safe. China is an orderly and respectful society. At times it may look a bit chaotic on the surface but there is a strong moral code, and if that fails to restrain then there is a real fear of authority.

On most of my walks I am alone and therefore, from a safety point of view, you might think quite vulnerable, especially when I can be seen to be carrying all my worldly possessions in my rucksack, including cash, cards, iPhone, camera, passport and computer. I once remember being given a stern briefing by a British Embassy security adviser in Sarajevo; he estimated that I was walking around with at least 1,000 euros in easily realizable cash/items on my back, which can make you a bit of a target, especially to drug addicts.

I am not blasé when it comes to personal safety. I do not like to walk in dusk or dark or in very heavy rain. I like to walk facing the oncoming traffic so that I can eyeball the driver to see if he/she is aware of me. That said, in China you must walk 'with the direction of traffic' but also most of the time I was walking with other people, so we created a greater presence on the road.

When I am walking around towns and cities at night, I try to stick to well-lit areas. When I do come across suspicious groups or individuals, then I always avoid eye contact. Eye contact is critical to conflict in the animal kingdom because making eye contact with a human or animal can be seen as threatening. Also humans (perhaps all animals do this) use eye contact as a means of weighing up the weakness/strength of someone whom they might attack; avoid eye contact and you at least create a doubt in their mind over your capabilities to defend yourself if attacked.

I have walked through 18 countries on my walks to date and China is as safe as any and safer than most. I wanted to test this perception in numbers, so I went to check out the international ranking of countries by murder/homicide rates and this seemed to confirm my instinct about China. With a rate of murders per 100,000 of population of 1.0, that puts it among the lowest rates in the world – 188th out of 218, in fact. The rate is the same as the UK (190th) and France (191st).

To show just how relatively safe those countries are, it is worth noting that India has a murder rate of 3.5 per 100,000, the United States is 111th with a murder rate of 4.7 (compared to 1.0 in China), the rate in the Philippines is 8.8 per 100,000, Russia 9.2, South Africa 31, Jamaica 39.3, Venezuela 53.7 and Honduras 90.4. To show just how bad the murder rate is in countries like Honduras, Venezuela, Jamaica and South Africa, consider the murder rate in Iraq, which is 8.8 per 100,000 population and in Afghanistan, which is 6.5.

Most countries with high violent crime rates are those in which there is a drug trade or other form of organized crime and high levels of alcoholism. People addicted to drugs will do anything to get their next fix. People under the influence of drugs or excessive alcohol lose their sense of inbuilt personal restraint. People involved in gang cultures will do almost anything to retain the respect of other gang members.

The fact that China has relatively low rates of violent crime may be due to the fact that it has managed to control the driving forces behind crime. It takes a very tough stance, of course, and China executed over 550 prisoners (2014), which is the largest number of executions in the world – twice as many as Iran and the United States, which executed 35. Of course, I am switching statistical methods to make a point here: when expressed in executions per 1 million population, China falls to 10th.

The Chinese people might fairly point to the fact that every 1.0 per 100,000 rise in the murder rate is 13,410 innocent people who are killed per year, compared to 550 executed. However, I have always been opposed to the death penalty, because I believe that life is sacred and no one has the right to take it away; because courts can make mistakes – we frequently receive reports that new evidence has been found which proves the innocence of someone convicted of a murder – it is bad enough that someone may have been deprived of his or her liberty for 10 or 15 years but they can be released – not so if they were executed; and because I believe in personal redemption. I believe that basically good people in a moment of madness can do bad things, but they are capable of facing up to the evil they have done and working for the remainder of their lives (albeit mostly in prison) to try and make amends.

Those doubting this latter point might read or watch Victor Hugo's *Les Misérables* and reflect on the encounter between Jean Valjean and Bishop Myriel. (I choose Victor Hugo because he is a highly respected figure in China. He was one of the few Western thinkers at the time to call the burning and looting of the Old Summer Palace in Beijing in 1860 by Anglo-French forces an act of 'barbarism', which on reflection was probably an understatement.)

URL http://www.walkforpeace.eu/day-69-personal-safety/

October 4 Day 70

Mother-in-law's Question Goes to the Heart of the Matter

Route: Deqingxian, Huzhou – Yuhang District, Hangzhou
Walked today: 26.30 miles / 42.30 km
Total walked: 1,036.00 miles / 1,667.70 km
Donated today: £400.00 / ¥170,288.00
Total donations: £5,460.27 and ¥574,469.45

It was raining hard during the day as we set off from Donglinzhen and followed a path along a riverbank, which became progressively muddier. The grips on the soles of my new walking shoes in Beijing have been completely worn down by the walk, so I was slipping around like a ballerina, or more like an elephant on roller skates. This slowed progress, with only one day to go. At lunchtime we had only done 12 km, whereas we should have done 18 km.

Xuelin did not want me to miss the target point for Day 70, which was Renhezhen. Her reasons were not only that we did not want to leave more than 35 km to do on the final day but also because she wanted us be able to stay at her home and have dinner with her mother and brother-in-law. We had a bit of a debate with rain-soaked maps as to which was the best route into Hangzhou – the river or the high-speed rail line? The rail line won, and it proved to be a good decision, as it brought us into Renhezhen at 5 pm.

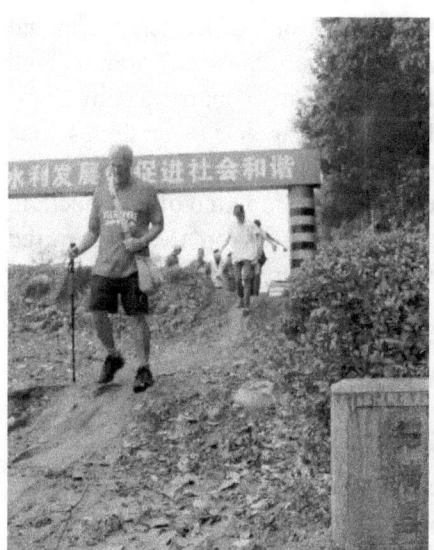
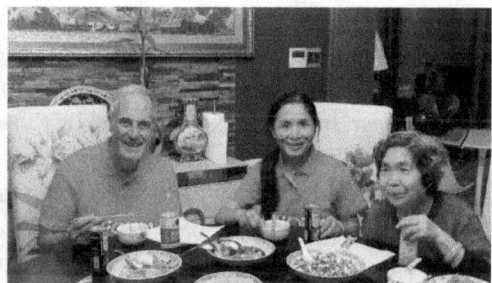
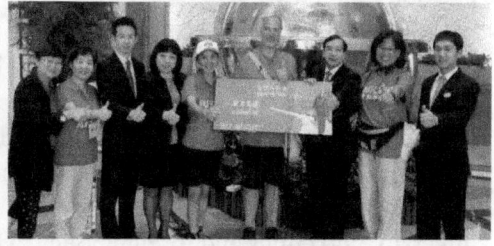

Left: Walking towards Renhezhen. Top right: Dinner with Mrs Wu, Lady Bates's mother. Bottom right: Welcome committee in Renhezhen.

It was wonderful to walk through the door of Xuelin's mother's beautiful home. It is one of my favourite places on the planet. It is an oasis of green in a sea of concrete. The wonderful array of trees and flowers in the garden attracts birds from far and wide. You are woken up with a wonderful dawn chorus. I think birdsong is the most beautiful music in the world for its melody and the fact that it is from living creatures communicating with each other.

I am proud to be a son-in-law of Hangzhou and proud that Mrs Wu is my mother-in-law. She is always so cheerful, gives me a hug and then pats my stomach and asks how my Chinese is coming along. Fortunately, on the walk I have managed to pick up about 50 new phrases or words, which I spill out in random fashion to try to impress her. Sadly, my attempts seem to produce more laughter than admiration.

A beautiful dinner was prepared and enjoyed. As the plates were being cleared away, Mrs Wu looked at me with sadness in her eyes and spoke at some length. I asked Xuelin what her mother had said and her response surprised me: 'My mum said, why do you trade your life for this walk? Your health is the most important thing; why would you risk it for this walk? Why put yourself through such hardship when you should be enjoying this time of life?' Mrs Wu and her daughter have a habit of being direct, but even so, this caught me off guard.

I had just slipped and slogged 42.3 km in the driving rain. I didn't enjoy one bit of it. I just wanted to finish. The fact that my shorts and shirt were soaked by the rain meant that I got friction burns in sensitive places and could only half sit on the seat at the dining room table. I feel guilty to say this, but I was tired and fed-up and Mrs Wu perhaps sensed this and asked the obvious question. Why?

I am in politics and am privileged to be a member of the UK Parliament and also to serve as a minister in the UK government. I regard these positions as both a remarkable honour and a heavy responsibility to serve my country and my party. I do my best, but politics is at times like wading through treacle to get things done – this probably says less about the political process in the UK and more about my lack of skill and ability within it. Walking therefore to me is a kind of direct action. At the end of each day, I can see the distance travelled on a map, the funds raised for charity online and opportunities to understand and share thoughts through conversations and blogs.

Moreover, the areas on which you are required to focus in the political arena are not necessarily the ones for which you have a burning passion. My passion is peace.

I became exposed to the world and the roots of conflict through a marvellous seven years as Director of Consultancy and Research at Oxford Analytica (www.oxan.com). This continued for two years of doctoral research at Durham University into ethics and foreign policy, which I failed to complete (insert: guilt). I continue to read and research extensively in this area. I believe we are on the verge of exposing the male lust for violence and the human glorification of war for what it is: a primaeval animal instinct. Its roots lie more in anthropology and tribal culture than in politics. Its antidotes are in the realms of competitive sport, education, cultural exchange and international systems of justice.

My core theory is that 'we are all the same'; there is good and evil in the world but it is not out there; it is in us. There are differences in culture, language and religion but these are explained not by some divine plan but by the simple accident of birth and our tribal roots. The more we see each other as human first and our adopted culture second, the less we will distrust, the less we will feel threatened by difference, the less we will feel superior or inferior and the more we may seek to resolve disputes through agreed systems of justice based on the fundamental principle of the equal value, worth, rights and responsibilities of each and every human being.

It sounds so improbable – a world without war? Yet I feel like some 15th-century explorer who senses in his bones there is a Northwest Passage between the Pacific and Atlantic Oceans but lacks the evidence to prove it. At some point, you just want to stop analysing the maps and get in a boat and go and find it. Well, for me, walking is 'getting in the boat'. In each country I walk through, 18 so far, what strikes me most are not our differences, which are trivial, entirely cultural and massively overstated, but our similarities, which are vast, awe-inspiring and largely unexplored.

I have yet to prove this theory or win an argument on its central premise, even among high school students, let alone political colleagues. I don't have the intellect or the words to even make the case, let alone win the argument, so I let my walk be my talk and hope.

URL http://www.walkforpeace.eu/day-70-mrs-wus-question/

October 5 Day 71

Crossing the Finishing Line

Route: Yuhang District – Zhejiang University, Hangzhou
Walked today: 21.70 miles / 35.00 km
Total walked: 1,057.70 miles / 1,702.70 km
Donated today: £195.83 / ¥37,986.00
Total donations: £5,656.10 and ¥612,455.45

The final day. Did I think it would ever come? In the plan, it was meant to be a rather symbolic walk of 10 km on to the campus of Zhejiang University, but slower progress over the past few days meant that I still had 35 km to walk.

Xuelin and Madam Zhang were in a whirlwind of activity organizing the closing ceremony, meeting points for people who wanted to come out and join us for a few miles on the final day and meeting points for press and media who were wanting to cover the final stages of the walk or present us with donations for the charitable causes. Apart from signing T-shirts, writing thank you notes and posing for photographs, all I had to concern myself with was walking 35 km.

Within a couple of hours, we were walking under the G2501 ring road and into the city of Hangzhou. Hangzhou is one of the most beautiful and prosperous cities in China. It has a population of over 21 million. It is surrounded by hills and mountains, which produce some of the finest and most expensive tea (Dragon well or longjing) in China and it was the centre of the silk trade. It is a city focused around the West Lake, which is a magnet for tourism and led Marco Polo to describe the city as the 'Venice of the East', and, as if that weren't enough praise, he added (in Italian of course). 'Hangzhou is the finest and most splendid city in the world.' Its location on the Yangtze River delta and at the southern end of the Grand Canal connecting it to Beijing added to its commercial and trading appeal and from there its wealth.

Today it retains those physical strengths, and it has also become a technology centre because of the leading universities and great living conditions and is the home to the Alibaba Group, one of the largest tech companies in the world. The prosperity is very obvious from the Western luxury cars, high fashions, huge Gucci and Luis Vuitton stores and flats with lake views that cost more than flats in London and New York.

When Xuelin and I had originally thought of a route for a walk in China, we had thought of following the Grand Canal through its entire length but then found that in many places there was no road or footpath to travel along. So when we came into the city, we quickly joined the footpath along the Jinghang Canal stretch of the Grand Canal and followed it down about 10 km to West Lake Plaza. The footpath along the canal was delightful, although the falling leaves and wet conditions made it quite challenging in places.

By now I was in top gear, walking with the end in sight and probably doing 6 km per hour. So quickly was I going that Xuelin had to come and tell us to slow down because they weren't expecting us to arrive at the university campus until 4.30 pm, and because of the rain they had needed to move the ceremony indoors.

Not needing much persuading to stop at a Starbucks, we sat down and checked the mileage on my pedometers. I carry two iPhones, both with the same app (Moves), which I can then cross-check to record an accurate distance. The apps were showing that I was going to finish having done 1,698 km (1,061 miles), and so we decided that, as we had time, instead of taking the direct route down Shuguang Road, we would walk around the edge of West Lake and this would take us just over 1,700 km (1,062.5 miles). It was a good idea, but this was National Holiday week and even in the rain the narrow paths and bridges around the lake were packed with tourists, which slowed us up a bit, but it was a good strategy all round.

Suddenly the crowds drifted away as we walked up from the West Lake up Yugu Road and through the famous Hangzhou Botanical Gardens. I was joined by Madam Zhang and Xuelin for the final couple of kilometres, which was what I wanted, for without them then this walk simply would not have happened. The number of Red Cross volunteers, Zhejiang University alumni, friends and supporters was now around 30–40, although I couldn't quite see the end of the group.

I wanted Xuelin to choose the end point of the walk in Hangzhou. Madam Zhang was right: this was a 'walk for peace' from Beijing to Nanjing and a 'walk for love' from Nanjing to Hangzhou. My partner in both walks is Xuelin. We met through my first walk for peace in 2011 and this is not just my passion, but ours. Xuelin was a student of architectural design at Zhejiang University – Yuquan Campus for seven years, completing two degrees, before coming to London to work in architectural practice.

For Xuelin, the association with Zhejiang University is a very special one. She is president of the alumni in the UK. Zhejiang is one of China's top-tier universities, usually coming in third in league tables, just behind Peking and Tsinghua. So Zhejiang University was the end point of the walk and the Temple of Heaven was the start.

As we approached the campus entrance, we saw a huge number of umbrellas and thought perhaps there had been an accident, but as we got closer it became clear they were there for us. We walked up to the finish line together to loud cheers and then, after a short pause, I pushed through the red ribbon marking the end of the walk. Students stepped forward with bouquets of flowers. Officials came to offer their congratulations. Everyone wanted a photo and we were only too happy to oblige. It was a truly memorable homecoming. I felt incredibly proud to be a 'son-in law' of this great city, university and very proud of my wife.

That wasn't quite it, though …

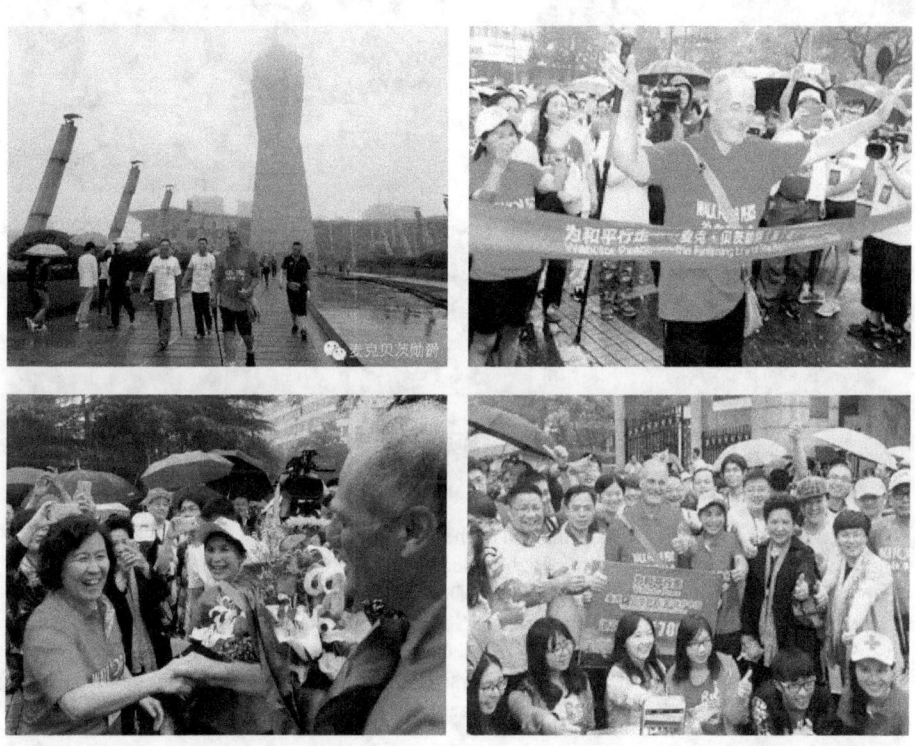

Top left: Wulin Square, Hangzhou. Top right: 1702.7 km in 71 days: the 'Walk for Peace' successfully ended at Zhejiang University. Bottom left: Welcome committee in the campus of Zhejiang University. Bottom right: Lord and Lady Bates with people at the gate of the University.

After the photos, people started heading to the main hall for the formal welcome ceremony. With great organization, Xuelin had booked a room at a hotel next door, where I could go for a shower and change of clothes. As we entered the room, I sat on a chair and Xuelin and I just looked at each other and smiled. It was like the scene you see when a Formula One race is over and the winners go into the small room to put on their official caps and get weighed. Words are few. The race is over – no words are necessary.

Ten minutes later and we were back on the university campus and ushered into a formal seated area with what seemed like a couple of hundred people seated in front of a large Walk for Peace banner. Madam Zhang, our host for the ceremony, Project Director from the Red Cross, constant companion on the walk and friend, had everything organized to the last detail.

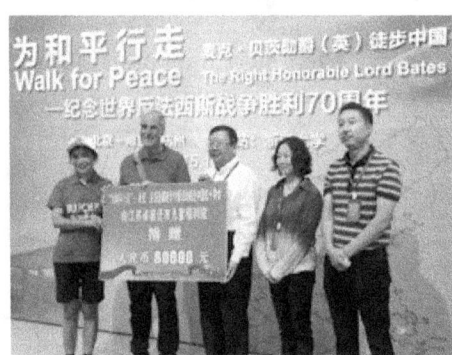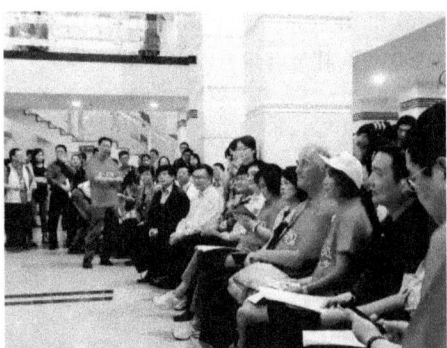

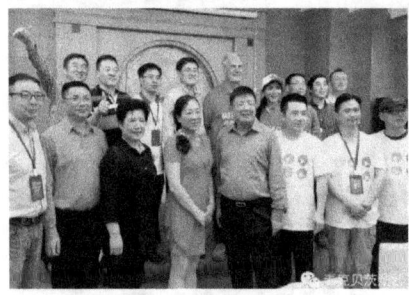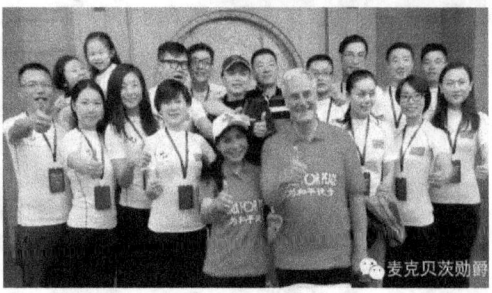

Top left: At the ceremony to mark the end of the Walk for Peace, Lord Bates presents cheques for the money raised by the walk to: Pizhou Red Cross's 'Hope House', Xuzhou City, Jiangsu Province; Linyi County Veteran Care Project, Dezhou City, Shandong Province; the Red Cross Veteran Care Project, Zhejiang Province; the Suqian Orphanage, Jiangsu Province; and Qing County Liusha Middle School Project, Cangzhou City, Hebei Province.
Top right: Closing ceremony at Zhejiang University. Bottom: Lord and Lady Bates and groups of supporters during the closing ceremony at Zhejiang University

There were kind and generous speeches from Wu Jing, Vice Chairman of the Zhejiang Provincial Committee of the CPPCC, and Madam Hao Linna, Deputy Head of the Red Cross Society of China, who had been with us at the start and visited us in Nanjing and was now here at the close. There were welcomes from the Dean and Secretary of the university committee of the Communist Party of China (CPC). Most important of all, we were able to hand over the first cheque for £50,000 (500,000 yuan) to Hope House, Pizhou, the Suqien Orphanage and Zhejiang Elderly Care. The leaders of these organizations had all made the journey down to receive the cheque, which made the presentation all the more special.

The total of pledges came to £70,000 (700,000 yuan), but in good accounting style the Red Cross wanted to make sure the monies had been received before they were distributed. There was also £5,706 which had been collected for the British Red Cross through the JustGiving site in the UK. The Red Cross had covered all its costs for the walk centrally, so that all the funds raised could go to the causes we identified, a wonderful gesture, and, of course, Xuelin and I had covered all our costs personally also. Our hope is that the total may increase still further in the days to come.

In my remarks, I added our thanks to Madam Zhang for her inspirational work. We were blessed to have her with us and it had been a privilege to get to know her. I also thanked those who had walked with us – over 700 – and those who had donated to the charitable causes – over 1,000. I thanked the 20 Red Cross teams who had guided us through their city, district or province. I thanked the Zhejiang alumni, the support team back in London, who had done such an amazing job of translating these blogs in record time, and the documentary team from CCTV, who had followed us all the way from Beijing.

I had one final message and that was for those in the audience and in the media who had listened to the generous tributes. I was worried that they might take this as about how special I am, which is to miss the point. The point is that we are all special and capable of doing truly amazing things. It matters not your age, your education, your social or professional status, your health and your wealth: if we follow our passion, focus on what we have rather than what we have not and have the courage to take the first step, then we can all achieve extraordinary things. If you think that is far-fetched, then perhaps you should take a trip to Pizhou and Hope House, and you will meet people with severe disabilities whose focus is not on the limitations of their wheelchair but on their dreams of achieving Paralympic Gold medals. If you want a lesson in inspiration, forget about me, celebrate them and do something yourself – today.

URL http://www.walkforpeace.eu/day-71-crossing-the-finishing-line/

Homecoming Reflection

London, UK

Total donations: £6,056.10 and ¥813,704.45

I was expecting a few friends, but we arrived at the New Imperial on Lisle Street, Chinatown, London, to find a room packed with 70 well-wishers and decked out with 'welcome home' banners and a large screen scrolling pictures from the walk. I got quite a lump in my throat. Xuelin smiled; she was in on the surprise, but it was as much recognition of her achievement as mine.

The event was the work of the Zhejiang UK Association, our dear friends Ping Huang and her committee. I have stopped asking how the Chinese people seem capable of putting on the most complex, professional events at incredibly short notice.

Xuelin and I took our place at a table and were flabbergasted to see so many leading figures from the UK Chinese community: C. T. Tang OBE, Chairman of the Chinatown Association and owner of the New Imperial, who had been our first donor to the Red Cross; Chinese community leader Dr Shan and his wife, Sherry; Counsellor General Fei and Counsellor Li from the Chinese Embassy; Christine Li from the British China Project; Charlie Wang, Chairman of the Chinese Finance Association; Zhu Mingming, President of the UK Chinese Business Association, and even Mr Hung Ng MBE, President of the Association for the Promotion of Chinese Education, who had travelled down from Newcastle especially.

Ping Huang told us that all the places had gone in a couple of days and there were actually more who had wanted to be there. There was something more than mere geography that seemed to have touched the hearts of the Chinese community in the UK about our walk this year. I know they feel that they are often forgotten or taken for granted. There are around 600,000 British Chinese in the UK, about 1% of the population. It is one of the oldest ethnic communities in the UK, with its origins in maritime trade in the 19th centuries in London and Liverpool.

The British Chinese make a positive contribution to UK society. They are rightly proud of both their Chinese roots and their British identity. It is very rare to see Chinese involved in crime or stirring up community divisions; their children are the highest achievers by ethnic group in education, their grandparents are among the lowest users of the NHS thanks to their healthy lifestyles and entrepreneurship, and hard work is in their DNA. Because they keep a low profile (except at Chinese New Year) and because they aren't to be found airing grievances in the media, the British Chinese often feel invisible. It seemed therefore that this 'crazy fellow Brit' taking time to get to know their ancestral country and culture was something they genuinely appreciated.

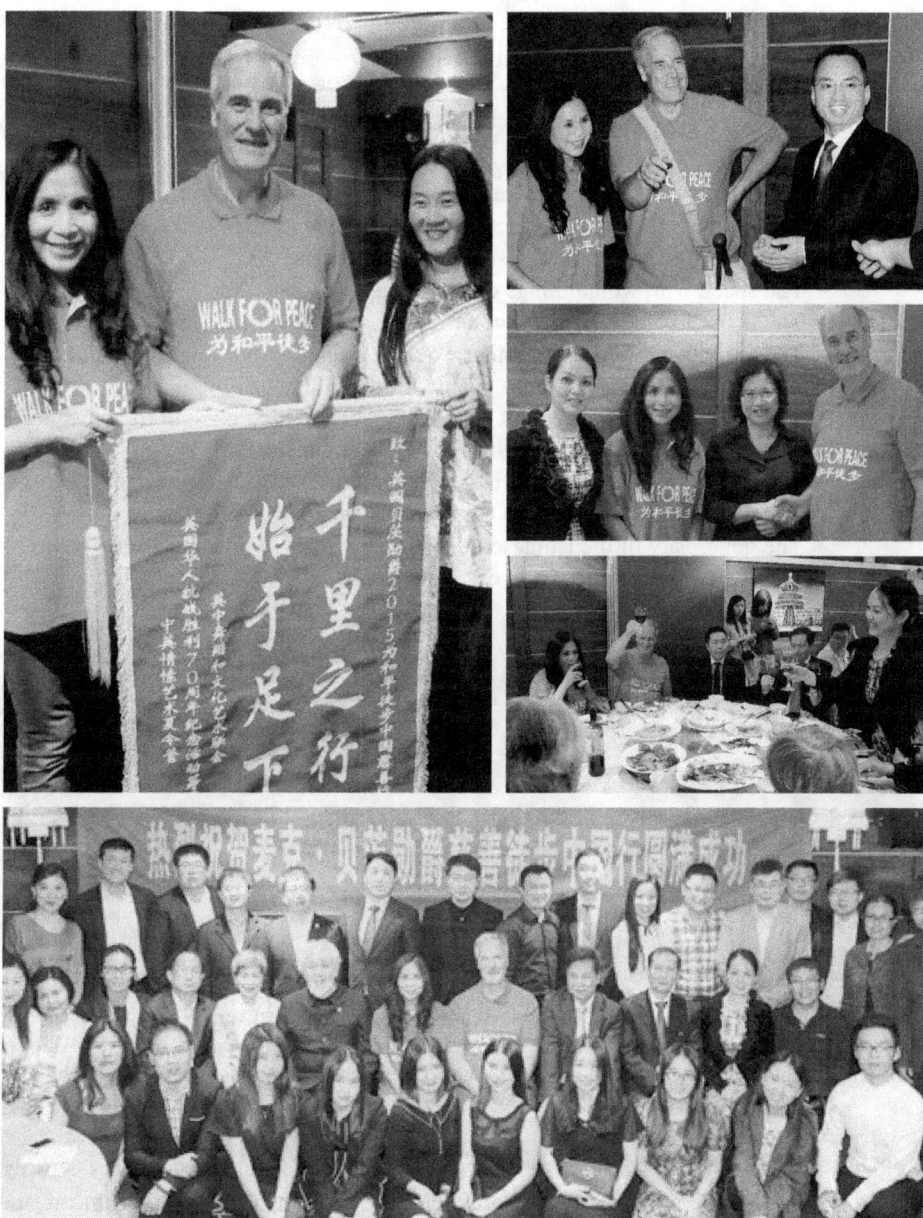

Top left: 'A journey of a thousand miles begins with a single step'
Top right: Lord and Lady Bates with FEI Mingxing, Counsellor General Fei of the Chinese
Embassy. Middle right: Lord and Lady Bates with Ping Huang, Senior Vice President of the
Zhejiang-UK Association. Lower middle right: A toast to the success of the Walk.
Bottom: 'Welcome home' event put on by the Zhejiang–UK Association to celebrate the
successful completion of the Walk for Peace.

Normally, when I speak, I see eyes glazing over with utter boredom after three minutes, but I spoke for 20 minutes and they seemed to still be interested – music to a politician's soul!

What were my standout reflections?

- The quality of the infrastructure.
- The vastness of the rural spaces in between urban zones.
- The cheerfulness and kindness of ordinary people.
- The speed with which things can happen.
- The incredible beauty of the countryside, mountains, lakes and rivers.
- The rediscovery of ancient Chinese culture and philosophy, which is underway.
- The real affection of Chinese people for the UK.
- The centrality of children in Chinese society and their passion for education.
- The inter-generational strength of Chinese society.
- The innocence of Chinese society and their sentimentality rather than cynicism.
- The pain and suffering of the Chinese during World War II.
- The generosity of the Chinese people – over 99% of donors and donations to the Red Cross charities were Chinese people.

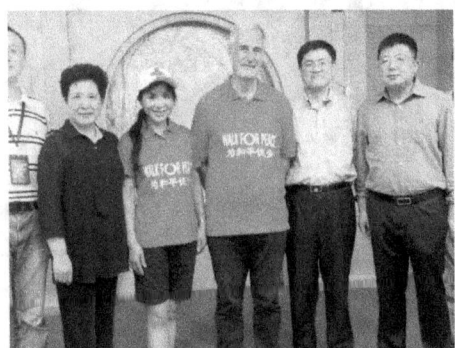 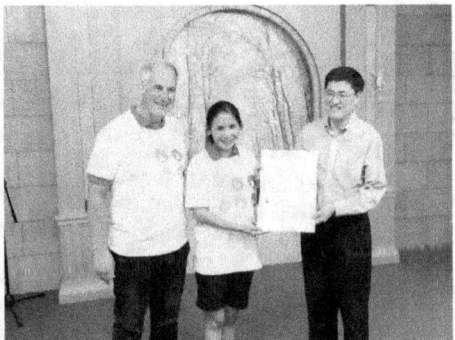

Left: The end of the ceremony, with deputy secretary of Zhejiang University Party committee Ren Shaobo (Third from right), assistant principal, vice president of Zhejiang University Alumni Association Zhang Meifeng (second from left) and alumni association secretary general Hu Wei (second from right). Right: Presentation from Ren Shaobo to Lord and Lady Bates

I closed my remarks with a personal tribute to Xuelin, without whom I simply would not have been able to embark on such an expedition. I recalled that on our final night, Zhejiang University had put on a banquet for us, which was attended by about 120 alumni and faculty from the university. At the end of the evening the Dean produced a special gift for Xuelin; it was her confidential report and score card over the seven years of study. There was only one occasion when her grades fell below 90% – she was described as an 'outstanding student with great promise'. I concluded by saying that I hope they felt that she had realized their ambition for her but, from what I had seen, I believed she is capable of even more, a bit like China itself.

URL http://www.walkforpeace.eu/homecoming-reflection/

Epilogue

The problem with travel is the cultural baggage we bring with us: the cultural baggage that shapes our worldview and by which we form judgements of the places we see and the people we meet; the cultural baggage that is neatly packed for us by social elites from second-hand sources to save us the trouble our 'little minds' have in figuring things out for ourselves. But what if that baggage was lost in transition and you needed to enter the country and just embrace its people the way you found them rather than the way you have been told you should find them? This I did in China during 2015, the official first UK–China Year of Cultural Exchange. This book tells you what I found.

My chosen mode of getting around on my three-month visit to China was an unusual one – walking. I was undertaking a charity walk from Beijing to Hangzhou, roughly following the Grand Canal connecting the two cities and extending some 1,000 miles (1,600 km). I was supported by my wife, and friends from the Red Cross would be my guides. This was not my first long walk for charity; it was our fourth. We had walked through 18 countries – now 23, having walked from Buenos Aires to Rio de Janeiro in 2016. When you walk, you need to engage with the communities you walk through in a real way – seeking food, water, shelter and advice on directions.

Breaking free from my heavy cultural baggage and with an opportunity to fully immerse myself in the country over the next 71 days, I set off from the Temple of Heaven in Beijing. On previous walks there would perhaps be a handful of family and friends coming out to see us off, but for this walk we had around 150. Chinese people, officials and media seemed genuinely touched that a 'crazy foreigner' would choose to embark upon such an expedition. People wanted to give us gifts of beads and flowers. Small bells were attached to my rucksack, and only a photo requested in return.

This was perhaps the first and most striking impression of the real China I encountered: deeply sentimental, nostalgic and believing of the best. British culture, at least in metropolitan elite circles, is much more cynical. This finding was backed up by a recent YouGov opinion poll, which found that the Chinese were the most optimistic people in the world, with 41% saying they thought that the world was getting better and 33% saying it was getting worse; the figures for Britain were 4% and 65%, respectively. I realized that if I were to accurately view the real China, I would need to change the lens I was observing it through, from cynical and pessimistic to sentimental and optimistic. Not to do so would be akin to trying to understand the meaning of Chinese characters using the Latin alphabet.

In Qufu, the home and final resting place of Confucius, I was to discover how deep the roots of the philosophy/religion of Confucianism go in modern China. The concepts of social hierarchy, political order and harmonious living give Chinese culture its shape and form, every bit as much as Greek philosophy and the Christian religion have formed Western civilization. It has not always been so. In the Cultural Revolution there was an attempt to eradicate social and cultural history, with catastrophic effect. Roots, be they cultural, national or familial, give us a sense of identity and belonging, which is necessary for social stability and growth. It was a notable feature of my walk to note how, in many, many places, temples and ancient buildings were being rebuilt and history was being re-embraced as the Chinese rediscovered their history – a truly extraordinary history not just over the past 70 but over the previous 5,000 years.

This sense of history, social order, duty and harmony permeates everything, from where you sit to eat to what you eat, whom you meet and how you are received. Whereas Western culture, especially Anglo-American, places strong emphasis on the potential of the individual and pleasing yourself, Chinese culture would have its starting point closer to your obligations to your family and wider community and pleasing others. Here I am not making a value judgement, just simply observing that they exist and shape the way we see the world and ourselves in it.

In the evenings, after a long, hot day walking, we would often stroll out into the local town or village to have some fresh noodles or dumplings. I was struck by how safe and unthreatening the atmosphere was. I am sure that China has its problems with crime and excessive drinking, but it was not visible in the public places I saw. The market squares were full of families – young children being pushed around in toy cars or scooters, men playing board games, women doing synchronized dancing and everyone drinking tea.

Nowhere do these combinations of sentimentality, duty and obligation come together more powerfully than in the home and in particular in their attitudes to children. Children are the centre of the universe for the Chinese. I used to think this was because of the 'one child' policy, now relaxed to 'two children', but I began to realize that this ran far deeper. I noticed that in villages and towns you rarely saw children alone, but instead they were surrounded by immediate and extended family and were the constant focus of attention.

We know how important early years development is for children. In China, children receive a wonderful head start. This then feeds through into the education system, where the sense of order in the classroom and duty to please others leads to respectful, compliant and industrious students, who in turn grow up to become respectful, compliant and industrious citizens. I saw this expressed in a thousand different ways on my travels through China, and it became not just a reason for admiration but also an underlying explanation for the strength and stability of Chinese society.

The Programme for International Student Assessment (PISA), undertaken by the OECD in 65 countries and regions, finds Shanghai, China, first in maths and science and reading, with the USA and the UK ranking in the mid-20s or early 30s. What makes this performance all the more remarkable is that it is produced in a country that is still ranked only 72nd in the world in terms of nominal GDP per capita. China is not just manufacturing its way in the world, but is also developing itself through education.

This strong academic performance is reflected in a vast growth in the number of students studying overseas, accounting for one-third of the total overseas student numbers around the world. In the UK there were 89,540 Chinese students enrolled at universities in 2014–2015, more than any other country. The next largest cohort was from India, 18,320 students, and in the United States,16,895 Chinese students were enrolled.

These numbers are interesting for a number of reasons. First, British universities are acknowledged as being, after the United States, the best in the world. Hence, the academic requirements required for entry into those universities will again be among the highest in the world. The Chinese are meeting those standards in ever-increasing numbers – and studying in a foreign language. Next, given that the costs of being a foreign student in the UK or the US are extraordinarily high, it reveals not just the wealth of parents sending children to study abroad but also their desire to sacrifice all they have to give their child the best education possible.

Education for the Chinese is a national obsession. In small towns in rural areas, you would see new schools spring up as the Chinese leadership 'shares the proceeds of economic growth', to coin a phrase. Their domestic universities are surging up the international rankings. What is more, 70–80% of graduates now return to China as 'turtles', as they are known, because they see their best career prospects at home. The high proportion of Chinese students studying at the world's leading universities is a superb reserve of intellectual capital, which will be deployed to develop China in the decades ahead.

On this theme of 'sharing the proceeds of growth', it is notable that huge efforts are made to raise the standard of living for all Chinese. In many economies that have grown fast, the profits have been skimmed off by the political leadership and deployed in Swiss and British bank accounts and properties. The result is that great divides open up between rich and poor, which become a festering sore of social injustice. I don't know the extent to which 'skimming' has happened in China, but it is very clear to see how the vast majority of wealth has been redistributed to raise the conditions of ordinary people in the areas which I was walking through.

In every village, you would see not only new roads and infrastructure but new homes being built or occupied and new schools and hospitals being built, with utility connections. The people I spoke to were often speaking of the great improvements in their lives, which is unusual in developing countries, where talk is often of wasteful schemes and corrupt officials.

At this point, my cultural baggage would be telling me that these people were oppressed and simply concealing the truth, but that can't be so. I was walking a route over which I was in complete control: a route that would vary randomly through villages and towns and stopping to meet people when and where I wanted. China has lifted more people out of poverty than any country in human history – 680 million. Three-quarters of the reduction in poverty identified by the United Nations under the Global Millennium Development Goals was achieved by China alone. Its extreme poverty rate has been reduced from 84% in 1980 to 10% now. For those passionate about reducing poverty, public infrastructure and improving life chances, China must surely be a glowing example on a scale of the Industrial Revolution in the UK.

The landscape of China is beautiful, especially when you escape the big cities. On my walk of 1,000 miles I would guess about 100 miles would have been urban or industrial and the rest rural and agricultural. I would walk for days through farms dedicated to growing one particular crop such as dates, garlic, pomegranates, water chestnuts or (of course) mandarin oranges. I would get to talk to the farmers and the workers and understand something about the farming process and prices at market on the way. It was a scene that was far from the fast-paced development, hustle and bustle of the metropolitan areas.

One day I was climbing in the Taishan Mountains. It was a hot August day and we arrived in a small village called Xingjiatun. There was a great tree offering shade from the midday sun and seats underneath. We sat down and villagers came out to talk. They told me the tree was 500 years old and the well beside it was 700 years old. They drew cold water out of the well to refresh me and even a treat of cool watermelon that had been kept in the well. It was a scene from where time had stood still.

As we talked, I asked how many foreign visitors they had had to their village. The answer surprised me – I was the first. To record this historic moment, we asked if we could take a picture with the villagers. The Chinese love photographs so they didn't need much persuading as we crowded together under the great tree. I felt perhaps I should explain what a camera was or a phone. What happened next was took me by complete surprise.

After the photo was taken, young and old pulled out their own smartphones and started asking for individual pictures and scanning QS codes so they could share pictures on WeChat and WeiBo. It was a seamless and harmonious integration of the ancient and modern worlds, made possible because telecom coverage and wifi access are just part of the critical infrastructure that has been built in all parts of the country and which has become indispensable to young and old alike.

Walking is a good way to see national infrastructure. In my walks I have certainly seen the good, the bad and the ugly. Infrastructure in China is impressive. The road surfaces I walked along were of an extremely high standard. The hedges, gutters and verges were meticulously maintained – each village took responsibility for looking after its section, and there seemed to be competition as to who could maintain it best. Roads, especially the local roads I was walking on, are only one small part of the infrastructure miracle in China.

According to McKinsey & Company management consultants, China has now overtaken the United States and the European Union in terms of annual cash spent on infrastructure. It shows China has the largest high-speed rail network in the world – some 12,500 miles (20,000 km) as of 2016. That is about twice the total high-speed rail in Europe either built or currently under construction. It compares to 67.5 miles (108 km) of HSR track we have in the UK. Moreover, by the time the UK expands its HSR network by a further 140 miles (225 km) (HSR2) in 2026, China will have built a further 11,250 miles (18,000 km). Even with this scale of development in China, there is still a need to book tickets well in advance, such is the demand. It is not just rail that is undergoing rapid expansion. Since 2007, China has seen a 62% increase in the number of airports, a 157% increase in the length of expressways and a 132% increase in the number of container terminals.

Not surprisingly, with such epic development of infrastructure in China, its civil engineers and construction companies have become in demand around the world. The return on capital employed in infrastructure is notoriously long-term, which can often make governments struggling with short-term election cycles shy away from such commitments. China is spared such limits on its thinking and instead sets its sights on 2049 and the centenary of the founding of the People's Republic, by which time it expects to be the leading economy in the world. Few would now doubt that it is on track to achieve this, with time to spare. This was not always the case.

I recall making visits to China in the early years of the new century while working for a respected firm of political and economic analysts. We would look at the extraordinary pace of growth that had occurred in China between 1991 and 2001 and how it had continued despite the 1997 Asian financial crisis and the bursting of the 'dot.com bubble' in 2000. We looked ahead and concluded that China's economic growth was simply 'unsustainable' and that it would require a massive correction to asset prices, which in turn could trigger social and political upheaval.

So, when the rest of the world watched awestruck by the quality of the Beijing Olympic Games, economists and political commentators were scratching their heads and wondering how China seemed to be rewriting the economic rule book. Far from crashing, the Chinese economy had quickened its pace of growth from 8.3% in 2001 to 14.2% in 2007.

To be fair, not all commentators got it so hopelessly wrong. Thomas Friedman, in his classic 2008 *New York Times* op-ed, 'The Biblical Seven Years', suggested that China had outperformed the United States because it had not been diverted into costly though necessary military conflicts. He also made the cultural observation on the source of the Chinese economic miracle, stating, 'And, I repeat, they got all this not by discovering oil. They got it by digging inside themselves.' This was a courageous statement by a Western liberal commentator, as it went against the grain of accepted cultural stereotypes of the time, and he was widely criticized for it.

Well, that was 2008. The Games were over and soon, we all thought, so would be the Chinese 'economic miracle'. The first sign came as economic data suggested that the Chinese economic growth was slowing down from its peak of 14.2% in 2007 to 9.6% in 2008, but this was soon realized not be a reflection of problems with asset prices or the banking system in China but rather in the West. What happened over the next four years was the greatest economic crisis in the West since the Great Depression. Its effects are still being felt as Western governments come to terms with high levels of national debt and consumer debt and banks seek to repair their balance sheets.

During the period between the Beijing Olympic and Paralympic Games and this year's G20 meetings in Hangzhou (2008–2016), UK annual economic growth averaged +0.92% per annum – the best in the G7 economies; in China, average annual growth in GDP was 8.54%, remarkably in line with average growth rates over the preceding 25 years. Just the annual growth of China, now the second largest economy in the world, is equivalent to the entire GDP of the Netherlands and greater than that of Switzerland. Still, commentators will refer to the 'Chinese economic slowdown'. In China, growth of 8.54% is called a 'slowdown', while growth of less than 1% in Europe is called a 'recovery' – time to check that baggage again.

The chief economist of Goldman Sachs, Jim O'Neil, wrote a paper identifying the exciting 'newly industrializing economies' of the world in 2001 – Brazil, Russia, India, China and South Africa – which became known by the acronym 'BRICS'. Together, these five economies accounted for half the world's population. It was suggested that growth rates would be roughly similar, as each country was at a similar stage of development, and yet that was not the case. Where the average growth rate in China was 8.54% per annum between the Beijing Olympics and the Hangzhou G20 (2008 and 2016), the comparative average figures were 2.2% per annum for India, 2.04% per annum for Brazil, 1.9% per annum in South Africa and 0.98% per annum for Russia. This adds to the suggestion that, to explain the extraordinary performance of China, we need to look deeper.

There is one other Chinese characteristic that we should mention in addition to education: a passion for infrastructure and love of technology, because it is, I believe, fundamental to understanding how all these elements are bound together to explain their exceptional success. Hard work. There is a culture of belief in the nobility of work and the duty of work. I recall, at the end of a long, hot day, meeting an elderly man raking a roadside embankment outside Suqian in the early evening. I asked him how old he was and he said he was 85. I asked him if this was his land or his job. He looked puzzled and said, 'No.' I asked why, therefore. he was doing such a demanding task and his reply was, 'Work is good for you.' This passion and belief in work as being as critical to noble living as resting run deep in Chinese culture. Work is literally worshipped, whether it is in the classroom, on the factory floor or on a roadside in Suqian.

Seventy-one days after leaving Beijing, I arrived in Hangzhou, the birthplace of many great people, the greatest of which, in my view, is Xuelin Li, my wife. The original walk was planned between Beijing (the northern capital) and Nanjing (the southern capital), but we had arrived a couple of weeks early and so I was persuaded by Xuelin to walk on to Hangzhou. We walked through six provinces, hundreds of villages and cities, and met thousands of people along the way.

When I had visited China before, I had often stayed within the major cities of Beijing, Shanghai and Hangzhou, but I had come in search of the real China, and I knew that this would lie outside the main cosmopolitan centres. I wasn't searching for a mythical 'Shangri-la', a Utopian dream from Hilton's classic novel, *Lost Horizon*. China has its problems and inconsistencies like the rest of us. It is certainly no Utopia. But it is said that to begin to understand someone else's world, you need to walk a mile in their shoes. Well, I may have brought my own shoes, but I had walked over 1,000 miles on their roads.

It was a phenomenal privilege. I was overwhelmed by the kindness and generosity of the people I met, especially of the poorest people. It transformed my understanding of this country and the lives of its people. I am privileged to live in another wonderful country, Britain. Without getting too uncharacteristically sentimental, I can honestly say that I love my country, but I believe we can still do better, especially if we are prepared learn from others. The Chinese have a deep respect and fascination with Britain and what this small island has managed to achieve in the world. The Chinese want to learn from British education, business, creative industries, the National Health Service. I am convinced that my fellow countrymen and women could achieve even greater things if they were to view China's successes and culture in the same way. Our view of China may still be obscured by those preconceptions packed for us in our cultural baggage. The first Year of UK–China Cultural Exchange and my walk through the 'real China' would seem a very good time to examine what we are packing and why. And ask ourselves the question how, through cultural exchange and mutual respect, we can use the best of each culture to strengthen both.

DOI https://doi.org/10.24103/TETE.en.cn.2017.1.4

Afterword

In the years since I started accompanying Michael walking, people have often asked about our marriage. Michael and I became attached while Michael walked 'for Greece and the Olympic Truce' between 2011 and 2012. Before this, I was fortunate enough to have success in the business world, while Michael is a senior British politician. At first, I was just intrigued by his idea of walking for the Olympic Truce, and then deeply moved by his spirit and perseverance. We got married on the day of the start of the London Olympics Truce, July 20, 2012. On our wedding day, we set up a charitable foundation for the Walk for Peace, and agreed to do something meaningful for world peace every year. We chose to walk in our appeal for world peace, and to raise money for charity.

From July to October 2015, to commemorate the 70th anniversary of victory in World War II and the first Sino-British cultural exchange year, I suggested to Michael that he undertake a Walk for Peace in China. He readily agreed. With the help of the Red Cross, he walked for 71 days from summer to autumn, from Beijing, via Nanjing and on to Hangzhou. Step by step, walking through the six provinces of China, Michael experienced the real China. To our amazement, President Xi Jinping mentioned Michael's peace walk in his speech in the British Parliament during his state visit to the United Kingdom: 'Recently, Lord Bates went on a charity walk for over two months in China. He covered about 1,700 kilometres on foot under the scorching sun to raise money for charity in China and call on people to cherish peace. Thanks to such efforts by numerous Chinese and Britons, Sino-British relations have made steady progress, despite the vast distance between our two countries.'

In 2016, in order to promote world peace and the Olympic Truce, Michael once again embarked on a long journey. It took him 115 days to walk from Buenos Aires in Argentina to Rio de Janeiro in Brazil, and he covered 3,025 kilometres (1,890 miles) through Argentina, Uruguay, Paraguay and Brazil, raising more than £260,000 for the United Nations Children's Fund. In the last five years, we have enjoyed the support of Ban Ki-moon, the Pope, Jacques Rogge, Thomas Bach, David Cameron, Her Majesty Queen Elizabeth II and many politicians. This book also includes information and photos from, Michael's Walks for Peace since 2011. The impact of these Walks for Peace is global, and the walk journal he shares with us is also the experience of transculturality.

Michael has written, 'Life is a journey, not just a destination. This is the story of a remarkable journey I was privileged to undertake in China last year from Beijing to Hangzhou. During the 71 days of walking, I encountered some truly amazing places, but most amazing were the people I met along the way. I invite you to join me on this memorable journey and experience the real China.'

While sorting out all the manuscripts, including Chinese translations, a large number of pictures and related information and completing the editing of this book, I have come to the view that the purpose that drives all the friends involved in its publication is to invite readers to experience what this Chinese foreign son-in-law has experienced physically and psychologically in China. The book is published in English, Chinese and a bilingual version.

I would like to take this opportunity to extend my sincere thanks to the volunteers who translated journal entries and maintained social media during the walk in China (in alphabetical order by family name): Huang Jia, 轩则喁, Liu Jiatong, Li Yongxuan, Ma Liweiqi, Ma Wanqing, Wu Yuheng, Xiao Meng and Xiao Xiao.

Special thanks are due to the Chinese Red Cross for their constant strong support along the way: for example, Chen Zhu, the Red Cross President, Xu Ke, Chinese Red Cross Party Secretary and Executive Vice President, came to Tai'er-zhuang specifically to visit us; Hao Linna and Wang Rupeng, both Vice Presidents of the Red Cross, visited us several times and walked with us; Ms Zhang Ming, Director of the Red Cross Liaison Department, accompanied us all the way and coordinated help from the local Red Cross Society; she was also involved in the planning and coordination of this book's publication and pleased to write a Preface. And of course, we cannot forget that the Red Cross arranged more than 700 volunteers to take part in the walk in different places.

Finally, I would like to express my respect and gratitude to my colleagues in the publishing industry who have lent their intellectual and professional skills to the publication of this book. Under the leadership of Ms Zhang Haiou, the editor-in-chief of New World Publishing House, Ms Li Sha-sha, editor of this book, Ms He Yuting, Li Yiming and Mr Huang Houqing, the art editors, made great efforts to publish this Chinese and English bilingual book. Professor Chen Lixing from Kansai University in Japan, honorary professor Chang Xiangqun from University College London in UK, have taken the wise decision to include this book in their co-edited 'Three Eyes' book series, published by Global China Press. In order to bring this book to more English-speaking readers, Global China Press will publish it in both English and Chinese. It is touching that, in a short period of time, the English editor, Ms Ingrid Cranfield, art editor, Mr Mark Lee, and translator, Ms Costanza Pernigotti, as well as Xu Haiyan, associate professor at Nanchang University and part-time translator for CCPN Global, have cooperated to ensure that the English version of this book will be published in time for the Third Global China Dialogue to be held at the British Academy on December 2-3, 2016.

Lady Xuelin Li Bates
November 2016

DOI https://doi.org/10.24103/TETE.en.cn.2017.1.5

Postscript

At the 2017 London Book Fair, New World Press and Global China Press launched their joint publication of the English edition of *Walk for Peace* by Lord Bates for Western readers.

First, I should point out that Lady Xuelin Li Bates, editor of *Walk for Peace*, was the linchpin of the whole enterprise. Without her influence and help, Lord Bates's walk across China would simply not have happened. If she had not collected and sorted out the entries, organized the translation and proofread the journal of the walk, the book would have not seen the light of day. Moreover, if she had not helped coordinate the Red Cross and New World Press, publication would not have been possible. The former head of the Public Relations Department of the Chinese Red Cross, Ms Zhang Ming, fittingly wrote the First Preface of this book, having been involved from start to finish in Lord Bates's walk across China, and she gathered together a great quantity of material and photos, helped coordinate communications between the author and the publishing house and even produced an updated version of the Preface for our English version, despite her busy schedule. Colleagues at New World Press and Global China Press designed the cover, sorted out the material, proofread it repeatedly and finally published the book within a very short time, which reflects their impressive dedication, professionalism and work ethic.

Second, it took almost eight years from my initial meeting with Ms Xuelin Li in 2010 and discussion about supporting our activities to commemorate the 100th anniversary of the birth of Fei Xiaotong, to bringing *Walk for Peace* to a state of readiness for promoting both its publication and at the same time Chinese social scientific work in the West, with the assistance of New World Press and scholars of China studies worldwide.

- In 2010 I got to know Xuelin Li by chance, and I was hoping to gain the support of the Zhejiang UK Association (ZJUKA), which she heads, for activities to commemorate the 100th anniversary of the birth of Fei Xiaotong at LSE[1]. Although our activities did not gain financial support, being purely academic, the ZJUKA did come to our assistance, helping us publicize the events and publishing reports about them in Chinese media.
- China was Market Focus at the 2012 London Book Fair, and China in Comparative Perspective Network (CCPN) at LSE held jointly with the

---

[1] The publications from the event: Stephan Feuchtwang, Xiangqun Chang et al. 'Fei Xiaotong studies', in *Globalization of Chinese Social Sciences* (vols 1 and 2, in English and Chinese). London: Global China Press; Beijing: New World Press, 2016. Details of the event: http://www.ccpn-global.com/cms.php?artid=64&catid=87.

China International Publishing Group (CIPG) an 'East–West Dialogue on Public Diplomacy: New Books from Zhao Qizheng', and launched the book *Why and How the CPC Works in China*. Lord Michael Bates was invited to deliver a speech at this event.

- Lord Bates was also invited to give a keynote speech at the international convention 'How Do Migrants from the BRIC Countries Participate in Shaping Global Society?' held on 2 March 2013 by CCPN at LSE.[2]

- Global China Press published the English edition of this book, formally launching it at the Third Global China Dialogue[3] forum on 2 December 2016. Lord Bates spoke at the reception held at the UK Parliament that evening, and signed copies of his book.

- Lord and Lady Bates participated in the launch of the English edition of *Walk for Peace: Transcultural Experiences in China* at the 2017 London Book Fair, organized jointly by the New World Press and Global China Press. Lord Michael Bates engaged in a conversation entitled 'Walking into a Transcultural Era' with Professor Kerry Brown (King's College London) and Professor Hugo de Burgh (University of Westminster). After the book launch, New World Press and Global China Press signed contracts for the joint publication of three books by the renowned Chinese sociologist, anthropologist, ethnologist and social activist Fei Xiaotong: *Towards a People's Anthropology, Chinese Village Close-Up* and *Small Towns in China: Functions, Problems and Prospects*. Lord Bates and Lady Bates witnessed the signing ceremony.

There are many similarities between Professor Fei Xiaotong and Lord Bates. As a pioneering Chinese sociologist and anthropologist, Fei was Vice-Chairman of the Standing Committee of the National People's Congress and Vice-President of the Chinese People's Political Consultative Conference, and Bates was vice-Chairman of the UK House of Lords, and is State Minister of International Development in the UK government. At the launch of Bates' *Walk for Peace* at the 2017 London Book Fair, Global China Press and New World Press signed a publishing agreement to jointly publish three social scientific popular books by Fei. Bates's *Walk for Peace* has similar features to Fei's books. Fei's work had a great influence on China's social economic development, and Bates's book provides some useful thoughts and information for understanding China from a comparative perspective.

Third, while the book was being prepared for publication, the editors raised several questions about issues such as the title and the cover, which are briefly discussed in the following sections.

---

[2] Details of the event: http://www.ccpn-global.com/cms.php?artid=46&catid=64.
[3] The Third Global China Dialogue was centred on the theme of Sustainable Development and Global Governance for Climate Change, and was held on 2–3 December 2016 at the British Academy.

Title

The Chinese and English dual-language edition, titled *Walk for Peace* in English and *Tubu Zhongguo: Ai yu heping de xinyang zhengtu* (《徒步中国——爱与和平的信仰征途》, *Walk across China: A Journey of Faith between Love and Peace*) in Chinese, was published by New World Press. There is, however, another book entitled *The Longest Way*[4] in English and *Tubu Zhongguo* (徒步中国, *Walk across China*) in Chinese, by Christoph Rehage, published in June 2013 by Hunan Literature and Art Publishing House. Therefore, we had to change the English title to *Walk for Peace: Transcultural Experiences in China* and the Chinese title to *Wei heping tubu: Zhongguo zhilu de chaowenhua tiyan* (《为和平徒步——中国之路的超文化体验》).

Cover

The proverb 'Don't judge a book by its cover' is similar to the Chinese saying *Bu yao jin cong biaomian kan ren* (不要仅从表面看人, lit. 'Don't just look at the surface'). Both imply that it is in our nature to give importance to appearances. Thus, the design of a book cover must be meaningful and be executed meticulously. Global China Press does not publish standalone books; that is to say, all our books become part of a book series. Therefore, we design only certain specific styles of book covers, and the image on the cover of each series tries to represent as much as possible the content of the series. We decided to solicit the support of French painter François Bossière, who provides his work free of charge for us to use for our covers. François's wife is the Chinese historical anthropologist Professor Yu Shuo[5], so François can also be considered 'culturally Chinese' and his paintings are characterized by a strong sense of transculturality. For instance, the title of the painting we chose for the cover of the Transcultural Experiences with 'Three Eyes' book series is *Tonus local*, which reflects the harmonization and symbiosis of transculturality.

Photos

In our haste to publish the Chinese and English dual-language edition, New World Press adopted the conventional method of inserting photos at the beginning of the book. In order to provide a better understanding of the content of the journal in the English edition, we distributed the photos so that they matched up with each entry of the journal. However, we discovered that only one photo had been taken by the

---

[4] The German and Russian editions of this book have already been translated, and I hope that it will be possible to publish their English translation, because Christoph Rehage is a fruit of transculturality himself, being of German, Hungarian, Danish, Russian, French–Swiss and Armenian descent. When he was a child, his dream job was to be a truck driver and a writer, and now he engages in commentary on current Chinese politics. He is also the author of *Chinese Characteristics*, Contemporary China Publishing House, 2014.

[5] Professor YU Shuo is founding Director and European Representative of the Centre for China–Europe Transcultural Communication at Hong Kong Polytechnic University, and former co-founder and first director of the China–Europa Forum (France).

author himself: this was the last photo, placed at the end of the diary, Day 49, 13 September, 'Fashion in Xuyi county'. This means that the pictures accompanying the journal do not, by and large, reflect the point of view of the author: the book thus represents the subjective view of the author of the text and the objective view of the photographer or photographers.

Thanks are due to Costanza Pernigotti, Assistant Editor of Global China Press, who went through all the published blogs and inserted all the photos back in their appropriate positions with respect to the blogs, and added the relevant captions and URLs at the end of each blog. Some photos taken by the author provide readers with a view of China and the Chinese people as the author would have seen it. Thus this book contains more than 400 photos in different sizes.

In addition to this, we should like to thank Xuelin for forwarding some of the pictures saved on Lord Bates's phone, which contributed to the addition of Appendix 1. We contemplated interviewing the author to explore the background of each photo so as to write captions or to gain more information about some parts of the journal and add annotations. However, we were not able to pursue this idea, for lack of time, and since 'the perfect is the enemy of the good'[6], we are content with our situation.

Table of contents

When comparing the original English version of the journal with its Chinese translation, we realized that the Chinese edition was missing 15 entries. Comparing these entries with others, I realized that the reason why they were not included by New World Press was perhaps that the translation of the headings is particularly faithful to the original English text. To preserve the integrity[7] of this journal, we

---

[6] The word 'perfect' in the expression 'the perfect is the enemy of the good' is universally translated as *wanmei* 完美 in Chinese. However, it is not really possible to translate this saying into Chinese, which is said to have been originally uttered by an Italian sage and was then used by French author Voltaire in his *La Bégueule* (1772). It can be literally translated as *wanmei shi hao dongxi de diren* 完美是好东西的敌人. It means that all good things are lost in the pursuit of perfection, and we end up achieving nothing. My version of translation of this saying is: *jian hao jiu chu, zhi zu chang le* 见好就收，知足常乐 (lit. Those who quit while they are ahead will be satisfied with what they have).

[7] According to the *Cambridge Dictionary*, 'integrity' means 'honesty' and 'wholeness', which seems very concise, but does not convey the gist and spirit of a single concept. The definition given by the *Oxford Dictionary* is 'the quality of being honest and having strong moral principles; the state of being whole and undivided'. If we Google 'integrity', the English definition that comes up is identical to that of the *Oxford Dictionary*, while the Chinese translation is *lianzheng he qijie* 廉正和气节 (lit. incorruptness and moral righteousness). Google's online translation tool translates 'integrity' as *chengxin* 诚信. The two translation systems operated by Google do not reflect the other layer of meaning of the word 'integrity', thawhicht is 'a whole that has not been divided'. The online dictionary iCiba translates 'integrity' as *zhengzhen, chengshi, wanzheng* 正直, 诚实; 完整 (honest, honourable, complete) [computer] *baocun* 保存 (to save) and *jianquan* 健全 (robust, sound): by if one lookings at the characters, this definition could be expressed by *wanzheng* (complete). However, to this day I have never seen a single Chinese concept that could express the precise meaning of 'integrity'. Indeed, in the Chinese version of this Epilogue I have kept the word 'integrity' in English.

decided to include these entries in our edition. We edited the headings of the 15 entries to give a more precise indication of their content and thus appeal more to readers. Some titles differ slightly between Chinese and English editions, while others are the same.

Comments

Among all the opinions expressed throughout the book, I would beg to differ with only two of them: the first is that Traditional Chinese Medicine is cheap (Day 63, 27 September, Moon Festival); the other concerns 'the generosity of the Chinese people – 99% of donations to the Chinese Red Cross come from Chinese donors' (dated 9 October, the last of the 12 things he will never forget in 'Homecoming, reflection'). We saw the Chinese being generous in many ways throughout the book but if we refer to Appendix III, showing a complete list of distances walked and donations received, and compare this data with data from the following walk that Lord Bates undertook in 2016, we cannot conclude that the Chinese people are generous based simply on amounts of money donated.

Time	Places	Distance covered on foot	Total amount of donations	Daily donation average	Donations per km
6 May–29 July 2016, 115 days	Argentina, Buenos Aires – Brazil, Rio de Janeiro	3,025 km 1,880 miles	£260,000	£2,260	£86
27 July–5 October 2015, 71 days	China, Beijing – Hangzhou	1,703km 1,058 miles	£90,000	£1,268	£53

This is what Bill Gates observed in 2014, when he called on China's wealthy to do more for charity, saying that China lacks systematic acts of charity and the government should consider adopting policies to encourage charity, such as tax relief.[8] Comparative studies on the concept of charity with regard to Chinese and non-Chinese people are valuable and interesting, but that is a topic for another time.

Finally, *Walk for Peace: Transcultural Experiences in China* collects the 71 entries of Lord Bates's journal, in addition to an Introduction, Preparation for the Walk, Reflection, Epilogue and Afterword. Each entry expresses unique opinions, original points of view and abundant information, sharing myriad sensations and experiences, altogether making for a very readable and inspiring book. We at Global China Press are proud to be publishing it and I strongly recommend it, knowing that whoever picks it up will be impressed, engaged and uplifted.

Xiangqun Chang

Director of the Global China Institute; Editor-in-chief of Global China Press

Honorary Professor of University College London, UK

Revised June 2017

---

[8] 'Bill Gates called Chinese Tuhao do more charities rather than luxury things', *Qianzhan Business Information Times*: 2014-04-09 10:05:06. http://en.qianzhan.com/en/news/341/140409-53810987.html

Appendix I

Selected photos by the author of the 2015 walk[1]

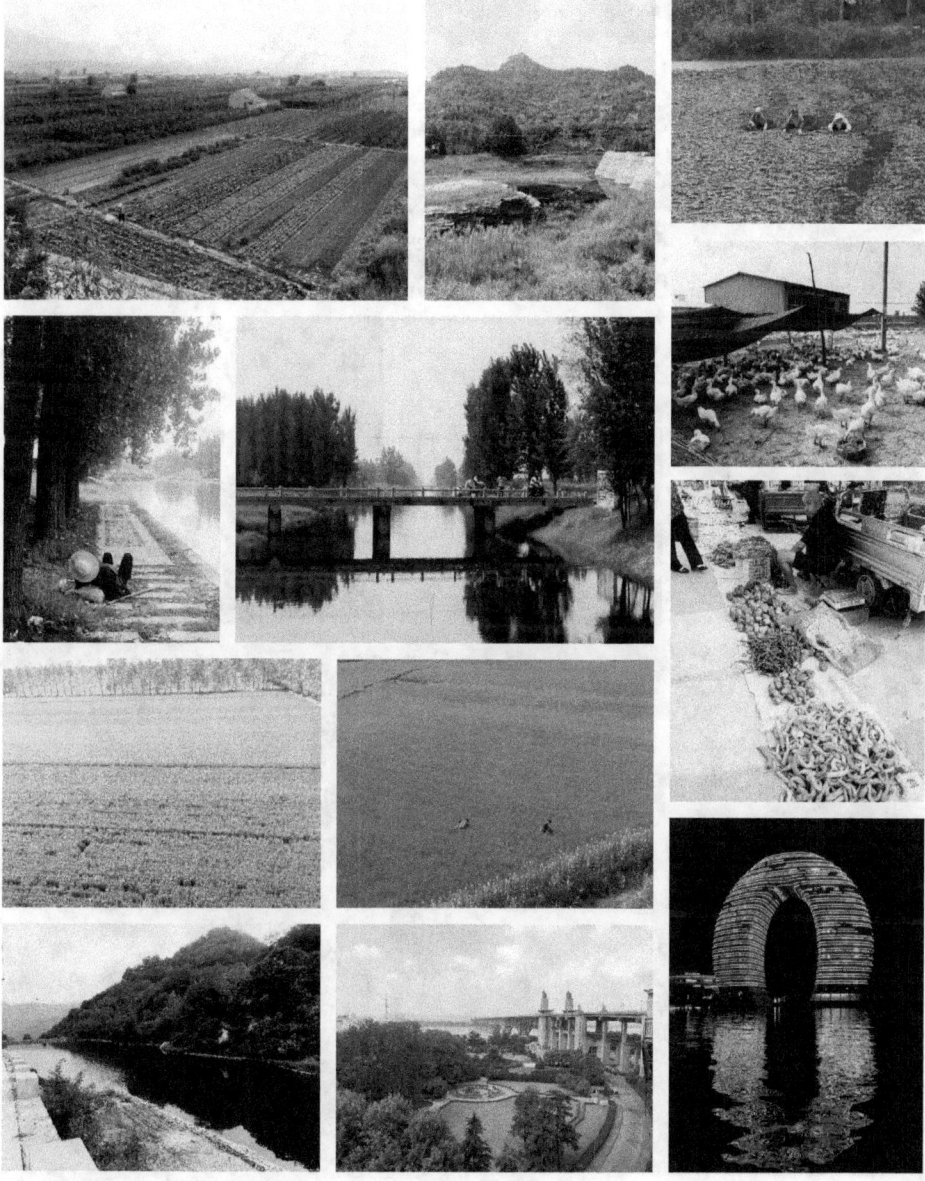

[1] Thanks to Lord and Lady Bates for providing the photos taken by the author. Our apologies for not supplying individual captions (see *Photos* in the Postscript).

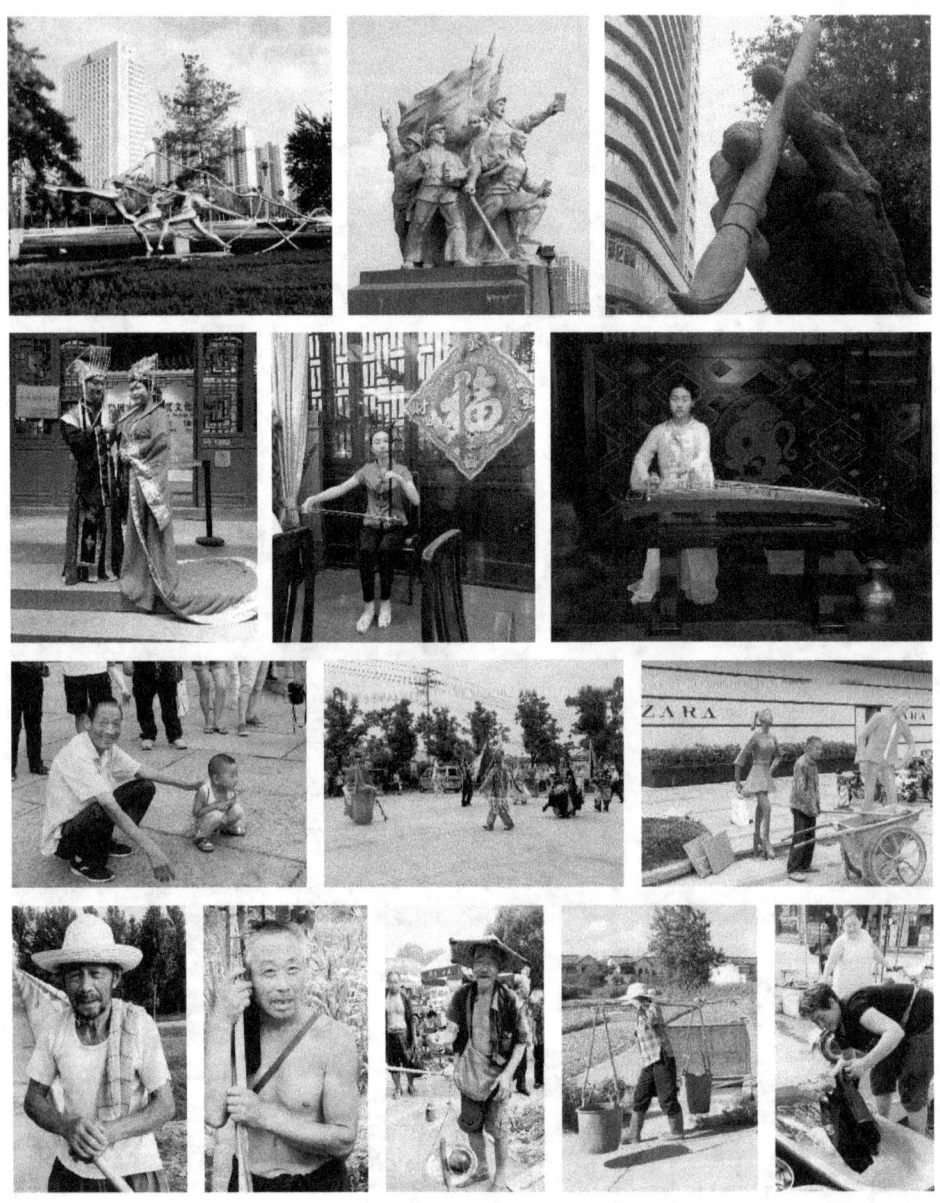

Appendix II

List of donors for the 2015 walk (incomplete)[1]

慈善学徒、国际学生实习计划、杭州海邦留学联盟、杭州花家山庄、江苏大众书局图书文化有限公司、江苏龙虎网信息科技股份有限公司、江苏泗州饭店有限公司经济分会、伦敦华埠商会、南京观睿文化传播有限公司、上海快鹿投资集团、协和华东、英国华商报、英中经济文化促进会、永兴特钢、浙江汇华房地产开发有限公司、浙江建工房地产开发集团、浙江康吉尔有限公司、浙江省对外服务公司、浙江省对外交流服务中心、浙江省发展侨务事业基金会、浙江省海外交流协会、Al. Neil & Dan, Alex Ge, Arthur & Catherine Bates, Bates Family, Becky Bao, Bella Zou, Binwei Lu, Couple Bates, Daibin David Bates, Dr Christina Zhang, Felix Xia, George Li, Gerry Langley, Grace Gu, Huali Tang, Hui Huang & Luke Jackson, Jachi Xiong, Jayne Douglass, Jihou Zheng, Joanna Zhong, John & Liz, Laura Wang, Linda Xiong, Longfellow Liu, Michael Liu, Mr. & Mrs. Emmanuel de Stoppani, Ou Zhang, Phoebe & Lily, Rob & Di Parsons, Rongrong, Silvia Ding, Simon Li, Stephen Bates, Tim, Ben & Ruth, Water Hu, Weijian Qi, William Wu, Xun Liu, Yammi, Yuhong, Zhenyu Yan, Zhong Wang, 安飞东、安宏娟、安志鹏、白建军、白小龙、包天钦、包铁民、包玉龙、北贝乐、毕敏、边莎莎、卞东辉、蔡传强、蔡赐河、蔡建华、蔡文男、曹春霞、曹庆峰、曹庆华、常春藤、常惠刚、常雷、车鉴、陈安、陈波、陈超平、陈成振、陈聪、陈琮文、陈大玲、陈东、陈峰烽、陈国良、陈海东、陈昊、陈昊男、陈洪、陈焕耀、陈辉、陈基细、陈佳、陈健勇、陈杰、陈金妹、陈静宜、陈军、陈坤林、陈兰、陈临江、陈旻、陈敏、陈明新、陈慕燕、陈七、陈谦、陈秋香、陈荣、陈瑞华、陈上荣、陈仕平、陈习龄、陈小钦、陈晓敏、陈秀荣、陈学英、陈艺敏、陈颖、陈映烈、陈余宽、陈远青、陈灼声、程厚博、程华九、程一峰、池清 & 金岳亨、池毓修、迟婧彦、迟乃河、迟志强、崔军、崔丽娟、崔亚涛、代建国、戴立、戴润昌、单声博士 & 单秋桂林、稻谷、邓宝金、邓君剑、邓明、邓柱廷、狄玲、习杰明、丁德坤、丁维娜、董成舟、董慧芬、杜玉娟、范红梅、范建勇、范俊、范瑞坤、范铁、方柏山、方侃、方向、方元弟、芳菲、冯国震、冯建、冯美兰、冯善忠、付艾伦、付峰、付维幸、傅明、傅赛凤、傅蔚冈、傅献玉、傅振球、高洪凯、高玲玲、高翔、高艳红、郜俊林、葛爱玲、龚魏、龚向阳、顾炳元、顾红、顾建华、顾秾、顾庆新、顾叶仁、顾迎化、关频杰、关炆奇、冠一、贵体谦、郭建涛、郭洁瑜、郭力杰、郭年明、郭强、郭尉、郭跃、哈里森、海丽曼、海燕、寒静、韩方敏、韩鹏飞、杭剑平、郝林娜、何洪杭、何玲玲、何明耿、何素、贺慧娟、贺湘、洪钢、洪冀宁、侯谨谦、胡斌、胡桂萍、胡娟红、胡倩、胡永群、黄冰、黄兵、黄浩忠、黄建刚、黄乐夫、黄萌、黄咪咪、黄伟、黄新建、黄馨、黄秀玉、黄宣

---

[1] Because of space limitations, only organisations and individuals who contributed more than 50 yuan are listed here. There are more than 600 donor names omitted here. This list of contributions is provided by Lord and Lady Bates.

武、黄晔、霍法如、姬乐乐、季建芳、家慧、简崇军、建云、江南雨、姜际春、姜若萍、姜晓玲、蒋晨、蒋盈盈、焦健、金朝龙、金剑辉、金王来、金伟钰、金永辉、津红、靖长华、瞿莹、康胜燕、柯砾、孔剑、孔庆秀、来镇、赖彩琳、赖国宾、赖小平、兰俭、兰蔻、乐辉、雷赛平、莉莉、李宝平、李潾、李春高、李道升、李德宏、李芳、李根、李汉进、李浩、李卉子、李嘉连、李建勇、李剑、李健、李金荣、李娟、李军、李立枝、李林、李芒 & 房艾玫、李孟波、李孟迁、李仁杰、李韧、李少方、李绍林、李唯佳、李熙琳、李相君、李欣安、李欣然、李秀生、李旭辉、李雪刚、李伊平、李怡琨、李永彤、李育青、李昱、李昭明、李真驹、厉春莲、厉秀华、郦菊红、连德江、梁剑、梁齐洋、梁月山、廖慧兰、廖秀琴、廖亦铭、林本诚、林波波、林超、林国荣、林航、林孔周、林莉、林理德、林美银、林明植、林年成、林年青、林钦、林群欣、林维贵、林伟斌、林宜利、凌云、刘常芳、刘贵赟、刘红丽、刘卉、刘键、刘鹏忠、刘姝娟、刘顺美、刘小华、刘晓华、刘新、刘新元、刘鑫、刘亚明、刘彦斌、刘艳林、刘胤宏、刘颖、刘永兵、刘永淼、刘芸芸、龙奕、楼晔、卢霖、卢晓丽、卢溢华、鲁祖统、陆其清、路映虹、璐璐、吕博涵、吕宏丽、吕洪凤、吕建生、吕丽丽、吕任东、罗嘉羽、罗琦、罗卿平、罗贤强、马宝山、马福荣、马嘉、马可奥勒留、马丽、马列、马秋梅、马文博、马月红、毛峰、毛力军、毛永锋、毛玉龙、毛植成、冒荔、梅月华、孟惠强、孟庆霞、缪峰、缪斯纯、缪艳萍、穆欣、倪小辉、宁志威、欧玉星、潘广儒、潘家驹、潘乐郡、潘勤敏、潘晓涵、潘旭华、潘仰知、彭少剑、戚华婧、钱萃阳、钱华峰、钱晓辉、钱昱、秦保红、邱意淳、裘建军、裘健、任德豹、任国才、任浩、任小鸿、阮锡长、邵建波、邵子睿、沈丹凤、沈德魁、沈国强、沈鸿霞、沈骏、沈琦明、沈文平、沈晓安、沈毅、盛国辉、施建基、施建日、施小伟、石坚、寿培平、舒晓华、宋舒、苏玲燕 & 董丹申、苏伟志、苏云芝、孙宝频、孙斌、孙红艳、孙威、孙晓丹、孙幸福、孙志祥、谭艳玲、汤政、唐谦一家、陶锦辉、田长桉、田力、田明、田征、佟帅、童志锋、万萍、汪博、汪建文、汪可雯、汪荣勋、汪胜忠、汪雪琴、王峥、王斌、王炳辉、王泊雅、王昌南 & 黄萍、王朝辉、王聃、王东明、王广宇、王浩飞、王红果、王继利、王家厚、王嘉宏、王建华、王建杰、王建利、王进学、王京辉、王兰英、王莉、王璐璐、王梦迪、王民、王强、王清、王全爱、王权、王荣娟、王若凡、王书恺、王滔、王伟、王小丽、王晓杰、王晓霞、王昕坤、王鑫、王星、王旭明、王怡发、王艺霏、王渊、王云汛、王中杰、韦臻、魏德毅、魏静、魏忠东、温红媚、温起、温兴建、文江、翁纪远、翁岚、翁茜、翁绳飞、吴超英、吴晨、吴丹花、吴海伦、吴建滨、吴建忠、吴剑、吴晶、吴敏芳、吴奇、吴清秀、吴思齐、吴燕、吴一心、吴雨霞、吴玉光、吴跃玲、伍善雄、奚灵平、夏小虎、项秀英、项秀玉、肖焕跃 & 肖杨、肖珺、肖立程、肖奇凤、肖茜、肖炜、谢斌、谢东奎、谢濚、忻立靖、辛斌、辛承军、熊亚伟、熊永华、徐琛凤、徐道睦、徐惠忠、徐坚真、徐璐、徐强、徐秀香、徐旭昶、徐燕、徐燕峰、徐正安、许蓓、许德钦、许伟良、许旭波、许雅香、薛建君、薛世文、闫志纯、严求真、严永军、严振羽、羊大雄、杨国忠、   杨海、杨建光、杨金坤、杨柳、杨晓敏、杨耀宇、杨玉龙、杨振岗、杨忠红、姚桂海、姚军、叶龙海、叶楠、叶佩善、叶青、叶青青、叶素珍、叶学强、叶学群、叶竹民、叶子、宜卓、易才拾、因扎东、殷杰、殷茵、应黎灿、应泉、永军、游鸿强、游淑淋、于丽颍、于佩、于燕如、余爱钦、余彩霞、余春桂、余良珍、余少华、余晚晚、俞祁平、宇山、袁芳、袁慧光、袁九根、袁云贵、曾剑琴、曾莉娜、曾灵敏、曾肖微、曾云、曾子、瞿永泉、詹雪梅、占福文、张必来、张兵、张灿燕、张潮、张岱、张典、张东平、张光和、张国权、张菡、张红娟、张红军、张虎、张晖、张嘉显、张建农、张建平、张杰、张金萱、张飕、张娟、张君豪、张磊、张力、张立、张立峰、张丽丽、张美凤、张明、张鹏、张巧巧、张巧中、张锐、张尚鑫、张少琴、张维仁、张伟、张文德、张文军、张祥荣、张小帆、张小颖、张绪军、张阳、张养发、张烨坤、张伊、张颐、张轶龙、张鉴、张瑛俏、张媛、张振新、张政平、张志华、张智颖、章利勇、赵滨、赵承良、赵国卫、赵凯、赵克强、赵倩、赵琴、赵胜男、赵顺禄、赵卫、赵晓村、赵学法、赵志强、珍珍、郑碧玲、郑炳克、郑光、郑惠茹、郑慧、郑培强、郑霞意、郑在峰、周縂光、周佳、周俭、周建文、周科、周莉、周明、周奇鹏、周琦、周淑颖、周维、周宵飞、周雪琴、周妍、周颖、周愉飞、周宇、周跃武、朱海红、朱恺、朱黎、朱力克、朱南松 & 杨荔雯、朱世哲、朱巍、朱卫平、朱小久、朱雪昌、朱禺、朱悦、朱跃龙、竺涛、祝建武、祝敏、庄克服、庄文元、卓建方、卓旭东、左廷

Appendix III

A complete list of distances walked and donations received

Day	Walked today (miles)	Total walked (miles)	Walked today (km)	Total walked (km)	Donated today (GBP)	Total donations (GBP)	Donated today (RMB)	Total donations (RMB)
25-Jul	0.0	0.0	0.0	0.0	0.00	0.00	0.00	0.00
26-Jul	0.0	0.0	0.0	0.0	0.00	0.00	0.00	0.00
27-Jul	11.5	11.5	18.4	18.4	120.00	120.00	0.00	0.00
28-Jul	26.3	37.8	42.3	60.7	185.88	305.88	0.00	0.00
29-Jul	21.1	58.9	59.7	120.4	100.00	405.88	0.00	0.00
30-Jul	0.0	58.9	0.0	120.4	0.00	405.88	0.00	0.00
31-Jul	31.0	89.9	49.9	170.3	0.00	405.88	0.00	0.00
1-Aug	30.2	120.1	48.7	219.0	0.00	405.88	0.00	0.00
2-Aug	20.7	140.8	32.7	251.7	525.00	930.88	0.00	0.00
3-Aug	0.0	140.8	0.0	251.7	20.00	950.88	1,000.00	1,000.00
4-Aug	26.9	167.7	43.3	295.0	50.00	1,000.88	0.00	1,000.00
5-Aug	21.9	189.6	36.4	331.4	0.00	1,000.88	2,100.00	3,100.00
6-Aug	24.6	214.2	39.6	371.0	0.00	1,000.88	0.00	3,100.00
7-Aug	0.0	214.2	0.0	371.0	0.00	1,000.88	0.00	3,100.00
8-Aug	23.5	237.7	37.8	408.8	100.00	1,100.88	0.00	3,100.00
9-Aug	25.4	263.1	40.9	449.7	0.00	1,100.88	0.00	3,100.00
10-Aug	0.0	263.1	0.0	449.7	1,007.25	2,108.13	200.00	3,300.00
11-Aug	0.0	263.1	0.0	449.7	600.00	2,708.13	1,000.00	4,300.00
12-Aug	24.7	287.8	39.8	489.5	0.00	2,708.13	500.00	4,800.00
13-Aug	23.8	311.6	38.3	527.8	600.00	3,308.13	3,000.00	7,800.00
14-Aug	0.0	311.6	0.0	527.8	10.00	3,318.13	2,000.00	9,800.00
15-Aug	25.9	337.5	41.7	569.5	0.00	3,318.13	0.00	9,800.00
16-Aug	17.5	355.0	28.6	598.1	50.00	3,368.13	0.00	9,800.00
17-Aug	0.0	355.0	0.0	598.1	61.95	3,430.08	0.00	9,800.00
18-Aug	29.7	384.7	47.8	645.9	0.00	3,430.08	10,000.00	19,800.00
19-Aug	23.5	408.2	37.8	683.7	0.00	3,430.08	0.00	19,800.00
20-Aug	0.0	408.2	0.0	683.7	0.00	3,430.08	0.00	19,800.00
21-Aug	18.7	426.9	30.2	713.9	143.23	3,573.31	5,000.00	24,800.00
22-Aug	0.0	426.9	0.0	713.9	50.00	3,623.31	5,288.00	30,088.00
23-Aug	25.3	452.2	40.8	754.7	0.00	3,623.31	900.00	30,988.00
24-Aug	23.3	475.5	37.5	792.2	0.00	3,623.31	0.00	30,988.00
25-Aug	0.0	475.5	0.0	792.2	0.00	3,623.31	6,100.00	37,088.00
26-Aug	25.8	501.3	41.5	833.7	100.00	3,723.31	0.00	37,088.00
27-Aug	20.2	521.5	32.6	866.3	50.00	3,773.31	13,000.00	50,088.00
28-Aug	0.0	521.5	0.0	866.3	0.00	3,773.31	200.00	50,288.00
29-Aug	14.3	535.8	23.0	889.3	0.00	3,773.31	1,200.00	51,488.00
30-Aug	10.6	546.4	17.0	906.3	80.00	3,853.31	2,421.31	53,909.31
31-Aug	23.7	570.1	38.2	944.5	0.00	3,853.31	6,100.00	60,009.31

Day	Walked today (miles)	Total walked (miles)	Walked today (km)	Total walked (km)	Donated today (GBP)	Total donations (GBP)	Donated today (RMB)	Total donations (RMB)
1-Sep	0.0	570.1	0.0	944.5	0.00	3,853.31	15,827.00	75,836.31
2-Sep	20.5	590.6	33.1	977.6	0.00	3,853.31	5,100.00	80,936.31
3-Sep	22.5	613.1	36.2	1013.8	50.00	3,903.31	2,000.00	82,936.31
4-Sep	26.0	639.1	41.9	1055.7	0.00	3,903.31	5,000.00	87,936.31
5-Sep	0.0	639.1	0.0	1055.7	0.00	3,903.31	200.00	88,136.31
6-Sep	0.0	639.1	0.0	1055.7	0.00	3,903.31	1,000.00	89,136.31
7-Sep	25.5	664.6	41.1	1096.8	0.00	3,903.31	1,999.00	91,135.31
8-Sep	20.6	685.2	33.2	1130.0	0.00	3,903.31	10,700.00	101,835.31
9-Sep	0.0	685.2	0.0	1130.0	0.00	3,903.31	3,800.00	105,635.31
10-Sep	21.6	706.8	34.7	1164.7	50.00	3,953.31	940.00	106,575.31
11-Sep	23.0	729.8	37.0	1201.7	0.00	3,953.31	0.00	106,575.31
12-Sep	0.0	729.8	0.0	1201.7	0.00	3,953.31	91.00	106,666.31
13-Sep	21.5	751.3	34.6	1236.3	113.64	4,066.95	0.00	106,666.31
14-Sep	23.3	774.6	37.5	1273.8	50.00	4,116.95	0.00	106,666.31
15-Sep	0.0	774.6	0.0	1273.8	0.00	4,116.95	0.00	106,666.31
16-Sep	23.6	798.2	37.9	1311.7	0.00	4,116.95	0.00	106,666.31
17-Sep	19.8	818.0	31.8	1343.5	0.00	4,116.95	51,348.50	158,014.81
18-Sep	8.8	826.8	14.2	1357.7	0.00	4,116.95	1,000.00	159,014.81
19-Sep	0.0	826.8	0.0	1357.7	0.00	4,116.95	0.00	159,014.81
20-Sep	0.0	826.8	0.0	1357.7	0.00	4,116.95	4,761.00	163,775.81
21-Sep	0.0	826.8	0.0	1357.7	300.00	4,416.95	7,450.00	171,225.81
22-Sep	25.1	851.9	40.3	1398.0	28.32	4,445.27	5,500.00	176,725.81
23-Sep	25.7	877.6	41.3	1439.3	50.00	4,495.27	12,125.64	188,851.45
24-Sep	0.0	877.6	0.0	1439.3	30.00	4,525.27	161,320.00	350,171.45
25-Sep	0.0	877.6	0.0	1439.3	0.00	4,525.27	50,000.00	400,171.45
26-Sep	0.0	877.6	0.0	1439.3	0.00	4,525.27	0.00	400,171.45
27-Sep	25.3	902.9	40.7	1480.0	15.00	4,540.27	0.00	400,171.45
28-Sep	26.2	929.1	42.2	1522.2	0.00	4,540.27	4,010.00	404,181.45
29-Sep	0.0	929.1	0.0	1522.2	0.00	4,540.27	0.00	404,181.45
30-Sep	28.3	957.4	45.5	1567.7	0.00	4,540.27	0.00	404,181.45
1-Oct	23.9	981.3	38.4	1606.1	0.00	4,540.27	0.00	404,181.45
2-Oct	0.0	981.3	0.0	1606.1	520.00	5,060.27	0.00	404,181.45
3-Oct	27.9	1009.2	45.0	1651.1	0.00	5,060.27	0.00	404,181.45
4-Oct	26.3	1035.5	42.3	1693.4	400.00	5,460.27	170,288.00	574,469.45
5-Oct	21.7	1057.2	35.0	1728.4	195.83	5,656.10	37,986.00	612,455.45
6-Oct	0.0	1057.2	0.0	1728.4	200.00	5,856.10	0.00	612,455.45
7-Oct	0.0	1057.2	0.0	1728.4	0.00	5,856.10	0.00	612,455.45
8-Oct	0.0	1057.2	0.0	1728.4	150.00	6,006.10	0.00	612,455.45
9-Oct	0.0	1057.2	0.0	1728.4	0.00	6,006.10	0.00	612,455.45
10-Oct	0.0	1057.2	0.0	1728.4	0.00	6,006.10	0.00	612,455.45
11-Oct	0.0	1057.2	0.0	1728.4	50.00	6,056.10	201,249.00	813,704.45
Total	1057.2		1728.4		6,056.10		813,704.45	

Appendix IV

Launch of the English edition of *Walk for Peace: Transcultural Experiences in* China by Lord Michael Bates, and publishing agreement signing ceremony
London Book Fair 2017

This event took place on Tuesday, 14 March 2017, at the stand of the China International Publishing Group (CIPG).

Organizers
- New World Press, China
- Global China Press, UK

Co-organizers
- Global China Institute, UK
- The China Media Centre, University of Westminster, UK

Chair: Mrs Ingrid Cranfield, President of Global China Press

Programme
14:00–14:05 Mrs Ingrid Cranfield: Welcome and introduction of guests
14:05–14:10 Prof Xiangqun Chang: Introducing *Walk for Peace: Transcultural Experiences in China*
14:10–14:15 Mr XIANG Xiaowei: Greeting remarks
14:15–14:20 Mr MA Rujun: Greeting remarks
14:20–14:25 Professor Martin Albrow: Address
14:25–15:00 Walking into a Transcultural Era: a conversation between Lord Bates, author of *Walk for Peace*, Professor Kerry Brown and Professor Hugo de Burgh
15:00–15:15 Q & A
15:15–15:25 Signing of contracts between New World Press and Global China Press, followed by group photo for all the speakers and guests

Speakers (in alphabetical order)
- Professor Martin Albrow FAcSS, Honorary Vice-President of the British Sociological Association, Professor Emeritus of the University of Wales, UK
- The Rt Hon Lord Bates, author; Minister of International Development, UK Government
- Professor Kerry Brown, Director of Lau China Institute, King's College London, UK

- Professor Xiangqun Chang, Director of Global China Institute, Honorary Professor of UCL, UK
- Professor Hugo de Burgh, Director of the China Media Centre, University of Westminster, UK
- Dr M. A. Rujun, Vice-President of New World Press, China
- Mr XIANG Xiaowei, Minister Counsellor, Cultural Office, Chinese Embassy to the UK

About the author and editor of *Walk for Peace*

Author: The Rt Hon. Lord Michael Bates, Member of the House of Lords, current Minister of State for Department of International Development, former Deputy Chairman of the Conservative Party, former Minister of State at the Home Office, former Deputy Speaker and Deputy Chairman of the House of Lords. Charitable walks include:

- Walked 1,865 miles from Buenos Aires to Rio de Janeiro for the Olympic Truce, raising over £250,000 for UNICEF (2016).
- Walked 1,059 miles from Beijing to Hangzhou, raising over £90,000 for the Red Cross (2015). This walk is the subject of *Walk for Peace*.
- Walked 1,041 miles from London to Berlin, raising over £40,000 for Friedensdorf International (2014).
- Walked 518 miles from London to Derry, raising over £50,000 for Save the Children (2013).
- Walked 2,916 miles from Olympia to London to raise awareness for the 2012 Olympic Truce (2012).

Editor: Lady Xuelin Li Bates, Chairman of Walk for Peace Foundation UK, Senior Vice Chairman & Secretary General of UK Chinese Business Association, Chairman of Zhejiang UK Association.

About the book

Walk for Peace by The Rt Hon. Lord Michael Bates, edited by Lady Xuelin Li Bates, has appeared in several editions:

- Chinese–English combined edition, published by New World Press, Oct 2016 (ISBN 978-7-5104-6029-6)
- As *Walk for Peace: Transcultural Experiences in China*, English edition, published by Global China Press, Dec 2016 (ISBN 978-1-910334-38-6 DOI https://doi.org/10.24103/TETE.en.2016.1)
- As *Walk for Peace: Transcultural Experiences in China*, Chinese edition, published by Global China Press, Dec 2016 (ISBN 978-1-910334-39-3 DOI https://doi.org/10.24103/TETE.cn.2017.1)
- English–Chinese combined edition, published jointly by Global China Press and New World Press 2017 (ISBN 978-1-910334-44-7 DOI https://doi.org/10.24103/TETE.en.cn.2017.1)

In 2015, Lord Michael Bates walked 1,059 miles from Beijing to Hangzhou, raising over £90,000 for the Chinese Red Cross. The book consists of 71 diary entries and dozens of photos taken of and by the author on the walk. It also includes five Appendices, which provide information related to the 'Walk for Peace' series.

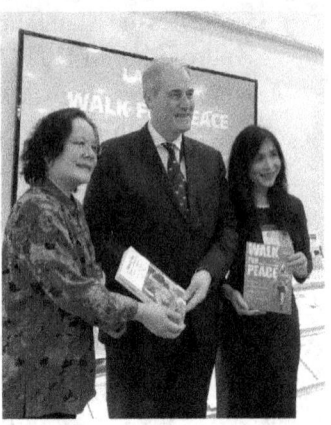

This is the second book in the Transcultural Experiences with 'Three Eyes' book series, jointly edited by Lixing Chen, Professor of Sociology, Kwansei Gakuin University, and former President of the Japan–China Sociological Society (JCSS), Japan; and Xiangqun Chang, Director of Global China Institute and Honorary Professor of University College London, UK.

Xiangqun Chang, Editor-in-Chief of Global China Press, with Lord and Lady Bates, the author and editor of the book.

Extracts from *Walk for Peace*

'The recent YouGov Opinion Poll found that the Chinese were the most optimistic people in the world, with 41% responding to say they thought that the world was getting better and 33% responding to say it was getting worse; the figures for Britain were that only 4% thought the world was getting better and 65% thought it was getting worse. I realised that if I were to accurately view the real China, then I needed to change the lens I was observing it through, from cynical and pessimistic to sentimental and optimistic. Not to do so would be akin to trying to understand the meaning of Chinese characters using the Latin alphabet.'

'My chosen mode of getting around on my three-month visit to China was an unusual one – walking. I was undertaking a charity walk from Beijing to Hangzhou, roughly following the Grand Canal connecting the two cities and extending some 1,000 miles … When you walk, you need to engage with the communities you walk through in a real way – seeking food, water, shelter and advice on directions.'

'In each country I walk through, 23 so far, what strikes me most are not our differences, which are trivial, entirely cultural and massively over-stated, but our similarities, which are vast, awe-inspiring and largely unexplored.'

Other invited guests and journalists (in alphabetical order)

- Ms Yuezhu Cheng, Cameraman, The Golden Age News Group, UK
- Mr Neil Clarke, Student, University of York, UK; Research Assistant, Global China Institute, UK
- Ms Sophie Ford, Graphic designer and typesetter, Global China Press, UK
- Mr Kaushal Goyal, Editor-in-Chief & CEO, GBD Books, India

- Mr Arjun Goyal, General Manager, GBD Books, India
- Dr Chiho Ivan Hon, Translator, Global China Institute, UK
- Mrs Yue Parkinson, Special Correspondent, *Financial Times*, UK
- Mr Mark Lee, Graphic designer and typesetter, Global China Press, UK
- Mr Li Ning, General Manager, The Golden Age News Group, UK
- Mr LIANG Xizhi, Correspondent, Xinhua News Agency, London
- Ms MA Lei, Second Secretary, Cultural Office, Chinese Embassy to the UK
- Ms Mengyi Ning, Cameraman, The Golden Age News Group, UK
- Ms RU Jing, General Manager, Cypress Books Ltd, UK
- Mr Zhiyong Wang, Correspondent, China Net, UK
- Ms Coco Wei, Master's student, University of Westminster, UK
- Dr Belinda Wu, Research Fellow, Development Policy and Planning, Open University, UK
- Mr Xiaoxing Wu, Producer and Cameraman, Phoenix TV, UK
- Mr Donghai Yang, General Manager, Fortune International Ltd, UK; Secretary of the Chinese Veterans' Society, UK
- Ms Emily Zhao, Reporter, Phoenix TV, UK
- Dr ZHOU Qingping, Visiting Fellow, China Media Centre, University of Westminster; Associate Professor, College of Journalism and Communication, Hunan University, China

Launch of English edition of *Walk for Peace: Transcultural Experiences in China*[1]

On 14 March 2017, at the London Book Fair, New World Press and Global China Press launched the English edition of *Walk for Peace: Transcultural Experiences in China* and held a publishing agreement signing ceremony.

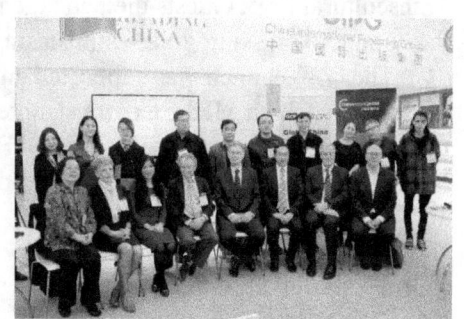

Walk for Peace: Transcultural Experiences in China is the UK edition of the Chinese–English combined edition

Participants at the book launch event.

published by New World Press in 2016, *Walk for Peace*.

Lord Bates started undertaking his charitable walks in 2009, from 2011 with the help of his wife, Xuelin. In 2015, he walked from Beijing to Hangzhou, raising

---

[1] This session is adapted from Chinese news. Source: http://news.china.com.cn/world/2017-03/15/content_40458880.htm

£90,000 for the Chinese Red Cross. So far, he has walked across 23 countries, including Argentina, Brazil, China, UK, Germany, and Greece. During his charitable walks, he has met with Ban Ki Moon, Jacques Rogge, the Pope, Thomas Bach, David Cameron and Queen Elizabeth II, and he has been praised by President Xi Jinping.

The launch event was chaired by the President of Global China Press, Mrs Ingrid Cranfield. Professor Xiangqun Chang, Director of the Global China Institute, Chief Editor at the Global China Press, and Honorary Professor of University College London, gave an introduction to the joint publication of *Walk for Peace: Transcultural Experiences in China*. Mr Xiang Xiaowei, Minister Counsellor at the Cultural Office of the Chinese Embassy to the UK, and Mr M. A. Jurun, Vice-President of New World Press, then delivered their opening re-

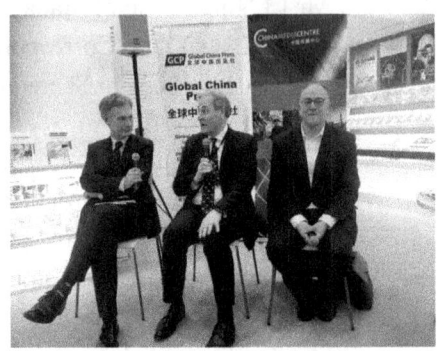

Walking into a Transcultural Era: a conversation between Lord Bates, author of *Walk for Peace*, Professor Kerry Brown and Professor Hugo de Burgh

marks. Professor Martin Albrow FAcSS, Honorary Vice-President of the British Sociological Association and Professor Emeritus of the University of Wales, followed with his address. A wide-ranging conversation then took place between Lord Bates, Professor Kerry Brown, Director of the Lau China Institute (King's College London), and Professor Hugo de Burgh, Director of the China Media Centre (University of Westminster), centred around the theme 'Walking into a Transcultural Era'. Guests then engaged in a lively debate with these scholars and the author, expressing great enthusiasm for the launch of the book.

The book launch was supported and co-organized by the Global China Institute and the China Media Centre (University of Westminster). The event attracted the attention of numerous Chinese and British media outlets, including the Xinhua News Agency London Bureau, the Golden Age News Group, the *Financial Times* and Phoenix TV.

After the book launch, New World Press and Global China Press signed contracts for the joint publication of three books by renowned Chinese sociologist, anthropologist, ethnologist, and social activist Fei Xiaotong: *Towards a People's Anthropology*, *Chinese Village Close-Up* and *Small Towns in China: Functions, Problems and Prospects*.

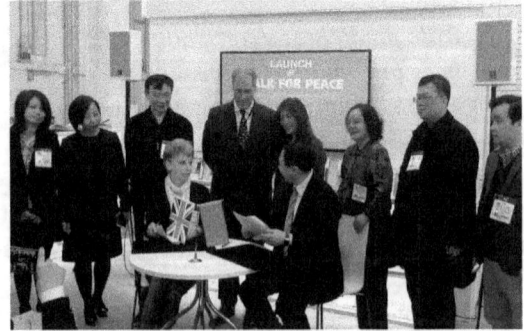

New World Press is a subsidiary of the China International Publishing Group, which has always been dedicated to explaining China to the rest of the world. With its experience and excellent resources for the publication of books in multiple languages, this publisher is constantly working towards an export-oriented, internationalized, multilingual and multimedia model. On the other hand, Global China Press focuses on bilingual publications (English and Chinese) about China. The cooperation between the two publishing houses will enable them to concentrate their resources to promote quality publications, expanding the field of cooperative publishing, enhancing the level of publishing and promoting the worldwide circulation of quality books, helping the world to gain a better understanding of China.

Mrs Ingrid Cranfield: Welcome and introduction of guests

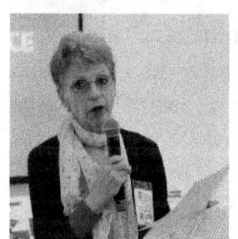

Lord and Lady Bates, ladies and gentlemen

As the President of Global China Press, I feel both privileged and thrilled to be here today to launch Global China Press's publication of *Walk for Peace* by Lord Michael Bates.

We are honoured to be joined by Lord Bates himself, who undertook a momentous walk through China, and his wife, Lady Bates, who edited the journal of the walk.

Professor Xiangqun Chang, editor-in-chief of Global China Press, was intrigued by the walk from the very beginning and was determined that an English edition of the book should be published as part of the Transcultural Experiences with 'Three Eyes' book series. It is thanks to her herculean efforts that *Walk for Peace* now becomes available to British and English-language readers, who will undoubtedly be enthralled and inspired by it.

Global China Press is the world's first publisher focusing on bilingual publications about China in comparative perspective, Chinese perspectives of the world and human knowledge and non-Chinese perspectives of China in a global context. We publish academic journals, conference proceedings, research monographs, learning materials for Chinese language for social sciences and reference books. We also publish several book series. As a part of Global China Institute, whose mission is education in the broadest sense and social change towards global governance, our output may be described as serving 75% academic purposes and 25% social activities. These also include the annual Global China Dialogue forum and social consultancy.

Among our book series, Transcultural Experiences with 'Three Eyes' is the only popular series concerned with the social sciences. The 'Three Eyes' of the title refer to the three perspectives from which an issue may be seen – Chinese, non-Chinese and professional.

We are proud to have in our programme this afternoon some distinguished speakers, including Lord Bates and Professor Chang, whom I have already mentioned. Part of the programme features a conversation between Lord Bates and Professors Kerry Brown and Hugh de Burgh. I will introduce them and our other speakers more fully at the time. Mr Xiang Xiaowei, Minister Counsellor in the Cultural Office of the Chinese Embassy to the UK, has several engagements today but will join us a little later to deliver some remarks in greeting.

First, however, may I hand over to Professor Chang, who is Honorary Professor at UCL and Director of the Global China Institute, but who will address us now in her role as editor-in-chief at Global China Press.

Prof Xiangqun Chang:
Introducing Walk for Peace: Transcultural Experiences in China
Walking into a transcultural era

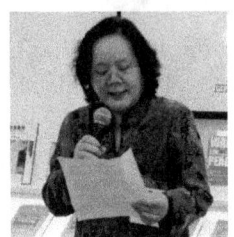

Lord Bates's *Walk for Peace* was an immensely important undertaking and his record of it has resulted in a book that has huge significance for all us. I became fascinated by the story even before the walk began, and while the walk was underway I read Lord Bates's journal, day by day. Nobody could fail to be staggered by his perseverance and willpower in completing his walk, or to be deeply impressed by his views on topics that affect us all. Let me give an example from 4 October, Day 70 of the walk, where he writes:

> 'I believe we are on the verge of exposing the male lust for violence and the human glorification of war for what it is: "a primeval animal instinct". Its roots lie more in anthropology and tribal culture than in politics. ... My core theory is that "we are all the same" ... The more we see each other as human first and our adopted culture second, the less we will distrust, the less we will feel threatened by difference, the less we will feel superior or inferior and the more we may seek to resolve disputes through agreed systems of justice based on the fundamental principle of the equal value, worth, rights and responsibilities of each and every human being.'

This passage calls to my mind the concept of 'cultural consciousness' developed by the renowned Chinese anthropologist and sociologist Fei Xiaotong. He interpreted the concept with 16 Chinese characters, which can be translated as 'cherishing one's own cultural beauty', 'openly appreciating others' beauties', 'letting different beauties coexist' and 'being blessed with harmony but diversity under the same heaven'. It means 'we are all the same' but 'we are all different'. True, we all have a tendency to love and hate; but we are all different in their proportions in us. We all experience fear: but some of us run away, some of us freeze and some of us fight. So, world order is not deducible from human nature, but from principles of organization that belong to the nature of existence, more specifically for human beings, human society in its environment.

In the early 1990s, some sociologists began to explore globalization, but since then the limitations of the concept of globalization have become more apparent and sociologists now hope to find a conceptual tool that can interpret and analyse current and future global patterns as we enter the post-global or transcultural age.

Walk for Peace is a chronicle of multi-directional participation in global governance, and in publishing it, we hope that a larger number of readers will gain new insights from it, helping them understand transcultural ideas. Lord Bates's walk was an individual action, and yet it was undertaken, as he points out in the book, in the hope that 'these steps may celebrate what connects the UK and China through culture and history. That they will raise funds to support the work of those who seek to bring peace and comfort in a world of conflict and pain.'

These hopes and goals are shared by many people from different cultural contexts. During the UK–China Year of Cultural Exchange, Lord and Lady Bates obtained the support of the governments of both countries, and thanks to the coordination efforts of the Chinese Red Cross, they successfully completed a walk of 1,700 km across six Chinese provinces, raising £90,000 for charity projects recommended by the Chinese Red Cross. Lord Bates's journey across China achieved many successes – it was an impressive feat of physical determination and endurance, a triumph of social interaction and an inspiring charitable enterprise – and it has set for all of us an example of 'transcultural cooperation for shared goals'.

Mr Xiang Xiaowei: Greeting remarks[2]

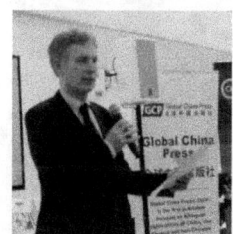

Lord and Lady Bates, Dr Ma Rujun, Mrs Cranfield, Professors Albrow, Brown, Chang, de Burgh, Ladies and Gentlemen

Good afternoon! Today, on the first day of the London Book Fair 2017, we celebrate the launch of the English version of Lord Bates's wonderful book, *Walk for Peace: Transcultural Experiences in China*. On behalf of the Chinese Embassy, I would like to extend our sincere congratulations to the author, the editor and to the publishers, New World Press and Global China Press.

As we all know, Chinese President Xi Jinping's successful state visit to the UK one and a half years ago marked the beginning of a 'Golden Era' in the relationship between China and the UK. The milestone visit also marked a flourishing of the cultural exchanges and cooperation between our two countries. Cooperation in the area of book publishing is an important part of this overall cultural cooperation.

However, you may not remember that in President Xi's address to the UK Parliament he said, 'Lord Bates, a British peer, went on a walk for charity in China, lasting over two months. He covered more than 1,700 kilometres on foot under the scorching sun, to raise money for charity in China and to call on the people to cherish peace. It is thanks to such efforts made by numerous Chinese and Britons

[2] In the absence of the speaker, this speech was read by Professor Hugo de Burgh.

that China–UK relations have made steady progress, despite the vast distance between our two countries.'

One of characteristics of this book is that the author recorded in his blog everything he saw, heard and experienced on his walk, with a triple perspective. His perspectives are a reflection of his three roles: a British person, a son-in-law of China because his wife is Chinese and a professional, as he is Minister of State at the Department for International Development. The walk and the resulting book are undoubtedly a very remarkable achievement.

The significance of Lord Bates's several walks for peace across 23 countries is that they revealed not the cultural differences, which have always been exaggerated, but the great similarities that exist between different countries. These similarities and increasing numbers of transcultural phenomena are the basis of the peace that we all desire.

I am very confident that with the launch of the English edition of this book, together with the dialogue between Lord Bates, Professor Brown and Professor de Burgh on 'Walking into a Transcultural Era', people in the UK and around the world will gain a deeper understanding of the vision and actions of the Walk for Peace.

With further such joint efforts among our friends in publishing and the press, we will undoubtedly be able to contribute increasingly to enhancing the cultural exchanges and cooperation between China and the UK.

Thank you!

Mr Ma Rujun: Greeting remarks

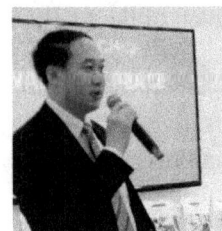

Ladies and gentlemen

First of all, I'd like to extend my gratitude to Lord Michael Bates and his wife Lady Xuelin Li Bates for attending the event today to launch the Global China Press edition of *Walk for Peace*.

The year 2015 marked the 70th anniversary of the victory against fascism and Nazism. To commemorate this anniversary and mark the first UK–China Year of Cultural Exchange, Lord Michael Bates came to China to undertake his Walk for Peace. Starting on July 27, he walked south from Beijing to Hangzhou, taking 71 days, and covering more than 1,700 kilometres. In the process, he raised nearly 780,000 yuan, which has all been donated to charity projects in China recommended by the Red Cross. On 20 October 2015, Chinese President Xi Jinping delivered a speech to the UK Parliament, in which he specifically mentioned Lord Michael Bates, and commended him for his contribution to the friendship between the people of China and the UK.

Lord Bates recorded his journey in China in daily logs, which Lady Bates edited and translated into Chinese. In order to celebrate this great philanthropic endeavour and make it more widely known among the Chinese, New World Press decided to publish this extraordinary diary. In October 2016, the Chinese and English versions of *Walk for Peace* were published in China.

Today, at the London Book Fair, we are glad to see that a new version of the book has been published by Global China Press. I'd like to express my thanks to Dr Xiangqun Chang for her unremitting efforts to make this happen.

Our partner Global China Press is committed to the publication of English–Chinese bilingual academic works covering a wide range of fields and adopting various forms. These publications have contributed to promoting Chinese culture overseas and achieved recognition and praise among the academic community.

In 2014, New World Press signed a letter of intent for cooperation with Global China Press in international publishing. Although our cooperation does not date back very far, we have made some remarkable achievements. In the form of copyright export or co-publishing, we have signed cooperation agreements for more than 40 titles. Among them, the Chinese and English versions of five books, including *Globalization of Chinese Social Sciences, Society Building* and *China's Urbanization* have already been published in the UK. This year, we will continue to deepen our cooperation.

The Chinese version of *Walk for Peace* has conveyed to many Chinese the significance of the outstanding enterprise of Lord Bates, a messenger for world peace. With the publication of its British version, more readers in the UK will understand China seen through the eyes of an Englishman. There is one sentence in the book I agree with wholeheartedly, and I'd like to end today by reading it to you:

'In each country I walk through, 23 so far, what strikes me most are not our differences, which are trivial, entirely cultural and massively overstated, but our similarities, which are vast, awe-inspiring and largely unexplored.'

Let us work together to explore the similarities between our countries through more cooperation in publishing and cultural exchanges.

Thank you!

Professor Martin Albrow: Address

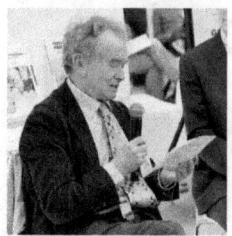

This is a rare and wonderful occasion to be present and, still more, have the privilege of speaking at the launch of a book that has so many lessons for the world and for each of us personally.

The book is full of profound reflections on peace and living together and Chinese philosophy and world affairs. But throughout it is the person and people who shine through.

It is the story of a walk and is of a quality that reminds me of another masterpiece, close to my heart, written over 150 years ago, *Wild Wales* by George Borrow. He came from Norfolk, as I do and he had fallen in love with the Welsh language as a boy. I lived in Wales and fell in love with a Welsh woman.

At the age of 51, Borrow resolved to visit Wales for the first time and walked from North to South recording, as does Michael Bates, the daily encounters that become extraordinary when seen through that third eye that Professor Xiangqun Chang describes.

Borrow tells how in a village inn between Mount Snowdon and Llangollen he happened to meet an Italian businessman who sold weather glasses, and in conversation they discovered he had a business associate from Milan, from whom, it just so happened, Borrow had once bought a diamond for his daughter.

Small world: just as Michael tells how in Zhejiang he meets Li Huizi, a well-known artist from Huzhou who showed him a picture of her son on her phone, who just happened to be working with his wife Xuelin in London.

From the beginnings of literature it is travel and encounters with the other that have prompted reflections on one's own place in creation and the purpose of life.

Borrow quotes an old Welsh saying: 'Three things come unawares upon a man, sleep, sin and old age.' Like a good Victorian, Borrow was quite certain God would never punish sins if they were committed unawares, but yes, sleep and old age could creep up on you – old age had already done so.

Michael also says he is old, at more or less at the same age as Borrow was then. All I can say is that the old must be the new young, for since his China walk he has walked from Buenos Aires to Rio de Janeiro.

His walks for peace are his way of combatting the sins of the world, of all the rest of us, and we are all in his debt. Thank you Michael, Xuelin, the Red Cross, and all who helped to make this possible.

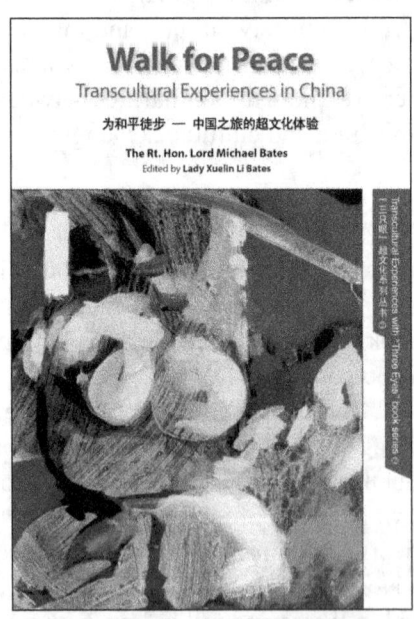

Appendix V

British Lord: Seeing the world on a walk for peace[1]

The fruits of this gentle, refined English gentleman's labours have been reaped, with his trek spanning 7 years, 23 countries and 12,000km rapidly becoming his defining achievement.

As a member of the House of Lords, Bates is a man of life peer, and has held positions as Deputy Chairman of the House of Lords, Parliament Under-Secretary of State at the Home Office and as a Member of Parliament for England's Conservative Party. In 2015, with the Conservative victory at the general election, Lord Bates was named Minister of State at the Home Office and appointed to Her Majesty's Most Honourable Privy Council.

However, just 10 months after his appointment, the 55 year old aristocrat resigned from his position and threw himself into his 'walking career'. The reason why we use the word 'career' is because over the past seven years Lord Bates has raised a total of more than 3.5 million RMB in donations, all of which was donated to UNICEF, the Red Cross, Save the Children and other similar charities, to aid orphans, children with disabilities and other such children who have suffered war, hunger and sickness.

When asked why he wanted to resign and do charity work, Bates steadfastly replied: 'Action speak louder than words'. In truth, in charity work only actions can create real change. Over the last seven years, Bates has been unwaveringly using his own actions to fulfil his promise.

Since 2009, Lord Bates has been involved in the 'Walk for Peace' initiative. From 2011 to 2012, he campaigned for the 'Olympic Truce', setting out on a 'Walk for Truce' from Olympia, Greece to London, England, during which he braved 300 days of trials and hardships. In 2013 he travelled from London to Derry, Northern Ireland, where he raised nearly 444,000 RMB for Save the Children in aid of Syrian children. In 2014, to commemorate the centenary of the First World War, he travelled from London to Berlin, raising more than 350,000 RMB for the German charity Friedensdorf International (Peace Village International) who provide emergency medical attention for child victims of conflict.

Last year, to celebrate the 70th Anniversary of the Allied victory and to celebrate the UK-China Year of Cultural Exchange , Lord Bates came to China. From the 27th July, Lord Bates walked all the way from Beijing to Hangzhou. His trek lasted 71 days and spanned 1704km, and raised nearly 780,000 RMB for projects identified by the Red Cross Society in China.

---

[1] Reporter: Lan Liyao, China Net 30th September, 2016 https://kknews.cc/world/94vbgb.html

Before the opening of this year's Rio Olympics, Lord Bates once again laid down his footprints, this time in Brazil, South America. In the last four months of 115 days of trekking, he raised a total of over 1.72 million yuan in support of UNICEF work with Children in Danger around the world.

Aside from his work with children, Lord Bates' primary goal with his walking is to promote the maintaining of peace. He said, 'I am pleased to see that during the 2012 London Olympic Games all 193 United Nations member states have joined the 'Olympic Truce' and promised to ceasefire during the Games and, in accordance with the spirit of the Charter of the United Nations, to resolve all international disputes.

As of late, his campaigns 'Walk for Peace' and the 'Olympic Truce' have both strengthened friendships between different countries and are an important link in promoting world peace. On the 20th October last year, when President Xi Jinping delivered a speech at the British Parliament, he specifically mentioned Lord Bates, praising and thanking him for his mutual understanding and support for the friendship between the Chinese and British peoples as well as his outstanding contributions to improving international relations.

We do not live in a world of peace. There are still many countries and regions of the world torn apart by the suffering of war. Lord Bates stated that 'World peace comes from friendship between countries, but the main thing is still friendship between the people. It is as Mr. Gandhi once said, 'be the change that you wish to see in the world'. Lord Bates firmly believes that although a single person may not have much power, if one can see one's every step can bring a change for the world, it would make him sincerely pleased.

With a voice tinged with palpable sentiment Lord Bates said: 'I have already journeyed across 23 countries, and the most shocking thing to me isn't the subtle differences between countries, for those are merely cultural differences, ones that are often prone to exaggeration. No, what truly shocked me to my very core was the unwavering similarities between all people, the kind of similarities that leave one in awe, and inspire one to continue exploring. I hope that all the young people of the world can carry out their dreams and take a solid first step. Using our actions we can create a better world.'

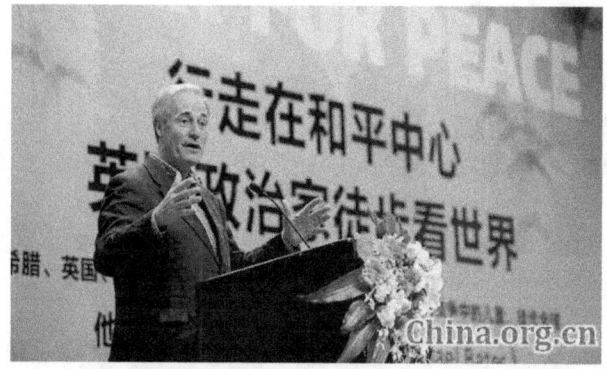

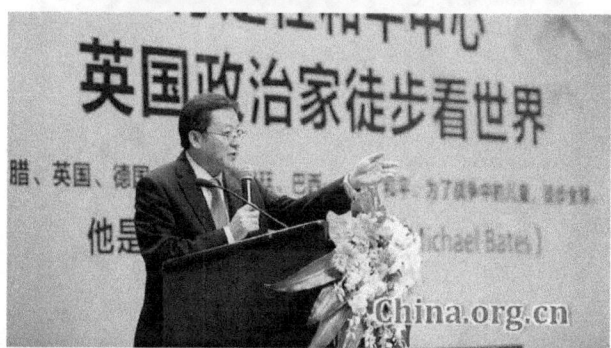

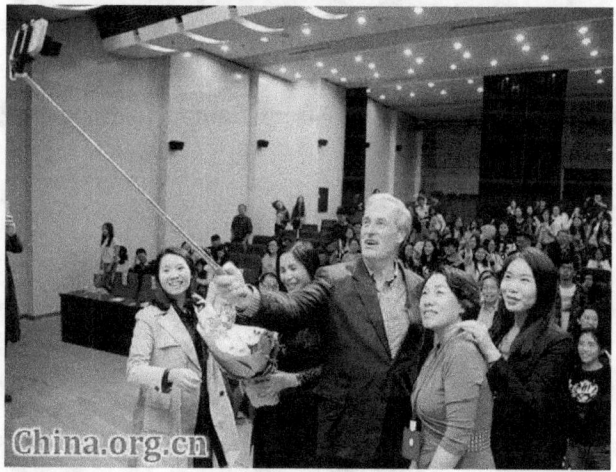

Top: On the 29th September, Lord Michael Bates gave his first talk on Walk for Peace at the book's preview in Beijing. Photography by Zhang Ruomeng, China Net

Middle: Lord Bates' first talk on Walk for Peace was held by the New World Press and China Daily, with China Net editor-in-chief Wang Xiaohui chairing the event. Photography by Zhang Ruomeng of China Net.

Bottom: After the speech, Bates took a selfie with 500 guests as well as various journalists. Photography by Zhang Ruomeng, China Net

Appendix VI

Charitable walks undertaken by Lord Michael Bates since 2011

2016: Walked 1,880 miles (3025km) from Buenos Aires to Rio de Janeiro for the Olympic Truce and raised over £260,000 for UNICEF

Dates: April 6 – July 29 (115 days)

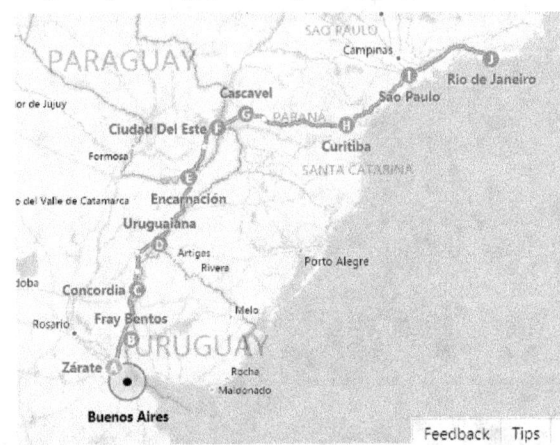

2015: Walked 1,059 miles (1702.7km) from Beijing to Hangzhou, raising over £90,000 for the Red Cross

Dates: July 27 – October 5 (71 days)

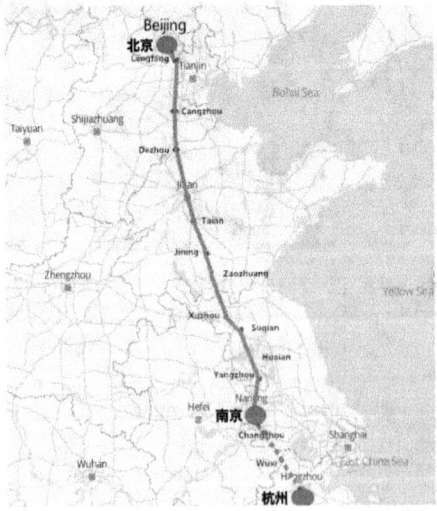

2014: Walked 1,041 miles (1697.5) from London to Berlin, raising over £40,000 for Friedensdorf International

Dates: August 4 – September 27 (54 days)

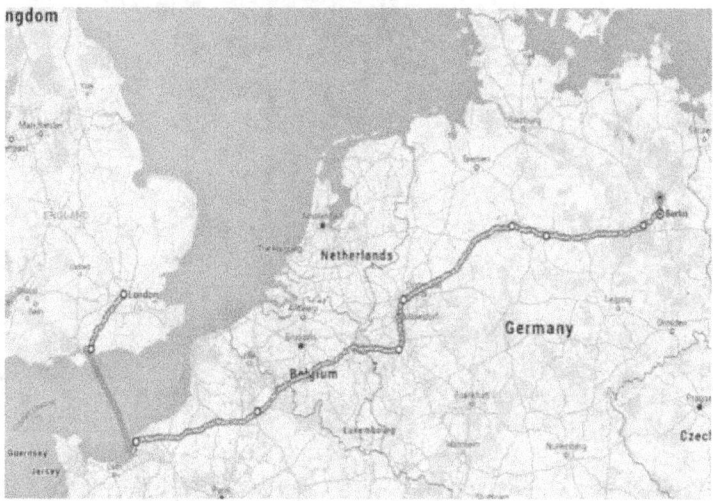

2013: Walked 518 miles (834.9km) from London to Derry, raising over £50,000 for Save the Children

Dates: July 27 – September 9 (35 days)

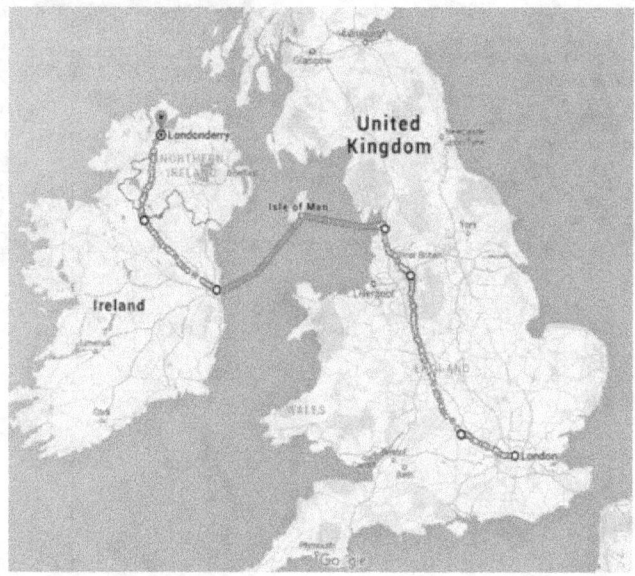

2011–12: Walked 2,916 miles (4693.1km) from Olympia to London to raise awareness of the 2012 Olympic Truce

Dates: April 22, 2011 – February 15, 2012 (300 days)

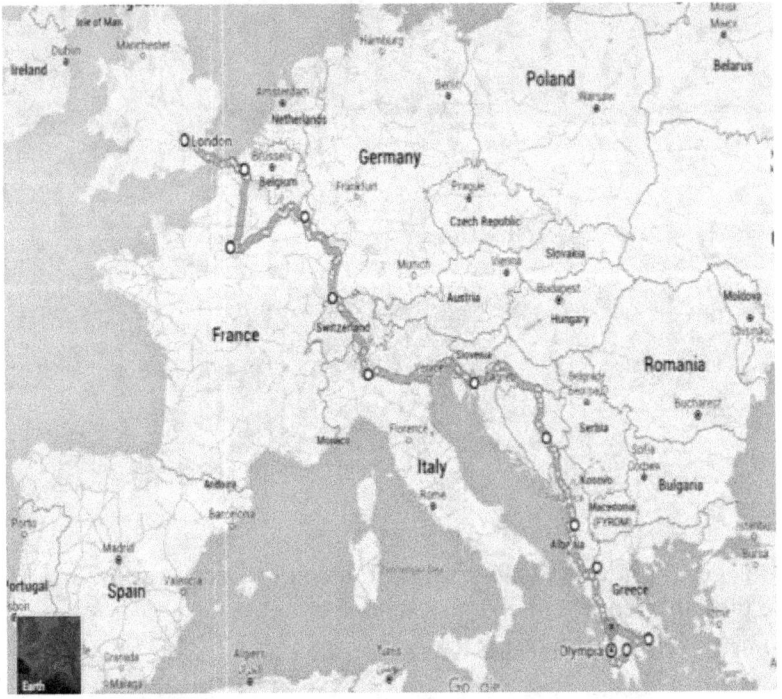

Appendix VII

VIP supporters

I: Photos

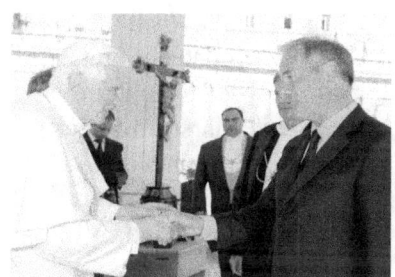
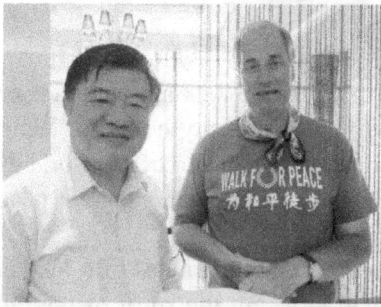
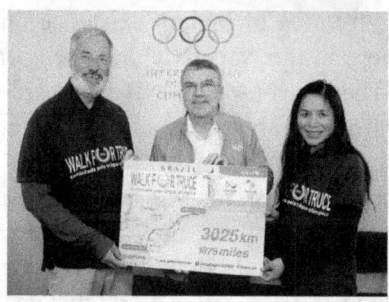
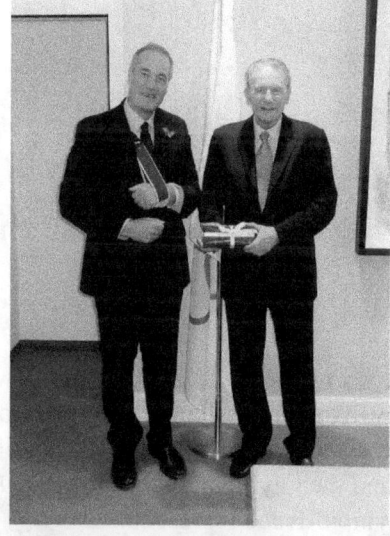
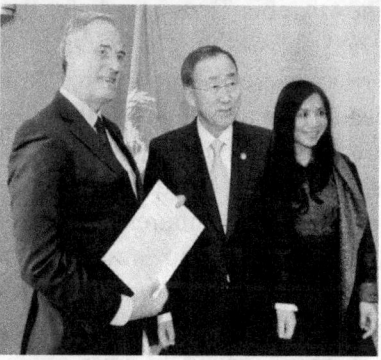

Top left: In 2011, Pope Benedict XVI granted an audience in the Vatican to Lord Bates, who was returning to London from Greece. Top right: In November 2011, on the way back to London from Greece, Michael was greeted by the then International Olympic Committee President, Jacques Rogge. Noting that Michael had insisted on walking every day, even with an injured arm, M Rogge, an expert in this area, offered relevant advice. Middle left: On August 30, 2015, the Vice Chairman of the Standing Committee of the National People's Congress and President of the Chinese Red Cross Society, Chen Zhu, visited Lord Michael Bates in Zaozhuang. Bottom left: Lord and Lady Bates with Thomas Bach, the current President of the International Olympic Committee. Bottom right: On the occasion of the Walk for Olympic Truce in 2012, Lord and Lady Bates met the UN Secretary-General, Ban Ki-moon.

II: Letters

International Olympic Committee

10 March 2016

The President

Lord Michael Bates
The Rt Hon the Lord Bates
Minister of State
The Home Office
2 Marsham Street
London
SW1P 4DF
Great Britain

Dear Lord Bates,

As you set out on the Walk for Peace, I wish you good luck and fortitude on your journey. You have a long walk ahead of you, but it is my hope that every step along the way will be a step towards building a peaceful and better world through sport and the Olympic ideal. Thank you for spreading the message of peace that the Olympic Truce represents.

The Olympic Truce stands for the common human values of tolerance, solidarity and peace. Sport is in a unique position to put the spirit of the Olympic Truce into practice because sport is the only area of human existence that has achieved universal law. Regardless of where in the world we practise sport, the rules are the same and apply to everyone. They are based on universal values that define our common humanity. In this way, sport is always about building bridges between people and cultures.

Thank you for your initiative to raise awareness for this noble ancient tradition of the Olympic Truce. Like all journeys, walking the 1,750 miles from Buenos Aires to Rio de Janeiro also begins with a single step. With your Walk for Peace, you are carrying the spirit of the Olympic Truce into a world that needs the values of tolerance, solidarity and peace more than ever before.

Yours Sincerely
Thomas Bach

The Prime Minister

18 March 2016

Dear Michael,

I want to take this opportunity to write and thank you for your Ministerial service, following your decision to step down from the Government to undertake a solo walk across South America in support of the UN Olympic Truce and to raise funds for UNICEF – a cause so close to your heart. It must have been a very tough decision to decide to stand down – and a deeply personal one – but I understand completely your wish to pursue this venture and you do so with my warmest blessing.

In particular, I would like to pay tribute to your parliamentary service, and your outstanding contribution to date. Your most recent work as Minister of State at the Home Office has been hugely valued and I have no doubt that your input will be greatly missed across the department, as well as by colleagues across the House. I am immensely grateful for your efforts in steering many important pieces of government legislation through the House of Lords, including the Modern Slavery Bill, the Psychoactive Substances Bill and, most recently, the Immigration Bill. This, in addition to your routine work as our Minister of State, taking questions and representing the Home Office in the House of Lords so effectively.

I am also immensely grateful for your hard work and service to the Conservative Party over so many years. Having previously played a leading role on the Northern Board and served as Deputy Party Chairman, you have always brought great passion and commitment to your work. You have been such a loyal and dedicated colleague throughout, and – whether it be for the Government or our party – you can be extremely proud of all that you have achieved.

Yours Sincerely
David Cameron

Buckingham Palace

18 April, 2016.

Dear Lord Bates,

Thank you for your letter of 23rd March, addressed to Sir Christopher Geidt, informing The Queen that you have stepped down from your role as a Minister in Her Majesty's Government.

I have shown your letter to The Queen, who was grateful to be kept informed and wishes you all the best for your 2000 mile solo walk from Buenos Aires to Rio de Janeiro to raise awareness for the 2016 Olympic Truce and to raise funds for Unicef's 'Children in Danger' initiative.

This letter comes with Her Majesty's warmest good wishes.

Yours Sincerely,
Samantha Cohen
Assistant Private Secretary to The Queen

The Rt. Hon. Lord Bates of Langbaurgh

The Secretary General

30 June 2016

Dear Lord Bates,

Congratulations on your latest Walk for the Olympic Truce, from Buenos Aires, host city for the 2018 Youth Summer Olympic Games, to Rio de Janeiro, host city of the 2016 Olympic and Paralympic Games. I fondly recall meeting you in Geneva in 2011, when the London 2012 Olympic Truce was adopted by the General Assembly. At the time, you and your wife, Xuelin, were in the middle of a prodigious trek from Olympia to London.

I thoroughly commend your dedication to the Truce and your contribution to the implementation of the United Nations General Assembly resolution 70/4, 'Building a peaceful and better world through sport and the Olympic ideal'. Sport is a powerful tool for education, health, sustainable development and peace. This has most recently been recognized in the newly adopted 2030 Agenda for Sustainable Development, which aims to promote peaceful and inclusive societies.

Your current walk is a wonderful initiative to encourage the observance of the Olympic Truce and to advocate for dialogue and mutual understanding among people and nations. I admire your commitment and fortitude, and that of your wife, whose support is, I know, indispensable.

Please accept my very best wishes for a successful conclusion to your latest walk, and my sincere gratitude for your continued efforts on behalf of world peace.

Yours sincerely,
BAN Ki-moon

The Right Honourable Lord Bates of Langbaurgh
House of Lords
London

Appendix VIII

Photos from the 2016 Walk for Olympic Truce

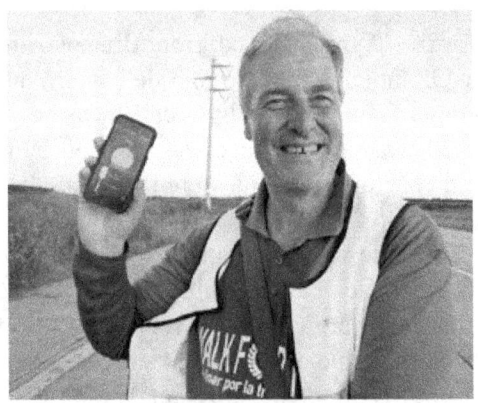
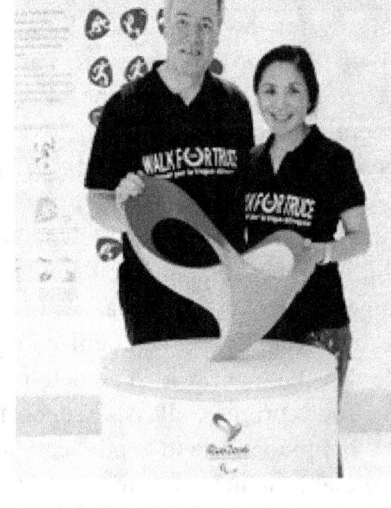
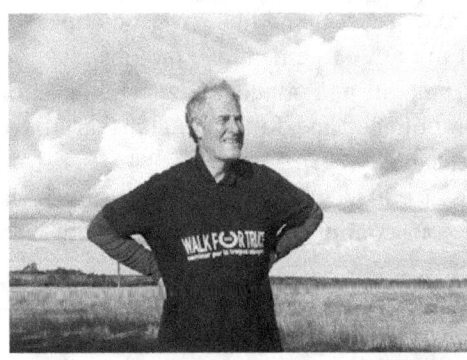
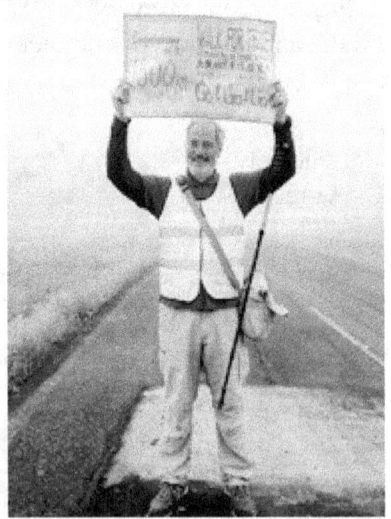
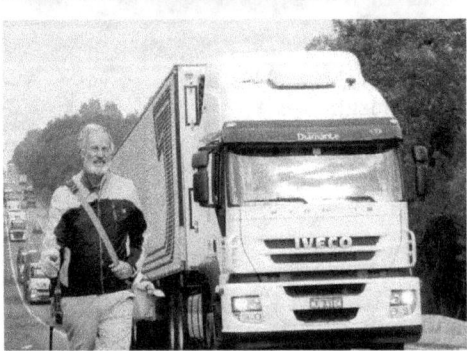

Top left: Lord Bates celebrating his day's walk of more than 48.3 kilometres
Top right: April 23: Before the start of the walk, Lord and Lady Bates visited the Rio Olympic
Organizing Committee. They are pictured behind the Paralympic logo
Centre left: Lord Bates at the end of the walk on that day, in sweat-soaked clothes
Bottom left: Walking on main national roads on the way to Brazil
Bottom right: Celebrating the milestone of 1,500 km on the walk on June 3

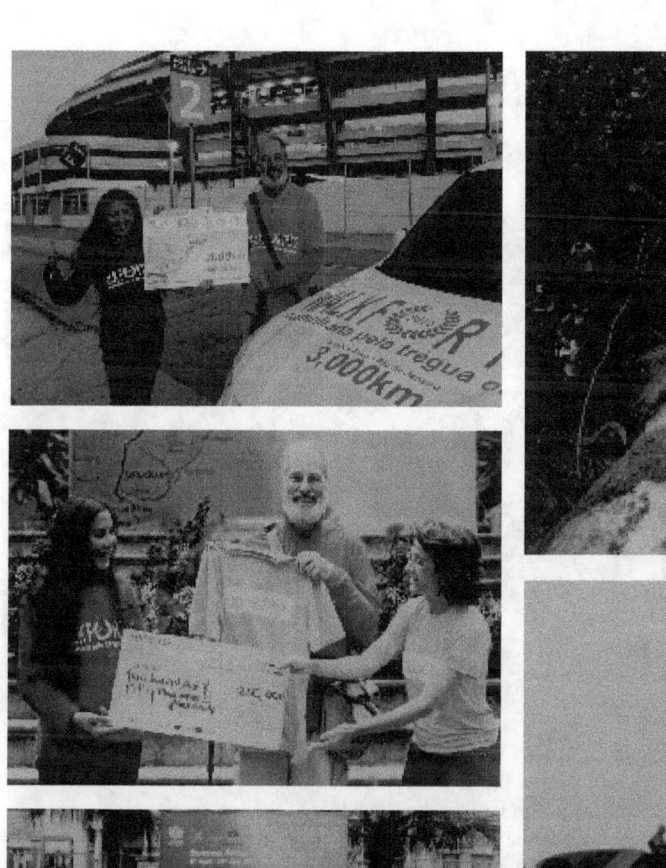

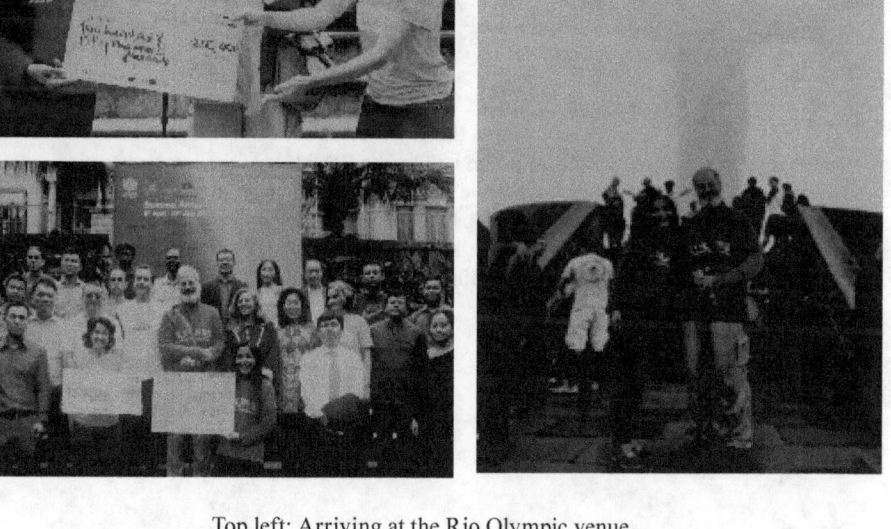

Top left: Arriving at the Rio Olympic venue
Top right: Nearing the top of Corcovado, Rio de Janeiro
Centre left: Lord and Lady Bates with Thomas Bach, after reaching the 3,000 km milestone
Bottom left: Celebrating the end of the walk
Bottom right: Marking the successful completion of the 2016 Walk at the summit of Corcovado

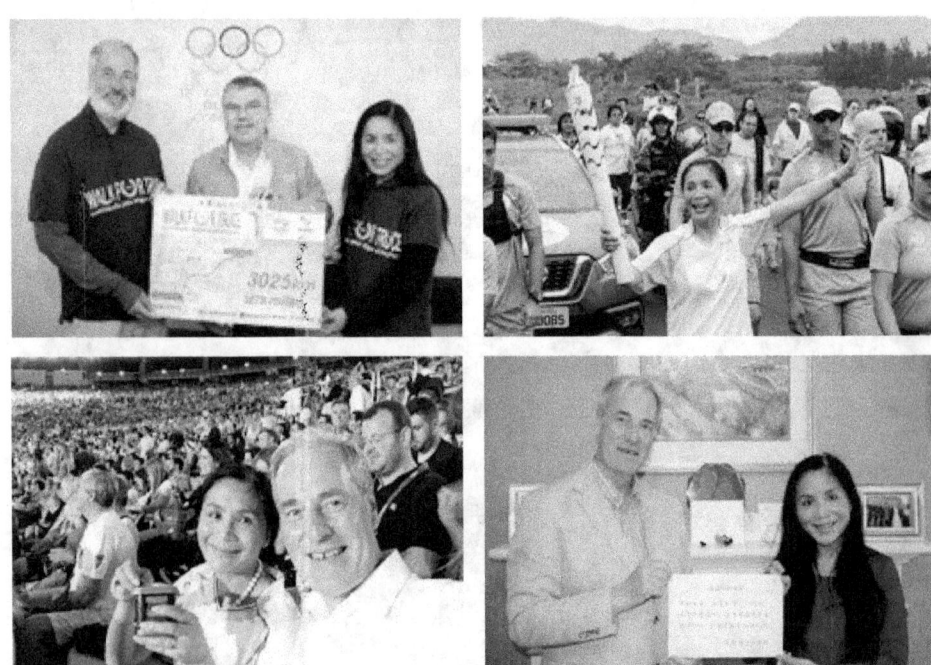

Top left: International Olympic Committee President Thomas Bach invited
Lady Bates to carry one of the Olympic torches, August 4, 2016.
Top right: Lord and Lady Bates were invited by the President of the International Olympic
Committee, Thomas Bach, to watch the Opening Ceremony of the Rio Olympic Games.
Bottom left: Donating money raised from the Walk to UNICEF
Bottom right: Back in London after the Walk for Peace in China, Lord Bates sent a G20 message
to his wife Xuelin's hometown, Hangzhou.

www.ingramcontent.com/pod-product-compliance
Lightning Source LLC
Chambersburg PA
CBHW081554220526
45468CB00010B/2660